21世纪高等学校规划教材 | 物联网

物联网专业英语教程

张强华 司爱侠 吕淑文 张千帆 编著

清华大学出版社
北京

内 容 简 介

本书的目的在于切实提高物联网行业人士的专业英语能力。

以物联网专业应用实际为依据，采集难度适中、覆盖面广的实用性和前瞻性材料，组成单元。每个单元包括：Text A 及 Text B——这些课文包括了基础知识和基本概念；New Words——给出课文中出现的新词，读者由此可以积累基本专业词汇；Phrases——给出课文中的常用词组；Abbreviations——给出课文中出现的、业内人士必须掌握的缩略语；Exercises——针对课文练习，巩固学习效果；Reading Material——可进一步扩大读者的视野；参考答案——读者可对照检查学习效果；词汇总表——供读者记忆单词和长期查询之用。

本书既可作为高等院校的专业英语教材，优秀高职高专院校也可选用；还可作为培训班教材或供从业人员自学。

本书封面贴有清华大学出版社防伪标签，无标签者不得销售。
版权所有，侵权必究。举报：010-62782989，beiqinquan@tup.tsinghua.edu.cn。

图书在版编目（CIP）数据

物联网专业英语教程/张强华等编著. —北京：清华大学出版社，2015（2024.1重印）
（21 世纪高等学校规划教材·物联网）
ISBN 978-7-302-39361-0

Ⅰ.①物… Ⅱ.①张… Ⅲ.①互联网络-应用-英语-教材 ②智能技术-应用-英语-教材 Ⅳ.①H31

中国版本图书馆 CIP 数据核字（2015）第 031615 号

责任编辑：魏江江　赵晓宁
封面设计：傅瑞学
责任校对：时翠兰
责任印制：宋　林

出版发行：清华大学出版社
网　　址：https://www.tup.com.cn，https://www.wqxuetang.com
地　　址：北京清华大学学研大厦 A 座　　邮　编：100084
社 总 机：010-83470000　　邮　购：010-62786544
投稿与读者服务：010-62776969，c-service@tup.tsinghua.edu.cn
质 量 反 馈：010-62772015，zhiliang@tup.tsinghua.edu.cn
课 件 下 载：https://www.tup.com.cn，010-62795951

印 装 者：三河市铭诚印务有限公司
经　　销：全国新华书店
开　　本：185mm×260mm　　印　张：20　　字　数：484 千字
版　　次：2015 年 9 月第 1 版　　印　次：2024 年 1 月第 10 次印刷
印　　数：8301～8800
定　　价：39.50 元

产品编号：051667-01

出版说明

随着我国改革开放的进一步深化，高等教育也得到了快速发展，各地高校紧密结合地方经济建设发展需要，科学运用市场调节机制，加大了使用信息科学等现代科学技术提升、改造传统学科专业的投入力度，通过教育改革合理调整和配置了教育资源，优化了传统学科专业，积极为地方经济建设输送人才，为我国经济社会的快速、健康和可持续发展以及高等教育自身的改革发展做出了巨大贡献。但是，高等教育质量还需要进一步提高以适应经济社会发展的需要，不少高校的专业设置和结构不尽合理，教师队伍整体素质亟待提高，人才培养模式、教学内容和方法需要进一步转变，学生的实践能力和创新精神亟待加强。

教育部一直十分重视高等教育质量工作。2007年1月，教育部下发了《关于实施高等学校本科教学质量与教学改革工程的意见》，计划实施"高等学校本科教学质量与教学改革工程（简称'质量工程'）"，通过专业结构调整、课程教材建设、实践教学改革、教学团队建设等多项内容，进一步深化高等学校教学改革，提高人才培养的能力和水平，更好地满足经济社会发展对高素质人才的需要。在贯彻和落实教育部"质量工程"的过程中，各地高校发挥师资力量强、办学经验丰富、教学资源充裕等优势，对其特色专业及特色课程（群）加以规划、整理和总结，更新教学内容、改革课程体系，建设了一大批内容新、体系新、方法新、手段新的特色课程。在此基础上，经教育部相关教学指导委员会专家的指导和建议，清华大学出版社在多个领域精选各高校的特色课程，分别规划出版系列教材，以配合"质量工程"的实施，满足各高校教学质量和教学改革的需要。

为了深入贯彻落实教育部《关于加强高等学校本科教学工作，提高教学质量的若干意见》精神，紧密配合教育部已经启动的"高等学校教学质量与教学改革工程精品课程建设工作"，在有关专家、教授的倡议和有关部门的大力支持下，我们组织并成立了"清华大学出版社教材编审委员会"（以下简称"编委会"），旨在配合教育部制定精品课程教材的出版规划，讨论并实施精品课程教材的编写与出版工作。"编委会"成员皆来自全国各类高等学校教学与科研第一线的骨干教师，其中许多教师为各校相关院、系主管教学的院长或系主任。

按照教育部的要求，"编委会"一致认为，精品课程的建设工作从开始就要坚持高标准、严要求，处于一个比较高的起点上；精品课程教材应该能够反映各高校教学改革与课程建设的需要，要有特色风格、有创新性（新体系、新内容、新手段、新思路，教材的内容体系有较高的科学创新、技术创新和理念创新的含量）、先进性（对原有的学科体系有实质性的改革和发展，顺应并符合21世纪教学发展的规律，代表并引领课程发展的趋势和方向）、示范性（教材所体现的课程体系具有较广泛的辐射性和示范性）和一定的前瞻性。教材由个人申报或各校推荐（通过所在高校的"编委会"成员推荐），经"编委会"认真评审，最后由清华大学出版社审定出版。

目前，针对计算机类和电子信息类相关专业成立了两个"编委会"，即"清华大学出版社计算机教材编审委员会"和"清华大学出版社电子信息教材编审委员会"。推出的特色精品教材包括：

（1）21世纪高等学校规划教材·计算机应用——高等学校各类专业，特别是非计算机专业的计算机应用类教材。

（2）21世纪高等学校规划教材·计算机科学与技术——高等学校计算机相关专业的教材。

（3）21世纪高等学校规划教材·电子信息——高等学校电子信息相关专业的教材。

（4）21世纪高等学校规划教材·软件工程——高等学校软件工程相关专业的教材。

（5）21世纪高等学校规划教材·信息管理与信息系统。

（6）21世纪高等学校规划教材·财经管理与应用。

（7）21世纪高等学校规划教材·电子商务。

（8）21世纪高等学校规划教材·物联网。

清华大学出版社经过三十多年的努力，在教材尤其是计算机和电子信息类专业教材出版方面树立了权威品牌，为我国的高等教育事业做出了重要贡献。清华版教材形成了技术准确、内容严谨的独特风格，这种风格将延续并反映在特色精品教材的建设中。

清华大学出版社教材编审委员会
联系人：魏江江
E-mail:weijj@tup.tsinghua.edu.cn

前言

物联网是继计算机、互联网之后信息产业发展的第三次浪潮，它通过智能感知、识别技术与普适计算，结合网络化应用，创造性地拓展和变革了众多行业。其影响的深度与广度都十分巨大，物联网人才需求旺盛。因此，我国数百所高校开设了相关专业。由于物联网各组成部分均处于高速发展之中，国际化特征尤为明显，从业人员必须提高专业英语水平，以便及时获得最新、最先进的专业知识。从某种意义上说，专业英语的水平决定了专业技能的水平。因此，几乎所有开设物联网专业的高校都开设了相应的专业英语课程。

我们以物联网专业应用实际为依据，采集难度适中、覆盖面广的实用性和前瞻性材料，组成单元。每个单元包括 Text、New Words、Phrases、Abbreviations、Notes、Exercises、Reading Material 等部分。其中，Text A 及 Text B 是课文，包括了基础知识和基本概念；New Words 给出课文中出现的新词，读者由此可以积累基本的专业词汇；Phrases 给出课文中的常用词组；Abbreviations 给出课文中出现的、业内人士必须掌握的缩略语；Exercises 提供针对课文的练习及扩展练习，以巩固学习效果、扩展能力；Reading Material 可进一步扩大读者的视野。附录 A 提供了参考答案，读者可对照检查学习效果，附录 B 提供了词汇总表，供读者记忆单词和长期查询之用。

我们提供的参考教案，可从清华大学出版社网站免费下载。

在使用本书的过程中，如有问题，都可以通过 E-mail 与我们交流。邮件标题请注明姓名及"物联网专业英语教程（清华大学版）"字样。E-mail 为 zqh3882355@163.com 或 zqh3882355@sina.com。

望大家不吝赐教，让我们共同努力，使本书成为一部"符合学生实际、切合行业实况、知识实用丰富、严谨开放创新"的优秀教材。

编 者
2015 年 5 月

Unit 1 ··· 1

    Text A   The Internet of Things: How It'll Revolutionise Your Devices ········· 1

    New Words ·· 4

    Phrases ··· 6

    Abbreviations ··· 7

    Exercises ·· 7

    Text B   The Internet of Things -- This Is Where We're Going ················· 9

    New Words ·· 12

    Phrases ··· 14

    Exercises ·· 15

    Text C   What Does the Internet of Things Mean for Today's Culture? ········· 16

    参考译文   Text A   物联网：它会如何改变你的设备 ······················ 18

Unit 2 ··· 21

    Text A   What is M2M? ·· 21

    New Words ·· 23

    Phrases ··· 25

    Abbreviations ··· 25

    Exercises ·· 26

    Text B   How Machine to Machine Communication Works ······················ 28

    New Words ·· 31

    Phrases ··· 32

    Exercises ·· 33

    Text C   Machine To Machine ··· 34

    参考译文   Text A   什么是 M2M? ·· 38

Unit 3 ··· 40

    Text A   How Smart Homes Work ··· 40

    New Words ·· 45

    Phrases ··· 46

    Abbreviations ··· 47

Exercises ··· 47
　　Text B　What is GPS? ·· 50
　　New Words ·· 53
　　Phrases ··· 54
　　Abbreviations ·· 55
　　Exercises ··· 55
　　Text C　Smart Home and Technology ··· 57
　　参考译文　Text A　智能家居如何工作 ·· 59

Unit 4 ·· 64

　　Text A　Network Architecture ·· 64
　　New Words ·· 68
　　Phrases ··· 69
　　Abbreviations ·· 70
　　Exercises ··· 70
　　Text B　Network Topology ·· 73
　　New Words ·· 78
　　Phrases ··· 79
　　Abbreviations ·· 80
　　Exercises ··· 80
　　Text C　Internet Terms ··· 82
　　参考译文　Text A　网络体系结构 ··· 85

Unit 5 ·· 88

　　Text A　Networking Hardware ··· 88
　　New Words ·· 92
　　Phrases ··· 93
　　Abbreviations ·· 94
　　Exercises ··· 94
　　Text B　Network Switch ··· 96
　　New Words ·· 103
　　Phrases ··· 104
　　Abbreviations ·· 105
　　Exercises ··· 106
　　Text C　Router ··· 107
　　参考译文　Text A　组网硬件 ·· 113

Unit 6 ·· 116

　　Text A　Wireless Sensor Network ··· 116

New Words	120
Phrases	121
Abbreviations	122
Exercises	123
Text B　Applications of WSN	125
New Words	128
Phrases	130
Abbreviations	130
Exercises	131
Text C　Sensor Web	132
参考译文　Text A　无线传感器网络	135

Unit 7 ... 138

Text A　How Wireless Networks Work	138
New Words	141
Phrases	142
Abbreviations	143
Exercises	143
Text B　RFID	145
New Words	148
Phrases	149
Abbreviations	150
Exercises	150
Text C　What is Wireless Internet Service?	152
参考译文　Text A　无线网络如何工作	155

Unit 8 ... 157

Text A　WiFi	157
New Words	163
Phrases	164
Abbreviations	165
Exercises	165
Text B　How Bluetooth Works	167
New Words	171
Phrases	172
Abbreviations	173
Exercises	173
Text C　Electronic Product Code (EPC)	174
参考译文　Text A　WiFi	179

Unit 9 ... 183

    Text A   Barcode ... 183

    New Words ... 187

    Phrases ... 189

    Abbreviations ... 190

    Exercises ... 190

    Text B   QR Code ... 193

    New Words ... 201

    Phrases ... 203

    Abbreviations ... 203

    Exercises ... 204

    Text C   Choosing the Right Barcode Scanner ... 205

    参考译文   Text A   条形码 ... 209

Unit 10 ... 213

    Text A   What is ZigBee? ... 213

    New Words ... 217

    Phrases ... 219

    Abbreviations ... 219

    Exercises ... 219

    Text B   3G and 4G ... 222

    New Words ... 225

    Phrases ... 227

    Abbreviations ... 228

    Exercises ... 228

    Text C   NFC ... 229

    参考译文   Text A   ZigBee 是什么？ ... 233

附录 A   参考答案 ... 236

    Unit 1 ... 236

        Text A ... 236

        Text B ... 237

    Unit 2 ... 239

        Text A ... 239

        Text B ... 240

    Unit 3 ... 242

        Text A ... 242

        Text B ... 243

Unit 4 ··· 244
    Text A ··· 244
    Text B ··· 246
Unit 5 ··· 248
    Text A ··· 248
    Text B ··· 249
Unit 6 ··· 251
    Text A ··· 251
    Text B ··· 253
Unit 7 ··· 254
    Text A ··· 254
    Text B ··· 256
Unit 8 ··· 257
    Text A ··· 257
    Text B ··· 259
Unit 9 ··· 260
    Text A ··· 260
    Text B ··· 262
Unit 10 ··· 263
    Text A ··· 263
    Text B ··· 265

附录 B　词汇总表 ··· 267

Unit 1

Text A

The Internet of Things: How It'll Revolutionise Your Devices

Forget the cliché idea of fridge that sends you a text when you run out of milk. Try one that senses what's inside, chooses your next fortnight's meal plans, orders what it needs via an online supermarket, and syncs a delivery slot with your Gmail calendar.

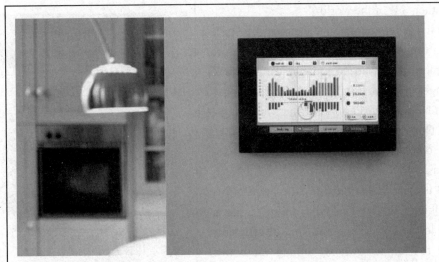

Energy-saving whole home control is already on offer from the likes of Niko, but it's a pricey custom installation.

You might have a smart TV and you've almost certainly got a smartphone, perhaps even one that syncs content to an iPad, but such 'smart' devices are just the beginning of what's loosely termed the 'Internet of Things', or IoT for short. Also (perhaps more correctly) called 'machine to machine', the IoT isn't owned or controlled by any one group or company, it comprises no single idea, and it certainly isn't on any of our gadget wish lists. But it will change all of our lives.

The uses for gadgets that communicate with each other on our behalf are huge and varied. How about a farmer that gets a text if any of his cows -- each sporting a wireless sensor[1] -- gets sick or pregnant. It already happens, and we're next: pacemakers that feed data through to a GP will be possible, and it could even send a text to relatives if the wearer falls ill.

More likely first uses include prescriptions that automatically get reordered and delivered without any need for trips to the doctors or pharmacy, and web-connected scales (WiFi models already exist) monitored remotely by a GP.

Smartphone apps are likely to provide an important window on the world of IoT, but tablets and other devices will also join in. The device itself is immaterial -- it's the internet connection that's critical.

Some already use live traffic updates on sat nav devices, but in the future your alarm clock will let you sleep in if your train is delayed, rearrange a taxi, and even email your boss if you're stuck on a motorway.

If you have the money, it's already possible to have lights with motion sensors that track your movements, and blinds that slide up and down to help regulate temperature and lighting levels. The intercom that rings your mobile phone, whether you're home or not, has been around a while. Ditto the security camera you can monitor from the other side of the world.

"The IoT is removing mundane repetitive tasks or creating things that just weren't possible before, enabling more people to do more rewarding tasks and leaving the machines to do the repetitive jobs", says Grant Notman, Head of Sales and Marketing at Wood & Douglas, a company that manufactures wireless communications hardware for IoT applications.

What is clear is that there is little point in two gadgets talking to each other if that doesn't bring an advantage to the owner, or some kind of efficiency gain. The IoT on its own is nothing more than back-office admin.

"The consumer won't be interested in the Internet of Things, just as they are not interested in an Internet of Computers," says Jean-Paul Edwards, Head of Media Futures at global creative media agency Manning Gottlieb OMD London.

Fancy a washing machine that monitors your fashion sense and suggests when your jeans need upgrading?

---

[1] Any device that receives a signal or stimulus (as heat or pressure or light or motion etc.) and responds to it in a <u>distinctive</u> ([dis'tiŋktiv]adj.与众不同的，有特色的) manner.

"They will be interested in what the IoT allows them to do or what it saves them from doing. Passive environmental monitoring, remote management and connectivity to everything will help us do what we used to do, but faster, cheaper and better."

Could these catch on? The self repairing washing machine that can be fixed remotely or at least with only one visit by an engineer who has the correct parts, or the Nest Thermostat that learns when you are in or out to better control home heating.

"The technology is complex," says Edwards of the latter, "but a claimed 20% saving on energy bills is a simple idea." Self repairing gadgets? Now there's a tasty idea that could take customer service, currently a frustrating blockage in the system, to new heights of efficiency.

Based around embedded RFID chips, barcodes and sensors, the Internet of Things is, at its most impressive, helping create smart cities. The aspects here are endless and begin with banal time saving activities in homes. However, the IoT is at its best when predicting human behaviour.

Is a city's free bike renting scheme being used? Stick a RFID chip on the handlebars and someone can plot exactly who are riding these bikes, where those bikes go, and when. At night streetlights could switch on only when a car approaches -- thus saving electricity -- but more impressively, data could be collected to map urban travel patterns.

Designed to cut fuel bills, the Nest Thermostat can be adjusted from a PC or smartphone app.

There is a city where a joined-up IoT already exists, albeit in embryonic form. New Songdo City, 40 miles south of Seoul in South Korea, has a super-smart way to use 1500 acres of reclaimed land.

A Cisco-powered concept called U.Life is based on a city wide wired broadband network that allows the current 60,000 residents to use their smartphones, tablets and other touchscreen[1] devices to control their homes' heating, lighting and air conditioning, with TelePrescence devices throughout the city free video calling. Cars talk to roads, which talk to streetlights, while rubbish is sucked away via an underground network of pipes, without the need for garbage trucks.

The aim is to build a low energy, incredibly efficient city with private investment, and there's good reason why it's being seen as a global template; of the world's seven billion population more than half now lives in cities, with 6.3 billion predicted to do so by 2050.

---

[1] A touchscreen is an electronic visual display that can detect the <u>presence</u> (['preznz]n.发生，存在) and location of a touch within the display area. The term generally refers to touching the display of the device with a finger or hand. Touchscreens can also sense other passive objects, such as a <u>stylus</u> (['staɪləs]n.尖笔).

"The M2M market is growing rapidly and unlike any other, it is one technology that can surpass human interaction," says Macario Namie, VP of marketing at Jasper Wireless, which is working with mobile operators such as O2 in the UK and AT&T in the US on IoT communications. "Its limitless reach means it's set to be prevalent in connecting future societies."

That 'double whammy' of population growth and ever-increasing urbanisation means that the IoT has the job of streamlining our cities, but in theory it will allow each of us to dispense with a lot of daily chores. Of course, that's exactly what is said about the home computer.

New Words

device	[di'vais]	n. 装置，设备
cliché	['kli:ʃei]	n. 口头禅，陈词滥调
fridge	[fridʒ]	n. 冰箱
sense	[sens]	vt. 感知
fortnight	['fɔ:tnait]	n. 两星期
order	['ɔ:də]	n. 次序，顺序，命令，定购，订单
		vt. 命令，定购，定制
supermarket	['sju:pə,ma:kit]	n. 超级市场
sync	[siŋk]	n. 同时，同步
delivery	[di'livəri]	n. 递送，交付，交货
calendar	['kælində]	n. 日历
smart	[sma:t]	adj. 智能的，敏捷的
smartphone	['sma:tfəun]	n. 智能电话
content	['kɔntent]	n. 内容
term	[tə:m]	vt. 把……称为；把……叫作
comprise	[kəm'praiz]	vt. 包含，包括；由……组成；由……构成
control	[kən'trəul]	n.& vt. 控制，支配，管理
gadget	['gædʒit]	n. 小器具，小配件，小玩意
huge	[hju:dʒ]	adj. 巨大的，极大的，无限的
varied	['vɛərid]	adj. 各式各样的
sport	[spɔ:t]	vt. 佩戴
wireless	['waiəlis]	adj. 无线的
pregnant	['pregnənt]	adj. 怀孕
pacemaker	['peismeikə]	n. 领跑者，带头人
wearer	['wɛərə]	n. 穿用者，佩戴者

relative	[ˈrelətiv]	n. 亲戚
prescription	[priˈskripʃən]	n. 指示，规定
automatically	[ɔːtəˈmætikli]	adv. 自动地，机械地
pharmacy	[ˈfɑːməsi]	n. 药剂学，配药业，制药业
scale	[skeil]	n. 刻度，衡量，比例
monitor	[ˈmɔnitə]	vt. 监控
		n. 监视器，监控器
remotely	[riˈməutli]	adv. 遥远地，偏僻地
app (=application)	[ˌæpliˈkeiʃən]	n. 应用
immaterial	[ˌiməˈtiəriəl]	adj. 非实质的
critical	[ˈkritikəl]	adj. 评论的，危急的，临界的
delay	[diˈlei]	v. & n. 耽搁，延迟，迟滞
rearrange	[ˌriːəˈreindʒ]	vt. 再排列，重新安排
motorway	[ˈməutəwei]	n. 汽车高速公路
blind	[blaind]	adj. 瞎的，盲目的
		vt. 使失明，缺乏眼光或判断力
slide	[slaid]	v.（使）滑动，（使）滑行
regulate	[ˈregjuleit]	vt. 控制，调节，校准
intercom	[ˈintəkɔm]	n. 内部通信联络系统
ditto	[ˈditəu]	n. 同上，同上符号，很相似的东西
		vt. 重复 adv. 与前同地
mundane	[ˈmʌndein]	adj. 世界的，世俗的，平凡的
repetitive	[riˈpetitiv]	adj. 重复的，反复性的
manufacture	[ˌmænjuˈfæktʃə]	vt. 制造，加工
		n. 制造，制造业，产品
complex	[ˈkɔmpleks]	adj. 复杂的，合成的，综合的
		n. 联合体
tasty	[ˈteisti]	adj. 有品味的；有趣的
frustrate	[frʌsˈtreit]	v. 挫败，阻挠，阻止
frustrating	[frʌsˈtreitiŋ]	adj. 令人灰心的；使人沮丧的；让人懊恼的
blockage	[ˈblɔkidʒ]	n. 妨碍，封锁
embed	[imˈbed]	vt. 使插入，使嵌入，深留，嵌入
embedded	[emˈbedid]	adj. 嵌入的，嵌入式
chip	[tʃip]	n. 芯片
handlebar	[ˈhændlbɑː]	n. 把手
plot	[plɔt]	vt. 标绘出，绘制……的图表（或平面图）
barcode	[ˈbɑːkəud]	n. 条形码
endless	[ˈendlis]	adj. 无止境的，无穷的

pattern	[ˈpætən]	n.	式样，模式，图案
		vt.	模仿，仿造
albeit	[ɔːlˈbiːit]	conj.	尽管；即使
broadband	[ˈbrɔːdbænd]	n.	宽带
network	[ˈnetwəːk]	n.	网络
touchscreen	[ˈtʌtʃskriːn]	n.	触摸屏
investment	[inˈvestmənt]	n.	投资
template	[ˈtemplit]	n.	模板（=templet）
population	[ˌpɔpjuˈleiʃən]	n.	人口
predict	[priˈdikt]	vt.	预言，预测
surpass	[səːˈpɑːs]	vt.	远远超出
interaction	[ˌintərˈækʃən]	n.	交互
prevalent	[ˈprevələnt]	adj.	普遍的，流行的
urbanisation	[ˈəːbənaizeiʃən]	n.	都市化
chore	[tʃɔː]	n.	家务杂事

Phrases

Internet of Things (IoT)	物联网
run out of	用完，耗尽
meal plan	用餐计划
delivery slot	交货时间段；交货槽，输送槽
for short	简称，缩写
machine to machine	机器对机器
communicate with …	与……通信，与……沟通
on one's behalf …	为……的利益，代表
get sick	生病
be likely to	可能；倾向于
sat nav	卫星导航
sleep in	多睡一会
motion sensor	运动传感器
be stuck	卡住了，动不了；被困住了，被难住了
up and down	上下地，到处，前前后后
on its own	本身
nothing more than	仅仅，只不过
back-office admin	后台管理
be interested in	对……感兴趣

save sb. from	省得某人做某事；使某人摆脱……
catch on	流行；抓牢，理解
self repair	自修复
customer service	客户服务
smart city	智慧城市
in embryonic form	在酝酿之中
reclaimed land	开垦地，开荒地，新生地
be based on	基于
wired broadband network	有线宽带网络
air conditioning	空调
video calling	视频电话
garbage truck	垃圾车
double whammy	祸不单行，双重打击，双重灾难
in theory	理论上
dispense with	免除，省却，无需

Abbreviations

GP (General Practioner)	全科医生
RFID (Radio Frequency IDentification)	无线射频识别技术
VP (Vice President)	副总裁；副总统
O2	英国一家通信公司
AT&T (American Telephone & Telegraph)	美国电话电报公司

Exercises

【EX.1】**Answer the following questions according to the text.**

1. What does IoT stand for?
2. What are smartphone apps likely to provide?
3. What will your alarm clock do in the future?
4. What is the IoT doing according to Grant Notman?
5. What is the IoT on its own?
6. Will the consumer be interested in the Internet of Things according to Jean-Paul Edwards? What will they be interested in?
7. What is the Internet of Things based around?
8. How can someone find out exactly who are riding these free renting bikes, where those bikes go, and when?

9. What is the city that has a joined-up IoT? Where is it?

10. What is a Cisco-powered concept called U.Life based on? What is its aim?

【EX.2】 Translate the following terms or phrases from English into Chinese and vice versa.

1. interaction
2. network
3. template
4. broadband
5. barcode
6. motion sensor
7. self repair
8. wired broadband network
9. smart city
10. device
11. vt. 感知
12. n. 同时，同步
13. adj. 智能的，敏捷的
14. adj. 无线的
15. adv. 自动地，机械地

【EX.3】 Translate the following sentences into Chinese.

1. The printer is the most commonly used output device after the monitor.

2. The communication system uses the wired mode and wireless mode.

3. Bluetooth is an open specification for short-range wireless data and voice communication.

4. The hardware and the software of sensor node are introduced in this passage.

5. You can search the information of all sorts of monitors on the net.

6. As our technological powers grow, the portability and flexibility of our computer hardware grows, too.

7. The chip is the most valuable part in the computer.

8. Recently the company launched the industry's first combined RFID and barcode unit.

9. My computer has a network interface, which allows me to get to other computers.

10. Overall, broadband access technology is developing towards high bandwidth, fiber and wireless.

【EX.4】 Complete the following passage with appropriate words in the box.

development	embedded	technologies	tagged	check
applications	tracked	computing	concept	network

The Internet of Things (IoT) is a scenario in which every thing has a unique identifier and the ability to communicate over the Internet or a similar wide-area network (WAN).

The ___1___ for an Internet of Things are already in place. Things, in this context, can be people, animals, servers, ___2___, shampoo bottles, cars, steering wheels, coffee machines, park benches or just about any other random item that comes to mind. Once something has a unique identifier, it can be ___3___, assigned a uniform resource identifier (URI) and monitored over a ___4___ network. The Internet of Things is an evolutionary outcome of the trend towards ubiquitous ___5___, a scenario in which processors are ___6___ in everyday objects.

Although the ___7___ wasn't named until 1999, the Internet of Things has been in ___8___ for decades. The first Internet appliance was a Coke machine at Carnegie Melon University in the early 1980s. Programmers working several floors above the vending machine wrote a server program that ___9___ how long it had been since a storage column in the machine had been empty. The programmers could connect to the machine over the Internet, ___10___ the status of the machine and determine whether or not there would be a cold drink awaiting them, should they decide to make the trip down to the machine.

【EX.5】 **Translate the following passage into Chinese.**

What does Internet of Things (IoT) mean?

The Internet of Things (IoT) is a computing concept that describes a future where everyday physical objects will be connected to the Internet and will be able to identify themselves to other devices. The term is closely identified with RFID as the method of communication, although it could also include other sensor technologies, other wireless technologies, QR codes, etc.

IoT is significant because an object that can represent itself digitally becomes something greater than the object existed by itself. No longer does the object relate just to you, but now it is connected to objects around it, data from a database, etc. When many objects act in unison, they are referred to as having "ambient intelligence."

Most of us think about being connected in terms of computers, tablets and smartphones. IoT describes a world where just about anything can be connected and communicate in an intelligent fashion. In other words, with the Internet of Things, the physical world is becoming one big information system.

Text B

The Internet of Things -- This Is Where We're Going

In one vision of the future, every "thing" is connected to the internet. This "Internet of Things "will bring about revolutionary change in how we interact with our environment and more importantly, how we live our lives.

The idea of everything being connected to the internet is not new, but it's increasingly becoming a reality. The Internet of Things came into being in 2008 when the number of things connected to the internet was greater than the number of people who were connected.

The technical utopians have portrayed the Internet of Things as a good thing that will bring untold benefits. They are supported by all the companies that stand to benefit by the increasing connectedness of everything.

Universal connectivity, sensors and computers that are able to collect, analyse and act on this data will bring about improvements in health, food production. In a roundabout way, it might even alleviate poverty.

On the other side are the sceptics who warn of the dangers inherent in not only having an ever growing Internet of Things, but our increasing reliance on it.

The problems range from the difficulties in actually scaling the internet to be capable of supporting the vast number of things and how these things (and the internet itself) are powered to issues of security, privacy and safety.

1. How many things are connected?

Today, there are nine billion devices connected to the internet. By 2020, this will have increased to 24 billion although some estimates place the number at 100 billion.

The parallel change is that the human-generated data being transported on the internet will be dwarfed by the data being generated by machines.

In fact, much of this communication will be between machines. Again, Cisco estimates that by the end of this year, 20 typical households could generate more traffic than the traffic of the entire internet in 2008.

2. What are we connecting?

The Internet of Things is not just about devices that are directly connected to the internet. Sensors and identifiers such as RFID (radio frequency identification) tags[1] also provide data through an intermediary such as a mobile phone, RFID reader, or internet-connected base station.

This means an RFID-tagged cereal box may be considered as one of the "things" on the internet. Theoretically, the RFID would have been used in conjunction with other sensors to record the full life-history of that particular box of cereal, from the time it was manufactured to how it was transported and how long it took for it to be empty.

Sparked, a company in the Netherlands, has developed a sensor that measures a cow's vital signs as well as movement and interactions with other cows. The sensor will transmit approximately 200MB of data per cow every year to allow farmers to monitor the health and wellbeing of their herds.

Sensors in the home and in cars are becoming ubiquitous. A modern car may have as many as 200 sensors, measuring everything from engine performance to tyre pressures. The data are being collected and analysed by on-board computers connected to the car's internal network.

These data can now be communicated to the internet and made available to not only the

---

[1] Radio-frequency identification (RFID) is the use of a wireless noncontact (['nɔn'kɔntækt]adj.没有接触的) system that uses radio- frequency electromagnetic fields to transfer data from a tag attached to an object, for the purposes of automatic identification ([ai,dentifi'keiʃən]n.识别, 辨认) and tracking.

driver of the car but also to companies that own or manage it on the driver's behalf. The sensor data can not only be used to detect problems but also to give statistics on the use of the car.

Tied in with real-time artificial intelligence, the car's network could be providing the driver with feedback and advice, and interacting with the internet for route information, for example.

3. Health-related sensors

Cars and houses are not the only things being wired up with sensors. There are numerous devices that monitor blood pressure, heart rate, levels of hormones and blood components and the like.

Sensors are now being connected directly to the internet or to a smart phone and stored in the Cloud for monitoring and analysis. Again, the estimates are that there will be about 400 million wearable wireless sensors by 2014.

4. And the catch?

Everybody has experienced that moment when a computer or phone has defeated all your attempts to do something basic such as connecting to a wireless network. At times like these, it's hard to imagine a technology-driven utopian world in which billions of devices are all communicating seamlessly and controlling everything around us to improve our lives.

But it really isn't as simple as that. The recent major outage of the BlackBerry Messaging Network serves as a reminder that something as relatively simple as delivering messages from one phone to another over a network that is supposed to be robust and fault tolerant can still be difficult to get right.

NetGear's Connected Lifestyle Survey has recently shown that in Australia, there are 18 million internet-enabled devices that are not connected. These devices include TVs, games consoles, and music and media players.

It's not clear from the report, though, if they are not connected because of the technical difficulty in connecting them or simply because the owners didn't know or care about the benefits of doing so. Clearly the growth and sustainability of the Internet of Things will not be able to rely on the ordinary consumer for connectivity and maintenance.

A recent blog on The Economist highlights issues with the infrastructure, privacy and the danger of a catastrophic failure in an Internet of Things world. Perhaps the most pressing concern Schumpeter raises is that who will end up owning and controlling the data from the Internet of Things.

We are rapidly proceeding to a point where the range of data being collected can literally be used to reconstruct a person's life. The privacy issues brought about by the Internet of Things will make concerns about our interactions on social media giants such as Facebook seem trivial by comparison.

The recent furore over the German Government's use of spyware to watch its citizens is also a harbinger of the amount of information that can be obtained by controlling connectedness to the internet.

The Internet of Things can ultimately be used for the benefit or detriment of individuals and society as a whole. Although business will argue benefits that include increasing efficiency, safety and health, these need to be balanced by safeguards and controls.

The ethics of mass connectivity have yet to be developed.

New Words

connect	[kə'nekt]	v. 连接，联合
revolutionary	[,revə'luːʃənəri]	adj. 革命的
environment	[in'vaiərənmənt]	n. 环境，外界
increasingly	[in'kriːsiŋli]	adv. 日益，愈加
reality	[ri(ː)'æliti]	n. 真实，事实
technical	['teknikəl]	adj. 技术的，技术上的
utopian	[juː'təupjən]	n. 乌托邦，空想家，理想主义者
		adj. 乌托邦的，理想化的，不切实际的
portray	[pɔː'trei]	v. 描绘
untold	[ʌn'təuld]	adj. 未透露的，数不清的
connectedness	[kə'nektidnes]	n. 连通性
collect	[kə'lekt]	v. 收集，聚集，集中，搜集
universal	[,juːni'vəːsəl]	adj. 普遍的，全体的，通用的
analyse	['ænəlaiz]	vt. 分析，分解
		n. 分析
improvement	[im'pruːvmənt]	n. 改进，进步
roundabout	['raundəbaut]	adj. 迂回的，转弯抹角的
poverty	['pɔvəti]	n. 贫穷，贫困，贫乏，缺少
alleviate	[ə'liːvieit]	vt. 使（痛苦等）易于忍受，减轻
sceptic	['skeptik]	n. 怀疑论者
inherent	[in'hiərənt]	adj. 固有的，内在的，与生俱来的
reliance	[ri'laiəns]	n. 信任，信心，依靠
vast	[vɑːst]	adj. 巨大的，大量的
issue	['isjuː]	n. 问题
security	[si'kjuəriti]	n. 安全
privacy	['praivəsi]	n. 隐私
safety	['seifti]	n. 安全，保险，安全设备，保险装置
estimate	['estimeit]	v. & n. 估计，估价，评估
parallel	['pærəlel]	adj. 并行的，平行的，并联的；相同的，类似的
transport	[træns'pɔːt]	vt. 传送，运输
dwarf	[dwɔːf]	vt. 使显得矮小；使相形见绌

		n. 矮子；侏儒
traffic	[ˈtræfik]	n. 通信量；流量
identifier	[aiˈdentifaiə]	n. 标识符
cereal	[ˈsiəriəl]	n. 麦片
theoretically	[θiəˈretikəli]	adv. 理论上，理论地
develop	[diˈveləp]	vt. 发展，开发
measure	[ˈmeʒə]	vt. 测量，测度，估量
		n. 量度器，量度标准，测量，措施
vital	[ˈvaitl]	adj. 生死攸关的，重大的，至关重要的
sign	[sain]	n. 标记，符号，记号
		v. 签名（于），署名（于），签署
wellbeing	[welˈbiːiŋ]	n. 幸福，福利，安乐
herd	[həːd]	n. 兽群，牧群
		v. 把……赶在一起放牧，成群
ubiquitous	[juːˈbikwitəs]	adj. 到处存在的，（同时）普遍存在的
engine	[ˈendʒin]	n. 发动机
available	[əˈveiləbl]	adj. 可用到的，可利用的，有用的
detect	[diˈtekt]	vt. 探测，发现
statistic	[stəˈtistik]	n. 统计数字
hormone	[ˈhɔːməun]	n. 荷尔蒙，激素
wearable	[ˈwɛərəbl]	adj. 可穿用的，可佩带的
experience	[iksˈpiəriəns]	n. & vt. 经验，体验，经历
defeat	[diˈfiːt]	n. & v. 击败
attempt	[əˈtempt]	n. 努力，尝试，企图
		vt. 尝试，企图
feedback	[ˈfiːdbæk]	n. 反馈，反应
seamless	[ˈsiːmlis]	adj. 无缝的
message	[ˈmesidʒ]	n. 消息，通信，信息
		vt. 通知
outage	[ˈautidʒ]	n. 储运损耗
reminder	[riˈmaində]	n. 提醒的人，暗示
robust	[rəˈbʌst]	adj. 健壮的
sustainability	[səˌsteinəˈbiləti]	n. 持续性，能维持性，永续性
maintenance	[ˈmeintənəns]	n. 维护，保持
consumer	[kənˈsjuːmə]	n. 消费者，客户
blog	[blɔg]	n. 博客
highlight	[ˈhailait]	vt. 加亮，使显著，突出
		n. 加亮区，最显著（重要）部分
infrastructure	[ˈinfrəˌstrʌktʃə]	n. 基础

pressing	['presiŋ]	adj. 紧迫的
		v. 挤压
concern	[kən'sə:n]	vt. 涉及，关系到
		n.（利害）关系，关心，关注
literally	['litərəli]	adv. 照字面意义，逐字地
reconstruct	[,ri:kən'strʌkt]	v. 重建；重造，修复
giant	['dʒaiənt]	n. 巨人
		adj. 庞大的，巨大的
trivial	['triviəl]	adj. 琐细的，价值不高的，微不足道的
furore	[fju:'rɔ:ri]	n. 狂热
spyware	['spaiwɛə]	n. 间谍软件
harbinger	['hɑ:bindʒə]	n. 先驱，预兆
		vt. 预告，做……的前驱
ultimately	['ʌltimətli]	adv. 最后，终于，根本，基本上
detriment	['detrimənt]	n. 损害，损害物
individual	[,indi'vidjuəl]	n. 个人
		adj. 个人的
balance	['bæləns]	vt. 平衡
safeguard	['seif,gɑ:d]	n. 保护，保卫；防护措施；安全设施
		vt. 保护

Phrases

bring about	使发生，致使
interact with …	与……相合
come into being	形成，产生
warn of	警告，告诫
be capable of	能够
cereal box	麦片盒子
in conjunction with …	与……协力
tyre pressure	轮胎气压
on-board computer	车载计算机
artificial intelligence	人工智能
blood pressure	血压
heart rate	心率
serve as	充当，担任
fault tolerant	容错
games console	游戏控制台
media player	媒体播放器

rely on 依赖，依靠
catastrophic failure 灾难性故障，突变失效
end up 结束，死
proceed to … 向……进发
social media 社交媒介
as a whole 总体上

Exercises

【EX.1】Answer the following questions according to the text.

1. When did the Internet of Things come into being?
2. What do the technical utopians think of the Internet of Things as?
3. What do the sceptics warn us?
4. How many devices will be connected to the internet by 2020?
5. What has Sparked developed?
6. What could the car's network be providing the driver with when tied in with real-time artificial intelligence?
7. How many wearable wireless sensors will there be by 2014?
8. What has everybody experienced?
9. What is the most pressing concern Schumpeter raises?
10. What can the Internet of Things ultimately be used for?

【EX.2】Translate the following terms or phrases from English into Chinese and vice versa.

1. media player _____   1. _____
2. connectedness _____   2. _____
3. parallel _____   3. _____
4. traffic _____   4. _____
5. spyware _____   5. _____
6. infrastructure _____   6. _____
7. message _____   7. _____
8. robust _____   8. _____
9. environment _____   9. _____
10. social media _____   10. _____
11. 灾难性故障，突变失效 _____ 11. _____
12. 容错 _____   12. _____
13. 人工智能 _____   13. _____
14. v.连接，联合 _____   14. _____
15. v.收集，聚集，集中，搜集 _____ 15. _____

【EX.3】Translate the following sentences into Chinese.

1. You must connect this wire with that one.

2. A variable is an identifier whose value can change at runtime.

3. A ubiquitous Internet will make every computer your office.

4. The designed signal processing system can detect signal effectively.

5. You need feedback to monitor progress.

6. Realizing the seamless handover is the key technology to support mobile network.

7. We should encode the message for security reasons.

8. The detector must be operationally simple, reliable and robust.

9. Finally, good standards can lead to reduced maintenance costs and improved reuse of design and code.

10. This is a hidden cost to the Internet device: the infrastructure cost.

Text C

What Does the Internet of Things Mean for Today's Culture?	
Today we are living in an era of "permanent revolution" thanks to the configuration of new media, entertainment and culture. Without doubt, the technological developments that are setting up in record time are creating a new ecosystem[1], where leading Internet-connected devices are changing the way consumers' access content.	[1] [i:kə'sistəm] n. 生态系统
Smartphones, tablets, e-readers, personal navigation[2] devices, wireless products and gaming units are among the driving factors for creating new applications, products and services that can improve people's daily lives.	[2] [ˌnævi'geiʃən] n. 导航，领航
1. Internet of Things	
The rapid transition to new content experiences online through the latest generation of devices has been given by several factors[3], among which are access to mobile broadband, increased investment in data centers and cloud computing, innovation in data mining[4] software, high use of social networking sites and intuitive interfaces on Smart TV's, tablets and game consoles that have brought innovations to the audience.	[3] ['fæktə] n. 因素，要素 [4] data mining：数据挖掘
Though global demand for Smart TVs is scarce[5] today, the demand is growing. It's expected that over 45 percent of people will	[5] [skɛəs] adj. 缺乏的，不足的

have a connected TV by 2014. At the same time, the total market of connected devices could grow another 60 percent in the same period.

Devices that can access the Internet have gained wide acceptance among users. Connected devices -- smartphones and tablets as well as cars and refrigerators -- will grow more than fourfold[6] in 2020. In addition, increased use of video will be assumed that the total Internet traffic will quadruple in 2014, according to latest Cisco report.

Furthermore, the concept of "Internet of Things" is leading to connect other gadgets, machine-to-machine (M2M) and even appliances or vehicles.

For example, S-class Mercedes have nearly as many embedded computers as an Airbus A380 to make driving a more pleasant[7] experience. Ford Sync, one of the most popular systems in its class, provides access to the climate control and entertainment functions with voice commands in the form of natural speech for car drivers. MyFord Mobile for iPhone is another mobile app offering from Ford Motors that link up[8] cars via an embedded AT&T wireless module[9] for remote communication.

Then, there is Siri-Car integration. Apple's voice control system will drive the next generation of cars in near future. General Motors is not far behind: the company is developing a series of apps that will transform the way we drive.

2. Future Connected Devices

A new startup, Everything, is exploring unique online profiles for products and other objects to make them part of the Web, so that every physical thing can be digitally[10] connected.

"We're looking to solve a problem that manufacturers didn't think there was a solution to. How do I get closer to my customers when I don't know who most of them are?" says Andy Hobsbawm, everything's cofounder[11] and chief marketing officer.

Every product can be packaged using a unique identifying tag like simple QR codes or NFC. Everything will then scan or swipe the product using smartphones to instantly connect to Internet, creating personalized[12] online services for customers.

Other services like AirBnB and the US private car sharing/rental company Relay Rides are already taking advantage of connected devices. Relay Rides provides private cars rent to travelers on a

[6] ['fɔːfəʊld]
adj. 四倍的

[7] ['plezənt]
adj. 令人愉快的，舒适的

[8] link up: 连接
[9] ['mɔdjuːl]
n. 模块

[10] ['dɪdʒɪtəli]
adv. 数字地

[11] [kəʊ'faʊndə]
n. 共同创办人，共同创始人

[12] ['pɜːsənəlaɪzd]
adj. 私人化的

journey-by-journey basis. The company is now using online network that allows same car to effectively share among different owners. This can lead to better planning, monitoring, parking, maintaining service history, seat positions as well as catering to[13] individual needs.	[13]cater to：迎合
"The web of things has been coming for a long time and people have been talking about products having a presence online," notes Hobsbawm. "Now you're entering a zone where the cost per unit of tagging a unit is becoming affordable for scale and where bandwidth is continuing to fall."	
New categories[14] of connected devices seem to be continually added to the M2M device mix. According to Berg Insight, shipped consumer M2M devices with cellular[15] connectivity grew to 7.1 million worldwide in 2011, up from 6.4 million in the previous year.	[14]['kætigəriz] n. 种类 [15]['seljulə] adj. 细胞的
The report says, "This relatively new breed[16] of connected devices -- neither classified as handsets, PCs, tablets nor traditional M2M devices, includes E-readers and personal navigation devices. Handheld[17] gaming consoles, personal tracking devices and wellness devices are promising categories as well."	[16][bri:d] n. 品种，种类 [17] ['hændheld] adj. 手持的
This will ensure that consumers are always connected and, therefore, be more and more accessible[18] to information, which will affect the ability to compare products and services to make decisions in a more thoughtful way and to influence other consumers.	[18][ək'sesəbl] adj. 易接近的，可访问的

参考译文

Text A 物联网：它会如何改变你的设备

当牛奶喝完了，冰箱就给你发送文本。忘了这个过时的想法吧。试想有这样一台冰箱，它能够感知冰箱里有什么、选择下两周的膳食计划、通过网上超市订购并按照 Gmail 日历同步配送。

也许你有一台智能电视，你一定会有一个智能手机，甚至是可以把内容同步到 iPad 的智能手机上，但这样的"智能"设备只能算初级的"物联网"设备，物联网也可简称为 IoT。物联网也称为"机器对机器"（也许更正确），它不由任何一个集团或公司所有或控制，也不是单一的想法，当然也不是我们想要的产品清单中的一项。但是，它将改变我们的生活。

我们用来相互沟通的设备是多种多样的。例如，给每个母牛佩戴一个无线传感器，农场主就可以得知它们是否生病或怀孕。这个已经实现了，下一步是能把数据发送给医生的心脏起搏器，它甚至在佩戴者生病时可以给亲属发短信。

更可能首先实现的应用包括自动订购处方药品。你无须到医生或药房去开处方单，而是由医生通过联网实现远程监控（已经有了 WiFi 模型）。

智能手机的应用程序可能提供物联网世界的重要窗口，但平板计算机和其他设备也将加入。装置本身是不重要的——Internet 连接才是关键。

一些卫星导航设备已经使用实时更新的交通信息，但在未来，如果你的列车晚点闹钟会让你继续睡，并重新安排一辆出租车；如果你被困在高速公路上甚至会发电子邮件给你的老板。

如果你有资金，已经可以用带运动传感器的灯跟踪你的活动，并通过上下滑动百叶窗来调节温度和照明水平。无论你是否在家，内部通话系统都可以呼叫你的手机。这种内部通话系统也已经存在一段时间了。同样，你可以从世界的另一边监控安全摄像机。

"物联网可以消除简单重复的任务或创造以前不可能的东西，使更多的人完成更有价值的任务，让机器去做重复的工作"，格兰特·诺文说，他在伍德和道格拉斯公司负责市场营销，该公司生产物联网应用的无线通信硬件。

显然，两个设备互相的交谈如果不能给所有者带来好处或增加某种效率，那就没有意义。物联网本身只不过是后台管理。

全球创意媒体机构 Manning Gottlieb OMD London 未来传媒部门的领导保罗·爱德华兹说："消费者不会对物联网感兴趣，就像他们对计算机的互联网不感兴趣一样。"

"他们会感兴趣的是物联网能让他们做什么或他们可以少做什么。无源环境监测、远程管理和万物相连都将帮助我们做我们曾经所做的一切，但会更快、更便宜而且更好。"

下面这些会流行吗？可以远程修理的洗衣机，或者，如果工程师有正确的部件只要运行一次就可自我修复的洗衣机，或 Nest 恒温器，可以知道你是否在家来更好地控制家里的暖气。

"技术是复杂的"，爱德华兹就后者而言，"但要求节省 20%的能源花费是一个简单的想法。"自我修复的产品吗？现在有一种有趣的想法，可以提供客户服务，消除系统中的障碍并提高效率。

基于嵌入式 RFID 芯片、条形码和传感器的物联网给人印象最深刻的是有助于创建智慧城市。其用途不可尽数，而且通常从节省家务活动的时间开始。然而，要预测人类的行为，物联网是最佳的。

一个城市在使用免费自行车租赁方案？把一个 RFID 芯片插入车把，就可以精确测定那些自行车去往何处、何时使用以及被谁所用。晚上，路灯可以仅当车子接近时开启——节省电力——令人印象更深刻的是，可以收集数据来确定城市交通模式。

有一个城市已经有了物联网，但还在初始阶段。韩国汉城以南 40 英里的松岛市，已利用超级智能的方式使用 1500 亩的填海土地。

基于城域有线宽带网络的叫作 U.Life 的思科动力概念使目前的 60 000 居民使用他们的智能手机、平板计算机和其他的触摸屏装置来控制他们家庭的供热、照明和空调，与全市的 TelePrescence 设备免费进行视频通话。汽车可以与道路对话，道路可与路灯对话，垃圾通过管道的地下网络被吸走，而不需要垃圾车。

其目标是建立一个私人投资的低能耗、非常高效的城市，并有很好的理由称为全球样板；全球 70 亿人口的一多半现在居住在城市，预计到 2050 年会达到 63 亿。

"M2M 市场不同于其他任何市场，它在迅速增长，它是一种可以超越人类交互的技术"，Jasper Wireless 的营销副总裁马卡里奥·奈美惠说。该公司在物联网通信领域与移动运营商（如英国的 O2 和美国的 AT&T）合作。"其不限范围意味着未来社会中连接无所不在。"

人口增长和日益增加的城市化的"双重打击"意味着物联网的任务就是使我们的城市流程化，但在理论上它会让我们省去很多日常事务。当然，这就是我们所说的家庭计算机的作用。

Unit 2

Text A

What is M2M?

M2M refers to data communications between two or more machines. M2M is most commonly translated as Machine to Machine but sometimes it is translated as Man to Machine, Machine to Man and others. Cellular telephone service providers use public wireless networks to accomplish M2M, Telemetry or Telematics[1].

Most often, M2M systems are task-specific, meaning that a given system is purpose-built for just one specific device, or a very restricted class of devices in an industry. This is one of the indicators of the M2M market which is still in its infancy, as a unified intercommunication standard has yet to evolve. Functions are duplicated -- each purpose-built system repeats many functions already implemented in similar systems.

Wireless M2M is machine to machine communication through wireless technologies such as CDMA.

1. Where can M2M be used?

M2M provides benefits to many individuals, companies, communities and organizations in the public and private sectors across various industries. Below are a few "emerging segments" that are gaining growth benefits through leveraging M2M solutions:

- Telecommunication - IP Internetworking / Wireless WAN / Mobile Learning
- Manufacturing - Supply Chain / Inventory Management / Factory Automation
- Light Industry - Sensor Monitoring / Remote Access Control / Utilities
- Transportation - Asset Tracking / Logistics Management
- Retail - Point-of-Sale / Kiosk / Digital Content Signage
- Telematics - Aftermarket / In-Vehicle Solutions

---

[1] Telematics typically is any integrated use of telecommunications and informatics, also known as ICT (Information and Communications Technology,信息与通信技术).

- e-Business / m-Business Solutions
- Real Estate - Building Automation
- Security - Video Surveillance

2. What are the benefits of M2M?

These are just some of the benefits that are gained through leveraging M2M to solve business challenges:

- Cost-effective preventive maintenance and quality of service
- Fast response through outsourcing troubleshooting
- Centralized service support and data management
- On-going revenues throughout product lifecycle
- Increased revenues from minimized downtime
- Remote diagnostics

3. What makes up an M2M solution?

Usually an M2M solution is made up of several components:

- Device(s) or sensor(s) to collect data and/or monitor changes
- An application and database to process the data sent and received
- A central server to send and / or receive data transmitted by the device(s) or sensor(s)
- Connectivity (either fixed line or wireless) to connect the device or sensor to a central server
- A modem to allow data exchange between the device(s) or sensor(s) and the central server
- An application to ensure security of the data transmitted and to monitor and manage the connectivity to the device or sensor network

4. What are the benefits of wireless M2M?

4.1 Flexibility

Devices that are wirelessly connected to a network are not limited to a physical location. This gives you the flexibility to move them should you need to, for example if a vending machine is not getting much footfall, you can simply place it elsewhere. Devices in remote locations where it's difficult to run cables can also be attached to a wireless network quickly and easily.

4.2 Mobility

Mobile devices can connect into a network, which is not possible with a fixed line network, allowing data communication with all devices.

4.3 Access to information

Wireless networks deliver real-time information to mobile devices enabling information to be received or sent whenever and wherever it is required, so organizations have access to live information for effective and fast decision making.

4.4 Independent network

A wireless network can be quickly and easily deployed into a building or location without the need for integration with the existing fixed line network, thereby delivering an independent secure network.

4.5 Speed

A wireless network can be deployed much more quickly than a fixed network as no cabling is needed between devices. This allows devices to be active more quickly and can provide cost savings.

4.6 Cost

There are cost savings related to the speed of deployment, the elimination of cabling costs, and the reduction in communication costs, as CDMA-cellular is more cost effective than PSTN/fixed line.

4.7 How do wireless M2M machines communicate?

M2M wireless solutions use wireless modems to communicate using always-on CDMA cellular, allowing it to communicate data immediately, and at much higher speeds. CDMA airtime/data usage is billed according to the amount of data used and not the amount of time the connection lasts.

New Words

accomplish	[ə'kɔmpliʃ]	vt. 完成，达到，实现
telemetry	[tə'lemətri]	n. 遥感勘测，自动测量记录传导
telematics	[ˌteli'mɑːtiks]	n. 信息通信业务，远程信息处理
purpose-built	['pəːpəsbilt]	adj. 为特定目的建造的
specific	[spi'sifik]	n. 细节
		adj. 详细而精确的，明确的，特殊的
restrict	[ri'strikt]	vt. 限制，约束，限定
industry	['indəstri]	n. 行业
indicator	['indikeitə]	n. 指标；指示器
infancy	['infənsi]	n. 幼年
intercommunication	[ˌintəkəˌmjuːni'keiʃən]	n. 双向（或多向）通信
evolve	[i'vɔlv]	v. （使）发展，（使）进展，（使）进化
function	['fʌŋkʃən]	n. 功能，作用
duplicate	['djuːplikeit]	vt. 使成双，使加倍；复制
		n. 复制品；复印件
		adj. 复制的，副本的；成对的，二倍的
implement	['implimənt]	v. 实施，实现

emerging	[iˈməːdʒiŋ]	adj. 新兴的，不断出现的，涌现的
gain	[gein]	vt. 获得，得到
leverage	[ˈliːvəridʒ]	vt. 杠杆作用
		n. 杠杆
retail	[ˈriːteil]	n. 零售
		adj. 零售的
		v. 零售
automation	[ɔːtəˈmeiʃən]	n. 自动控制，自动操作
utility	[juːˈtiləti]	n. 效用，有用
logistic	[ləˈdʒistik]	adj. 物流的，后勤的
kiosk	[ˈkiːɔsk]	n. 亭子
aftermarket	[ˈɑːftəˌmɑːkit]	n. 贩卖修理用零件的市场
surveillance	[səːˈveiləns]	n. 监视，监督
preventive	[priˈventiv]	adj. 预防性的
centralize	[ˈsentrəlaiz]	vt. 集聚，集中
revenue	[ˈrevənjuː]	n. 收入，税收
downtime	[ˈdauntaim]	n. 停工期
component	[kəmˈpəunənt]	n. 成分
		adj. 组成的，构成的
database	[ˈdeitəbeis]	n. 数据库，资料库
ensure	[inˈʃuə]	v. 确保，保证
connectivity	[kənekˈtiviti]	n. 连通性
server	[ˈsəːvə]	n. 服务器
modem	[ˈməudəm]	n. 调制解调器
exchange	[iksˈtʃeindʒ]	vt. 交换
flexibility	[ˌfleksəˈbiliti]	n. 弹性，适应性，灵活性
footfall	[ˈfutfɔːl]	n. 客流量
attach	[əˈtætʃ]	vt. 缚上，系上，贴上
mobility	[məuˈbiliti]	n. 活动性，移动性，机动性
live	[laiv]	adj. 活的，生动的，精力充沛的
effective	[iˈfektiv]	adj. 有效的，被实施的
independent	[indiˈpendənt]	adj. 独立的，不受约束的
deploy	[diˈplɔi]	v. 部署，展开，配置
integration	[ˌintiˈgreiʃən]	n. 综合，集成
deliver	[diˈlivə]	vt. 递送，交付
elimination	[iˌlimiˈneiʃən]	n. 排除，除去，消除
reduction	[riˈdʌkʃən]	n. 减少，缩影，变形，缩减量
immediately	[iˈmiːdjətli]	adv. 立即，马上，直接地

Phrases

refer to	指；涉及；查阅；有关
cellular telephone	移动电话
public wireless network	公共无线网络
in one's infancy	初期，早期
mobile learning	移动学习
supply chain	供应链
inventory management	库存管理
factory automation	工厂自动化
light industry	轻工业
sensor monitoring	传感器监测
remote access control	远程访问控制
asset tracking	资产跟踪
logistics management	物流管理
digital content signage	数字标牌
in-vehicle solutions	车载解决方案
m-business solutions	移动商务解决方案
real estate	房地产
building automation	楼宇自动化
video surveillance	视频监视
preventive maintenance	预防性维修，定期检修
outsourcing troubleshooting	外包的故障排除
data management	数据管理
product lifecycle	产品生命周期
remote diagnostics	远程诊断
vending machine	自动贩卖机
real time	实时
mobile device	移动设备
decision making	决策，判定
cost saving	节约成本
communication cost	通信成本

Abbreviations

M2M (Machine to Machine)   机器对机器

CDMA (Code Division Multiple Access)　　码分多址
WAN (Wide Area Network)　　广域网
PSTN (Public Switched Telephone Network)　　公共开关电话网络

Exercises

【EX.1】Answer the following questions according to the text.

1. What does M2M refer to?
2. What is the characteristic of M2M systems? What does it mean?
3. What is wireless M2M?
4. How many fields can M2M be used in the text?
5. Can M2M offer centralized service support and data management?
6. Are devices that are wirelessly connected to a network limited to a physical location?
7. What do wireless networks deliver to mobile devices?
8. Which one can be deployed more quickly, a wireless network or a fixed one? Why?
9. Which one is less cost effective, CDMA-cellular or PSTN/fixed line?
10. How is CDMA airtime/data usage billed?

【EX.2】Translate the following terms or phrases from English into Chinese and vice versa.

1. centralize　　　　　　　1. _____
2. modem　　　　　　　　2. _____
3. mobility　　　　　　　　3. _____
4. server　　　　　　　　　4. _____
5. logistic　　　　　　　　5. _____
6. ensure　　　　　　　　　6. _____
7. automation　　　　　　　7. _____
8. remote access control　　8. _____
9. building automation　　　9. _____
10. product lifecycle　　　　10. _____
11. 移动设备　　　　　　　　11. _____
12. n.功能，作用　　　　　　12. _____
13. n.信息通信业务，远程信息处理　　13. _____
14. n.停工期　　　　　　　　14. _____
15. v.部署，展开，配置　　　15. _____

【EX.3】Translate the following sentences into Chinese.

1. Developments in electronic, sonic, and laser technology will provide telemetry that will increase accuracy and timely management response.

2. Have VLAN function is an important indicator to measure LAN switches.

3. Wireless area network (WLAN) is an important part in computer networks.

4. Automation of the factory has greatly increased its productivity.

5. What is the difference between logistics and supply chain management?

6. Logic simulation is an important component of automatic design of digital circuits.

7. In database, a field contains information about an entity.

8. You can then distribute your custom components, or you can move them from test to production.

9. With a 10 Mbps Cable modem, that same file can be downloaded in 8 seconds.

10. These error messages will appear when remote access control has failed.

【EX.4】 Complete the following passage with appropriate words in the box.

| waste | services | adapted to | changed | public |
| security | free | transportation | optimize | urban |

Statistics, forecasts and population studies confirm the continuous migration of population towards cities. There, people find jobs, better access to ___1___ and better living conditions. The current ___2___ environment is not ___3___ this massive migration. This means, new challenges in the fields of ___4___, environmental issues, ___5___ systems, water distribution and – more general – resource management will rapidly occur.

Today, large cities are faced with problems such as ___6___ or misuse of resources, which could be ___7___ by increased in-time information. In Digital Cities, people will arrive just in time for their ___8___ transportation as exact information is provided to their device in due time. Even parking your car will be easier as ___9___ parking spots around you are shown on your device.

Real time information that is always available will ___10___ time, save energy and make life easier.

【EX.5】 Translate the following passage into Chinese.

Digital city

The term Digital City or Digital Community (Smart Community, information city and e-city are also used) refers to a connected community that combines broadband communications infrastructure; flexible, service-oriented computing infrastructure based on open industry standards; and innovative services to meet the needs of governments and their employees, citizens and businesses. The geographical dimension (space) of digital communities vary: they can be extended from a city district up to a multi-million metropolis.

While wireless infrastructure is a key element of Digital City infrastructure, it is only a first step. The Digital City may require hard-wired broadband infrastructure, and it is much more than just the network. A Digital City provides interoperable, Internet-based government services that enable ubiquitous connectivity to transform key government processes, both internally across departments and employees and externally to citizens and businesses. Digital City services are accessible through wireless mobile devices and are enabled by services oriented enterprise architecture including Web services, the Extensible Markup Language (XML), and mobilized software applications.

Text B

How Machine to Machine Communication Works

A car's microchip tells the engine how to operate under various conditions so that the car can achieve the best fuel economy. Computers link production plants together to monitor and maximize production.

For years, the machines used to make our life easier have been getting smarter as their internal computer processors and software tell them what to do based on the parameters we provide.

When machines "talk" they do so in a language known as "telemetry". The concept of telemetry -- remote machines and sensors collecting and sending data to a central point for analysis, either by humans or computers -- certainly isn't new. But an emerging concept is taking that idea to a whole new level by applying modern-networking technology.

Three very common technologies -- wireless sensors, the Internet and personal computers -- are coming together to create Machine to Machine communications, or M2M. The concept holds great promise in promoting telemetry's use by business, government and private individuals.

M2M communications, for instance, can be used to more efficiently monitor the condition of critical public infrastructure, such as water treatment facilities or bridges, with less human intervention. It can help businesses maintain inventory or make it easier for scientists to conduct research. Because it relies on common technology, it also could help a homeowner maintain the perfect lawn or create a shopping list at a button's touch.

M2M communications expands telemetry's role beyond its common use in science and engineering and places it in an everyday setting. People are already using M2M, but there are many more potential applications as wireless sensors, networks and computers improve, and the concept is closely combined with other technology.

How have M2M communications developed? How is it different from traditional telemetry? And what are the various applications for M2M communications? Read on to find out more about M2M.

1. Telemetry vs. M2M Communications

In Machine to Machine communications, a remote sensor gathers data and sends it wirelessly to a network, where it's next routed, often through the Internet, to a server such as a personal computer. At that point, the data is analyzed and acted upon, according to the software in place.

Older systems worked similarly, using "telemetry". Telemetry technology, in many ways, was the forerunner of the more advanced M2M communications systems. Both telemetry communication and M2M communications transmit data through a sensor. The major difference between the two is that rather than a random radio signal, M2M communications uses existing networks, such as wireless networks used by the public, to transmit the data.

Telemetry systems were once the province of scientists, government agencies and other organizations. Still, telemetry technology found many uses, including in aerospace, agriculture, water treatment monitoring and wildlife science. A radio collar wildlife scientists fit onto a captured animal sends telemetry about that animal's movement and habits.

The sensors in older telemetry communications, however, were highly specialized and often needed strong power sources to transmit data. Also, data collection could be spotty if a remote sensor was located in a "dead spot". Of course, any data analysis was conducted by what we now consider antiquated computers.

Modern M2M communications represent vast improvements over these systems. Remote sensor technology advances offer increased sensitivity and accuracy. The explosive growth of public wireless networks is probably the biggest change that has opened M2M communications to many more sectors.

Using wireless networks makes it easier to transmit telemetry for several reasons. One of them is that radio signals don't need to be as powerful as they once did, as cellular towers are spread over large areas to provide coverage. The other is older telemetry systems didn't always rely on radio signals -- some used dedicated phone lines, for instance -- but the wireless aspect allows for easier remote placement of sensors.

2. How M2M Works

Making a Machine to Machine communications system work is a step by step process. The main elements involved are sensors (usually the kind that can send telemetry wirelessly), a wireless network and a computer connected to the Internet.

Let's take the case of a water treatment facility. City engineers are responsible for supplying the community with fresh drinking water. They need to monitor the raw water supply, the treatment process and the end product, which is drinkable water.

First, the engineers would place sensors in strategic locations. This includes placing sensors that can detect contaminants near or around the raw water supply, such as a lake or river, as well as near the water plant's main intakes. They also would place sensors at various stages of the treatment process and more sensors on the plant's outflow pipes, which supply the treated water to the community.

These sensors will send real-time data to a wireless network, which are connected to the Internet. Engineers then monitor this incoming streaming data using computers loaded with specialized software.

The data from the lake sensors might tell them, for instance, that a plume of oil has appeared in the lake, perhaps from a spill. The engineers might then switch to a different intake location to avoid pulling the contaminated water into the treatment plant.

Data from the treatment plant will give information about the water's condition as it enters the process. For instance, some communities experience high levels of chemical runoff during certain times of the year, causing engineers to use special processes to purify the water at those times. If the sensors detect that, it can alert engineers to treat the water for that issue. By only using that treatment process when needed, however, it saves the city's money.

Finally, engineers can monitor the outflow water to ensure their treatment process is indeed resulting in high quality drinking water for the community.

3. Applications of M2M Communications

It's easy to see why Machine to Machine communications have so many applications. With better sensors, wireless networks and increased computing capability, M2M is applied in many sectors.

Utility companies, for instance, use M2M communications both in harvesting energy products, such as oil and gas, and in billing customers. In the field, remote sensors can detect important parameters at an oil drill site. The sensors can send information wirelessly to a computer with specific details about pressure, flow rates and temperatures or even fuel levels in on-site equipment. The computer can automatically adjust on-site equipment to maximize efficiency.

Traffic control is another dynamic environment that can benefit from M2M communications. In a typical system, sensors monitor variables such as traffic volume and speed. The sensors send this information to computers using specialized software that controls traffic-control devices, like lights and variable informational signs. Using the incoming data, the software manipulates the traffic control devices to maximize traffic flow. Researchers are studying ways to create M2M networks that monitor the status of infrastructure, such as bridges and highways.

Telemedicine offers another use. For instance, some heart patients wear special monitors that gather information about the way their heart is working. The data is sent to implanted devices that deliver a shock to correct an errant rhythm.

Businesses also can use M2M communications for tracking inventory and security. Late in 2007, M2M communications helped break up a heavy equipment theft ring. A rental company noticed sensors on its equipment showed the bulldozers were almost 100 miles from where they were supposed to be. Checking on other equipment rented the same day at different locations showed a similar trend, and the business used its M2M communications to disable the engines on the equipment and contacted the law enforcement agency. Officers found that the company's equipment, along with a dozen other stolen pieces, was headed for the Mexican border.

Machine to Machine communication appears to have a bright future. It's a flexible technology that uses common equipment in new ways. Every day, businesses, engineers, scientists, doctors and many others are finding new ways to use this new communications tool.

New Words

microchip	[ˈmaikrəutʃip]	n. 微芯片
engine	[ˈendʒin]	n. 发动机；引擎
achieve	[əˈtʃiːv]	vt. 得到，获得
fuel	[fjuəl]	n. 燃料
economy	[iːˈkɔnəmi]	n. 经济，节约，节约措施，经济实惠
maximize	[ˈmæksimaiz]	vt. 取……最大值，最佳化
software	[ˈsɔftwɛə]	n. 软件
parameter	[pəˈræmitə]	n. 参数，参量
promote	[prəˈməut]	vt. 促进，发扬，提升
facility	[fəˈsiliti]	n. 设备，工具
intervention	[ˌintə(ː)ˈvenʃən]	n. 干涉
homeowner	[ˈhəumˌəunə]	n. 自己拥有住房者，（住自己房子的）私房屋主
lawn	[lɔːn]	n. 草地，草坪
expand	[iksˈpænd]	vt. 使膨胀，扩张 vi. 发展
remote	[riˈməut]	adj. 遥远的，远程的
gather	[ˈgæðə]	n. 集合，聚集 vi. 集合，聚集 vt. 使聚集，搜集
similarly	[ˈsiniləli]	adv. 同样地，类似于
forerunner	[ˈfɔːˌrʌnə]	n. 先驱（者）
random	[ˈrændəm]	n. 随意，任意 adj. 随机的，任意的，随便的
province	[ˈprɔvins]	n. 范围，职责
aerospace	[ˈɛərəuspeis]	n. 航空航天学
wildlife	[ˈwaildlaif]	n. 野生动植物
fit	[fit]	vt. 安装
specialized	[ˈspeʃəlaizd]	adj. 专门的
spotty	[ˈspɔti]	adj. 多污点的，质量不一的
antiquated	[ˈæntikweitid]	adj. 老式的，陈旧的
sensitivity	[ˈsensiˈtiviti]	n. 敏感，灵敏（度），灵敏性
accuracy	[ˈækjurəsi]	n. 精确性，正确度
explosive	[iksˈpləusiv]	adj. 爆炸（性）的，爆发（性）的

signal	['signl]	n. 信号 adj. 信号的 v. 发信号
coverage	['kʌveridʒ]	n. 覆盖
process	[prə'ses]	n. 过程，作用，方法，程序，步骤 vt. 加工，处理
element	['elimənt]	n. 要素，元素，成分，元件
contaminant	[kən'tæminənt]	n. 致污物，污染物
intake	['inteik]	n.（水管、煤气管等的）入口，进口
treatment	['tri:tmənt]	n. 处理
avoid	[ə'vɔid]	vt. 避免，消除
runoff	['rʌnɔ:f]	n. 流量，溢流
purify	['pjuərifai]	v. 净化
alert	[ə'lə:t]	n. 警惕，警报 adj. 提防的，警惕的
outflow	['autfləu]	n. 流出
capability	[,keipə'biliti]	n. 性能，容量
manipulate	[mə'nipjuleit]	vt.（熟练地）操作，巧妙地处理
telemedicine	['teli,medisin]	n.（通过遥测、电话、电视等手段求诊的）远距离医学
errant	['erənt]	adj. 漂泊的；偏离正道的，错误的
rhythm	['riðəm]	n. 节奏，韵律
bulldozer	['buldəuzə]	n. 推土机
trend	[trend]	n. 倾向，趋势
contact	['kɔntækt]	vt. 联系

Phrases

production plant	生产工厂
personal computer	个人计算机，缩写为 PC
water treatment	水处理，水的净化
conduct research	进行研究
shopping list	购物单
at a button's touch	只按一键，一触即成
different from …	异于……
government agency	政府部门
dead spot	哑点，死点，（接收机）盲点，非灵敏区
explosive growth	爆炸性增长
cellular tower	蜂窝塔

spread over…	遍布在……，覆盖在……
dedicated line	专用线
step by step	按部就班的
be responsible for	负责
drinking water	饮用水
raw water	未净化的水
drinkable water	可饮用水
strategic location	优越的地理位置，战略要地
outflow pipe	出水管
a plume of	一股，一团，一缕
treatment plant	污水处理厂
result in	引起，导致，以……为结局
utility company	公共事业公司
at the time	当时，在那个时候
oil drill site	石油钻井现场
traffic volume	交通量，运输量，运输密度，行车量
heart patient	心脏病患者
break up	打碎，破碎，分裂，结束
rental company	租赁公司
law enforcement agency	执法部门

Exercises

【EX.1】Answer the following questions according to the text.

1. What does a car's microchip tell the engine?

2. How do machines "talk"?

3. What are the three very common technologies that are coming together to create Machine to Machine communications?

4. Why could M2M communications help a homeowner maintain the perfect lawn or create a shopping list at a button's touch?

5. What is the same thing for telemetry communication and M2M communications?

6. What is the major difference between telemetry communication and M2M communications?

7. What is said about the sensors in older telemetry communications?

8. What is probably the biggest change that has opened M2M communications to many more sectors?

9. What does the example of a water treatment facility show?

10. What are the sectors M2M is applied in?

【EX.2】 Translate the following terms or phrases from English into Chinese and vice versa.

1. break up   1. _____
2. dedicated line   2. _____
3. result in   3. _____
4. personal computer   4. _____
5. at a button's touch   5. _____
6. microchip   6. _____
7. maximize   7. _____
8. parameter   8. _____
9. facility   9. _____
10. sensitivity   10. _____
11. n. 精确性，正确度   11. _____
12. n. 流出   12. _____
13. vt.（熟练地）操作，巧妙地处理 13. _____
14. n. 性能，容量   14. _____
15. n. 覆盖   15. _____

【EX.3】 Translate the following sentences into Chinese.

1. The average microchip is about the size of a grain of rice.
2. The processor itself has traditionally required one or more boards of logic.
3. Future computer development depends greatly upon software.
4. One declaration of the function contains a variable parameter list.
5. These error messages will appear when remote access control has failed.
6. The computer applies control action directly to the process without manual intervention.
7. This sensor has high sensitivity, short response time and good stabilization.
8. The signal will be converted into digital code.
9. How fast does the computer process the data?
10. Most commercial routers have some kind of built - in packet filtering capability.

Text C

Machine To Machine

M2M is about enabling the flow of data between machines and machines and ultimately machines and people. Regardless of the type of machine or data, information usually flows in the same general way

-- from a machine over a network, and then through a gateway to a system where it can be reviewed and acted on[1].

Within that basic framework[2], there are many different choices to make such as how the machine is connected, what type of communication is used, and how the data is used. Even though it can be complex, once a company knows what it wants to do with the data, the options[3] for setting up the application are usually straightforward[4].

When it comes to the detailed points of machine to machine communication, every deployment is unique. However, there are four basic stages that are common to just about every M2M application. Those components are:

- Collection of data
- Transmission of selected data through a communication network
- Assessment of the data
- Response to the available information

1. Collection of Data

The intelligence of a monitored machine may be as simple as a temperature sensor, level indicator[5] or contact closure[6], or it may be an industrial computer system with a Modbus communication port.

The process of M2M communication begins with taking data out of a machine so that it can be analyzed and sent over a network. Monitoring a "dumb" machine may mean directly connecting to and monitoring one or more limit switches[7], contact closures or analog outputs[8]. With an intelligent electronic device, it may be possible to simply connect it to the equipment's serial port[9] and ask for the data.

The goal of the M2M hardware is to bridge the intelligence in the machine with the communication network.

An intelligent wireless data module is physically integrated with the monitored machine and programmed to understand the machine's protocol (the way it sends and receives data).

If the monitored machine is configured as an intelligent master device[10], it may treat the M2M device as a simple wireless modem, loading it up with data and then instructing it to transmit that data to the network. If the machine is just a collection of switches and sensors or an intelligent slave device, the M2M device can act as the master device[11]. In this mode, it takes charge by periodically[12] polling the device by reading the sensors and switches or by sending data requests

---

[1] act on: 对……起作用，作用于
[2] ['freimwə:k] n. 构架，框架，结构
[3] ['ɔpʃən] n. 选项，选择权
[4] [streit'fɔ:wəd] adj. 简单的，易懂的，直截了当的

[5] level indicator: 液面指示器
[6] contact closure: 接点闭合

[7] limit switch: 限位开关，极限开关
[8] analog outputs: 模拟输出
[9] serial port: 串行端口

[10] master device: 主设备
[11] slave device: 从设备
[12] [ˌpiəri'ɔdikəli] adv. 周期性地，定时

through the serial port.

In a high end application like a major electric utility substation, it may be necessary to send a constant[13] stream of real time data describing the machine or process. But in many cases, this is not necessary or worth the cost. In these cases, the M2M device should minimize the amount of data to be sent by constantly reviewing the data, comparing it against programmable[14] alarm limits or set points, and then only transmitting real time information when a reading is out-of-limits.

In addition, the application will typically be programmed to send complete data updates on a time scheduled basis or anytime upon request from the web server.

2. Transmission of data through a communication network

There are several good options for transporting data from the remote equipment to the network operation center. The cellular network, telephone lines, and communication satellites are all common solutions.

The telephone may be the best choice if a line is already installed and the cost can be shared with other uses. Its disadvantage is usually the ongoing monthly cost and sometimes the cost and difficulty of installation.

Satellite may be the most expensive solution, but it is often the best or only solution for monitoring equipment in very remote areas.

The wide spread coverage of the cellular network is the main reason M2M is getting so much attention these days, and it's usually the method that fits best. There are several methods of sending data over the cellular network. CDMA and GPRS[15] are both widespread in North America today and their coverage areas continue to grow. The advantage of these systems is the ability to send large amounts of data frequently. The costs continue to drop.

Connecting to the cellular or satellite network typically requires the use of a gateway. A gateway receives the data from the wireless communication network and converts[16] it so that it can be sent to the network operation center, often over the Internet or by a frame relay[17] (phone line) connection. Data security features such as authentication and access control can be managed by the gateway and the application software.

The gateway also has an important role when the flow of data is

[13]['kɔnstənt]
n. 常数，恒量
adj. 不变的，持续的

[14]['prəʊɡræməbl]
adj. 可编程的

[15]通用分组无线业务
General Packet Radio Service

[16][kən'və:t]
vt. 使转变，转换……

[17]frame relay:
帧中继

reversed, going from a network to the machine for data requests and remote control. The gateway still functions as a protocol converter, but this time it takes high-bandwidth Internet protocols and converts them to low-bandwidth wireless protocols so the data is optimized for transfer over a cellular network.

For companies deploying an M2M application, the gateway, the application software, and the data warehouse[18] can be housed internally or can be hosted by a third party in a network operations center. In many cases, the hosted model may be more attractive because of the high cost involved in setting up the infrastructure and managing the network. Since the upfront cost[19] is often lower with the hosted model, the payback can be faster and the solution can be deployed in less time.

[18]['wɛəhaus] n. 仓库

[19]upfront cost: 先期成本

3. Assessment of the data

Data from a company's networked machines usually shows up in one of two places: in an enterprise software application the company already uses, or in a standalone system designed specifically for M2M.

Today's deployments tend to favor standalone systems for applications such as remote monitoring because most M2M application providers specialize in providing these and there can be additional costs involved with integrating new data into existing systems.

Still, the vast majority of opportunities for M2M center around taking data out of machines and integrating it with operational data. For example, remote monitoring data can be incorporated into customer-relationship management systems[20] for logging service and maintenance history.

[20]customer-relationship management system: 客户关系管理系统

4. Response to the available information

Whether the application is standalone or part of a larger system, the common goal is to automate a business process by automating the flow of data to the people and systems that need to know. The technology should enable sending the right data to the right place in the right way depending on the circumstances[21]. It should also present data to individual users based on their specific function in the business process.

A modern farmer who has automated irrigation[22] systems operating in different locations can now be constantly aware of their operation based on short messages that are relayed to his pager or cell phone.

[21]['sə:kəmstəns] n. 环境，境况

[22][ˌiri'geiʃən] n. 灌溉，冲洗

Of course, none of this technology is specific to M2M; the whole purpose of business software is to keep people from having to do everything manually. The new element that M2M brings to the picture is that now companies have new data to work with, data that is central to the way they operate and the value they provide.

参考译文

Text A 什么是 M2M？

M2M 指两个或更多的机器之间的数据通信。M2M 最普遍的翻译是机器对机器，有时也译为人对机器、机器对人等。蜂窝电话服务提供商使用公共无线网络实现 M2M、遥测和远程信息处理。

通常，M2M 系统执行具体的任务，这意味着一个给定的系统只为一个特定的设备而建立，或只为一个行业中非常有限的一类设备而建立。这只是 M2M 市场的一个特点，该市场尚在起步阶段，还没有形成一个统一的标准。功能重复——每个专用系统都重复类似系统已经实现了的许多功能。

无线 M2M 是通过无线技术（如 CDMA）实现的机器对机器通信。

1. 何处可用 M2M？

M2M 使各个行业中的众多个体、公司、社区和组织受益。下面是一些利用 M2M 解决方案获得更多好处的"新兴领域"：

- 电信——IP 网络互连/无线广域网/移动学习；
- 制造——供应链/库存管理/工厂自动化；
- 轻工业——传感器监测/远程访问控制设施/应用；
- 运输——资产跟踪/物流管理；
- 零售——销售点/亭/数字内容标牌；
- 信息技术——售后市场/车载解决方案；
- 电子商务/移动商务解决方案；
- 不动产——楼宇自动化；
- 安全——视频监控。

2. M2M 有何益处？

以下只是通过 M2M 解决业务挑战可得到的一些好处：

- 成本-效益的预防性维护和服务质量；
- 通过外包的故障排除实现快速响应；
- 集中服务支持和数据管理；
- 在整个产品生命周期不断获得收入；
- 通过使停机时间最短来获得收入；

- 远程诊断。

3. M2M 解决方案由什么组成？

通常，M2M 解决方案是由以下几部分构成：
- 收集数据和/或监测变化的装置或传感器；
- 发送和接收数据的应用程序和数据库；
- 发送和/或接收传感器数据的中央服务器；
- （用固定线路或无线）连接到一个中央服务器的装置或传感器；
- 在设备、传感器和中央服务器设备之间交换数据的调制解调器；
- 保证数据传输安全性以及监控和管理设备或传感器网络连通性的应用程序。

4. 无线 M2M 有何益处？

4.1 灵活性

以无线方式连接到网络的设备不受物理位置的限制。当需要时可以灵活地移动这些设备。例如，如果一个自动售货机处客流不足，只需搬到他处即可。在偏远的难以布置电缆的地方，可以快速和容易地把设备连接到无线网络。

4.2 移动性

移动设备可以连接到不能用固定线路连接的网络，实现了所有设备的数据通信。

4.3 访问信息

无线网络给移动设备提供实时信息，使得这些设备能按需要随时随地接收或发送信息，这样组织就可以访问即时信息，以便有效和快速地决策。

4.4 独立网络

无线网络可以快速方便地部署到一个建筑内或不需要与现有的固定线路网络整合的地方，从而提供一个独立的安全网络。

4.5 速度

由于无须在设备之间布线，所以无线网络的部署比有线网络快得多。这样能够更快地使用设备，并节约成本。

4.6 成本

节约成本与部署速度、消除电缆成本和降低通信成本相关，因为 CDMA 蜂窝网比 PSTN/固定线路更划算。

4.7 无线 M2M 机器如何通信？

M2M 无线解决方案通过无线调制解调器使用即通的 CDMA 蜂窝通信，可以实现数据的即时通信，速度更快。CDMA 通话/数据将根据所使用的数据量而不是根据持续连接的时间收费。

Unit 3

Text A

How Smart Homes Work

When you're not at home, nagging little doubts can start to crowd your mind. Did I turn the coffee maker off? Did I set the security alarm? Are the kids doing their homework or watching television?

With a smart home, you could quiet all of these worries with a quick trip online. When you're at home, the house takes care of you by playing your favorite song whenever you walk in or instantaneously dimming the lights for a movie. Is it magic? No, it's home automation. Smart homes connect all the devices and appliances in your home so they can communicate with each other and with you.

Anything in your home that uses electricity can be put on the home network and at your command. Whether you give that command by voice, remote control or computer, the home reacts. Most applications relate to lighting, home security, home theater and entertainment and thermostat regulation.

The idea of a smart home might make you think of George Jetson and his futuristic abode or maybe Bill Gates, who spent more than $100 million building his smart home. Once a draw for the tech-savvy or the wealthy, smart homes and home automation are becoming more common. About $14 billion was spent on home networking in 2005, and analysts predict that figure will climb to more than $85 billion by 2015.

1. Smart Home Software and Technology

Smart home technology was developed in 1975, when a company in Scotland developed X10. X10 allows compatible products to talk to each other over the already existing electrical wires of a home. All the appliances and devices are receivers, and the means of controlling the system, such as remote controls or keypads, are transmitters. If you want to turn off a lamp in another room, the transmitter will issue a message in numerical code that includes the following:

- An alert to the system that it's issuing a command

- An identifying unit number for the device that should receive the command and
- A code that contains the actual command, such as "turn off"

All of this is designed to happen in less than a second, but X10 does have some limitations. Communicating over electrical lines is not always reliable because the lines get "noisy" from powering other devices. An X10 device could interpret electronic interference as a command and react, or it might not receive the command at all. While X10 devices are still around, other technologies have emerged to compete for your home networking dollar.

Instead of going through the power lines, some systems use radio waves to communicate, which is also how WiFi and cell phone signals operate. However, home automation networks don't need all the juice of a WiFi network because automation commands are short messages. Two most prominent radio networks in home automation are ZigBee and Z-Wave. Both of these technologies are mesh networks, meaning there's more than one way for the message to get to its destination.

Z-Wave uses a Source Routing Algorithm to determine the fastest route for messages. Each Z-Wave device is embedded with a code, and when the device is plugged into the system, the network controller recognizes the code, determines its location and adds it to the network. When a command comes through, the controller uses the algorithm to determine how the message should be sent. Because this routing can take up a lot of memory on a network, Z-Wave has developed a hierarchy between devices: Some controllers initiate messages, and some are "slaves," which means they can only carry and respond to messages.

ZigBee's name illustrates the mesh networking concept because messages from the transmitter zigzag like bees, looking for the best path to the receiver. While Z-Wave uses a proprietary technology for operating its system, ZigBee's platform is based on the standard set by the Institute for IEEE (Electrical and Electronics Engineers) for wireless personal networks. This means any company can build a ZigBee-compatible product without paying licensing fees for the technology behind it, which may eventually give ZigBee an advantage in the marketplace. Like Z-Wave, ZigBee has fully functional devices and reduced function devices.

Using a wireless network provides more flexibility for placing devices, but like electrical lines, they might have interference. Insteon offers a way for your home network to communicate over both electrical wires and radio waves, making it a dual mesh network. If the message isn't getting through on one platform, it will try the other. Instead of routing the message, an Insteon device will broadcast

This keypad will send a message to your lamp.

the message, and all devices pick up the message and broadcast it until the command is performed. The devices act like peers, as opposed to one serving as an instigator and another as a receptor. This means that the more Insteon devices that are installed on a network, the stronger the message will be.

2. Setting Up a Smart Home

X10, Insteon, ZigBee and Z-Wave just provide the technology for smart home communication. Manufacturers have made alliances with these systems to create the products that use the technology. Here are some examples of smart home products and their functions.

- Cameras will track your home's exterior even if it's pitch-black outside.
- Plug your tabletop lamp into a dimmer instead of the wall socket, and you can brighten and dim at the push of a button.
- A video door phone provides more than a doorbell -- you get a picture of who's at the door.
- Motion sensors will send an alert when there's motion around your house, and they can even tell the difference between pets and burglars.
- Door handles can open with scanned fingerprints or a four-digit code, eliminating the need to fumble for house keys.
- Audio systems distribute the music from your stereo to any room with connected speakers.
- Channel modulators take any video signal -- from a security camera to your favorite television station -- and make it viewable on every television in the house.
- Remote controls, keypads and tabletop controllers are the means of activating the smart home applications. Devices also come with built-in web servers that allow you to access their information online.

This keypad will send a message to your lamp. These products are available at home improvement stores, electronics stores, from technicians or online. Before buying, check to see what technology is associated with the product. Products using the same technology should work together despite different manufacturers, but joining up an X10 and a Z-Wave product requires a bridging device.

In designing a smart home, you can do as much or as little home automation as you want. You could begin with a

With smart home security, you can check on your little one from anywhere.

lighting starter kit and add on security devices later. If you want to start with a bigger system, it's a good idea to design carefully how the home will work, particularly if rewiring or renovation will be required. In addition, you'll want to place strategically the nodes of the wireless networks so that they have a good routing range.

3. Smart Home Benefits

Smart homes obviously have the ability to make life easier and more convenient. Who wouldn't love being able to control lighting, entertainment and temperature from their couch? Home networking can also provide peace of mind. Whether you're at work or on vacation, the smart home will alert you to what's going on, and security systems can be built to provide an immense amount of help in an emergency. For example, the smart home will not only wake up a resident with notification of a fire alarm, but also unlock doors, dial the fire department and light the path to safety.

Here are a few more examples of cool smart home tricks:
- Light a path for nighttime bathroom trips
- Instantly create mood lighting
- Program your television so that your children can watch only at certain times
- Access all your favorite DVDs from any television in the home
- Have your thermostat start warming the bedroom before you get out of bed so that it's nice and toasty when you get up
- Turn on the coffee maker from bed

Smart homes also provide some energy efficiency savings. Because systems like Z-Wave and ZigBee put some devices at a reduced level of functionality, they can go to "sleep" and wake up when commands are given. Electric bills go down when lights are automatically turned off when a person leaves the room, and rooms can be heated or cooled based on who's there at any given moment. Some devices can track how much energy each appliance is using and command it to use less. One smart homeowner boasted her heating bill was about one-third less than a same-sized normal home.

Smart home technology promises tremendous benefits for an elderly person living alone. Smart homes can notify the resident when it is time to take medicine, alert the hospital if the resident fall and track how much the resident is eating. If the elderly person is a little forgetful, the smart home will perform tasks such as shutting off the water before a tub overflows or turning off the oven if the cook has wandered away. One builder estimates that this system could cost $20,000, which is less expensive than a full-time nursing home. It also allows people who might live elsewhere to participate in the care of their aging parent. Easy-to-control automated systems will provide similar benefits to those with disabilities or a limited range of movement.

4. Smart Home Challenges

A smart home probably sounds like a nightmare to those people not comfortable with computers. Those who routinely fumble around with a remote control just trying to change the television channel might have stopped reading by now.

It may be your fear that if you try to turn on the television in your smart home, lights will start flashing, and this does happen occasionally. (Power outages, however, activate backup battery and safe mode, which means you can still perform tasks like unlocking a door manually). One of the challenges of installing a smart home system is balancing the complexity of the system against the usability of the system. When planning the system, it's important to consider a few factors:

- How large will the system be?
- What kinds of components are used in the system? Are they basic, such a light dimmer, or more imposing, like an alarm system or a video camera?
- How intuitive will the system be to a non-user?
- How many people will be required to use the system?
- Who will know how to operate the system? Who will know how to maintain the system and address failures? How often will people who can only operate the system be left alone in the home?
- How easy is it to make changes to the interface? For example, if your house is programmed to wake you up at 7 a.m., how will you let it know that you're away overnight on business or sleeping in on a Saturday?

For these reasons, it may be easier to start with a very basic home network and expand as enhancements are needed or desired. However, there's some concern that with the market so new, technologies are developing all the time, sometimes leaving old versions of products useless. If you invest too soon, you may end up with a model that has impossible-to-find components and spare parts. Like many new technologies, smart homes require a significant investment to keep up.

Smart homes also come with some security concerns. Hackers who access the network will have the ability to turn off alarm systems and lights, leaving the home vulnerable to a break-in, or the theft could be more electronic. If music is saved on a hard drive so that it can be played around the house, make sure that sensitive information, such as passwords or identifying numbers, are saved elsewhere.

Some smart home devices also raise ethical questions about privacy. It's great to be able to check in on a four-year-old in his room while you're cooking dinner in the kitchen, but how will that child feel when he's constantly monitored through puberty? The information that a smart home collects might feel like a weapon to a teenager who gets caught sneaking in after a late-night party. When setting up a smart home, it's a good idea to discuss it with the whole family first.

Of course, there's also the question of whether an individual needs all this technology. Is our society really so lazy that we can't turn flip a light switch? It's an interesting argument, but smart homes are coming. The good news is that with all the time we save from home automation, we'll have time to work on other pursuits.

New Words

nagging	[ˈnægiŋ]	adj. 唠叨的，挑剔的
crowd	[kraud]	v. 群集，拥挤，挤满
quiet	[ˈkwaiət]	vt. 使平静，使安心
		vi. 平静下来
instantaneous	[ˌinstənˈteinjəs]	adj. 瞬间的，即刻的，即时的
dim	[ˈdim]	adj. 暗淡的，模糊的，无光泽的
		vt. 使暗淡，使失去光泽
appliance	[əˈplaiəns]	n. 用具，器具
command	[kəˈmɑːnd]	n. 命令，掌握
		v. 命令，支配
entertainment	[entəˈteinmənt]	n. 娱乐
thermostat	[ˈθəːməstæt]	n. 自动调温器，温度调节装置
regulation	[regjuˈleiʃən]	n. 调节，校准
futuristic	[fjuːtʃəˈristik]	adj. 超现代化的，超时髦的，最先进的
abode	[əˈbəud]	n. 住所，住处
draw	[drɔː]	n. 有吸引力的人（或事物）
compatible	[kəmˈpætəbl]	adj. 兼容的，一致的
receiver	[riˈsiːvə]	n. 接收者，接收器
keypad	[ˈkiːpæd]	n. 小键盘，键区
transmitter	[trænzˈmitə]	n. 发射机，转送者，变送器
limitation	[ˌlimiˈteiʃən]	n. 限制，局限性
noisy	[ˈnɔizi]	adj. 噪声的，嘈杂的
juice	[dʒuːs]	n. 电，动力来源
prominent	[ˈprɔminənt]	adj. 卓越的，显著的，突出的
recognize	[ˈrekəgnaiz]	vt. 认可，承认，公认
hierarchy	[ˈhaiərɑːki]	n. 层次，层级
initiate	[iˈniʃieit]	vt. 开始，发动
		v. 开始，发起
eventually	[iˈventjuəli]	adv. 最后，终于
dual	[ˈdjuː(ː)əl]	adj. 双的，二重的，双重
peer	[piə]	n. 同等的人
		vt. 与……同等
instigator	[ˈinstigeitə]	n. 发动器
receptor	[riˈseptə]	n. 接收器，感受器
exterior	[eksˈtiəriə]	adj. 外部的，外在的，表面的

		n. 外部，表面，外形
plug	[plʌg]	vt. 插上，插栓
		n. 插头，插销
dimmer	['dimə]	n. 调光器
burglar	['bə:glə]	n. 夜贼
fingerprint	['fiŋgəprint]	n. 指纹，手印
		vt. 采指纹
distribute	[dis'tribju(:)t]	vt. 分发，分配，分布，分类，分区
audio	['ɔ:diəu]	adj. 音频的，声频的，声音的
modulator	['mɔdjuleitə]	n. 调节器
starter	['stɑ:tə]	n. 起动器，起动钮
kit	[kit]	n. 成套工具，用具包，工具箱
rewire	[ri:'waiə]	vt. 再接电线，改电路
renovation	[ˌrenəu'veiʃən]	n. 革新
strategically	[strə'ti:dʒikəli]	adv. 战略上
immense	[i'mens]	adj. 极广大的，无边的，<口>非常好的
emergency	[i'mə:dʒnsi]	n. 紧急情况，突然事件，非常时刻，紧急事件
notification	[ˌnəutifi'keiʃən]	n. 通知，布告，告示
tremendous	[tri'mendəs]	adj. 极大的，巨大的
node	[nəud]	n. 节点
disability	[ˌdisə'biliti]	n. 无力，无能，残疾
nightmare	['naitmeə]	n. 梦魇，噩梦，可怕的事物
comfortable	['kʌmfətəbl]	adj. 舒适的
hacker	['hækə]	n. 黑客
vulnerable	['vʌlnərəb(ə)l]	adj. 易受攻击的
password	['pɑ:swə:d]	n. 密码，口令
lazy	['leizi]	adj. 懒惰的，懒散的
pursuit	[pə'sju:t]	n. 追求，追赶；工作

Phrases

security alarm	安全警报器
smart home	智能家居
take care of	照顾
home network	家庭网络
at one's command	听某人指挥，在某人的掌握之中
remote control	遥控，遥控装置，遥控操作

relate to	涉及
home theater	家庭影院
electrical wire	电线
numerical code	数字编码，数字代码
interpret…as	把……看作；把……理解为
radio wave	无线电波
short message	短信
mesh network	网状网络
Source Routing Algorithm	源路由算法
proprietary technology	专利技术
wireless personal network	无线个人网络
licensing fee	授权使用费用，许可证费用
dual mesh network	对偶网格网络
make alliances with	与……结成联盟；与……联合
fumble for	笨手笨脚地去摸索，摸索
web server	网络服务器
bridging device	桥接设备
in an emergency	在紧急的时候
fire alarm	火警
coffee maker	咖啡壶
shut off	关掉，切断
nursing home	疗养院
safe mode	安全模式
spare part	备件

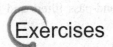

Abbreviations

IEEE (Institute for Electrical and Electronics Engineers)　　电气和电子工程师协会

Exercises

【EX.1】Answer the following questions according to the text.

1. When was smart home technology developed?
2. What does a message in numerical code include?
3. What are two most prominent radio networks in home automation?
4. What is ZigBee's platform based on?
5. What will motion sensors?

6. What does it require when joining up an X10 and a Z-Wave product?

7. What are the benefits smart homes bring?

8. What does a smart home probably sound like to those people not comfortable with computers?

9. What is one of the challenges of installing a smart home system?

10. What are the questions raised by smart homes?

【EX.2】Translate the following terms or phrases from English into Chinese and vice versa.

1. home network   1. _____
2. security alarm   2. _____
3. remote control   3. _____
4. radio wave   4. _____
5. mesh network   5. _____
6. Source Routing Algorithm 6. _____
7. crowd   7. _____
8. regulation   8. _____
9. Web server   9. _____
10. 网络服务器   10. _____
11. 关掉，切断   11. _____
12. adj. 兼容的，一致的 12. _____
13. n. 调节器   13. _____
14. n. 节点   14. _____

【EX.3】Translate the following sentences into Chinese.

1. Back in the days of command lines and character-based menus, interfaces indirectly offered services to users.

2. The system and the hardware of this computer are not compatible.

3. We didn't have a receiver sensitive enough to pick up the signal.

4. Do you want to use your numeric keypad instead of the mouse?

5. The transmitter circuit consists of a pulse signal generator circuit, band-pass filters and power amplifiers.

6. There's only a modest association between these two measures of inequality, according to our statistical analysis.

7. For example, some websites embed video players, games, and other interactive experiences on site pages.

8. The video and audio signals might be compressed during transmission or not.

9. The new version of the program comes with a much better user interface than the original.

10. Check that the user name is correct, then type the password again.

【EX.4】Complete the following passage with appropriate words in the box.

| transmitter | switch | installed | receive | plugged |
| standardize | convey | entertainment | smart | coded |

A smart home or building is a home or building, usually a new one, that is equipped with special structured wiring to enable occupants to remotely control or program an array of automated home electronic devices by entering a single command. For example, a homeowner on vacation can use a Touchtone phone to arm a home security system, control temperature gauges,___1___appliances on or off, control lighting, program a home theater or entertainment system, and perform many other tasks.

The field of home automation is expanding rapidly as electronic technologies converge. The home network encompasses communications,___2___, security, convenience, and information systems.

A technology known as Powerline Carrier Systems (PCS) is used to send___3___signals along a home's existing electric wiring to programmable switches, or outlets. These signals ___4___commands that correspond to "addresses" or locations of specific devices, and that control how and when those devices operate. A PCS___5___, for instance, can send a signal along a home's wiring, and a receiver plugged into any electric outlet in the home could___6___that signal and operate the appliance to which it is attached.

One common protocol for PCS is known as X10, a signaling technique for remotely controlling any device___7___into an electrical power line. X10 signals, which involve short radio frequency (RF) bursts that represent digital information, enable communication between transmitters and receivers.

In Europe, technology to equip homes with___8___devices centers on development of the European Installation Bus, or Instabus. This embedded control protocol for digital communication between smart devices consists of a two-wire bus line that is___9___along with normal electrical wiring. The Instabus line links all appliances to a decentralized communication system and functions like a telephone line over which appliances can be controlled. The European Installation Bus Association is part of Konnex, an association that aims to___10___. home and building networks in Europe.

【EX.5】Translate the following passage into Chinese.

What Is a "Smart House"?

A smart house is a house that has highly advanced automatic systems for lighting, temperature control, multi-media, security, window and door operations, and many other functions.

A smart home appears "intelligent" because its computer systems can monitor so many aspects of daily living. For example, the refrigerator may be able to inventory its contents, suggest menus, recommend healthy alternatives, and order groceries. The smart home systems might even take care of cleaning the cat's litter box and watering the plants.

However, smart home technology is real, and it's becoming increasingly sophisticated. Coded signals are sent through the home's wiring to switches and outlets that are programmed to operate appliances and electronic devices in every part of the house. Home automation can be especially useful for elderly and disabled persons who wish to live independently.

Text B

What is GPS?

The GPS (Global Positioning System) is a satellite-based navigation system made up of a network of 24 satellites placed into orbit by the U.S. Department of Defense. GPS was originally intended for military applications, but in the 1980s, the government made the system available for civilian use. GPS works in any weather conditions, anywhere in the world, 24 hours a day. There are no subscription fees or setup charges to use GPS.

1. How It Works

GPS satellites circle the earth twice a day in a very precise orbit and transmit signal information to the earth. GPS receivers take this information and use triangulation to calculate the user's exact location. Essentially, the GPS receiver compares the time a signal is transmitted by a satellite with the time it is received. The time difference tells the GPS receiver how far away the satellite is. Now, with distance measurements from a few more satellites, the receiver can determine the user's position and display it on the unit's electronic map.

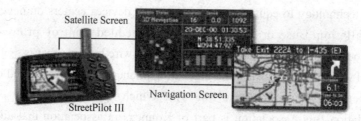

A GPS receiver must be locked on to the signal of at least three satellites to calculate a 2D position (latitude and longitude) and track movement. With four or more satellites in view, the receiver can determine the user's 3D position (latitude, longitude and altitude). Once the user's position has been determined, the GPS unit can calculate other information, such as speed, bearing, track, trip distance, distance to destination, sunrise and sunset time and more.

2. How Accurate GPS is

Today's GPS receivers are extremely accurate, thanks to their parallel multichannel design. Garmin's 12 parallel channel receivers are quick to lock onto satellites when first turned on and they maintain strong locks, even in dense foliage or urban settings with tall buildings. Certain atmospheric factors and other sources of error can affect the accuracy of GPS receivers. Garmin

GPS receivers are accurate to within 15 meters on average.

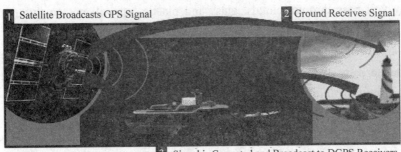

Newer Garmin GPS receivers with WAAS (Wide Area Augmentation System) capability can improve accuracy to less than three meters on average. No additional equipment or fees are required to take advantage of WAAS. Users can also get better accuracy with Differential GPS (DGPS), which corrects GPS signals to within an average of three to five meters. The U.S. Coast Guard operates the most common DGPS correction service. This system consists of a network of towers that receive GPS signals and transmit a corrected signal by beacon transmitters. In order to get the corrected signal, users must have a differential beacon receiver and beacon antenna in addition to their GPS.

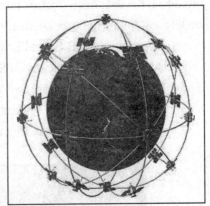

3. The GPS Satellite System

The 24 satellites that make up the GPS space segment are orbiting the earth about 12,000 miles above us. They are constantly moving, making two complete orbits in less than 24 hours. These satellites are travelling at a speed of roughly 7,000 miles an hour.

GPS satellites are powered by solar energy. They have backup batteries onboard to keep them running in the event of a solar eclipse, when there's no solar power. Small rocket boosters on each satellite keep them flying in the correct path.

Here are some other interesting facts about the GPS satellites (also called NAVSTAR, the official U.S. Department of Defense name for GPS):

- The first GPS satellite was launched in 1978.
- A full constellation of 24 satellites was achieved in 1994.
- Each satellite is built to last about 10 years. Replacements are constantly being built and launched into orbit.
- A GPS satellite weighs approximately 2,000 pounds and is about 17 feet across with the solar panels extended.
- Transmitter power is only 50 watts or less.

4. What the Signal Is

GPS satellites transmit two low power radio signals, designated L1 and L2. Civilian GPS uses the L1 frequency of 1575.42 MHz in the UHF band. The signals travel by line of sight, meaning they will pass through clouds, glass and plastic but will not go through most solid objects such as buildings and mountains.

A GPS signal contains three different bits of information--a pseudorandom code, ephemeris data and almanac data. The pseudorandom code is simply an I.D. code that identifies which satellite is transmitting information. You can view this number on your Garmin GPS unit's satellite page, as it identifies which satellites it's receiving.

Ephemeris data, which is constantly transmitted by each satellite, contains important information about the status of the satellite (healthy or unhealthy), current date and time. This part of the signal is essential for determining a position.

The almanac data tells the GPS receiver where each GPS satellite should be at any time throughout the day. Each satellite transmits almanac data showing the orbital information for that satellite and for every other satellite in the system.

5. Sources of GPS Signal Errors

Factors that can degrade the GPS signal and thus affect accuracy include the following:

- Ionosphere and troposphere delays -- The satellite signal slows as it passes through the atmosphere. The GPS system uses a built-in model that calculates an average amount of delay to partially correct for this type of error.

- Signal multipath -- This occurs when the GPS signal is reflected off objects such as tall buildings or large rock surfaces before it reaches the receiver. This increases the travel time of the signal, thereby causing errors.
- Receiver clock errors -- A receiver's built-in clock is not as accurate as the atomic clocks onboard the GPS satellites. Therefore, it may have very slight timing errors.
- Orbital errors -- Also known as ephemeris errors, these are inaccuracies of the satellite's reported location.
- Number of satellites visible -- The more satellites a GPS receiver can "see," the better the accuracy. Buildings, terrain, electronic interference, or sometimes even dense foliage can block signal reception, causing position errors or possibly no position reading at all. GPS units typically will not work indoors, underwater or underground.
- Satellite geometry/shading -- This refers to the relative position of the satellites at any

given time. Ideal satellite geometry exists when the satellites are located at wide angles relative to each other. Poor geometry results when the satellites are located in a line or in a tight grouping.
- Intentional degradation of the satellite signal -- Selective Availability (SA) is an intentional degradation of the signal once imposed by the U.S. Department of Defense. SA was intended to prevent military adversaries from using the highly accurate GPS signals. The government turned off SA in May 2000, which significantly improved the accuracy of civilian GPS receivers.

New Words

satellite	[ˈsætəlait]	n. 人造卫星
navigation	[ˌnæviˈgeiʃən]	n. 导航，领航
orbit	[ˈɔːbit]	n. 轨道
		vt. 绕……轨道而行
		vi. 进入轨道，沿轨道飞行
military	[ˈmilitəri]	adj. 军事的，军用的
civilian	[siˈviljən]	adj. 民间的，民用的
subscription	[sʌbˈskripʃən]	n. 签署，同意
charge	[tʃɑːdʒ]	n. 电荷，充电
		v. 充电
precise	[priˈsais]	adj. 精确的，准确的
		n. 精确
triangulation	[traiˌæŋjuˈleiʃən]	n. 三角测量，分成三角形
transmit	[trænzˈmit]	vt. 传输，转送，传达，发射，传播
		vi. 发射信号，发报
location	[ləuˈkeiʃən]	n. 位置，场所，特定区域
position	[pəˈziʃən]	n. 位置
		vt. 安置，决定……的位置
latitude	[ˈlætitjuːd]	n. 纬度，范围
longitude	[ˈlɔndʒitjuːd]	n. 经度，经线
altitude	[ˈæltitjuːd]	n.（尤指海拔）高度
accurate	[ˈækjurit]	adj. 精确的，正确的
bearing	[ˈbɛəriŋ]	n. 方位
multichannel	[ˌmʌltiˈtʃænl]	adj. 多通话线路的，多通道的，多波段的
dense	[dens]	adj. 密集的，浓厚的
atmospheric	[ˌætməsˈferik]	adj. 大气的
factor	[ˈfæktə]	n. 因素，要素，因数

backup	['bækʌp]	n. 后援，支持 vt. 做备份 adj. 备份的，支持性的
onboard	['ɔn'bɔ:d]	adj. 随带的，板载的
constellation	[kɔnstə'leiʃən]	n. [天]星群，星座，灿烂的一群
replacement	[ri'pleismənt]	n. 替换，复位，交换，代替者
launch	[lɔ:ntʃ, lɑ:ntʃ]	vi. 发射，投放市场
approximately	[əprɔksi'mətli]	adv. 近似地，大约
watt	[wɔt]	n. 瓦特
frequency	['fri:kwənsi]	n. 频率，周率
ephemeris	[i'feməris]	n. 历书
almanac	['ɔ:lmənæk]	n. 历书，年鉴
orbital	['ɔ:bitl]	adj. 轨道的
degrade	[di'greid]	v.（使）降级，（使）退化
ionosphere	[ai'ɔnəsfiə]	n. 电离层
troposphere	['trɔpəusfiə]	n. 对流层
atmosphere	['ætməsfiə]	n. 大气，空气
built-in	['bilt'in]	adj. 内置的，固定的，嵌入的 n. 内置
inaccuracy	[in'ækjurəsi]	n. 错误
terrain	['terein]	n. 地形
reception	[ri'sepʃən]	n. 接收
geometry	[dʒi'ɔmitri]	n. 几何学，几何形状；几何图形
angle	['æŋgl]	n. 角度
degradation	[,degrə'deiʃən]	n. 降级，降格，退化
adversary	['ædvəsəri]	n. 敌手，对手
significantly	[sig'nifikəntli]	adv. 意味深长地，值得注目地

Phrases

Department of Defense	国防部
civilian use	民用
subscription fee	预付费
time difference	时差
distance measurement	距离测量，远距测量
electronic map	电子地图
lock on	锁定，用雷达跟踪
on average	平均，均值

take advantage of	利用
beacon transmitter	信标发送机
differential beacon receiver	差分信标接收器，微分信标接收器
beacon antenna	信标天线
solar energy	太阳能
backup battery	备用电源，备份电源
in the event of …	如果……发生
solar eclipse	日食
rocket booster	火箭加速器，火箭助推器
solar panel	太阳电池板，太阳能电池板
solid object	固体
ephemeris data	星历数据
almanac data	卫星年历
atomic clock	原子钟
timing error	同步误差，定时误差
relative position	相对位置
poor geometry	不良几何条件；不良几何图形

Abbreviations

GPS (Global Positioning System)	全球定位系统
2D (2 Dimension)	二维
3D (3 Dimension)	三维
WAAS (Wide Area Augmentation System)	广域增强系统
DGPS (Differential GPS)	差分 GPS，微分 GPS
UHF (Ultra High Frequency)	超高频
SA (Selective Availability)	选择可用性，选择性可靠度

Exercises

【EX.1】 **Fill in the blanks according to the text.**

1. GPS stands for _____. It is a satellite-based navigation system made up of a network of _____ placed into orbit by _____.

2. GPS satellites circle the earth _____ in a very precise orbit and transmit _____ to the earth.

3. A GPS receiver must be locked on to the signal of _____ to calculate a 2D position (latitude and longitude) and _____.

4. Today's GPS receivers are extremely accurate, thanks to _____.

5. The most common DGPS correction service is operated by _____. This system consists of _____ that receive GPS signals and transmit a corrected signal by _____.

6. GPS satellites are powered by _____. These satellites are travelling at a speed of _____.

7. The first GPS satellite was launched in _____.

8. GPS satellites transmit two low power radio signals, designated _____. Civilian GPS uses _____ in the UHF band.

9. A GPS signal contains _____ different bits of information. They are _____, _____ and _____.

10. Satellite geometry/shading refers to _____ at any given time. Ideal satellite geometry exists when the satellites are located _____ relative to each other. Poor geometry results when the satellites are located _____ or _____.

【EX.2】Translate the following terms or phrases from English into Chinese and vice versa.

1.	distance measurement	1.	_____
2.	backup battery	2.	_____
3.	take advantage of	3.	_____
4.	timing error	4.	_____
5.	solar panel	5.	_____
6.	navigation	6.	_____
7.	charge	7.	_____
8.	transmit	8.	_____
9.	factor	9.	_____
10.	onboard	10.	_____
11.	vt. 做备份 adj. 备份的，支持性的	11.	_____
12.	n. 频率，周率	12.	_____
13.	n. 替换，复位，交换，代替者	13.	_____
14.	n. 签署，同意	14.	_____
15.	信标发送机	15.	_____

【EX.3】Translate the following sentences into Chinese.

1. The great importance of the quality of equipment for navigation should never be neglected.

2. This is currently the most efficient way to transmit certain types of data like electronic mail.

3. Having the antenna at the bottom means less radio frequency waves are flooding the

sensors.

4. When the main system fails, the backup system takes over.

5. A subdirectory for each database is created to store the backup files.

6. This article first introduced the basic principle of radio frequency recognition technology.

7. Such energy transformation is also known as energy degradation.

8. A browser is a piece of computer software that you use to search for information on the Internet.

9. These currents can degrade the accuracy of low current measurements considerably.

10. Electric power is measured in watts, named after the famous British engineer James Watt.

Text C

Smart Home and Technology

1. What Is a Smart Home?

A Smart Home is one that provides its home owners comfort, security, energy efficiency (low operating costs) and convenience at all times, regardless of whether anyone is at home.

"Smart Home" is the term commonly used to define[1] a residence that has appliances, lighting, heating, air conditioning, TVs, computers, entertainment audio & video systems, security, and camera systems that are capable of communicating with one another and can be controlled remotely by a time schedule[2], from any room in the home, as well as remotely from any location in the world by phone or internet.

Installation of smart products give the home and its occupants various benefits -- the same benefits that technology and personal computing have brought to us over the past 30 years -- convenience and savings of time, money and energy.

Most homes do not have these appliances and systems built into them, therefore the most common and affordable approach is for the home owner to retrofit[3] smart products into their own finished home.

Most products are available in one of four protocols (the means of communication between themselves) and all of these are compatible with the internet, phone, and cell phones. These are the names for the four: X10, Z-Wave, UPB and EnOcean. Products that use the same protocol offer the ability to add products and hardware at the

[1][di'faɪn] vt. 定义

[2]['ʃedju:l] n. 时间表，进度表

[3]['retrə,fɪt] n. 式样翻新，花样翻新

homeowners' own pace and budget[4]. The system can grow to meet the needs of a changing family as time goes on[5]. All of these products can be selected from various manufacturers, preventing an expensive obsolescence[6] or non-competitive pricing.

The products SmartHomeUSA offers are all DIY[7] friendly and were created with retrofitting in mind (such as installation of smart lighting switches without needing to run any new wires). Our software offerings are homeowner friendly and can be installed on any existing PCs.

An emerging important feature of a smart home is conservation[8] of the earth's limited resources. More and more people are becoming aware of the ability to make their homes truly smart -- and green -- by utilizing home controllers integrated with all home sub-systems to increase savings by controlling lighting, window coverings, HVAC[9], irrigation[10] and by monitoring usage. Many home controllers have built-in monitoring systems whereby they calculate and log usage by all connected devices, giving the home owner heightened awareness and the knowledge to make changes as necessary. These systems can even be accessed over the Internet from anywhere in the world so the homeowner can adjust consumption any time, anywhere.

SmartHomeUSA offers phone and email product technical support to insure that you will always be successful in your installations and operation. We provide all our customers the information and personal guidance they may need to select the most appropriate products, taking budget, needs, and desired end-results into consideration.

2. What Is Smart Home Technology?

Smart home technology is an integrated home management system. Begin with functions that automatically regulate lights and house temperature. Smart security systems monitor web cameras containing motion and heat sensors and alert you and the security company if needed. You can also program appliances to operate automatically. Your smart entertainment system preselects[11] music for specific rooms, and monitors your children's video game and television use while you're away.

2.1 Design Considerations

You can design smart home technology into a new home, or retrofit an existing home as your budget allows. Park Place Installations recommends you implement smart technology in selected rooms of

[4]['bʌdʒit]
n. 预算
vi. 做预算
[5]as time goes on: 随着时间的推移
[6][,ɔbsə'lesns]
n. 荒废，退化
[7]DIY(Do It Yourself):自己动手做
[8][,kɔnsə(:)'veiʃən]
n. 保存，保持

[9]HVAC(Heating, Ventilation and Air Conditioning):供热通风与空气调节
[10][,iri'geiʃən]
n. 冲洗，灌溉

[11]['pri:si'lekt]
vt. 预先选择

your new home during construction. Pre-wire other rooms for your future needs. You'll find it more challenging to smart-wire an existing home; technicians are faced with structural[12] constraints and the challenges of working with existing wiring systems.

2.2 Benefits

Smart home technology offers two major benefits. Your pre-programmed settings for lighting, heating and other home systems help you to manage your environment without constantly worrying about the process. You'll also enjoy some energy-saving benefits. When you set environmental controls based on your needs and usage habits, you'll focus your energy resources on exactly where they're needed. This practice reduces your overall energy consumption[13].

2.3 Costs

You can implement some aspects of smart home technology without overextending[14] your budget. In 2010, Seattle Magazine notes that you can purchase a remote-controlled light dimmer switch[15] for $73. Wireless technology means you can automate lighting, security and other functions without significant structural expenditures[16]. Whole-house packages are more expensive. Washington-based Architechtronics estimates that audio and video equipment for a 1,500-square-foot home is placed on one remote controller for approximately $1,000.

2.4 Technology Advances

As smart home technology continues to evolve, you'll note two major advances in 2010. Ray Bell of Grid Net observes that washers, dryers, refrigerators and air conditioners are increasingly configured to easily mesh with smart home technology. Utility companies are also shifting the nature of their relationships with customers. Customers are given economic incentives and encouraged to voluntarily[17] shift consumption habits to increase energy efficiency.

[12]['strʌktʃərəl] adj. 结构的，建筑的

[13] overall energy consumption: 能耗总量

[14]['əuvəiks'tend] vt. 过分扩展，过分扩张

[15] dimmer switch: 变光开关

[16][iks'penditʃə] n. 支出，花费

[17]['vɔləntərili] adv. 自动地，以自由意志

Text A 智能家居如何工作

当你不在家，头脑中会不时闪现几许不安。关咖啡壶了吗？有没有设置安全报警？孩子在做作业还是看电视？

有了智能家居，迅速到网上看一下，就会消除这些担忧。当你在家的时候，你到哪个房间，那个房间就会播放你喜欢的歌曲。当你看电影时，会立即调暗光灯。这是魔术吗？不，这是家庭自动化。智能家庭连接你家中所有的设备和器具，所以它们可以相互通信，也能与你沟通。

你家里任何电气设备都可以加入家庭网络并由你控制。无论通过语音、远程控制还是计算机来下命令，家里都会有反应。大多数应用涉及照明、家庭安全、家庭影院、娱乐和温度调节。

一想起智能家居，你可能想到乔治·杰森和他那超现代化的住所，或许还会想到用一亿多美元建造自己智能家居的比尔·盖茨。智能家居和家庭自动化这个曾经只有技术专家或富豪们感兴趣的事情，正变得越来越普遍。2005年有大约140亿美元用于家庭网络，而分析师预测，在2015年这一数字将上升到超过850亿美元。

1. 智能家居的软件和技术

智能家居技术开发于1975年，当时苏格兰一家公司开发了X10。X10允许兼容产品通过家中现有的线路对话。所有的电器和设备都是接收器和发射器（如遥控器或键盘），这意味着可以控制系统。如果你想关闭在另一个房间的灯，发射器用数值代码发出消息，这些代码包括：

- 警告系统它在发出命令；
- 识别应接收命令装置的单元编号；
- 包含一个实际命令（如"关闭"）的代码。

所有这一切都在一秒钟内发生，但是X10也有一些局限性。通过电力线通信并不总是可靠的，因为线路上有为其他设备供电的"噪声"。X10装置可能会把电子干扰作为命令并做出反应，或它可能根本就收不到命令。虽然X10装置仍然存在，但其他技术已经出现，共同争夺家庭网络的投资。

有些系统不用电源线而是用无线电波来通信，WiFi和手机信号也使用无线电波。然而，家居自动化网络无须像WiFi这么大工程的网络资源，因为自动化命令都是短信息。家居自动化中最突出的两个无线网络是ZigBee和Z-Wave。它们的结构都是网状网络，也意味着信息到达目的地的路不止一条。

Z-Wave利用源路由算法来确定信息的最快途径。每个Z-Wave装置都嵌入一个代码，当设备插入系统，网络控制器就识别该代码，确定其位置并将它添加到网络。当一个命令到达时，控制器使用算法来确定如何发送消息。因为该路由可以占用网络上的许多内存，Z-Wave已经对设备分层：一些控制器发出消息，有些是"从属"设备，这意味着它们只能携带和响应消息。

ZigBee的名字表明了网状网络的概念，因为来自发射机的信息像蜜蜂扇动翅膀，寻找到接收机的最佳路径。Z-Wave使用专有技术来操作其系统，ZigBee平台是基于由IEEE（电气和电子工程师协会）建立的无线个人网标准。这意味着任何公司都可以构建一个ZigBee兼容的产品，而无须为支撑技术支付许可费，这最终可能使ZigBee赢得市场优势。像

Z-Wave 一样，ZigBee 具有功能齐全的设备和功能精简的设备。

使用无线网络为放置设备提供了更多的灵活性，但与使用有线一样，都可能会受到干扰。Insteon 技术为家庭网络提供了一个方法：通信电线和无线电波相互通信，使它成为一个双重网格网络。如果消息不能通过一个平台传输，它将尝试其他平台。一个 Insteon 装置将广播消息而不是通过路由传输消息，所有设备捡取消息和广播它直到该命令被执行。这些装置就像对等网，而不是一个作为发送者、另一个作为接收器。这意味着，一个网络安装的 Insteon 装置越多，传输消息的能力就越强。

2．建立一个智能家居

X10、Insteon、ZigBee 和 Z-Wave 只提供智能家居通信技术。制造商已建立了生产使用该技术产品的联盟。这里有一些智能家居产品的例子及其功能的示例。

- 即使外面漆黑一片，摄像机也将跟踪住宅外面的情景。
- 把桌面灯插到调光器中而不是插到墙上的插座中，可以通过按按钮调整亮度。
- 视频门电话远非门铃可比——可以看到门口那个人的图像。
- 当有东西在房子周围运动时，运动传感器会发出警报，甚至可以分辨出是宠物还是小偷。
- 门把手能够通过扫描指纹或输入 4 位数的代码来打开门，不用掏钥匙。
- 音频系统把音乐从你的立体声音响送入任何一个房间的扬声器上。
- 频道调节器捕捉任何视频信号——从摄像头到你喜欢的电视台——可以在家里的任一台电视上观看它。
- 远程控制，键盘和桌面控制器都能激活智能家居设备。它们都具有内置的 Web 服务器，可以在线访问其信息。

这个键盘将给灯发送一个消息。这些产品可在家装店、电子商店，从技术员那里购买或在线购买。购买前，看看产品与何种技术相关。使用相同技术的产品，即便由不同厂家生产，也可以协调工作，但连接 X10 和 Z-Wave 的产品需要一个桥接设备。

进行智能家居设计时，可以确定家庭自动化的程度。可以先用照明套件，以后再安装安全设备。如果一开始就想要更大的系统，就要精心设计智能家居尤其要考虑以后重新布线和改造。此外，可能会从长远考虑来建立无线网络的节点，以便路由范围更理想。

3．智能家居的优点

显然，智能家居使生活更容易和更方便。谁不喜欢坐在沙发上就能够控制照明、控制娱乐和温度？家庭网络也让人安心。无论你是在工作还是在度假，智能家居将提醒你正在发生什么事情，而且在紧急情况下安全系统会起很大作用。例如，智能家居不仅会向沉睡的居民报火警，而且还打开大门，拨打消防部门电话和照亮安全通道。

这里有更多的例子，来看看智能家居有多酷：

- 照亮夜间如厕路径；
- 立即营造气氛照明；

- 编制电视节目单，让孩子只能在特定的时间看特定内容的节目；
- 家里的任何一台电视机都可以播放所有您最喜爱的 DVD；
- 起床前打开自动调温器让卧室变暖，这样在你起床时会感到既舒心又温暖；
- 躺在床上即可打开咖啡壶电源。

智能家居能节约能源。因为像 Z-Wave 和 ZigBee 这类系统可以降低功能等级，进入"睡眠"状态，而命令到达时再被唤醒。人去灯关会少花电费，可以根据人在的时间来暖屋或冷屋。有些设备可以跟踪各电器使用能源的数量，并命令其少用能源。一个聪明的房主扬言她取暖账单大约不到同类家庭的三分之一。

智能家居技术对独居老人极有益处。智能家居可以通知老人按时服药并跟踪服药量，如果摔倒则给医院报警。如果老年人有点健忘，智能家居将执行一些任务，如水桶溢出前关闭水龙头或在厨师离开后关掉烤箱。一个建造者估计，该系统将花费 20000 美元，这比雇用一个全职护理还便宜。它还能让生活在别处的成年子女照顾他们年迈的父母。容易控制的自动化系统将为残障人士或活动范围受限的人提供类似的帮助。

4. 智能家居的缺点

智能家居对于不适应计算机用户来说听起来像是噩梦，那些经常手拿遥控器只是用来更换电视频道的人读到此处可能已经打住了。

如果在智能家居环境中想打开电视，灯光会开始闪烁，这可能让你害怕。而且的确偶尔会这样（然而停电时会启动备用电池和安全模式。这意味着你仍可做些手动开门之类的事情）。安装智能家居系统的挑战之一是如何平衡系统的可用性和系统的复杂性。当规划系统时，考虑以下因素尤为重要：

- 这个系统会有多大？
- 系统各部分有哪些部件？它们是基本的（如一个调光器）还是更高级的（如一个报警系统或视频摄像头）？
- 对非用户来说，系统的直观性如何？
- 多少人需要使用该系统？
- 谁知道如何操作系统？谁知道如何维护系统和处理故障？会去操作该系统的人有多少时间独自在家？
- 改变接口容易吗？例如，如果房子是编程在凌晨 7 点唤醒你，怎样让它知道你整夜在公司或在一个星期六睡懒觉？

由于这些原因，可能从一个基本的家庭网络起步会更容易，然后根据需要或期望进行扩展。然而有人担心，该市场如此新兴，而新技术又在不断地开发，有时旧版本的产品会失效。如果投资得太快，可能会因找不到与自己的模型相匹配的组件和备件而后悔。像许多新技术一样，智能家居的保养需要大量投资。

智能家居也存在一些安全问题。访问网络的黑客能关闭报警系统和灯，使住宅更容易被侵入，盗窃也可能更电子化。如果把音乐保存在硬盘上以便可以在家里播放，应确保把敏感信息（如密码或标识号）保存在其他地方。

一些家庭智能设备也会引发关于隐私的伦理道德问题。当你在厨房做饭时能够检查 4 岁的孩子是否在他的房间里，这很了不起。但当这孩子在青春期一直被监控时他会有什么样的感觉？智能家居收集的信息可能像一个工具，能够抓住一个在聚会后深夜偷偷溜进家的十几岁的年轻人。要建立一个智能家居时，最好先与全家人讨论一下。

当然，还是一个问题：个人是否需要这些技术。是不是我们的社会真的懒到了不能轻触一下电灯开关的地步？这是一个有趣的争议，然而智能家居正在到来。值得称赞的是，家庭自动化可以节省时间，我们就有时间实现其他追求。

Unit 4

Text A

Network Architecture

Network architecture is the design of a communications network. It is a framework for the specification of a network's physical components and their functional organization and configuration, its operational principles and procedures, as well as data formats used in its operation.

In telecommunication, the specification of network architecture may also include a detailed description of products and services delivered via a communications network, as well as detailed rate and billing structures under which services are.

1. OSI Network Model

The Open Systems Interconnection model[1] (OSI model) is a product of the Open Systems Interconnection effort at the International Organization for Standardization. It is a way of sub-dividing a communications system into smaller parts called layers. A layer is a collection of similar functions that provide services to the layer above it and receives services from the layer below it. On each layer, an instance provides services to the instances at the layer above and requests service from the layer below.

1.1 Physical Layer

The Physical Layer defines the electrical and physical specifications for devices. In particular, it defines the relationship between a device and a transmission medium, such as a copper or optical cable. This includes the layout of pins, voltages, cable specifications, hubs, repeaters, network adapters, host bus adapters (HBA used in storage area networks) and more. Its main task is the transmission of a stream of bits over a communication channel.

---

[1] The Open Systems Interconnection (OSI) model (ISO/IEC 7498-1) is a product of the Open Systems Interconnection effort at the International Organization for Standardization. It is a <u>prescription</u> ([prɪˈskrɪpʃən]n.指示, 规定) of characterizing and standardizing the functions of a communications system in terms of abstraction layers.

1.2 Data Link Layer

The Data Link Layer provides the functional and procedural means to transfer data between network entities and to detect and possibly correct errors that may occur in the Physical Layer. Originally, this layer was intended for point-to-point and point-to-multipoint media, characteristic of wide area media in the telephone system. Local area network architecture, which included broadcast-capable multi-access media, was developed independently of the ISO work in IEEE Project 802. In modern practice, only error detection, not flow control using sliding window, is present in data link protocols such as Point-to-Point Protocol (PPP)[1], and, on local area networks, the IEEE 802.2 LLC[2] layer is not used for most protocols on the Ethernet, and on other local area networks, its flow control and acknowledgment mechanisms are rarely used. Sliding window flow control and acknowledgment is used at the Transport Layer by protocols such as TCP, but is still used in niches where X.25[3] offers performance advantages. Simply, its main job is to create and recognize the frame boundary. This can be done by attaching special bit patterns to the beginning and the end of the frame. The input data is broken up into frames.

1.3 Network Layer

The Network Layer provides the functional and procedural means of transferring variable length data sequences from a source host on one network to a destination host on a different network, while maintaining the quality of service requested by the Transport Layer (in contrast to the data link layer which connects hosts within the same network). The Network Layer performs network routing functions, and might also perform fragmentation and reassembly, and report delivery errors. Routers operate at this layer--sending data throughout the extended network and making the Internet possible. This is a logical addressing scheme -- values are chosen by the network engineer. The addressing scheme is not hierarchical. It controls the operation of the subnet and determines the routing strategies between IMPs[4] and insures that all the packs are correctly received at the destination in the proper order.

1.4 Transport Layer

The Transport Layer provides transparent transfer of data between end users, providing

---

[1] In networking, the Point-to-Point Protocol (PPP) is a data link protocol commonly used in establishing a direct connection between two networking nodes. It can provide connection authentication, transmission encryption, and compression ([kəm'preʃən]n.压缩).

[2] In the seven-layer OSI model of computer networking, the logical link control (LLC) data communication protocol layer is the upper sublayer of the data link layer, which is itself layer 2.

[3] X.25 is an ITU-T standard protocol suite for packet switched wide area network (WAN) communication. An X.25 WAN consists of packet-switching exchange (PSE) nodes as the networking hardware, and leased lines (租用线,专用线), plain old telephone service connections or ISDN connections as physical links.

[4] The Interface Message Processor (IMP) was the packet-switching node used to interconnect participant ([pɑ:'tisipənt]adj.参与的) networks to the ARPANET from the late 1960s to 1989. It was the first generation of gateways, which are known today as routers.

reliable data transfer services to the upper layers. The Transport Layer controls the reliability of a given link through flow control, segmentation/desegmentation, and error control. Some protocols are state and connection oriented. This means that the Transport Layer can keep track of the segments and retransmit those that fail. The Transport layer also provides the acknowledgement of the successful data transmission and sends the next data if no errors occurred. Some Transport Layer protocols, for example TCP, but not UDP, support virtual circuits[1] and provide connection oriented communication over an underlying packet oriented datagram[2] network. The datagram transportation delivers the packets randomly and broadcasts it to multiple nodes.

Notes: The transport layer multiplexes several streams on to 1 physical channel. The transport header tells which message belongs to which connection.

1.5 The Session Layer

This Layer provides a user interface to the network where the user negotiates to establish a connection. The user must provide the remote address to be contacted. The operation of setting up a session between two processes is called "Binding". In some protocols it is merged with the transport layer. Its main work is to transfer data from the other application to this application so this application is mainly used for transferred layer.

1.6 Presentation Layer

The Presentation Layer establishes context between Application Layer entities, in which the higher-layer entities may use different syntax and semantics if the presentation service provides a mapping between them. If a mapping is available, presentation service data units are encapsulated into session protocol data units, and passed down the stack. This layer provides independence from data representation (e.g., encryption) by translating between application and network formats. The presentation layer transforms data into the form that the application accepts. This layer formats and encrypts data to be sent across a network. It is sometimes called the syntax layer. The original presentation structure used the basic encoding rules of Abstract Syntax Notation One (ASN.1), with capabilities such as converting an EBCDIC-coded text file to an ASCII-coded file, or serialization of objects and other data structures from and to XML.

1.7 Application Layer

The Application Layer is the OSI layer closest to the end user, which means that both the OSI application layer and the user interact directly with the software application. This layer interacts with software applications that implement a communicating component. Such

---

[1] In telecommunications and computer networks, a virtual circuit (VC), synonymous with virtual connection and virtual channel, is a connection oriented communication service that is delivered by means of packet mode communication. After a connection or virtual circuit is established between two nodes or application processes, a bit stream (位流) or byte stream may be delivered between the nodes; A virtual circuit protocol allows higher level protocols to avoid dealing with the division of data into segments, packets, or frames.

[2] A datagram is a basic transfer unit associated with a packet-switched network in which the delivery, arrival time, and order of arrival are not guaranteed by the network service.

application programs fall outside the scope of the OSI model. Application layer functions typically include identifying communication partners, determining resource availability, and synchronizing communication. When identifying communication partners, the application layer determines the identity and availability of communication partners for an application with data to transmit.

2. Distributed Computing

In distributed computing, the term network architecture often describes the structure and classification of distributed application architecture, as the participating nodes in a distributed application are often referred to as a network. For example, the applications architecture of the public switched telephone network (PSTN)[1] has been termed the Advanced Intelligent Network[2]. There are a number of specific classifications but all lie on a continuum between the dumb network[3] (e.g., Internet) and the intelligent computer network (e.g., the telephone network). Other networks contain various elements of these two classical types to make them suitable for various types of applications. Recently the context aware network[4], which is a synthesis of two, has gained much interest with its ability to combine the best elements of both.

A popular example of such usage of the term in distributed applications as well as PVCs (permanent virtual circuits) is the organization of nodes in peer-to-peer (P2P) services and networks. P2P networks usually implement overlay networks running over an underlying physical or logical network. These overlay network may implement certain organizational structures of the nodes according to several distinct models, the network architecture of the system.

---

[1] The public switched telephone network (PSTN) is the network of the world's public circuit-switched telephone networks. It consists of telephone lines, fiber optic cables, microwave (['maikrəuweiv] n. 微波) transmission links, cellular networks, communications satellites, and undersea telephone cables, all inter-connected by switching centers, thus allowing any telephone in the world to communicate with any other.

[2] The Intelligent Network (IN) is the standard network architecture specified in the ITU-T Q.1200 series recommendations. It is intended for fixed as well as mobile telecom networks. It allows operators to differentiate themselves by providing value-added services (增值服务) in addition to the standard telecom services such as PSTN, ISDN and GSM (Global System of Mobile communication, 全球移动通信系统) services on mobile phones.

[3] A dumb network is marked by using intelligent devices (i.e. PCs) at the periphery that make use of a network that does not interfere or manage with an application's operation / communication. The dumb network concept is the natural outcome of the end to end principle. The Internet was originally designed to operate as a dumb network.

[4] A context aware network is a network that tries to overcome the limitations of the dumb and intelligent network models and to create a synthesis (['sinθisis]n. 综合) which combines the best of both network models. It is designed to allow for customization and application creation while at the same time ensuring that application operation is compatible not just with the preferences of the individual user but with the expressed preferences of the enterprise or other collectivity ([,kəlek'tiviti] n. 全体, 总体) which owns the network. The Semantic Web is an example of a context aware network.

New Words

architecture	['ɑ:kitektʃə]	n.	体系结构
framework	['freimwə:k]	n.	构架，框架，结构
specification	[,spesifi'keiʃən]	n.	规范，详述，规格，说明书
functional	['fʌŋkʃənl]	adj.	功能的
configuration	[kən,figju'reiʃən]	n.	构造，结构，配置
principle	['prinsəpl]	n.	法则，原则，原理
procedure	[prə'si:dʒə]	n.	程序，过程
layer	['leiə]	n.	层
collection	[kə'lekʃən]	n.	集
instance	['instəns]	n.	实例，要求
		vt.	举……为例
request	[ri'kwest]	vt. & n.	请求，要求
repeater	[ri'pi:tə]	n.	转发器，中继器
storage	['stɔridʒ]	n.	存储
entity	['entiti]	n.	实体
multipoint	['mʌltipɔint]	adj.	多点（式）的，多位置的
characteristic	[,kæriktə'ristik]	adj.	特有的，表示特性的，典型的
		n.	特性，特征
broadcast	['brɔ:dkɑ:st]	n. & v.	广播
Ethernet	['i:θənet]	n.	以太网
acknowledgment	[ək'nɔlidʒmənt]	n.	确认，承认
niche	[nitʃ]	n.	合适的位置，小生境
performance	[pə'fɔ:məns]	n.	履行，执行，性能
sequence	['si:kwəns]	n.	次序，顺序，序列
fragmentation	[,frægmen'teiʃən]	n.	分段
reassembly	['ri:ə'sembli]	n.	重新装配
router	['ru:tə]	n.	路由器
hierarchical	[,haiə'rɑ:kikəl]	adj.	分等级的，分层的
subnet	['sʌb,net]	n.	子网络，分支网络
transparent	[træns'pɛərənt]	adj.	透明的，显然的，明晰的
segmentation	[,segmən'teiʃən]	n.	分割
connection	[kə'nekʃən]	n.	连接，接线，线路
retransmit	[,ri:trænz'mit]	v.	转播，转发
datagram	['deitəgræm]	n.	数据报
multiplex	['mʌltipleks]	v.	多路传输，多路复用；多重发信

		adj. 多元的
establish	[isˈtæbliʃ]	vt. 建立，设立
session	[ˈseʃən]	n. 会话
binding	[ˈbaindiŋ]	n. 绑定
semantics	[siˈmæntiks]	n. 语义
mapping	[ˈmæpiŋ]	n. 映射
map	[mæp]	vt. 映射
encapsulate	[inˈkæpsjuleit]	v. 封装
stack	[stæk]	n. 堆栈
		v. 堆叠
accept	[əkˈsept]	v. 接受，认可，承认
format	[ˈfɔːmæt]	n. 形式，格式
		vt. 安排……的格式
encrypt	[inˈkript]	v. 加密，将……译成密码
convert	[kənˈvəːt]	vt. 使转变，转换……
serialization	[ˌsiəriəlaiˈzeiʃən]	n. 序列化
synchronize	[ˈsiŋkrənaiz]	v. 同步
identity	[aiˈdentiti]	n. 身份，一致
continuum	[kənˈtinjuəm]	n. 连续统一体，闭联集
synthesis	[ˈsinθisis]	n. 综合，合成

Phrases

communication network	通信网络
Open Systems Interconnection model (OSI model)	开放式系统互联参考模型
International Organization for Standardization	国际标准化组织
physical layer	物理层
transmission medium	传输介质，传送介质
optical cable	光缆
stream of bits	比特流
data link layer	数据链路层
intend for …	趋向于……，倾向于……，想要……
Local area network	局域网
independent of …	不依赖，独立于……
Point-to-Point Protocol (PPP)	点对点协议
flow control	流控制
sliding window	滑动窗口
transport layer	传输层

bit pattern	位组合格式，位的形式
network layer	网络层
in contrast to …	和……形成对比，和……形成对照
logical addressing scheme	逻辑寻址方案
virtual circuit	虚拟线路，虚拟电路
session layer	会话层
presentation layer	表示层
abstract syntax notation one	抽象语法表示法1，抽象语法符号1
application layer	应用层
fall outside	超越，超出……
distributed computing	分布式计算
advanced intelligent network	高级智能网
suitable for …	适合……的
context aware network	情景感知网络
overlay network	覆盖网络，重叠网络，叠加网络

Abbreviations

HBA (Host Bus Adapter)	主机总线适配器
LLC (Logical Link Control)	逻辑链路控制
IMP (Interface Message Processor)	接口信息处理器
UDP (User Datagram Protocol)	用户数据报协议
EBCDIC (Extended Binary Coded Decimal Interchange Code)	扩充的二进制编码的十进制交换码
ASCII (American Standard Code for Information Interchange)	美国信息交换标准码
XML (eXtensible Markup Language)	可扩展标记语言
PVC (Permanent Virtual Circuit)	永久虚拟电路

Exercises

【EX.1】Answer the following questions according to the text.

1. What is the Open Systems Interconnection model (OSI model)?
2. What is a layer?
3. What does the Physical Layer define?
4. What does the Data Link Layer provide?
5. What does the Network Layer provide?
6. What does the Transport Layer control?

7. What is binding?

8. What does the Presentation Layer establish?

9. What do application layer functions typically include?

10. What does the term network architecture often describe in distinct usage in distributed computing?

【EX.2】 Translate the following terms or phrases from English into Chinese and vice versa.

1. data link layer   1. _____
2. Point-to-Point Protocol (PPP)   2. _____
3. transport layer   3. _____
4. logical addressing scheme   4. _____
5. Local area network   5. _____
6. session layer   6. _____
7. distributed computing   7. _____
8. virtual circuit   8. _____
9. presentation layer   9. _____
10. data link layer   10. _____
11. n. 构架，框架，结构   11. _____
12. adj. 功能的   12. _____
13. n. 转发器，中继器   13. _____
14. n. 进程，程序   14. _____
15. n. 路由器   15. _____

【EX.3】 Translate the following sentences into Chinese.

1. It is certified that the software architecture is universal and expandable.

2. In an object-oriented environment, a framework consists of abstract and concrete classes.

3. The software does something that the product specification says it shouldn't do.

4. An error has occurred during configuration of home networking on this computer.

5. A hub is a device that connects several nodes of a local area network.

6. The signal transmitted between the end facilities is relayed by the repeater.

7. You cannot disable the selected network adapter because it is used for network connectivity.

8. Only Ethernet facilitates the combination of components from different manufacturers.

9. Which command will configure a default route on a router?

10. Classifying the datagram on LANs can provide some evidences of NID (network intrusion detect).

【EX.4】 Complete the following passage with appropriate words in the box.

same	workstation	collision	decreased	captured
delay	token-passing	system	logical	node

The Ethernet protocol is by far the most widely used. Ethernet uses an access method called CSMA/CD (Carrier Sense Multiple Access/Collision Detection). This is a __1__ where each computer listens to the cable before sending anything through the network. If the network is clear, the computer will transmit. If some other __2__ is already transmitting on the cable, the computer will wait and try again when the line is clear. Sometimes, two computers attempt to transmit at the __3__ instant. When this happens a __4__ occurs. Each computer then backs off and waits a random amount of time before attempting to retransmit. With this access method, it is normal to have collisions. However, the __5__ caused by collisions and retransmitting is very small and does not normally effect the speed of transmission on the network.

The Ethernet protocol allows for linear bus, star, or tree topologies. Data can be transmitted over wireless access points, twisted pair, coaxial, or fiber optic cable at a speed of 10 Mbps up to 1000 Mbps.

The Token Ring protocol was developed by IBM in the mid-1980s. The access method used involves __6__. In Token Ring, the computers are connected so that the signal travels around the network from one computer to another in a __7__ ring. A single electronic token moves around the ring from one computer to the next. If a computer does not have information to transmit, it simply passes the token on to the next __8__. If a computer wishes to transmit and receives an empty token, it attaches data to the token. The token then proceeds around the ring until it comes to the computer for which the data is meant. At this point, the data is __9__ by the receiving computer. The Token Ring protocol requires a star-wired ring using twisted pair or fiber optic cable. It can operate at transmission speeds of 4 Mbps or 16 Mbps. Due to the increasing popularity of Ethernet, the use of Token Ring in school environments has __10__.

【EX.5】**Translate the following passage into Chinese.**

Network

A network is a group of two or more computer systems linked together. There are many types of computer networks, including:

- Local Area Networks (LANs): The computers are geographically close together.
- Wide Area Networks (WANs): The computers are farther apart and are connected by telephone lines or radio waves.
- Campus Area Networks (CANs): The computers are within a limited geographic area, such as a campus or military base.
- Metropolitan Area Networks (MANs): A data network designed for a town or city.
- Home Area Networks (HANs): A network contained within a user's home that connects a person's digital devices.
- In addition to these types, the following characteristics are also used to categorize different types of networks:
- Topology: The geometric arrangement of a computer system. Common topologies include a bus, star, and ring.

- Protocol: The protocol defines a common set of rules and signals that computers on the network use to communicate. One of the most popular protocols for LANs is called Ethernet. Another popular LAN protocol for PCs is the IBM token-ring network.
- Architecture: Networks can be broadly classified as using either a peer-to-peer or client/server architecture.

Computers on a network are sometimes called nodes. Computers and devices that allocate resources for a network are called servers.

Network Topology

Network topology is the arrangement of the various elements (links, nodes, etc.) of a computer or biological network. Essentially, it is the topological structure of a network, and may be depicted physically or logically. Physical topology refers to the placement of the network's various components, including device location and cable installation, while logical decreased topology shows how data flows within a network, regardless of its physical design. Distances between nodes, physical interconnections, transmission rates, and/or signal types may differ between two networks, yet their topologies may be identical.

A good example is a local area network (LAN)[1]: Any given node in the LAN has one or more physical links to other devices in the network; graphically mapping these links results in a geometric shape that can be used to describe the physical topology of the network. Conversely, mapping the data flow between the components determines the logical topology of the network.

There are two basic categories of network topologies:
1) Physical topologies
2) Logical topologies

The shape of the cabling layout used to link devices is called the physical topology of the network. This refers to the layout of cabling, the locations of nodes, and the interconnections between the nodes and the cabling. The physical topology of a network is determined by the capabilities of the network access devices and media, the level of control or fault tolerance desired, and the cost associated with cabling or telecommunications circuits.

The logical topology, in contrast, is the way that the signals act on the network media, or the way that the data passes through the network from one device to the next without regard to the physical interconnection of the devices. A network's logical topology is not necessarily the same as its physical topology. For example, the original twisted pair Ethernet[2] using repeater

---

[1] A local area network (LAN) is a computer network that interconnects computers in a limited area such as a home, school, computer laboratory, or office building using network media.

[2] The twisted pair Ethernet technologies use twisted-pair cables for the physical layer of an Ethernet computer network. Other Ethernet cable standards employ coaxial cable or optical fiber.

hubs was a logical bus topology with a physical star topology layout. Token Ring is a logical ring topology, but is wired a physical star from the Media Access Unit[1].

The logical classification of network topologies generally follows the same classifications as those in the physical classifications of network topologies but describes the path that the data takes between nodes being used. The logical topologies are generally determined by network protocols.

Logical topologies are often closely associated with Media Access Control[2] methods and protocols. Logical topologies are able to be dynamically reconfigured by special types of equipment such as routers and switches.

1. Point to Point

The simplest topology is a permanent link between two endpoints. Switched point-to-point topologies are the basic model of conventional telephony. The value of a permanent point-to-point network is unimpeded communications between the two endpoints. The value of an on-demand point-to-point connection is proportional to the number of potential pairs of subscribers, and has been expressed as Metcalfe's Law[3].

Permanent (dedicated): Easiest to understand, of the variations of point-to-point topology, is a point-to-point communications channel that appears, to the user, to be permanently associated with the two endpoints. A children's tin can telephone is one example of a physical dedicated channel.

Within many switched telecommunications systems, it is possible to establish a permanent circuit. One example might be a telephone in the lobby of a public building, which is programmed to ring only the number of a telephone dispatcher. "Nailing down" a switched connection saves the cost of running a physical circuit between the two points. The resources in such a connection can be released when no longer needed, for example, a television circuit from a parade route back to the studio.

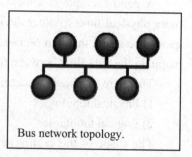

Bus network topology.

---

[1] A Media Access Unit (MAU, also called Multistation Access Unit, MSAU) is a device to attach multiple network stations in a star topology in a token ring network, internally wired to connect the stations into a logical ring.

[2] In the seven-layer OSI model of computer networking, media access control (MAC) data communication protocol is a <u>sublayer</u> (['sʌb'leɪə] n. 下层) of the data link layer, which itself is layer 2. The MAC sublayer provides addressing and channel access control mechanisms that make it possible for several terminals or network nodes to communicate within a multiple access network that incorporates a shared medium, e.g. Ethernet.

[3] Metcalfe's law states that the value of a telecommunications network is <u>proportional</u> ([prə'pɔːʃənl] adj. 成比例的) to the square of the number of connected users of the system (n^2).

Switched: Using circuit switching[1] or packet switching[2] technologies, a point-to-point circuit can be set up dynamically, and dropped when no longer needed. This is the basic mode of conventional telephony.

2. Bus

In local area networks where bus topology is used, each node is connected to a single cable. Each computer or server is connected to the single bus cable. A signal from the source travels in both directions to all machines connected on the bus cable until it finds the intended recipient. If the machine address does not match the intended address for the data, the machine ignores the data. Alternatively, if the data matches the machine address, the data is accepted. Since the bus topology consists of only one wire, it is rather inexpensive to implement when compared to other topologies. However, the low cost of implementing the technology is offset by the high cost of managing the network. Additionally, since only one cable is utilized, it can be the single point of failure. If the network cable is terminated on both ends and when without termination data transfer stop and when cable breaks, the entire network will be down.

2.1 Linear Bus

The type of network topology in which all of the nodes of the network are connected to a common transmission medium which has exactly two endpoints (this is the 'bus', which is also commonly referred to as the backbone, or trunk) -- all data that is transmitted between nodes in the network is transmitted over this common transmission medium and is able to be received by all nodes in the network simultaneously.

Note: The two endpoints of the common transmission medium are normally terminated with a device called a terminator[3]. It exhibits the characteristic impedance of the transmission medium and dissipates or absorbs the energy that remains in the signal to prevent the signal from being reflected or propagated back onto the transmission medium in the opposite direction, which would cause interference with and degradation of the signals on the transmission medium.

2.2 Distributed Bus

The type of network topology in which all of the nodes of the network are connected to a common transmission medium which has more than two endpoints that are created by adding branches to the main section of the transmission medium -- the physical distributed bus topology

---

[1] Circuit switching is a methodology of implementing a telecommunications network in which two network nodes establish a dedicated communications channel (circuit) through the network before the nodes may communicate. The circuit <u>guarantees</u> ([,gærən'tiː] vt. 保证) the full bandwidth of the channel and remains connected for the duration of the communication session. The circuit functions as if the nodes were physically connected as with an electrical circuit.

[2] Packet switching is a digital networking communications method that groups all transmitted data -- <u>regardless of</u> (不管，不顾) content, type, or structure -- into suitably sized blocks, called packets.

[3] Electrical termination of a signal involves providing a terminator at the end of a wire or cable to prevent an RF signal from being reflected back from the end, causing interference. The terminator is placed at the end of a transmission line or daisy chain bus, designed to match impedance and hence minimize signal reflections.

functions in exactly the same fashion as the physical linear bus topology (i.e., all nodes share a common transmission medium).

Notes:

1) All the endpoints of the common transmission medium are normally terminated using 50 ohm resistor.

2) The linear bus topology is sometimes considered to be a special case of the distributed bus topology -- i.e., a distributed bus with no branching segments.

3) The physical distributed bus topology is sometimes incorrectly referred to as a physical tree topology -- however, although the physical distributed bus topology resembles the physical tree topology, it differs from the physical tree topology in that there is no central node to which any other nodes are connected, since this hierarchical functionality is replaced by the common bus.

3. Star

In local area networks with a star topology, each network host is connected to a central hub with a point-to-point connection. In star topology every node (computer workstation or any other peripheral) is connected to the central node called the hub or the switch. The switch is the server and the peripherals are the clients. The network does not necessarily have to resemble a star to be classified as a star network, but all of the nodes on the network must be connected to one central device. All traffic that traverses the network passes through the central hub. The hub acts as a signal repeater[1]. The star topology is considered the easiest topology to design and implement. An advantage of the star topology is the simplicity of adding additional nodes. The primary disadvantage of the star topology is that the hub represents a single point of failure.

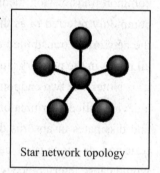
Star network topology

Notes:

1) A point-to-point link (described above) is sometimes categorized as a special instance of the physical star topology -- therefore, the simplest type of network that is based upon the physical star topology would consist of one node with a single point-to-point link to a second node. It is arbitrary to choose which node is the 'hub' and which node is the 'spoke'.

2) After the special case of the point-to-point link, the next simplest type of network that is based upon the physical star topology would consist of one central node -- the 'hub' -- with two separate point-to-point links to two peripheral nodes – the 'spokes'.

3) Although most networks that are based upon the physical star topology are commonly implemented using a special device such as a hub or switch as the central node (i.e., the 'hub' of

---

[1] A repeater is an electronic device that receives a signal and retransmits it at a higher level or higher power, or onto the other side of an <u>obstruction</u> ([əbˈstrʌkʃən] n. 阻塞, 障碍物), so that the signal can cover longer distances.

the star), it is also possible to implement a network that is based upon the physical star topology using a computer or even a simple common connection point as the 'hub' or central node.

4) Star networks may also be described as either broadcast multi-access or nonbroadcast multi-access (NBMA), depending on whether the technology of the network either automatically propagates a signal at the hub to all spokes, or only addresses individual spokes with each communication.

4. Ring

A network topology that is set up in a circular fashion in which data travels around the ring in one direction and each device on the right acts as a repeater to keep the signal strong as it travels. Each device incorporates a receiver for the incoming signal and a transmitter to send the data on to the next device in the ring. The network is dependent on the ability of the signal to travel around the ring.

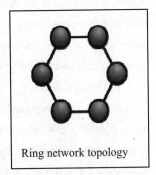

Ring network topology

5. Tree

The type of network topology in which a central 'root' node (the top level of the hierarchy) is connected to one or more other nodes that are one level lower in the hierarchy (i.e., the second level) with a point-to-point link between each of the second level nodes and the top level central 'root' node. Each of the second level nodes will also have one or more other nodes that are one level lower in the hierarchy (i.e., the third level) connected to it, also with a point-to-point link, the top level central 'root' node being the only node that has no other node above it in the hierarchy. The hierarchy of the tree is symmetrical. This tree has individual peripheral nodes.

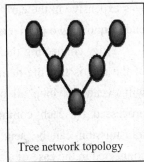

Tree network topology

Notes:

1) A network that is based upon the physical hierarchical topology must have at least three levels in the hierarchy of the tree, since a network with a central 'root' node and only one hierarchical level below it would exhibit the physical topology of a star.

2) A network that is based upon the physical hierarchical topology and with a branching factor of 1 would be classified as a physical linear topology.

3) The branching factor, f, is independent of the total number of nodes in the network and, therefore, if the nodes in the network require ports for connection to other nodes the total number of ports per node may be kept low even though the total number of nodes is large -- this makes the effect of the cost of adding ports to each node totally dependent upon the branching factor and may therefore be kept as low as required without any effect upon the total number of nodes that are possible.

4) The total number of point-to-point links in a network that is based upon the physical hierarchical topology will be one less than the total number of nodes in the network.

5) If the nodes in a network that is based upon the physical hierarchical topology are

required to perform any processing upon the data that is transmitted between nodes in the network, the nodes that are at higher levels in the hierarchy will be required to perform more processing operations on behalf of other nodes than the nodes that are lower in the hierarchy. Such a type of network topology is very useful and highly recommended.

6. Hybrid

Hybrid networks use a combination of any two or more topologies in such a way that the resulting network does not exhibit one of the standard topologies (e.g., bus, star, ring, etc.). For example, a tree network connected to a tree network is still a tree network topology. A hybrid topology is always produced when two different basic network topologies are connected. Two common examples for Hybrid network are: star ring network and star bus network.

7. Daisy Chain

Except for star-based networks, the easiest way to add more computers into a network is by daisy-chaining[1], or connecting each computer in series to the next. If a message is intended for a computer partway down the line, each system bounces it along in sequence until it reaches the destination. A daisy-chained network can take two basic forms: linear and ring.

Notes:

1) A linear topology puts a two-way link between one computer and the next. However, this was expensive in the early days of computing, since each computer (except for the ones at each end) required two receivers and two transmitters.

2) By connecting the computers at each end, a ring topology can be formed. An advantage of the ring is that the number of transmitters and receivers can be cut in half, since a message will eventually loop all of the way around. When a node sends a message, the message is processed by each computer in the ring. If the ring breaks at a particular link then the transmission can be sent via the reverse path, thereby ensuring that all nodes are always connected in the case of a single failure.

New Words

topology	[təˈpɔlədʒi]	n. 拓扑，布局
arrangement	[əˈreindʒmənt]	n. 排列，安排
link	[liŋk]	n. & vt. 链接
depict	[diˈpikt]	vt. 描述，描写
placement	[ˈpleismənt]	n. 放置，布置
interconnection	[ˌintə(:)kəˈnekʃən]	n. 互联

---

[1] In electrical and electronic engineering, a daisy chain is a <u>wiring scheme</u> (接线图，布线图) in which multiple devices are wired together in sequence or in a ring. Other than a full, single loop, systems which contain internal loops cannot be called daisy chains.

identical	[aiˈdentikəl]	adj. 同一的，同样的
telecommunication	[ˌtelikəmjuːniˈkeiʃən]	n. 电信，长途通信，无线电通信，电信学
dynamical	[daiˈnæmikəl]	adj. 动态的
reconfigure	[ˌriːkənˈfigə]	v. 重新装配，改装
permanent	[ˈpəːmənənt]	adj. 永久的，持久的
endpoint	[ˈendpɔint]	n. 端点，终点
unimpeded	[ˌʌnimˈpiːdid]	adj. 未受阻止的，没受到阻碍的
proportional	[prəˈpɔːʃənl]	adj. 相称的，均衡的
bus	[bʌs]	n. 总线
recipient	[riˈsipiənt]	n. 接收者
ignore	[igˈnɔː]	vt. 不理睬，忽略
utilize	[juːˈtilaiz]	vt. 利用
backbone	[ˈbækbəun]	n. 骨干，支柱
trunk	[trʌŋk]	n. 干线，树干，主干
simultaneously	[siməlˈteiniəsly]	adv. 同时地
terminator	[ˈtəːmineitə]	n. 终结器
impedance	[imˈpiːdəns]	n. 阻抗，电阻
dissipate	[ˈdisipeit]	v. 驱散，消耗
propagate	[ˈprɔpəgeit]	v. 传播
resistor	[riˈzistə]	n. 电阻器
peripheral	[pəˈrifərəl]	adj. 外围的
		n. 外围设备
hub	[hʌb]	n. 网络集线器，网络中心
spoke	[spəuk]	n. 轮辐
symmetrical	[siˈmetrikəl]	adj. 对称的，均匀的
branching	[ˈbrɑːntʃiŋ]	n. 分歧
		adj. 发枝的
port	[pɔːt]	n. 端口
partway	[ˈpɑːtwei]	v. 到中途，到达一半

Phrases

physical topology	物理拓扑
logical topology	逻辑拓扑
data flow	数据流
regardless of	不管，不顾
transmission rate	传输率
cable layout	电缆配线图，电缆敷设图

act on …	对……起作用，按……行动，作用于
without regard to	不考虑，不遵守
twisted pair Ethernet	双绞线以太网
star topology	星型拓扑
token ring	令牌网
Media Access Unit	媒体存取单元，媒体访问单元
Media Access Control	媒体存取控制，媒体访问控制
Metcalfe's Law	麦特卡夫定律
nail down	钉牢
circuit switching	线路交换，线路转接
packet switching	包交换技术
opposite direction	反向,相反方向
base upon	根据，依据
daisy chain	串式链接，链接式
in sequence	顺次，依次
cut in half	切成两半

Abbreviations

LAN (Local Area Network)	局域网

Exercises

【EX.1】Fill in the blanks according to the text.

1. Network topology is _____ of a computer or biological network.

2. There are two basic categories of network topologies: _____ and _____.

3. Physical topology refers to _____, including device location and cable installation, while logical topology shows _____, regardless of its physical design.

4. The value of a permanent point-to-point network is _____. The value of an on-demand point-to-point connection is _____.

5. Linear bus topology is the type of network topology in which _____ are connected to a common transmission medium which has exactly two endpoints. The two endpoints of the common transmission medium are normally terminated with a device called _____.

6. Distributed bus topology is the type of network topology in which all of the nodes of the network are connected to _____ which has more than two endpoints that are

created by adding branches to _____.

7. In star topology every node is connected to the central node called _____. An advantage of the star topology is _____. The primary disadvantage of the star topology is that _____.

8. A network that is based upon the physical hierarchical topology must have at least _____ in the hierarchy of the tree, since a network with a central 'root' node and only one hierarchical level below it would exhibit _____.

9. Two common examples for Hybrid network are _____ and _____.

10. The two basic forms a daisy-chained network can take are _____ and _____.

【EX.2】Translate the following terms or phrases from English into Chinese and vice versa.

1. physical topology   1. _____
2. circuit switching   2. _____
3. daisy chain   3. _____
4. packet switching   4. _____
5. topology   5. _____
6. placement   6. _____
7. telecommunication   7. _____
8. reconfigure   8. _____
9. backbone   9. _____
10. proportional   10. _____
11. n. 终结器   11. _____
12. n. 端口   12. _____
13. adj. 外围的 n. 外围设备   13. _____
14. n. 网络集线器，网络中心   14. _____
15. n. 终结器   15. _____

【EX.3】Translate the following sentences into Chinese.

1. Structural topology optimization method is a newly developing method and has achieved remarkable success.

2. Communication technology actually means the interconnection between equipment to equipment.

3. In a huge telecommunication network, there are many devices from different manufactures.

4. The network transport endpoint already has an address associated with it.

5. Today's Ethernet networks--particularly on the backbone--use switched rather than shared Ethernet.

6. This workstation does not have sufficient resources to open another network session.

7. PCI bus can interconnect peripheral components with CPU.

8. One way to stand out in a crowded category of electronic devices is to employ a novel hardware design.

9. Cable is not symmetrical: Downstream speeds far outpace upstream speeds.

10. It is a combination of information technology and management knowledge.

Text C

Internet Terms

1. Internet

The Internet, sometimes called simply "the Net," is a worldwide system of computer networks -- a network of networks in which users at any one computer can, if they have permission[1], get information from any other computer (and sometimes talk directly to users at other computers). It was conceived by the Advanced Research Projects Agency (ARPA)[2] of the U.S. government in 1969 and was first known as the ARPANet. The original aim was to create a network that would allow users of a research computer at one university to be able to "talk to" research computers at other universities. A side benefit of ARPANet's design was that, because messages could be routed or rerouted[3] in more than one direction, the network could continue to function even if parts of it were destroyed[4] in the event of a military attack or other disasters.

Today, the Internet is a public, cooperative, and self-sustaining[5] facility accessible to hundreds of millions of people worldwide. Physically, the Internet uses a portion of the total resources of the currently existing public telecommunication networks. Technically, what distinguishes the Internet is its use of a set of protocols called TCP/IP (Transmission Control Protocol/Internet Protocol). Two recent adaptations of Internet technology, the intranet[6] and the extranet[7], also make use of the TCP/IP protocol.

For many Internet users, electronic mail (e-mail) has practically replaced the Postal Service for short written transactions. Electronic mail is the most widely used application on the Net. You can also carry on live "conversations"[8] with other computer users, using Internet Relay Chat (IRC)[9]. More recently, Internet telephony hardware and

[1][pəˈmiʃən]
n. 许可，允许

[2]（美国国防部）高级研究计划署

[3][riˈruːt]
vt. 变更路程

[4][disˈtrɔi]
vt. 破坏，毁坏

[5][selfsəsˈteiniŋ]
adj. 自立的

[6][intrəˈnet]
n. 企业内部互联网

[7][ˈekstrənet]
n. 外联网

[8][ˌkɔnvəˈseiʃən]
n. 会话，交谈

[9]因特网在线聊天

software allows real-time voice conversations.

The most widely used part of the Internet is the World Wide Web (often abbreviated "WWW" or called "the Web"). Its outstanding feature is hypertext, a method of instant cross-referencing. In most Web sites, certain words or phrases appear in text of a different color than the rest; often this text is also underlined. When you select one of these words or phrases, you will be transferred to the site or page that is relevant to this word or phrase. Sometimes there are buttons[10], images, or portions of images that are "clickable[11]." If you move the pointer over a spot on a Web site and the pointer changes into a hand, this indicates[12] that you can click and be transferred to another site.

Using the Web, you have access to millions of pages of information. Web browsing is done with a Web browser[13], the most popular of which are Microsoft Internet Explorer and Netscape Navigator. The appearance of a particular Web site may vary slightly depending on the browser you use. Also, later versions of a particular browser are able to render more "bells and whistles[14]," such as animation, virtual reality, sound, and music files, than earlier versions.

2. TCP/IP (Transmission Control Protocol/Internet Protocol)

TCP/IP (Transmission Control Protocol/Internet Protocol) is the basic communication language or protocol of the Internet. It can also be used as a communications protocol in a private network[15] (either an intranet or an extranet). When you are set up with direct access to the Internet, your computer is provided with a copy of the TCP/IP program just as every other computer that you may send messages to or get information from also has a copy of TCP/IP.

TCP/IP is a two-layer program. The higher layer, Transmission Control Protocol, manages the assembling of a message or file into smaller packets that are transmitted over the Internet and received by a TCP layer that reassembles the packets into the original message. The lower layer, Internet Protocol, handles[16] the address part of each packet so that it gets to the right destination. Each gateway computer on the network checks this address to see where to forward the message. Even though some packets from the same message are routed differently than others, they'll be reassembled at the destination.

TCP/IP uses the client/server model of communication in which a computer user (a client) requests and is provided a service (such as sending a Web page) by another computer (a server) in the network.

---

[10]['bʌtn]
n. 按钮

[11][klik'eibl]
adj. 可点击的

[12]['indikeit]
vt. 指出,显示

[13][brauzə]
n. 浏览器

[14]bells and whistles: 花哨

[15]private network: 私有网络,专有网络

[16]['hændl]
vt. 处理,操作

TCP/IP communication is primarily point-to-point, meaning each communication is from one point or host computer[17] in the network to another point or host computer. TCP/IP and the higher-level applications that use it are collectively said to be "stateless" because each client request is considered a new request unrelated to any previous one (unlike ordinary phone conversations that require a dedicated connection for the call duration[18]). Being stateless frees network paths so that everyone can use them continuously. (Note that the TCP layer itself is not stateless as far as any one message is concerned. Its connection remains in place until all packets in a message have been received.)	[17]host computer: 主机 [18]for the duration: 在整段时期内
Many Internet users are familiar with[19] the even higher layer application protocols that use TCP/IP to get to the Internet. These include the World Wide Web's Hypertext Transfer Protocol (HTTP), the File Transfer Protocol (FTP), Telnet (Telnet) which lets you logon to remote computers, and the Simple Mail Transfer Protocol (SMTP[20]). These and other protocols are often packaged together with TCP/IP as a "suite[21]."	[19]be familiar with: 熟悉 [20]简单邮件传输协议
Personal computer users with an analog phone modem[22] connection to the Internet usually get to the Internet through the Serial Line Internet Protocol (SLIP[23]) or the Point-to-Point Protocol (PPP). These protocols encapsulate the IP packets so that they can be sent over the dial-up[24] phone connection to an access provider's modem.	[21][swi:t] n. 套件,套,组 [22]['məudəm] n. 调制解调器 [23]串行线路网际协议
Protocols related to TCP/IP include the User Datagram Protocol (UDP[25]), which is used instead of TCP for special purposes. Other protocols are used by network host computers for exchanging router information. These include the Internet Control Message Protocol (ICMP[26]), the Interior Gateway Protocol (IGP[27]), the Exterior Gateway Protocol (EGP[28]), and the Border Gateway Protocol (BGP[29]).	[24]['daiəlʌp] n. 拨号 [25]用户数据报协议 [26]因特网控制消息协议 [27]内部网关协议 [28]外部网关协议 [29]边界网关协议
3. HTTP (Hypertext Transfer Protocol) HTTP (Hypertext Transfer Protocol) is the set of rules for transferring files (text, graphic images, sound, video, and other multimedia[30] files) on the World Wide Web. As soon as a Web user opens their Web browser, the user is indirectly making use of HTTP. HTTP is an application protocol that runs on top of the TCP/IP suite of protocols (the foundation protocols for the Internet). HTTP concepts include (as the Hypertext part of the name	[30]['mʌltiˈmi:djə] n. 多媒体

implies) the idea that files can contain references to other files whose selection will elicit additional transfer requests. Any Web server machine contains, in addition to the Web page files it can serve, an HTTP daemon[31], a program that is designed to wait for HTTP requests and handle them when they arrive. Your Web browser is an HTTP client, sending requests to server machines. When the browser user enters file requests by either "opening" a Web file (typing in a Uniform Resource Locator or URL) or clicking on a hypertext link[32], the browser builds an HTTP request and sends it to the Internet Protocol address (IP address) indicated by the URL. The HTTP daemon in the destination server machine receives the request and sends back the requested file or files associated with the request.	[31]['di:mən] n. 精灵 [32]hypertext link：超链接

参考译文

Text A 网络体系结构

网络体系结构就是设计通信网络，是网络物理部件及其功能组织和配置、运作原理与过程以及运行中所用数据格式的规范框架。

在通信学科中，网络体系结构的规范还包括通过产品和通信网络交付的服务明细费率，也包括此服务详细的费率和收费体系。

1. OSI 网络模型

开放系统互连参考模型（OSI 模型）是由国际标准化组织提出的开放系统互连产品，它提供了一种把通信系统细分为"层"的更小部分的方法。层是相似功能的集合，它为其上的层提供服务并从其下的层接受服务。在每一层，一个实例为其上层实例提供服务并请求下层提供服务。

1.1 物理层

物理层定义设备的电子和物理规范，特别定义了设备和传输介质（如铜线或光缆）之间的关系，包括针的布局、电压、电缆规范、集线器、中继器、网络适配器、主机总线适配器（HBA 用于存储区域网络）等。物理层的主要任务是通过通信通道传输比特流。

1.2 数据链路层

数据链路层提供在网络实体之间传输数据的功能和方法，并检查和尽量改正物理层可能出现的错误。起初，该层打算供点对点和点对多点介质使用，这是电话系统中广域介质的特点。局域网体系包括可广播的多路访问介质，其开发不依赖 IEEE Project 802 中的 ISO。在当今的实践中，在数据链路协议（如点对点协议）只有错误检测而没有使用滑动窗口的流控制，并且，在局域网中，IEEE 802.2 LLC 层在以太网上没有使用太多的协议，在其他局域网中，它的流控制和确认机制也很少使用。滑动窗口流控制和确认由像 TCP 这样的协议用在传输层,但仍然用于 X.25 能够提供性能优势的情况下。简单地说,其主要任务是建立并识别帧边界。可以通过在帧头和帧尾附加特殊的位格式来实现该任务,这样输入数据就划分为帧。

1.3 网络层

网络层提供在不同网络中从源主机到目的主机之间传输可变长度数据序列的功能和方法,期间保持传输层要求的服务质量(与连接同一网络内主机的数据链路层对应)。网络层执行网络路由功能,也可实现信息的分解与重新装配,并报告传输错误。路由器运行在这一层——通过扩展的网络发送数据并使因特网成为可能。这是一个逻辑寻址方案——值由网络工程师选择。这个寻址方案不分层,它控制子层的运行、确定 IMP 之间的路由策略并确保所有数据包都在目的地按照适当的顺序被正确接收。

1.4 传输层

传输层提供端用户之间数据的透明传输,这样就可以把数据可靠地传输给上层。传输层管理某个流控制链路、分解/合并以及错误控制的可靠性。有些协议是面向状态和连接的,这就意味着传输层可以跟踪信息段并在传输失败后重发。传输层也提供对数据传输成功的确认,如果没有错误再发送之后的数据。某些协议(如 TCP 而不是 UDP)支持虚拟线路并通过下层的面向数据包的数据报网络来提供面向连接的通信。数据报传输随机发送数据包并向多个节点广播。

注意:传输层可以把多个流放入一个物理通道中。传输的头信息可以告知消息属于哪个连接。

1.5 会话层

该层提供用户接口以便用户可以建立会话连接。用户必须提供要联系的远程地址。在两个进程间建立会话的操作叫做"绑定"。在有些协议中,它被合并到传输层。其主要工作是从其他应用中向本应用传输数据,因此本应用主要用于传输层。

1.6 表示层

表示层建立应用层实体之间的语境关联,如果表示服务提供相应的映射,则高层实体可用不同的语法和语义。如果映射有效,可以把表示服务数据单元封装到会话协议数据单元,并传递到堆栈。该层通过在应用与网络格式之间转换而独立于数据表示(如加密)。表示层把数据转换为应用可以接受的形式。该层格式化和加密网络上要发送的数据,它有时也叫作语法层。最初的表现结构使用抽象语法标记(ASN.1)的基本编码规则,它能把 EBCDIC 编码的文本文件转换为 ASCII 编码的文件,或把对象和来自并用于 XML 的其他数据结构序列化。

1.7 应用层

应用层是离端用户最近的 OSI 层。这意味着 OSI 应用层和用户与软件应用程序直接交互。应用层与实现通信的软件应用程序交互。这样的应用程序超出了 OSI 模型的范围。应用层的功能通常包括识别通信伙伴、确定可用资源以及同步通信。当识别通信伙伴时,应用层确定通信伙伴的身份和有效性,以便传输数据。

2. 分布计算

在分布计算的独特应用中,术语"网络体系结构"通常用来描述分布应用体系的结构和种类,因为分布式应用中的参与节点通常被称为网络。例如,公用电话交换网络的应用体系被称为"高级智能网"。这有许多特殊种类，但都依赖于哑网络（如因特网）与智能计算机网络（如电话网）之间的通信。其他网络包含着两类网络的各种要素，以便满足各种应用。最近，情景感知网络——这两者的综合，能够结合两者中的最佳元素——已经获得了人们的更多关注。

在分布应用和 PVC（永久虚拟电路）中该术语的一个流行范例是点对点服务和网络中的节点组织。P2P 网络通常实现一个覆盖网络，运行在更低的物理或逻辑网络上。这些覆盖网络可以按照几种明确的模型（系统的网络体系）实现一些确定的节点组织结构。

Unit 5

Networking Hardware

Networking hardware includes all computers, peripherals, interface cards and other equipment needed to perform data processing and communications within the network.

This section provides information on the following components:
- File Servers
- Workstations
- Network Interface Cards
- Concentrators/Hubs
- Repeaters
- Bridges
- Routers

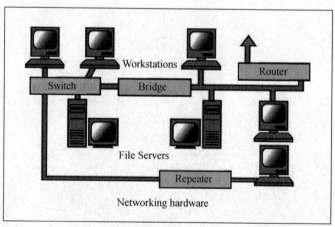

Networking hardware

1. File Servers

A file server stands at the heart of most networks. It is a very fast computer with a large amount of RAM and storage space, along with a fast network interface card. The network operating system software resides on this computer, along with any software applications and data files that need to be shared.

The file server controls the communication of information between the nodes on a network. For example, it may be asked to send a word processor program to one workstation, receive a database file from another workstation, and store an E-mail message during the same time period. This requires a computer that can store a lot of information and share it very quickly. File servers should have at least the following characteristics:

- 75 megahertz or faster microprocessor
- A fast hard drive with at least four gigabytes of storage
- A RAID (Redundant Array of Inexpensive Disks) to preserve data after a disk casualty
- A tape back-up unit
- Numerous expansion slots
- Fast network interface card
- At least of 32 MB of RAM

2. Workstations

All the computers connected to the file server on a network are called workstations. A typical workstation is a computer that is configured with a network interface card, networking software, and the appropriate cables. Workstations do not necessarily need floppy disk drives or hard drives because files can be saved on the file server. Almost any computer can serve as a network workstation.

3. Network Interface Cards

The Network Interface Card (NIC) provides the physical connection between the network and the workstation. Most NICs are internal, with the card fitting into an expansion slot inside the computer. Some computers, such as Mac Classics, use external boxes which are attached to a serial port or a SCSI port. Laptop computers generally use external LAN adapters connected to the parallel port or network cards that slip into a PCMCIA[1] slot.

Network interface cards are a major factor in determining the speed and performance of a network. It is a good idea to use the fastest network card available for the type of workstation you are using.

The three most common network interface connections are Ethernet cards, LocalTalk connectors, and Token Ring cards. According to an International Data Corporation, Ethernet is the most popular, followed by Token Ring and LocalTalk.

3.1 Ethernet Cards

Ethernet cards are usually purchased separately from a computer, although many computers

---

[1] Short for Personal Computer Memory Card International Association, and pronounced as separate letters, PCMCIA is an organization consisting of some 500 companies that has developed a standard for small, credit card-sized devices, called PC Cards. Originally designed for adding memory to portable (['pɔːtəbl]adj. 轻便的, 手提(式)的) computers, the PCMCIA standard has been expanded several times and is now suitable for many types of devices.

(such as the Macintosh) now include an option for a preinstalled Ethernet card. Ethernet cards contain connections for either coaxial or twisted pair cables (or both). If it is designed for coaxial cable, the connection will be BNC[1]. If it is designed for twisted pair, it will have a RJ-45 connection. Some Ethernet cards also contain an AUI[2] connector. This can be used to attach coaxial, twisted pair, or fiber optics cable to an Ethernet card. When this method is used there is always an external transceiver attached to the workstation.

3.2 Token Ring Cards

Token Ring network cards look similar to Ethernet cards. One visible difference is the type of connector on the back end of the card. Token Ring cards generally have a nine pin DIN type connector to attach the card to the network cable.

4. Concentrators/Hubs

A concentrator is a device that provides a central connection point for cables from workstations, servers, and peripherals. In a star topology, twisted-pair wire is run from each workstation to a central concentrator. Hubs are multi-slot concentrators into which a number of multi-port cards can be plugged to provide additional access as the network grows in size. Some concentrators are passive. They allow the signal to pass from one computer to another without any change. Most concentrators are active. They electrically amplify the signal as it moves from one device to another. Active concentrators, like repeaters, are used to extend the length of a network. Concentrators are:

- Usually configured with 8, 12, or 24 RJ-45 ports
- Often used in a star or star-wired ring topology
- Sold with specialized software for port management
- Also called hubs
- Usually installed in a standardized metal rack that also may store netmodems, bridges, or routers

5. Repeaters

When a signal travels along a cable, it tends to lose strength. A repeater is a device that boosts a network's signal as it passes through. The repeater does this by electrically amplifying the signal it receives and rebroadcasting it. Repeaters can be separate devices or they can be incorporated into a concentrator. They are used when the total length of your network cable

---

[1] The BNC connector is a miniature quick connect/disconnect RF connector used for coaxial cable. It features two bayonet lugs on the female connector; mating is achieved with only a quarter turn of the coupling nut (联结螺母). BNCs are ideally suited for cable termination for miniature-to-<u>subminiature</u> ([sʌbˈminjətʃə]adj. 超小型的，微型的) coaxial cable (e.g., RG-58, 59, to RG-179, RG-316).

[2] An Attachment Unit Interface (AUI) is a 15 pin connection that provides a path between a node's Ethernet interface and the <u>Medium Attachment Unit</u> (MAU, 介质连接单元), sometimes known as a transceiver. It is the part of the IEEE Ethernet standard located between the Media Access Control (MAC), and the MAU. An AUI cable may be up to 50 meters long, although frequently the cable is omitted altogether and the MAU and MAC are directly attached to one another.

exceeds the standards set for the type of cable being used.

A good example of the use of repeaters would be in a local area network using a star topology with unshielded twisted-pair cabling. The length limit for unshielded twisted-pair cable is 100 meters. The most common configuration is for each workstation to be connected by twisted-pair cable to a multi-port active concentrator. The concentrator regenerates all the signals that pass through it allowing for the total length of cable on the network to exceed the 100 meter limit.

6. Bridges

A bridge is a device that allows you to segment a large network into two smaller, more efficient networks. If you are adding to an older wiring scheme and want the new network to be up-to-date, a bridge can connect the two.

A bridge monitors the information traffic on both sides of the network so that it can pass packets of information to the correct location. Most bridges can "listen" to the network and automatically figure out the address of each computer on both sides of the bridge. The bridge can inspect each message and, if necessary, broadcast it on the other side of the network.

The bridge manages the traffic to maintain optimum performance on both sides of the network. You might say that the bridge is like a traffic cop at a busy intersection during rush hour. It keeps information flowing on both sides of the network, but it does not allow unnecessary traffic through. Bridges can be used to connect different types of cabling, or physical topologies. They must, however, be used between networks with the same protocol.

7. Routers

A router translates information from one network to another; it is similar to a super intelligent bridge. Routers select the best path to route a message, based on the destination address and origin. The router can direct traffic to prevent head-on collisions, and is smart enough to know when to direct traffic along back roads and shortcuts.

While bridges know the addresses of all computers on each side of the network, routers know the addresses of computers, bridges, and other routers on the network. Routers can even "listen" to the entire network to determine which sections are busiest -- they can then redirect data around those sections until they clear up.

If you have a school LAN that you want to connect to the Internet, you will need to purchase a router. In this case, the router serves as the translator between the information on your LAN and the Internet. It also determines the best route to send the data over the Internet. Routers can:

- Direct signal traffic efficiently
- Route messages between any two protocols
- Route messages between linear bus, star, and star-wired ring[1] topologies
- Route messages across fiber optic, coaxial, and twisted-pair cabling

---

[1] A star-wired ring topology may appear (externally) to be the same as a star topology. Internally, the MAU (multistation access unit, 多站访问部件) of a star-wired ring contains wiring that allows information to pass from one device to another in a circle or ring. The Token Ring protocol uses a star-wired ring topology.

New Words

concentrator	[ˈkɔnsentreitə]	n.	集中器
bridge	[bridʒ]	n.	桥接器
reside	[riˈzaid]	vi.	驻留
share	[ʃɛə]	n. & v.	分享，共享
workstation	[ˈwəːksteiʃən]	n.	工作站
megahertz	[ˈmegəˌhəːts]	n.	兆赫
microprocessor	[maikrəuˈprəusesə]	n.	微处理器
gigabyte	[ˈgigəbait]	n.	十亿字节，吉字节
preserve	[priˈzəːv]	vt.	保护，保持，保存
casualty	[ˈkæʒjuəlti]	n.	损坏，事故
configure	[kənˈfigə]	vi.	配置，设定
internal	[inˈtəːnl]	adj.	内在的，内部的
external	[eksˈtəːnl]	adj.	外部的
determine	[diˈtəːmin]	vt.	决定，断定
option	[ˈɔpʃən]	n.	选项，选择权
preinstall	[ˈpriːinˈstɔːl]	v.	预设，预安装
coaxial	[kəuˈæksəl]	adj.	同轴的，共轴的
transceiver	[trænˈsiːvə]	n.	收发器
connector	[kəˈnəktə]	n.	连接器
multislot	[ˈmʌltislɔt]	n.	多插槽，多插座
passive	[ˈpæsiv]	adj.	被动的
active	[ˈæktiv]	adj.	主动的，活动的
amplify	[ˈæmplifai]	vt.	放大，增强
standardized	[ˈstændəˌdaizd]	adj.	标准的
rack	[ræk]	n.	架，设备架
		vt.	放在架上
netmodem	[netˈməudəm]	n.	网络调制解调器
boost	[buːst]	v.	推进
rebroadcast	[riːˈbrɔːdkɑːst]	v. & n.	转播，重播
exceed	[ikˈsiːd]	vt.	超越，胜过
		vi.	超过其他
unshielded	[ʌnˈʃiːldid]		无防护的，无铠装的，无屏蔽的
regenerate	[riˈdʒenərit]	vt.	使新生，重建
segment	[ˈsegmənt]	v.	分割
		n.	段，节，片断

address	[əˈdres]	n. 地址
inspect	[inˈspekt]	v. 检查
optimum	[ˈɔptiməm]	n. 最适宜
		adj. 最佳的
intersection	[ˌintə(:)ˈsekʃən]	n. 十字路口
unnecessary	[ʌnˈnesisəri]	adj. 不必要的，多余的
intelligent	[inˈtelidʒənt]	adj. 聪明的，智能的
route	[ru:t]	v. 发送
		n. 路线，路程，通道
collision	[kəˈliʒən]	n. 碰撞，冲突
shortcut	[ˈʃɔ:tkʌt]	n. 捷径
redirect	[ˈri:diˈrekt]	vt. 重寄，使改道，使改变方向

Phrases

interface card	接口卡
Network Interface Card (NIC)	网卡
file server	文件服务器
storage space	存储空间
along with …	连同……一起，随同……一起
network operating system	网络操作系统
software application	软件应用程序
data file	数据文件
word processor	文字处理软件
database file	数据库文件
hard drive	硬盘驱动器
tape back-up unit	磁带备份机
be saved on …	被保存在……上
fit into	插入，装入
attach… to	附在
serial port	串行端口
laptop computer	膝上型计算机
floppy disk drive	软盘驱动器
parallel port	并行端口
network card	网卡
slip into	分成
twisted pair	双绞线
fiber optics cable	光导纤维电缆

port management	端口管理
be incorporated into	融入
unshielded twisted-pair	非屏蔽双绞线
information traffic	信息流量
on both sides	双方，两边
figure out	计算出，断定
traffic cop	<美口>交通警察
rush hour	高峰时间
be similar to …	与……相似
clear up	整理，消除

Abbreviations

RAM (Random Access Memory)	随机存储器
RAID (Redundant Array of Inexpensive Disks)	廉价磁盘的冗余阵列
MB (MegaByte)	兆字节
SCSI (Small Computer System Interface)	小型计算机系统接口
PCMCIA (Personal Computer Memory Card International Association)	个人计算机储存卡国际联盟
BNC (Bayonet Nut Connector)	同轴电缆接插件
AUI (Attachment Unit Interface)	连接单元接口
DIN (Deutsche Industrie-Norm (德文))	德国工业标准

Exercises

【EX.1】Answer the following questions according to the text.

1. What does networking hardware include?
2. What is a file server?
3. What does a file server do?
4. What is a typical workstation?
5. What does the Network Interface Card (NIC) do?
6. What are the three most common network interface connections?
7. What is a concentrator?
8. How does a repeater boost a network's signal as it passes through?
9. What does a bridge do?
10. If you have a school LAN that you want to connect to the Internet, What will you need to buy?

【EX.2】Translate the following terms or phrases from English into Chinese and vice versa.

1. network operating system
2. serial port
3. hard drive
4. fiber optics cable
5. unshielded twisted-pair
6. parallel port
7. bridge
8. microprocessor
9. preinstall
10. connector
11. n. 收发器
12. n. 地址
13. n. 碰撞，冲突
14. v. 分割 n. 段，节，片断
15. vi. 配置，设定

【EX.3】Translate the following sentences into Chinese.

1. Data transmit between the concentrator and the collector in the form of wireless ad hoc networks.
2. Normally demodulation frequency is inside the limits of a few hertz to hundreds of megahertz.
3. The second option is technically superior but it demands higher-performance equipment.
4. Coaxial cable is also used for undersea telephone lines.
5. We are using this transistor to amplify a telephone signal.
6. It can regenerate data in storage units where the process of reading data results in its destruction.
7. Please inspect all parts for damage prior to installation and start-up.
8. Microsoft developed an intelligent solution to this problem.
9. What function would you use to redirect the browser to a new page?
10. Filter route establishes the basic rules for connectivity through a firewall.

【EX.4】Complete the following passage with appropriate words in the box.

| provides | devices | host | surrounded | signals |
| carrier | random | amplify | electricity | designed |

CSMA/CA stands for Carrier Sense Multiple Access Collision Avoidance. It is a network access method in which each device signals its intent to transmit before it actually does so. This prevents other ___1___ from sending information, thus preventing collisions from occurring between ___2___ from two or more devices. This is the access method used by LocalTalk.

CSMA/CD stands for Carrier Sense Multiple Access Collision Detection. It is a network access method in which devices that are ready to transmit data first check the channel for a carrier. If no ___3___ is sensed, a device can transmit. If two devices transmit at once, a collision occurs and each computer backs off and waits a ___4___ amount of time before attempting to retransmit. This is the access method used by Ethernet.

Concentrator is a device that ___5___ a central connection point for cables from workstations, servers, and peripherals. Most concentrators contain the ability to ___6___ the electrical signal they receive.

Dumb Terminal refers to devices that are ___7___ to communicate exclusively with a host (main frame) computer. It receives all screen layouts from the host computer and sends all keyboard entry to the host. It cannot function without the ___8___ computer.

Fiber Optic Cable is a a cable which consists of a center glass core ___9___ by layers of plastic. It transmits data using light rather than ___10___. It has the ability to carry more information over much longer distances.

【EX.5】 Translate the following passage into Chinese.

Network Gateway

A network gateway is an internetworking system capable of joining together two networks that use different base protocols. A network gateway can be implemented completely in software, completely in hardware, or as a combination of both. Depending on the types of protocols they support, network gateways can operate at any level of the OSI model.

Because a network gateway, by definition, appears at the edge of a network, related capabilities like firewalls tend to be integrated with it. On home networks, a broadband router typically serves as the network gateway although ordinary computers can also be configured to perform equivalent functions.

Text B

Network Switch

A network switch is a computer networking device that links network segments or network devices. The term commonly refers to a multi-port network bridge that processes and routes data at the data link layer (layer 2) of the OSI model. Switches that additionally process data at the network layer (layer 3) and above are often called layer-3 switches or multilayer switches.

1. Function

A switch is a telecommunication device which receives a message from any device connected to it and then transmits the message only to the device for which the message is meant. This makes the switch a more intelligent device than a hub (which receives a message and then transmits it to all the other devices on its network). The network switch plays an integral part in most modern Ethernet local area networks (LANs). Mid-to-large sized LANs contain a number of linked managed switches. Small office/home office (SOHO) applications typically use a single switch, or an all-purpose converged device such as a residential gateway to access small office/home broadband services such as DSL or cable Internet. In most cases, the end-user device contains a router and components that interface to the particular physical broadband technology. User devices may also include a telephone interface for VoIP[1].

An Ethernet switch operates at the data link layer of the OSI model to create a separate collision domain[2] for each switch port. With 4 computers (e.g., A, B, C, and D) on 4 switch ports, any pair (e.g. A and B) can transfer data back and forth while the other pair (e.g. C and D) also do so simultaneously, and the two conversations will not interfere with one another. In full duplex[3] mode, these pairs can also overlap (e.g. A transmits to B, simultaneously B to C, and so on). In the case of a repeater hub, they will all share the bandwidth and run in half duplex[4], resulting in collisions, which will then necessitate retransmissions.

Using a bridge or a switch (or a router) to split a larger collision domain into smaller ones in order to reduce collision probability and improve overall throughput is called segmentation. In the extreme of microsegmentation, each device is located on a dedicated switch port. In contrast to an Ethernet hub, there is a separate collision domain on each of the switch ports. This allows computers to have dedicated bandwidth on point-to-point connections to the network and also to run in full duplex without collisions. Full duplex mode has only one transmitter and one receiver per 'collision domain', making collisions impossible.

2. Role of Switches in a Network

Switches may operate at one or more layers of the OSI model, including data link and network. A device that operates simultaneously at more than one of these layers is known as a multilayer switch.

---

[1] Voice over IP (VoIP, abbreviation of voice over Internet Protocol) commonly refers to the communication protocols, technologies, methodologies, and transmission techniques involved in the delivery of voice communications and multimedia sessions over Internet Protocol (IP) networks, such as the Internet.

[2] A collision domain is a section of a network where data packets can collide with (冲突) one another when being sent on a shared medium or through repeaters, in particular, when using early versions of Ethernet. A network collision occurs when more than one device attempts to send a packet on a network segment at the same time. Collisions are resolved using carrier sense multiple access (多路存取) with collision detection in which the competing packets are discarded and resent one at a time. This becomes a source of inefficiency ([ˌiniˈfiʃənsi] n. 无效率, 无能) in the network.

[3] A full-duplex (FDX), or sometimes double-duplex system, allows communication in both directions, and, unlike half-duplex, allows this to happen simultaneously. Land-line (陆上通信线路) telephone networks are full-duplex, since they allow both callers to speak and be heard at the same time.

[4] A half-duplex (HDX) system provides communication in both directions, but only one direction at a time (not simultaneously). Typically, once a party begins receiving a signal, it must wait for the transmitter to stop transmitting, before replying (antennas are of trans-receiver type in these devices, so as to transmit and receive the signal as well).

In switches intended for commercial use, built-in or modular interfaces make it possible to connect different types of networks, including Ethernet, Fibre Channel, ATM, ITU-T [1] G.hn [2] and 802.11[3]. This connectivity can be at any of the layers mentioned. While layer-2 functionality is adequate for bandwidth-shifting within one technology, interconnecting technologies such as Ethernet and token ring is easier at layer 3.

Devices that interconnect at layer 3 are traditionally called routers, so layer-3 switches can also be regarded as (relatively primitive) routers.

A modular network switch with three network modules (a total of 24 Ethernet and 14 Fast Ethernet ports) and one power supply.

Where there is a need for a great deal of analysis of network performance and security, switches may be connected between WAN routers as places for analytic modules. Some vendors provide firewall, network intrusion detection, and performance analysis modules that can plug into switch ports. Some of these functions may be on combined modules.

In other cases, the switch is used to create a mirror image of data that can go to an external device. Since most switch port mirroring provides only one mirrored stream, network hubs can be useful for fanning out data to several read-only analyzers, such as intrusion detection systems and packet sniffers.

3. Layer-Specific Functionality

While switches may learn about topologies at many layers, and forward at one or more layers, they do tend to have common features. Other than for high performance applications, modern commercial switches use primarily Ethernet interfaces.

At any layer, a modern switch may implement Power over Ethernet (PoE), which avoids the need for attached devices, such as a VoIP phone or wireless access point, to have a separate power supply. Since switches can have redundant power circuits connected to uninterruptible

---

[1] The ITU Telecommunication Standardization Sector (ITU-T) is one of the three sectors (divisions or units) of the International Telecommunication Union (ITU); it coordinates standards for telecommunications.

[2] G.hn is the common name for a home network technology family of standards developed under the International Telecommunication Union's Telecommunication Standardization sector (the ITU-T) and promoted by the HomeGrid Forum and several other organizations. The G.hn specification defines networking over power lines (电力线), phone lines and coaxial cables with data rates up to 1 Gbit/s.

[3] IEEE 802.11 is a set of standards for implementing wireless local area network (WLAN, 无线局域网) computer communication in the 2.4, 3.6 and 5 GHz frequency bands (频段).

power supplies, the connected device can continue operating even when regular office power fails.

3.1 Layer 1(Hubs Versus Higher-Layer Switches)

A network hub, or repeater, is a simple network device. Hubs do not manage any of the traffic that comes through them. Any packet entering a port is broadcast out or "repeated" on every other port, except for the port of entry. Since every packet is repeated on every other port, packet collisions affect the entire network, limiting its capacity.

A switch creates the -- originally mandatory -- Layer 1 end-to-end connection only virtually. Its bridge function selects which packets are forwarded to which port(s). The connection lines are not "switched" literally, it only appears like this on the packet level. "Bridging hub" or possibly "switching hub" would be more appropriate terms.

There are specialized applications where a hub can be useful, such as copying traffic to multiple network sensors. High end switches have a feature which does the same thing called port mirroring[1].

3.2 Layer 2

A network bridge, operating at the data link layer, may interconnect a small number of devices in a home or the office. This is a trivial case of bridging, in which the bridge learns the MAC address of each connected device.

Single bridges can also provide extremely high performance in specialized applications such as storage area networks.

Classic bridges may also interconnect using a spanning tree protocol[2] that disables links so that the resulting local area network is a tree without loops. In contrast to routers, spanning tree bridges must have topologies with only one active path between two points. The older IEEE 802.1D spanning tree protocol could be quite slow, with forwarding stopping for 30 seconds while the spanning tree would reconverge. A Rapid Spanning Tree Protocol was introduced as IEEE 802.1w. The newest standard Shortest Path Bridging (IEEE 802.1aq) is the next logical progression and incorporates all the older Spanning Tree Protocols (IEEE 802.1D STP, IEEE 802.1w RSTP, IEEE 802.1s MSTP) that blocked traffic on all but one alternative path. IEEE 802.1aq (Shortest Path Bridging SPB) allows all paths to be active with multiple equal cost paths, provides much larger layer 2 topologies (up to 16 million compared to the 4096 VLANs limit), faster convergence times, and improves the use of the mesh topologies through increase bandwidth and redundancy between all devices by allowing traffic to load share across all paths of a mesh network.

---

[1] Port mirroring is used on a network switch to send a copy of network packets seen on one switch port (or an entire VLAN) to a network monitoring connection on another switch port. This is commonly used for network appliances that require monitoring of network traffic, such as an intrusion detection system.

[2] The Spanning Tree Protocol (STP) is a network protocol that ensures a loop-free topology for any bridged Ethernet local area network. The basic function of STP is to prevent bridge loops and the broadcast radiation ([ˌreɪdiˈeɪʃən]n. 辐射，放射) that results from them.

While layer 2 switch remains more of a marketing term than a technical term, the products that were introduced as "switches" tended to use microsegmentation and full duplex to prevent collisions among devices connected to Ethernet. By using an internal forwarding plane which is much faster than any interface, they give the impression of simultaneous paths among multiple devices. 'Non-blocking' devices use a forwarding plane or equivalent method which is fast enough to allow full duplex traffic for each port simultaneously.

Once a bridge learns the addresses of its connected nodes, it forwards data link layer frames using a layer 2 forwarding method. There are four forwarding methods a bridge can use, of which the second through fourth method were performance-increasing methods when used on "switch" products with the same input and output port bandwidths:

- Store and forward: The switch buffers and verifies each frame before forwarding it.
- Cut through: The switch reads only up to the frame's hardware address before starting to forward it. Cut-through switches have to fall back to store and forward if the outgoing port is busy at the time the packet arrives. There is no error checking with this method.
- Fragment free: A method that attempts to retain the benefits of both store and forward and cut through. Fragment free checks the first 64 bytes of the frame, where addressing information is stored. According to Ethernet specifications, collisions should be detected during the first 64 bytes of the frame, so frames that are in error because of a collision will not be forwarded. This way the frame will always reach its intended destination. Error checking of the actual data in the packet is left for the end device.
- Adaptive switching: A method of automatically selecting between the other three modes.

While there are specialized applications, such as storage area networks, where the input and output interfaces are of the same bandwidth, this is not always the case in general LAN applications. In LANs, a switch used for end user access typically concentrates lower bandwidth and uplinks into a higher bandwidth.

3.3 Layer 3

Within the confines of the Ethernet physical layer, a layer-3 switch can perform some or all of the functions normally performed by a router. The most common layer-3 capability is the awareness of IP multicast[1] through IGMP snooping[2]. With this awareness, a layer-3 switch can increase efficiency by delivering the traffic of a multicast group only to ports where the attached device has signaled that it wants to listen to that group.

3.4 Layer 4

While the exact meaning of the term layer-4 switch is vendor-dependent, it almost always

---

[1] IP multicast is a method of sending Internet Protocol (IP) datagrams to a group of interested receivers in a single transmission. It is often employed for streaming media applications on the Internet and private networks. The method is the IP-specific version of the general concept of multicast networking. It uses specially reserved multicast address blocks in IPv4 and IPv6.

[2] IGMP snooping is the process of listening to Internet Group Management Protocol (IGMP) network traffic. The feature allows a network switch to listen in on the IGMP conversation between hosts and routers. By listening to these conversations the switch maintains a map of which links need which IP multicast streams.

starts with a capability for network address translation, but then adds some type of load distribution based on TCP sessions.

The device may include a stateful inspection firewall[1], a VPN concentrator, or be an IPSec[2] security gateway.

3.5 Layer 7

Layer-7 switches may distribute loads based on URL (Uniform Resource Locator) or by some installation-specific technique to recognize application-level transactions. A layer-7 switch may include a web cache and participate in a content delivery network[3].

4. Types of Switches

4.1 Form Factor

- Desktop, not mounted in an enclosure, typically intended to be used in a home or office environment outside of a wiring closet
- Rack mounted -- A switch that mounts in an equipment rack
- Chassis -- with swappable module cards
- DIN rail mounted -- normally seen in industrial environments or panels

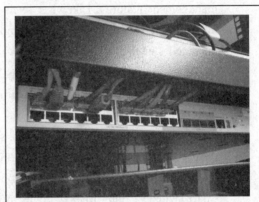

Rack-mounted 24-port 3Com switch.

4.2 Configuration Options

Unmanaged switches -- These switches have no configuration interface or options. They are plug and play[4]. They are typically the least expensive switches found in home, SOHO, or small businesses. They can be desktop or rack mounted.

Managed switches -- These switches have one or more methods to modify the operation of

---

[1] A firewall can either be software-based or hardware-based and is used to help keep a network secure. Its primary objective is to control the incoming and outgoing network traffic by analyzing the data packets and determining whether it should be allowed through or not, based on a predetermined <u>rule set</u> (规则集).

[2] Internet Protocol Security (IPsec) is a protocol suite for securing Internet Protocol (IP) communications by <u>authenticating</u> ([ɔː'θentikeit]v. 鉴别) and encrypting each IP packet of a communication session. IPsec also includes protocols for establishing <u>mutual</u> (['mjuːtjuəl]adj.相互的，共有的) authentication between agents at the beginning of the session and negotiation of <u>cryptographic</u> ([ˌkriptə'græfik]adj. 用密码写的) keys to be used during the session.

[3] A content delivery network (CDN) is a large distributed system of servers deployed in multiple data centers in the Internet. The goal of a CDN is to serve content to end-users with high availability and high performance. CDNs serve a large fraction of the Internet content today, including web objects (text, graphics, URLs and <u>scripts</u> ([skript]n. 脚本)), downloadable objects (media files, software, documents), applications (e-commerce, <u>portals</u> (['pɔːtəl]n. 门户)), live streaming media, on-demand streaming media, and social networks.

[4] In computing, a plug and play device or computer bus, is one with a specification that facilitates the discovery of a hardware component in a system without the need for physical device configuration or user <u>intervention</u> ([ˌintə(ː)'venʃən]n. 干涉) in resolving resource conflicts.

the switch. Common management methods include: a command-line interface (CLI) accessed via serial console, telnet or Secure Shell, an embedded Simple Network Management Protocol (SNMP) agent allowing management from a remote console or management station, or a web interface for management from a web browser. Examples of configuration changes that one can do from a managed switch include: enabling features such as Spanning Tree Protocol, setting port bandwidth, creating or modifying Virtual LANs (VLANs), etc. Two sub-classes of managed switches are marketed today:

- Smart (or intelligent) switches -- These are managed switches with a limited set of management features. Likewise "web-managed" switches are switches which fall in a market niche between unmanaged and managed. For a price much lower than a fully managed switch they provide a web interface (and usually no CLI access) and allow configuration of basic settings, such as VLANs, port-bandwidth and duplex.
- Enterprise Managed (or fully managed) switches -- These have a full set of management features, including CLI, SNMP agent, and web interface. They may have additional features to manipulate configurations, such as the ability to display, modify, backup and restore configurations. Compared with smart switches, enterprise switches have more features that can be customized or optimized, and are generally more expensive than smart switches. Enterprise switches are typically found in networks with larger number of switches and connections, where centralized management is a significant savings in administrative time and effort. A stackable switch is a version of enterprise-managed switch.

Traffic monitoring on a switched network -- Unless port mirroring or other methods such as RMON[1], SMON or sFlow[2] are implemented in a switch, it is difficult to monitor traffic that is bridged using a switch because only the sending and receiving ports can see the traffic. These monitoring features are rarely present on consumer-grade switches.

Two popular methods that are specifically designed to allow a network analyst to monitor traffic are:

- Port mirroring -- the switch sends a copy of network packets to a monitoring network connection.
- SMON -- "Switch Monitoring" is described by RFC 2613 and is a protocol for controlling facilities such as port mirroring.

Another method to monitor may be to connect a layer-1 hub between the monitored device and its switch port. This will induce minor delay, but will provide multiple interfaces that can be used to monitor the individual switch port.

---

[1] The Remote Network MONitoring (RMON) was developed by the IETF to support monitoring and protocol analysis of LANs.

[2] sFlow is a technology for monitoring network, wireless and host devices. The sFlow.org consortium is the authoritative source for the sFlow protocol specifications: previous version of sFlow, including RFC 3176, have been deprecated (['deprikeit] vt. 不赞成, 反对, 轻视).

New Words

switch	[swɪtʃ]	n.	交换机
multi-port	[ˈmʌlti-pɔːt]	n.	多口，多个端口
multilayer	[ˈmʌltiˌleɪə]	n.	多层
converge	[kənˈvəːdʒ]	v.	聚合，聚集
separate	[ˈsepəreit]	adj.	分开的，分离的，个别的，单独的
		v.	分开，隔离，分散，分别
domain	[dəuˈmein]	n.	范围，区域，领域
necessitate	[niˈsesiteit]	v.	成为必要
retransmission	[ˌriːtrænzˈmiʃən]	n.	转播，中继，重发
split	[split]	v.	分开，分裂，分离
probability	[ˌprɔbəˈbiliti]	n.	概率，或然性，可能性
microsegmentation	[ˈmaikrəˌsegmənˈteiʃən]	n.	微段
dedicated	[ˈdedikeitid]	adj.	专门的，专注的
modular	[ˈmɔdjulə]	adj.	模块化的，组合的
analysis	[əˈnælisis]	n.	分析，分解
analytic	[ˌænəˈlitik]	adj.	分析的，解析的
firewall	[ˈfaiəwɔːl]	n.	防火墙
intrusion	[inˈtruːʒən]	n.	闯入，侵扰
detection	[diˈtekʃən]	n.	侦查，探测
module	[ˈmɔdjuːl]	n.	模块
combine	[kəmˈbain]	v.	组合，（使）联合，（使）结合
analyzer	[ˈænəlaizə]	n.	分析者，分析器
forward	[ˈfɔːwəd]	vt.	转发，转寄，运送
redundant	[riˈdʌndənt]	adj.	多余的，冗余的
uninterruptible	[ʌnˌintəˈrʌptibl]	adj.	不可打断的，不可中断的
primarily	[ˈpraimərili]	adv.	首先，起初；主要地，根本上
capacity	[kəˈpæsiti]	n.	容量，才能
literally	[ˈlitərəli]	adv.	照字面意义，逐字地
convergence	[kənˈvəːdʒəns]	n.	集中，集合
reconverge	[rikənˈvəːdʒ]	v.	重新聚合
progression	[prəˈgreʃən]	n.	行进，级数
redundancy	[riˈdʌndənsi]	n.	冗余
buffer	[ˈbʌfə]	n.	缓冲器
verify	[ˈverifai]	vt.	检验，校验
uplink	[ˈʌpˌliŋk]	n.	向上传输，上行线，卫星上行链路

multicast	[ˈmʌltikɑːst]	n. 多点传送；多播，组播
snoop	[snuːp]	vi. 探听，调查
transaction	[trænˈzækʃən]	n. 办理，处理，事务
mount	[maunt]	v. 安装，放置
chassis	[ˈʃæsi]	n. 底盘
swappable	[ˈswɔpəbl]	adj. 可替换的
panel	[ˈpænl]	n. 面板，嵌板，仪表板
console	[kənˈsəul]	n. 控制台
agent	[ˈeidʒnt]	n. 代理
customize	[kʌstəmaiz]	v. 定制，用户化
optimize	[ˈɔptimaiz]	vt. 使最优化
stackable	[ˈstækəbl]	adj. 可堆叠的，易叠起堆放的
induce	[inˈdjuːs]	vt. 促使，导致，引起
minor	[ˈmainə]	adj. 较小的，次要的

Phrases

network switch	网络交换
network segment	网段
network bridge	网桥
switch port	交换端口
multilayer switch	多层交换
residential gateway	家庭网关
back and forth	来来往往地，来回地
full duplex	全双工
repeater hub	转发集线器
half duplex	半双工
collision probability	碰撞概率，冲突几率
in the extreme	非常，极端
commercial use	商业用途
be adequate for	适合，足够
mirror image	镜像，映像
external device	外部设备
fan out	扇出
intrusion detection system	入侵检测系统
packet sniffer	封包监听器，封包探测器
high performance	高精确性，高性能
commercial switch	商用交换机

power over Ethernet	用以太网供电
wireless access point	无线接入点
uninterruptible power supply	不间断电源（UPS）
network sensor	网络传感器
port mirroring	端口镜像，端口映射
storage area networks	存储区域网
except for …	除……以外
spanning tree protocol	生成树协议
forwarding plane	转发平面
store and forward	储存和转送
error checking	误差校验，错误校验
fall back	后退
fragment free	无分段
adaptive switching	自适应交换
within the confines of …	在……（范围）之内
network address translation	网络地址转换
load distribution	负荷分配
stateful inspection firewall	状态检测防火墙
web cache	网页快照，网页缓存
content delivery network	内容交付网络，内容分发网络
form factor	物理尺寸和形状，规格
rack mounted	安装在机架上的
equipment rack	设备架
plug and play	即插即用
management station	管理站
web browser	网络浏览器
smart switch	智能交换机
administrative time	修理准备时间，管理实施时间
stackable switch	可堆叠交换机

Abbreviations

SOHO (Small office/home office)	小型办公室/家庭办公室
ATM (Asynchronous Transfer Mode)	异步传输模式
ITU (International Telecommunication Union)	国际电信联盟
STP (Shielded Twisted Pair)	屏蔽双绞线
RSTP (Rapid Spanning Tree Protocol)	快速生成树协议
MSTP (Multi-Service Transfer Platform）	多业务传送平台

SPB (Shortest Path Bridging)　　　　　最短路径桥接
VLAN (Virtual Local Area Network)　　虚拟局域网
IGMP (Internet Group Management Protocol)　　因特网组管理协议
TCP (Transfer Control Protocol)　　　传输控制协议
URL (Uniform Resource Locator)　　　统一资源定位符
CLI (Command-Line Interface)　　　　命令行界面
SNMP (Simple Network Management Protocol)　　简单网络管理协议
RMON (Remote Network MONitoring)　　远程网络监控
SMON (Switch Monitoring)　　　　　　交换机监控
RFC (Request For Comments)　　　　　请求评议，请求注解

Exercises

【EX.1】Answer the following questions according to the text.

1. What is a network switch?
2. Which is more intelligent, a switch or a hub? Why?
3. Where does an Ethernet switch operate?
4. What is a multilayer switch?
5. Why can network hubs be useful for fanning out data to several read-only analyzers?
6. Why can the connected device continue operating even when regular office power fails?
7. Why do packet collisions affect the entire network, limiting its capacity?
8. What are the four forwarding methods a bridge can use?
9. What are the two sub-classes of managed switches marketed today?
10. What are the two popular methods that are specifically designed to allow a network analyst to monitor traffic?

【EX.2】Translate the following terms or phrases from English into Chinese and vice versa.

1.	network segment	1.	
2.	multilayer switch	2.	
3.	network bridge	3.	
4.	full duplex	4.	
5.	half duplex	5.	
6.	fan out	6.	
7.	wireless access point	7.	
8.	port mirroring	8.	
9.	error checking	9.	
10.	adaptive switching	10.	
11.	即插即用	11.	

12. 智能交换机 _____ 12. _____
13. adj. 模块化的，组合的 _____ 13. _____
14. n. 闯入，侵扰 _____ 14. _____
15. n. 防火墙 _____ 15. _____

【EX.3】**Translate the following sentences into Chinese.**

1. The viability of multilayer switches depends on the protocol supported.
2. The majority of these cable networks have been upgraded to broadband.
3. It separates the user's name from the domain name.
4. By default, this means that automatic retransmission is enabled.
5. The platform is built to a modular design, with good reusability.
6. A firewall acts like a virtual security guard for your network.
7. Memory organization relates to internal memory capacity and structure.
8. What is the initial capacity of the following string buffer?
9. Some UNIX system operations must be performed at the console.
10. Generally, wireless LAN is constituted by access point and workstation with wireless network card.

Text C

Router

A router is a device that forwards data packets between computer networks, creating an overlay internetwork[1]. A router is connected to

[1] [ˌin.təˈnetwəːk]
n. 网间网

A Cisco ASM/2-32EM router deployed at CERN[2] in 1987

[2] European Laboratory for Particle Physics: 欧洲粒子物理研究所

two or more data lines from different networks. When a data packet comes in one of the lines, the router reads the address information in the packet to determine its ultimate destination. Then, using information in its routing table[3] or routing policy, it directs the packet to the next network on its journey. Routers perform the "traffic directing" functions on the Internet. A data packet is typically forwarded from one router to another through the networks that constitute the internetwork until it gets to its destination node.

[3]routing table：路由表

A typical home or small office router showing the ADSL[4] telephone line and Ethernet network cable connections.

The most familiar type of routers are home and small office routers that simply pass data, such as web pages and email, between the home computers and the owner's cable or DSL[5] modem, which connects to the Internet through an ISP[6]. More sophisticated routers, such as enterprise routers, connect large business or ISP networks up to the powerful core routers that forward data at high speed along the optical fiber lines of the Internet backbone. Though routers are typically dedicated hardware devices, use of software-based routers has grown increasingly common.

[4]Asymmetrical Digital Subscriber Line：非对称数字用户环线
[5]Digital Subscriber Line：数字用户线
[6]Internet Server Provider：因特网服务提供商

1. Applications

When multiple routers are used in interconnected[7] networks, the routers exchange information about destination addresses, using a dynamic routing protocol. Each router builds up a table listing the preferred routes[8] between any two systems on the interconnected networks. A router has interfaces for different physical types of network connections, (such as copper cables[9], fiber optic, or wireless

[7][ˌɪntə(:)kəˈnektid] adj. 互相连接的
[8]preferred route：优先路径
[9]copper cable：铜质电缆

transmission). It also contains firmware[10] for different networking protocol standards. Each network interface uses this specialized computer software to enable data packets to be forwarded from one protocol transmission system to another.

Routers may also be used to connect two or more logical groups of computer devices known as subnets, each with a different sub-network address. The subnets addresses[11] recorded in the router do not necessarily map directly to the physical interface connections. A router has two stages of operation called planes:

- Control plane[12]: A router records a routing table listing what route should be used to forward a data packet, and through which physical interface connection. It does this using internal preconfigured addresses[13], called static routes.
- Forwarding plane: The router forwards data packets between incoming and outgoing interface connections.

It routes it to the correct network type using information that the packet header contains. It uses data recorded in the routing table control plane.

Routers may provide connectivity within enterprises, between enterprises and the Internet, and between Internet service providers (ISPs) networks. The largest routers (such as the Cisco CRS-1 or Juniper T1600) interconnect the various ISPs, or may be used in large enterprise networks. Smaller routers usually provide connectivity for typical home and office networks. Other networking solutions may be provided by a backbone Wireless Distribution System (WDS[14]), which avoids the costs of introducing networking cables into buildings.

All sizes of routers may be found inside enterprises. The most powerful routers are usually found in ISPs, academic and research facilities. Large businesses may also need more powerful routers to cope with ever increasing demands of intranet data traffic. A three-layer model is in common use, not all of which need be present in smaller networks.

1.1 Access routers

Access routers, including 'small office/home office' (SOHO) models, are located at customer sites such as branch offices that do not need hierarchical routing of their own. Typically, they are optimized for low cost. Some SOHO routers are capable of running alternative free Linux-based firmware like Tomato, OpenWrt or DD-WRT.

---

[10]['fə:m,wɛə] n. 固件，韧件

[11]subnet addresses：子网地址

[12]control plane：控制面板

[13]preconfigured address：预先配置地址

[14]无线分布式系统

A screenshot of the LuCI web interface used by OpenWrt.
This page configures Dynamic DNS[15].

1.2 Distribution routers

Distribution routers aggregate[16] traffic from multiple access routers, either at the same site, or to collect the data streams from multiple sites to a major enterprise location. Distribution routers are often responsible for enforcing quality of service across a WAN, so they may have considerable memory installed, multiple WAN interface connections, and substantial[17] onboard data processing routines. They may also provide connectivity to groups of file servers or other external networks.

1.3 Security routers

External networks must be carefully considered as part of the overall security strategy. Separate from the router may be a firewall or VPN handling device, or the router may include these and other security functions.

1.4 Core routers

In enterprises, a core router may provide a "collapsed backbone[18]," interconnecting the distribution tier[19] routers from multiple buildings of a campus, or large enterprise locations. They tend to be optimized for high bandwidth, but lack some of the features of Edge Routers[20].

1.5 Internet connectivity and internal use

Routers intended for ISP and major enterprise connectivity usually exchange routing information using the Border Gateway Protocol (BGP). RFC 4098 standard defines the types of BGP-protocol routers according to the routers' functions:

- Edge router: Also called a Provider Edge router, is placed at the

[15]Domain Name Server，域名服务器
[16]['ægrigeit] v. 聚集，集合

[17][səb'stænʃəl] adj. 坚固的，实质的

[18]collapsed backbone：折叠式骨干
[19][tiə]n. 行，排，层 vt. 使层叠
[20]edge router：边缘路由器

edge of an ISP network. The router uses External BGP to EBGP[21] protocol routers in other ISPs, or a large enterprise Autonomous System.

- Subscriber edge router: Also called a Customer Edge router, is located at the edge of the subscriber's network, it also uses EBGP to its provider's Autonomous System. It is typically used in an (enterprise) organization.
- Inter-provider border router: Interconnecting ISPs, is a BGP-protocol router that maintains BGP sessions with other BGP protocol routers in ISP Autonomous Systems[22].
- Core router: A core router resides within an Autonomous System as a backbone to carry traffic between edge routers.
- Within an ISP: In the ISPs Autonomous System, a router uses internal BGP protocol to communicate with other ISP edge routers, other intranet core routers, or the ISPs intranet provider border routers.
- "Internet backbone": The Internet no longer has a clearly identifiable backbone, unlike its predecessor[23] networks. The major ISPs system routers make up what could be considered to be the current Internet backbone core. ISPs operate all four types of the BGP routers described here. An ISP "core" router is used to interconnect its edge and border routers. Core routers may also have specialized functions in virtual private networks based on a combination of BGP and Multi-Protocol Label Switching[24] protocols.
- Port forwarding: Routers are also used for port forwarding between private internet connected servers.
- Voice/Data/Fax/Video Processing Routers: Commonly referred to as access servers or gateways[25], these devices are used to route and process voice, data, video, and fax traffic on the internet. Since 2005, most long-distance phone calls have been processed as IP traffic (VOIP) through a voice gateway. Use of access server type routers expanded with the advent of the internet, first with dial-up access, and another resurgence[26] with voice phone service.

2. Forwarding

For pure Internet Protocol (IP) forwarding function, a router is designed to minimize the state information associated with individual

[21] External Border Gateway Protocol: 外部边界网关协议

[22] Autonomous System: 自治系统

[23] ['pri:disesə]
n. 前辈，前任

[24] Multi-Protocol Label Switching: 多协议标签交换

[25] ['geitwei]
n. 网关

[26] [ri'sə:dʒəns]
n. 苏醒

packets. The main purpose of a router is to connect multiple networks and forward packets destined either for its own networks or other networks. A router is considered a Layer 3 device because its primary forwarding decision is based on the information in the Layer 3 IP packet, specifically the destination IP address. This process is known as routing. When each router receives a packet, it searches its routing table to find the best match between the destination IP address of the packet and one of the network addresses in the routing table. Once a match is found, the packet is encapsulated in the Layer 2 data link frame for that outgoing interface. A router does not look into the actual data contents that the packet carries[27], but only at the layer 3 addresses to make a forwarding decision, plus optionally other information in the header for hints on. Once a packet is forwarded, the router does not retain any historical information about the packet, but the forwarding action can be collected into the statistical data[28], if so configured.

Forwarding decisions can involve decisions at layers other than layer 3. A function that forwards based on layer 2 information is properly called a bridge. This function is referred to as layer 2 bridging, as the addresses it uses to forward the traffic are layer 2 addresses (e.g. MAC addresses on Ethernet).

Besides making decisions as which interface a packet is forwarded to, which is handled primarily via the routing table, a router also has to manage congestion[29], when packets arrive at a rate higher than the router can process. Three policies commonly used in the Internet are tail drop[30], random early detection (RED[31]), and weighted random early detection (WRED[32]). Tail drop is the simplest and most easily implemented; the router simply drops packets once the length of the queue[33] exceeds the size of the buffers in the router. RED monitors the average queue size and drops packets based on statistical probabilities[34]. If the buffer is almost empty, all incoming packets are accepted. As the queue grows, the probability for dropping an incoming packet grows too. When the buffer is full, the probability has reached 1 and all incoming packets are dropped. WRED requires a weight on the average queue size to act upon when the traffic is about to exceed the preconfigured size, so that short bursts[35] will not trigger[36] random drops.

Another function a router performs is to decide which packet should be processed first when multiple queues exist. This is managed

[27]['kæri]
vt. 携带，运送

[28]statistical data：
统计数据

[29][kən'dʒestʃən]
n. 拥塞
[30]tail drop：
尾部丢弃
[31]随机早期检测
[32]加权随机先期检测
[33][kju:] n. 队列
[34]statistical probability：统计概率

[35]short burst：
短脉冲群
[36]['trigə]
vt. 引发，引起，触发

through quality of service (QoS[37]), which is critical when Voice over IP is deployed, so that delays between packets do not exceed 150ms to maintain the quality of voice conversations.	[37]服务质量
Yet another function a router performs is called policy-based routing[38] where special rules are constructed[39] to override[40] the rules derived from the routing table when a packet forwarding decision is made.	[38]policy-based routing：策略路由 [39] [kənˈstrʌkt] vt. 建造，构造 [40] [əuvəˈraid] vt. 优先于，无视 [41]专用集成电路
These functions may be performed through the same internal paths that the packets travel inside the router. Some of the functions may be performed through an application-specific integrated circuit (ASIC[41]) to avoid overhead caused by multiple CPU cycles, and others may have to be performed through the CPU as these packets need special attention that cannot be handled by an ASIC.	

参考译文

Text A 组 网 硬 件

组网硬件包括全部的计算机、外部设备、接口卡以及进行数据处理和网内通信所需的其他设备。

本节提供以下设备的相关信息：
- 文件服务器；
- 工作站；
- 网卡；
- 集中器/集线器；
- 中继器；
- 网桥；
- 路由器。

1. 文件服务器

文件服务器是大多数网络的核心。它是一台速度很快的计算机，带有大容量随机存储器和存储空间并配有快速网卡。该机装载了网络操作系统及应用软件，还装载了需要共享的数据文件。

文件服务器管理网络各个节点之间的信息通信。例如，它可以同时把字处理软件发送给一个工作站、从另一个工作站接收数据库文件并存储一个电子邮件。这需要一台能够存储大量的信息并快速地分享这些信息的服务器。服务器至少要满足以下要求：
- 75MHz 或以上的微处理器；
- 容量至少有 4GB 的快速硬盘；

- 一个 RAID 以便在磁盘损坏后保存数据；
- 备份磁带机；
- 多个扩充插槽；
- 快速网卡；
- 至少 32 MB 的随机存储器。

2. 工作站

网络中所有连接到文件服务器的计算机都叫作工作站。一个典型的工作站是配有网卡、网络软件和适当电缆的计算机。工作站并不必须配置软盘驱动器或硬盘驱动器，因为文件可以存放在文件服务器上。几乎任何计算机都可以作为网络工作站。

3. 网卡

网卡提供网络和工作站之间的物理连接。大多数网卡都是内置的，插在计算机内的扩展槽上。有些计算机，如 Mac 这一类的计算机，使用连接到串口或 SCSI 接口的扩展箱。笔记本计算机通常使用连接到并口的外部 LAN 适配器或者插到 PCMCIA 槽的网卡。

网卡是决定网络速度和性能的重要因素，为你所用的工作站配备最快的网卡是个好主意。

三种最常见的网络接口连接是以太卡、LocalTalk 连接器和令牌网卡。一家国际数据公司指出：以太网最流行，其次是令牌网和 LocalTalk。

3.1 以太网卡

虽然许多计算机（如麦金塔计算机）可以选择预装以太网卡，但通常网卡与计算机是分别购买的。以太网卡要么连接同轴电缆要么双绞线（或两者都行）。如果要连接同轴电缆，就用 BNC 连接。如果要连接双绞线，就用 RJ-45 连接。有些网卡带有 AUI 连接器。这可以用来把同轴电缆、双绞线或光缆连接到以太网卡。当使用这种模式时，就需要一个连接到工作站上的外部收发器。

3.2 令牌网卡

令牌网卡看上去类似于以太网卡。明显的不同在于该卡背面的连接器类型。通常令牌网卡有针 DIN 型连接器把该卡与网络电缆相连。

4. 集中器/集线器

集中器是一个为工作站、服务器和外部设备提供中心连接点的设备。在星状拓扑中，使用双绞线把每个工作站连接到中心集中器上。集线器是内置了多口卡的多槽集中器，当网络规模增加时，可以提供新增的访问。有些连接器是被动式的。它们让信息无改变地从一个计算机传输到另一个计算机。大多数连接器是主动式的，当把信号从一个设备传输到另一个设备时，增强信号。主动式连接器（如中继器）用来扩展网络的长度。集中器是：

- 通常带有 8、12 或 24 个 RJ-45 端口；
- 通常用于星状或星状—环状拓扑；
- 有专门的端口管理软件销售；
- 也叫集线器；
- 通常安装在标准化的金属架上，该架上也安装网络调制解调器、网桥或路由器。

5. 中继器

当信号在电缆中传输时，强度会降低。中继器是一个增强所通过网络信号的设备。它增强并转发所接收的信号。中继器可以是一个独立设备，也可以集成到集中器中。当网络电缆的总长度超过所用标准规定的长度时，就可以使用中继器。

一个好例子就是在星状拓扑的非屏蔽双绞线局域网中使用中继器。非屏蔽双绞线电缆的长度限定在 100 米内。最常用的配置是用双绞线把每个工作站连接到多端口主动型集中器上。集中器重新生成所有经过它的信号，使网络电缆的总长度超过 100 米的限制。

6. 网桥

网桥是一个设备，可以把一个大网段分割成两个更小、更有效的网段。如果要给旧的布线方案中增加新网络并使这新网络最先进，网桥可以将新旧网络相连。

网桥监控网络两边通过的信息，以便把信息包传到正确的位置。大多数网桥可以"监听"网络并自动计算出网桥两边每个计算机的地址。如果必要，网桥可以检查每个信息，并把它广播给网络的另一端。

网桥管理流量以便使网络两边的性能最佳，也可以说网桥就像高峰期十字路口的交通警察。它管理网络两边的信息流，阻止不必要的信息通过。网桥可以连接不同类型的电缆或物理拓扑，但是必须用在使用相同协议的网络之中。

7. 路由器

路由器把信息从一个网络的传输给另一个网络，类似于超级智能的网桥。路由器根据目的地址和起始地址选择最佳路径来传递消息。路由器可以引导流量以防止正面冲突，也有足够的智能知道何时把流量引导到僻径和捷径上。

尽管网桥知道网络每一边全部计算机的地址，但路由器知道网络上计算机、网桥和其他路由器的地址。路由器甚至可以"监听"整个网络以便确定哪一段是最繁忙的——这样它们可以引导数据绕过这些路段，直到不再繁忙为止。

如果有连接到因特网的学校局域网，就需要买一个路由器。在这种情况下，路由器就在局域网和因特网之间翻译信息。它也可以确定通过因特网之间发送数据的最佳路径。路由器可以：

- 有效引导信号流量；
- 在两个协议之间发送消息；
- 在线状总线、星状总线和星状—环状拓扑之间发送消息；
- 在光缆、同轴电缆和双绞线之间传输消息。

Unit 6

Text A

Wireless Sensor Network

A wireless sensor network (WSN) consists of spatially distributed autonomous sensors to monitor physical or environmental conditions, such as temperature, sound, pressure, etc. and to cooperatively pass their data through the network to a main location. The more modern networks are bidirectional, and they are also enabling control of sensor activity. The development of wireless sensor networks was motivated by military applications such as battlefield surveillance; today such networks are used in many industrial and consumer applications, such as industrial process monitoring and control, machine health monitoring, and so on.

The WSN is built of "nodes"--from a few to several hundreds or even thousands, where each node is connected to one (or sometimes several) sensors. Each such sensor network node has typically several parts: a radio transceiver with an internal antenna or connection to an external antenna, a microcontroller, an electronic circuit for interfacing with the sensors and an energy source, usually a battery or an embedded form of energy harvesting. A sensor node might vary in size from that of a shoebox down to the size of a grain of dust, although functioning "motes" of genuine microscopic dimensions have yet to be created. The cost of sensor nodes is similarly variable, ranging from a few to hundreds of dollars, depending on the complexity of the individual sensor nodes. Size and cost constraints on sensor nodes result in corresponding constraints on resources such as energy, memory, computational speed and communications bandwidth. The topology of the WSNs can vary from a simple star network to an advanced multihop wireless mesh network. The propagation technique between the hops of the network can be routing or flooding.

In computer science and telecommunications, wireless sensor networks are an active research area with numerous workshops and conferences arranged each year.

1. Characteristics

The main characteristics of a WSN include:

- Power consumption constrains nodes using batteries or energy harvesting
- Ability to cope with node failures
- Mobility of nodes
- Communication failures
- Heterogeneity of nodes
- Scalability to large scale of deployment
- Ability to withstand harsh environmental conditions
- Ease of use
- Power consumption

Sensor nodes can be imagined as small computers, extremely basic in terms of their interfaces and their components. They usually consist of a processing unit with limited computational power and limited memory, sensors or MEMS (including specific conditioning circuitry), a communication device (usually radio transceivers or alternatively optical), and a power source usually in the form of a battery. Other possible inclusions are energy harvesting modules, secondary ASICs, and possibly secondary communication devices (e.g. RS-232 or USB).

The base stations are one or more components of the WSN with much more computational, energy and communication resources. They act as a gateway between sensor nodes and the end user as they typically forward data from the WSN on to a server. Other special components in routing based networks are routers, which are designed to compute, calculate and distribute the routing tables.

2. Platforms

2.1 Standards and Specifications

Several standards are currently either ratified or under development by organizations including WAVE2M[1] for wireless sensor networks. There are a number of standardization bodies in the field of WSNs. The IEEE focuses on the physical and MAC layers; the Internet Engineering Task Force works on layers 3 and above. In addition to these, bodies such as the International Society of Automation provide vertical solutions, covering all protocol layers. Finally, there are also several non-standard, proprietary mechanisms and specifications.

Standards are used far less in WSNs than in other computing systems which make most systems incapable of direct communication between different systems. However, predominant standards commonly used in WSN communications include:
- WirelessHART[2]

---

[1] WAVE2M is an international nonprofit (['nɔn'prɔfit] adj. 非赢利的) standard development organization founded to promote the global use and enhancement of WAVE2M, an emerging wireless communication technology standard for ultra-low-power (超低功耗) and long-range devices.

[2] WirelessHART is a wireless sensor networking technology based on the Highway Addressable Remote Transducer Protocol (HART, 可寻址远程传感器高速通道).

- IEEE 1451[1]
- ZigBee / 802.15.4
- ZigBee IP
- 6LoWPAN[2]

2.2 Hardware

One major challenge in a WSN is to produce low cost and tiny sensor nodes. There are an increasing number of small companies producing WSN hardware and the commercial situation can be compared to home computing in the 1970s. Many of the nodes are still in the research and development stage, particularly their software. Also inherent to sensor network adoption is the use very low power methods for data acquisition.

2.3 Software

Energy is the scarcest resource of WSN nodes, and it determines the lifetime of WSNs. WSNs are meant to be deployed in large numbers in various environments, including remote and wild regions, where ad-hoc communications are a key component. For this reason, algorithms and protocols need to address the following issues: lifetime maximization, robustness and fault tolerance and self-configuration.

Energy/Power Consumption of the sensing device should be minimized and sensor nodes should be energy efficient since their limited energy resource determines their lifetime. To conserve power the node should shut off the radio power supply when not in use.

Some of the important topics in WSN software research are operating systems, security and mobility.

Operating systems for wireless sensor network nodes are typically less complex than general-purpose operating systems. They more strongly resemble embedded systems for two reasons. First, wireless sensor networks are typically deployed with a particular application in mind rather than as a general platform. Second, a need for low costs and low power leads most wireless sensor nodes to have low-power microcontrollers ensuring that mechanisms, such as virtual memory, are either unnecessary or too expensive to implement.

It is, therefore, possible to use embedded operating systems such as eCos or uC/OS for sensor networks. However, such operating systems are often designed with real-time properties.

---

[1] IEEE 1451 is a set of smart transducer interface standards developed by the Institute of Electrical and Electronics Engineers (IEEE) Instrumentation and Measurement Society's Sensor Technology Technical Committee that describe a set of open, common, network-independent communication interfaces for connecting transducers (sensors or actuators) to microprocessors, instrumentation ([ˌinstrumen'teiʃən] n. 仪器, 仪表) systems, and control/field networks.

[2] 6LoWPAN is an acronym of IPv6 over Low power Wireless Personal Area Networks (用 IPv6 的低功率无线个人局域网络). 6LoWPAN is the name of a working group in the Internet area of the IETF.

The 6LoWPAN concept originated from the idea that "the Internet Protocol could and should be applied even to the smallest devices," and that low-power devices with limited processing capabilities should be able to participate in the Internet of Things.

TinyOS is perhaps the first operating system specifically designed for wireless sensor networks. TinyOS is based on an event-driven programming[1] model instead of multithreading[2]. TinyOS programs are composed of event handlers and tasks with run-to-completion semantics. When an external event occurs, such as an incoming data packet or a sensor reading, TinyOS signals the appropriate event handler to handle the event. Event handlers can post tasks that are scheduled by the TinyOS kernel some time later.

LiteOS is a newly developed OS for wireless sensor networks, which provides UNIX-like abstraction and support for the C programming language.

Contiki is an OS which uses a simpler programming style in C while providing advances such as 6LoWPAN and Protothreads[3].

3. Other Concepts

3.1 Distributed sensor network

If a centralized architecture is used in a sensor network and the central node fails, then the entire network will collapse. However the reliability of the sensor network can be increased by using distributed control architecture.

Distributed control is used in WSNs for the following reasons:
- Sensor nodes are prone to failure
- For better collection of data
- To provide nodes with backup in case of failure of the central node
- There is also no centralized body to allocate the resources and they have to be self organized.

3.2 Data Integration and Sensor Web

The data gathered from wireless sensor networks is usually saved in the form of numerical data in a central base station. Additionally, the Open Geospatial Consortium (OGC)[4] is specifying standards for interoperability interfaces and metadata encodings that enable real time integration of heterogeneous sensor webs into the Internet, allowing any individual to monitor or

---

[1] In computer programming, event-driven programming (EDP) or event-based programming (基于事件编程) is a programming paradigm (['pærədaim] n. 范例) in which the flow of the program is determined by events--e.g., sensor outputs or user actions (mouse clicks, key presses) or messages from other programs or threads ([θred] n. 线程).

[2] In computer science, a thread of execution is the smallest sequence of programmed instructions (程序指令) that can be managed independently by an operating system scheduler. A thread is a light-weight process.

[3] A protothread is a low-overhead mechanism for concurrent ([kən'kʌrənt] adj. 并发的，协作的) programming.
Protothreads function as stackless, lightweight threads providing a blocking context cheaply using minimal memory per protothread (on the order of single bytes).

[4] The Open Geospatial Consortium (OGC), an international voluntary (['vɔləntəri] adj. 自愿的) consensus standards organization, originated in 1994. In the OGC, more than 400 commercial, governmental, nonprofit and research organizations worldwide collaborate in a consensus process encouraging development and implementation of open standards for geospatial content and services, GIS data processing and data sharing.

control Wireless Sensor Networks through a Web Browser.

3.3 In-network Processing

To reduce communication costs some algorithms remove or reduce nodes redundant sensor information and avoid forwarding data that is of no use. As nodes can inspect the data they forward they can measure the average or directionality of readings from other nodes. For example, in sensing and monitoring applications, it is generally the case that neighbouring sensor nodes monitoring an environmental feature typically register similar values. This kind of data redundancy due to the spatial correlation between sensor observations inspires the techniques for in-network data aggregation and mining.

New Words

sensor	['sensə]	n.	传感器
spatially	['speiʃəli]	adv.	空间地
autonomous	[ɔː'tɔnəməs]	adj.	自治的
temperature	['tempritʃə]	n.	温度
cooperatively	[kəu'ɔpərətivli]	adv.	合作地，协力地
bidirectional	[,baidi'rekʃənəl]	adj.	双向的
activity	[æk'tiviti]	n.	活动，行动
antenna	[æn'tenə]	n.	天线
battlefield	['bæt(ə)lfiːld]	n.	战场，沙场
microcontroller	['maikrəukən'trəulə]	n.	微控制器
battery	['bætəri]	n.	电池
mote	[məut]	n.	尘埃，微粒
genuine	['dʒenjuin]	adj.	真实的，真正的
microscopic	[maikrə'skɔpik]	adj.	极小的，微小的
variable	['vɛəriəbl]	adj.	可变的，不定的
correspond	[kɔris'pɔnd]	vi.	符合，协调，通信，相应
computational	[,kɔmpjuː'teiʃənəl]	adj.	计算的
propagation	[,prɔpə'geiʃən]	n.	（声波，电磁辐射等）传播
flooding	['flʌdiŋ]	n.	泛洪法；涌入，流入
workshop	['wəːkʃɔp]	n.	车间，工场
conference	['kɔnfərəns]	n.	会议，讨论会，协商会
consumption	[kən'sʌmpʃən]	n.	消费，消耗
hop	[hɔp]	v.	跳跃
heterogeneity	[,hetərəudʒi'niːiti]	n.	异种，异质，不同成分
scalability	[,skeilə'biliti]	n.	可量测性
withstand	[wiθ'stænd]	vt.	抵挡，经受住

harsh	[hɑ:ʃ]	adj. 苛刻的，荒芜的
optical	[ˈɔptikəl]	adj. 视力的，光学的
platform	[ˈplætfɔ:m]	n. 平台
ratify	[ˈrætifai]	vt. 批准，认可
proprietary	[prəˈpraiətəri]	adj. 所有的 n. 所有者，所有权
incapable	[inˈkeipəbl]	adj. 无能力的，不能的
predominant	[priˈdɔminənt]	adj. 支配的，主要的，有影响的
tiny	[ˈtaini]	adj. 很少的，微小的
scarce	[skɛəs]	adj. 缺乏的，不足的，稀有的
ad-hoc	[ˈædˌhɔk]	adj. 特别
maximization	[ˌmæksəmaiˈzeiʃən]	n. 最大值化，极大值化
robustness	[rəˈbʌstnes]	n. 坚固性，健壮性，鲁棒性
conserve	[kənˈsə:v]	vt. 保存，保藏
particular	[pəˈtikjulə]	n. 细节，详细 adj. 特殊的，特别的，独特的
property	[ˈprɔpəti]	n. 性质，特性；财产，所有权
resemble	[riˈzembl]	vt. 像，类似
multithreading	[ˈmʌltiˈθrediŋ]	n. 多线程
task	[tɑ:sk]	n. 任务，作业 v. 分派任务
handler	[ˈhændlə]	n. 处理者，处理器
semantics	[siˈmæntiks]	n. 语义学
abstraction	[æbˈstrækʃən]	n. 提取
allocate	[ˈæləukeit]	vt. 分派，分配
protothread	[ˈprəutəuθred]	n. 轻量级线程
metadata	[ˈmetəˈdeitə]	n. 元数据
heterogeneous	[ˌhetərəuˈdʒi:niəs]	adj. 不同种类的，异类的
neighbouring	[ˈneibəriŋ]	adj. 附近的，毗邻的
spatial	[ˈspeiʃəl]	adj. 空间的
correlation	[ˌkɔriˈleiʃən]	n. 相互关系，相关性
inspire	[inˈspaiə]	vt. 激发，产生

Phrases

battlefield surveillance	战场侦察，战场监视
machine health monitoring	机器的健康监测
electronic circuit	电子电路

energy harvesting	能量采集
sensor node	传感器节点
a grain of	一粒；一点点，一些
communication bandwidth	通信带宽
star network	星状网络
multihop wireless mesh network	多跳无线网状网络
power consumption	能量消耗，功率消耗，动力消耗
cope with	应付
environmental condition	环境条件，环境状况
processing unit	处理部件，处理器
base station	基站，基地
special component	专有部件，专用附件
focus on	致力于；使聚焦于；对（某事或做某事）予以注意；把……作为兴趣中心
Internet Engineering Task Force	因特网工程工作小组
International Society of Automation	国际自动化学会
research and development	研究与开发，研发
data acquisition	数据获取
fault tolerance	容错
sensing device	灵敏元件，传感器
power supply	电源
embedded system	嵌入系统
virtual memory	虚拟内存
embedded operating system	嵌入式操作系统
event-driven programming model	事件驱动编程模型
be composed of	由……组成
event handler	事件处理器
be prone to …	有……的倾向，易于
in case of	假设，万一
in the form of …	以……的形式

Abbreviations

WSN (Wireless Sensor Network)	无线传感器网络
MEMS (MicroElectro Mechanical Systems)	微型机电系统
ASIC (Application Specific Integrated Circuit)	特定用途集成电路
USB (Universal Serial Bus)	通用串行总线架构
OGC (Open Geospatial Consortium)	开放地理信息联盟

Exercises

【EX.1】Answer the following questions according to the text.

1. What does a wireless sensor network (WSN) consist of ?
2. What can sensor nodes be imagined as?
3. What do base stations act as?
4. What do predominant standards commonly used in WSN communications include?
5. What is one major challenge in a WSN?
6. What is the scarcest resource of WSN nodes?
7. What are some of the important topics in WSN software research?
8. What is perhaps the first operating system specifically designed for wireless sensor networks? What is it based on?
9. What are the reasons for the use of distributed control in WSNs?
10. How is the data gathered from wireless sensor networks usually saved?

【EX.2】Translate the following terms or phrases from English into Chinese and vice versa.

1. sensor node   1. _____
2. communication bandwidth   2. _____
3. multihop wireless mesh network   3. _____
4. star network   4. _____
5. fault tolerance   5. _____
6. base station   6. _____
7. sensing device   7. _____
8. embedded operating system   8. _____
9. microcontroller   9. _____
10. computational   10. _____
11. n. 平台   11. _____
12. n. 坚固性，健壮性，鲁棒性   12. _____
13. n. 多线程   13. _____
14. n. 元数据   14. _____
15. n. 处理者，处理器   15. _____

【EX.3】Translate the following sentences into Chinese.

1. Border Gateway Protocol (BGP) provides loop-free inter domain routing between autonomous systems.
2. In many data communications ways, cable is an ideal Internet access technology in the

bidirectional.

3. Computational grid is a burgeoning high performance computing technique.

4. The new algorithm is also applicable to general relational database.

5. Robustness analysis attracts more and more attention in these years.

6. An event handler is the code you write to respond to event.

7. Metadata is the soul of data warehouse.

8. The core idea of heterogeneous database inter-operation is data sharing and transparent accessing.

9. The standards of Web Service solved interoperability puzzles among heterogeneous information systems.

10. It is essential to consider system level power consumption when designing current mobile devices.

【EX.4】Complete the following passage with appropriate words in the box.

| touching | voltmeter | aware | liquid | measure |
| indicates | sensitivities | manufactured | responds | converts |

A sensor (also called detector) is a converter that measures a physical quantity and converts it into a signal which can be read by an observer or by an (today mostly electronic) instrument. For example, a mercury-in-glass thermometer __1__ the measured temperature into expansion and contraction of a __2__ which can be read on a calibrated glass tube. A thermocouple converts temperature to an output voltage which can be read by a __3__. For accuracy, most sensors are calibrated against known standards.

Sensors are used in everyday objects such as touch-sensitive elevator buttons (tactile sensor) and lamps which dim or brighten by __4__ the base. There are also innumerable applications for sensors of which most people are never __5__. Applications include cars, machines, aerospace, medicine, manufacturing and robotics.

A sensor is a device which receives and __6__ to a signal when touched. A sensor's sensitivity __7__ how much the sensor's output changes when the measured quantity changes. For instance, if the mercury in a thermometer moves 1 cm when the temperature changes by 1°C, the sensitivity is 1cm/°C (it is basically the slope Dy/Dx assuming a linear characteristic). Sensors that __8__ very small changes must have very high __9__. Sensors also have an impact on what they measure; for instance, a room temperature thermometer inserted into a hot cup of liquid cools the liquid while the liquid heats the thermometer. Sensors need to be designed to have a small effect on what is measured; making the sensor smaller often improves this and may introduce other advantages. Technological progress allows more and more sensors to be __10__ on a microscopic scale as microsensors using MEMS technology. In most cases, a microsensor reaches a significantly higher speed and sensitivity compared with macroscopic approaches.

【EX.5】Translate the following passage into Chinese.

Sensor network

A sensor network is a group of specialized transducers with a communications infrastructure intended to monitor and record conditions at diverse locations. Commonly monitored parameters are temperature, humidity, pressure, wind direction and speed, illumination intensity, vibration intensity, sound intensity, power-line voltage, chemical concentrations, pollutant levels and vital body functions.

A sensor network consists of multiple detection stations called sensor nodes, each of which is small, lightweight and portable. Every sensor node is equipped with a transducer, microcomputer, transceiver and power source. The transducer generates electrical signals based on sensed physical effects and phenomena. The microcomputer processes and stores the sensor output. The transceiver, which can be hard-wired or wireless, receives commands from a central computer and transmits data to that computer. The power for each sensor node is derived from the electric utility or from a battery.

Potential applications of sensor networks include:
- Industrial automation
- Automated and smart homes
- Video surveillance
- Traffic monitoring
- Medical device monitoring
- Monitoring of weather conditions
- Air traffic control
- Robot control.

Text B

Applications of WSN

1. Area Monitoring

Area monitoring is a common application of WSNs. In area monitoring, WSN is deployed over a region where some phenomenon is to be monitored. A military example is the use of sensors to detect enemy intrusion; a civilian example is the geo-fencing[1] of gas or oil pipelines.

When the sensors detect the event being monitored (heat, pressure), the event is reported to one of the base stations, which then takes appropriate action (e.g., send a message on the Internet or to a satellite). Similarly, wireless sensor networks can use a range of sensors to detect the presence of vehicles ranging from motorcycles to tramcars.

2. Environmental/Earth Monitoring

The term Environmental Sensor Networks has evolved to cover many applications of WSNs

---

[1] A geo-fence is a <u>virtual perimeter</u>（虚拟边界） for a real-world geographic area. A geo-fence could be dynamically generated--as in a radius around a store or point location. Or a geo-fence can be a predefined set of boundaries, like school attendance zones or neighborhood boundaries.

to earth science research. This includes sensing volcanoes, oceans, glaciers forests, etc. Some of the major areas are listed below.

2.1 Air Quality Monitoring

To protect humans and the environment from damage by air pollution, it is of the utmost importance to measure the levels of pollutants in the air. Real time monitoring of dangerous gases is particularly interesting in hazardous areas, as the conditions can change dramatically quickly, with serious consequences. Air quality monitoring includes:

- Environmental magnitudes: Temperature, Humidity, Light
- Gas & particle concentration: O_2, CO, CO_2, SO_2, H_2S, NO, NO_2, NH_2, CH_2, PM-10, TVOC
- Ambient monitoring: Rainfall, Wind speed, Wind direction, UV levels, Atmospheric pressure
- Interior monitoring

The measurement of gas levels at hazardous environments requires the use of robust and trustworthy equipment that meets industrial regulations.

- Exterior monitoring

Outdoor monitoring of air quality not only requires the use of accurate sensors but also rain and wind resistant housing, as well as the use of energy harvesting techniques that ensure extended autonomy to equipment which will most probably have difficult access.

2.2 Air Pollution Monitoring

Wireless sensor networks have been deployed in several cities (Stockholm, London or Brisbane) to monitor the concentration of dangerous gases for citizens. These can take advantage of the ad-hoc wireless links rather than wired installations, which also make them more mobile for testing readings in different areas. There are various architectures, different kinds of data analysis and data mining that can be used for such applications.

2.3 Forest Fire Detection

A network of Sensor Nodes can be installed in a forest to detect when a fire has started. The nodes can be equipped with sensors to measure temperature, humidity and gases which are produced by fire in the trees or vegetation. The early detection is crucial for a successful action of the firefighters. Thanks to Wireless Sensor Networks, the fire brigade will be able to know when a fire is started and how it is spreading.

2.4 Landslide Detection

A landslide detection system makes use of a wireless sensor network to detect the slight movements of soil and changes in various parameters that may occur before or during a landslide. And through the data gathered it may be possible to know the occurrence of landslides long before it actually happens.

2.5 Water Quality Monitoring

Water quality monitoring involves analyzing water properties in dams, rivers, lakes, oceans, as well as underground water reserves. The use of many wireless distributed sensors enables the creation of a more accurate map of the water status, and allows the permanent deployment of monitoring stations in locations of difficult access, without the need of manual data retrieval.

2.6 Natural Disaster Prevention

Wireless sensor networks can effectively act to prevent the consequences of natural disasters, like floods. Wireless nodes have successfully been deployed in rivers where changes of the water levels have to be monitored in real time.

3. Industrial Monitoring

3.1 Machine Health Monitoring

Wireless sensor networks have been developed for machinery condition-based maintenance (CBM) as they offer significant cost savings and enable new functionalities. In wired systems, the installation of enough sensors is often limited by the cost of wiring. Previously inaccessible locations, rotating machinery, hazardous or restricted areas, and mobile assets can now be reached with wireless sensors.

3.2 Data Logging

Wireless sensor networks are also used for the collection of data for monitoring of environmental information. This can be as simple as the monitoring of the temperature in a fridge and the level of water in overflow tanks in nuclear power plants. The statistical information can then be used to show how systems have been working. The advantage of WSNs over conventional loggers is the "live" data feed that is possible.

3.3 Industrial Sense and Control Applications

In recent research a vast number of wireless sensor network communication protocols have been developed. While previous research was primarily focused on power awareness, more recent research have begun to consider a wider range of aspects, such as wireless link reliability, real-time capabilities, and quality-of-service. These new aspects are considered as an enabler for future applications in industrial and related wireless sense and control applications, partially replacing or enhancing conventional wire-based networks by WSN techniques.

3.4 Water/Wastewater Monitoring

Water monitoring involves many different activities, from ensuring the quality of surface or underground water, both for human beings and animal life, to the monitoring of a country's water infrastructure.

- Water Quality Magnitudes: Temperature, PH, specific electrical conductance (EC)
- Water Distribution Network Monitoring: Flow & pressure levels, leakage detection, water levels, remote metering
- Natural Disaster Prevention: Flood & drought preemptive warning

There are many opportunities for using wireless sensor networks within the water/wastewater industries. Facilities not wired for power or data transmission can be monitored using industrial wireless I/O devices and sensors powered using solar panels or battery packs and also used in pollution control board.

4. Agriculture

It is increasingly common to use wireless sensor networks within the agricultural industry. It frees the farmer from the maintenance of wiring in a difficult environment. Gravity feed water systems can be monitored using pressure transmitters to monitor water tank levels, pumps can be controlled using wireless I/O devices and water use can be measured and wirelessly transmitted back to a central control center for billing. Irrigation automation enables more efficient water use and reduces waste.

Wireless sensor networks are also used to control the temperature and humidity levels inside commercial greenhouses. When the temperature and humidity drops below specific levels, the greenhouse manager must be notified via e-mail or cell phone text message, or host systems can trigger misting systems, open vents, turn on fans, or control a wide variety of system responses.

5. Structural Monitoring

Wireless sensors can be used to monitor the movement within buildings and infrastructure such as bridges, flyovers, embankments, tunnels etc.. It enables engineers to monitor assets remotely without the need for costly site visits. They can get the daily data, whereas traditionally this data was collected weekly or monthly by physical site visits, involving either road or rail closure in some cases. It is also far more accurate than any visual inspection that would be carried out.

Real time monitoring of structures is an excellent field of application for wireless sensor networks. It includes structural health magnitudes which cover loads, fatigue, vibration and crack evolution. It is important in large bridges to perform simultaneous measurement of loads and effects of these loads, in order to estimate the loads and their effect, possible fatigue of the structure, and in general, the future evolution of the bridge conditions. It also includes environment conditions, such as wind and weather conditions, traffic & pollution effects.

New Words

phenomenon	[fi'nɔminən]	n.	现象
geo-fencing	[gjəu-'fensiŋ]	n.	地理围栏
pipeline	['paip,lain]	n.	管道，管线
tramcar	['træmkɑ:]	n.	电车，矿车
volcano	[vɔl'keinəu]	n.	火山
ocean	['əuʃən]	n.	大海，海洋
forest	['fɔrist]	n.	森林，林木
		adj.	森林的
		vt.	植树于
glacier	['glæsjə]	n.	冰河

utmost	[ˈʌtməust]	n. 极限，最大可能，极力
		adj. 极度的，最远的
pollutant	[pəˈluːtənt]	n. 污染物质
hazardous	[ˈhæzədəs]	adj. 危险的，冒险的
dramatically	[drəˈmætikəli]	adv. 戏剧地，引人注目地
magnitude	[ˈmægnitjuːd]	n. 数量，量级
humidity	[hjuːˈmiditi]	n. 湿度
particle	[ˈpɑːtikl]	n. 粒子，点，极小量
concentration	[ˌkɔnsenˈtreiʃən]	n. 浓度
ambient	[ˈæmbiənt]	adj. 周围的
		n. 周围环境
trustworthy	[ˈtrʌstˌwəːði]	adj. 可信赖的
autonomy	[ɔːˈtɔnəmi]	n. 自治
Stockholm	[ˈstɔkhəum]	n. 斯德哥尔摩（瑞典首都）
Brisbane	[ˈbrizbən]	n. 布里斯班（澳大利亚东部港市）
vegetation	[ˌvedʒiˈteiʃən]	n. 植物
landslide	[ˈlændslaid]	n. 山崩，泥石流
dam	[dæm]	n. 水坝
manual	[ˈmænjuəl]	n. 手册，指南
		adj. 手的，手动的，手工的
retrieval	[riˈtriːvəl]	n. 取回，恢复，修补，重获，挽救
consequence	[ˈkɔnsikwəns]	n. 结果
inaccessible	[ˌinækˈsesəbl]	adj. 达不到的，难以接近
feed	[fiːd]	n. & v. 输入，馈送
aspect	[ˈæspekt]	n. 方面
reliability	[riˌlaiəˈbiliti]	n. 可靠性
enable	[iˈneibl]	vt. 使能够
enhance	[inˈhɑːns]	vt. 提高，增强
preemptive	[priːˈemptiv]	adj. 有先买权的，有强制收购权的，抢先的
wastewater	[ˈweistwɔːtə]	n. 废水
greenhouse	[ˈgriːnhaus]	n. 温室
notify	[ˈnəutifai]	v. 通报
vent	[vent]	n. 通风孔
flyover	[ˈflaiəuvə]	n. 立交桥
embankment	[imˈbæŋkmənt]	n. 堤防
tunnel	[ˈtʌnl]	n. 隧道，地道
inspection	[inˈspekʃən]	n. 检查，视察
fatigue	[fəˈtiːg]	n. 疲劳
vibration	[vaiˈbreiʃən]	n. 振动，颤动，摇动，摆动

Phrases

area monitoring	区域监测
Environmental Sensor Network	环境传感器网络
air pollution	空气污染
air quality monitoring	空气质量监测
particle concentration	粒子浓度
atmospheric pressure	大气压力
data mining	数据挖掘
be used for ……	用作……
fire brigade	消防队
water quality monitoring	水质量监测
data retrieval	数据检索
natural disaster	自然灾害
rotating machinery	回转式机器
data logging	数据资料记录
nuclear power plant	核电站
underground water	地下水
leakage detection	泄露检测
drought warning	旱情预报
data transmission	信息传输，数据传输
battery pack	电池组
gravity feed water system	重力给水系统
control center	控制中心，调度室
irrigation automation	自动灌溉
misting system	喷雾系统
carry out	完成，实现，贯彻，执行

Abbreviations

TVOC (Total Volatile Organic Compounds)	总挥发性有机物
UV (UltraViolet)	紫外线
CBM (Machinery Condition-based Maintenance)	基于状态维修
EC (Electrical Conductance)	导电率
I/O (Input/Output)	输入输出

Exercises

【EX.1】 Fill in the blanks according to the text.

1. A military example of area monitoring is the use of sensors _____; a civilian example is _____.

2. To protect humans and the environment from damage by air pollution, it is utmost important to _____.

3. Outdoor monitoring of air quality not only requires _____ but also rain and wind resistant housing, as well as the use of energy harvesting techniques that ensure extended autonomy to equipment which will most probably have difficult access.

4. _____ can be installed in a forest to detect when a fire has started.

5. Water quality monitoring involves _____ in dams, rivers, lakes, oceans, as well as underground water reserves.

6. Wireless sensor networks can effectively act to prevent the consequences of _____, like floods.

7. The advantage of WSNs over conventional loggers is _____.

8. Water monitoring involves many different activities, from ensuring the quality of _____, both for human beings and animal life, to the monitoring of _____.

9. Wireless sensor network frees the farmer from _____ the. Irrigation automation enables _____.

10. Real time monitoring of structures is an excellent field of application for _____. It includes structural health magnitudes which cover _____, _____, _____ and _____.

【EX.2】 Translate the following terms or phrases from English into Chinese and vice versa.

1.	data retrieval	1.	_____
2.	data transmission	2.	_____
3.	intrusion	3.	_____
4.	utmost	4.	_____
5.	magnitude	5.	_____
6.	autonomy	6.	_____
7.	ambient	7.	_____
8.	retrieval	8.	_____
9.	feed	9.	_____
10.	reliability	10.	_____

11. 电池组	11. _____
12. n. 检查，视察	12. _____
13. 完成，实现，执行	13. _____
14. adj. 可信赖的	14. _____
15. n. 手册，指南	15. _____

【EX.3】Translate the following sentences into Chinese.

1. Network monitoring is one of the key technologies in network area.

2. Online auto monitoring is an application of information technique in environmental monitoring area.

3. Wireless sensor network (WSN) is widely used, which can instantly monitor, collect and process environmental information.

4. Wireless sensor network can collect and process real time environmental information, then forward the results to its users.

5. Data mining is generally divided into descriptive data mining and predictive data mining.

6. Data mining is a popular technology supporting for DSS.

7. Data Mining is acquire and mine knowledge from mass data.

8. Explosive increasing of storing data stimulates more demand of data mining.

9. The genetic algorithm plays an important role in the area of data mining.

10. Clustering is an efficient method of data mining and text mining.

Sensor Web

The concept of the "sensor web"[1]" is a type of sensor network that is especially well suited for environmental monitoring. The phrase "sensor web" is also associated with a sensing system which heavily utilizes the World Wide Web. OGC's Sensor Web Enablement (SWE)[2] framework defines a suite of web service interfaces and communication protocols abstracting from the heterogeneity of sensor (network) communication.	[1] sensor web: 传感器万维网 [2] 感测器网路赋能
1. Definition The term "sensor web" was first used by Kevin Delin of NASA in 1997 to describe a novel wireless sensor network architecture where the individual pieces could act and coordinate[3] as a whole. In this sense, the term describes a specific type of sensor network: an amorphous[4] network of spatially distributed sensor platforms	[3] [kəuˈɔːdineit] vt. 调整，整理 [4] [əˈmɔːfəs] adj. 无定形的，无组织的

(pods[5]) that wirelessly communicate with each other. This amorphous architecture is unique since it is both synchronous and router-free, making it distinct from the more typical TCP/IP-like network schemes. A pod as a physical platform for a sensor can be orbital[6] or terrestrial[7], fixed or mobile and might even have real time accessibility via the Internet. Pod-to-pod communication is both omnidirectional[8] and bidirectional[9] where each pod sends out collected data to every other pod in the network. Hence, the architecture allows every pod to know what is going on with every other pod throughout the sensor web at each measurement cycle. The individual pods (nodes) were all hardware equivalent and Delin's architecture did not require special gateways or routing to have each of the individual pieces communicate with one another or with an end user. Delin's definition of a sensor web was an autonomous, stand-alone, sensing entity -- capable of interpreting and reacting to the data measured -- that does not necessarily require the presence of the World Wide Web to function. As a result, on-the-fly data fusion, such as false-positive identification and plume tracking, can occur within the sensor web itself and the system subsequently reacts as a coordinated, collective whole to the incoming data stream. For example, instead of having uncoordinated smoke detectors, a sensor web can react as a single, spatially dispersed, fire locator.

The term "sensor web" has also morphed into, sometimes being associated with an additional layer connecting sensors to the World Wide Web. The Sensor Web Enablement (SWE) initiative of the Open Geospatial Consortium (OGC[10]) defines service interfaces which enable an interoperable usage of sensor resources by enabling their discovery, access, tasking, as well as eventing and alerting. By defining standardized service interfaces, a sensor web based on SWE services hides the heterogeneity[11] of an underlying sensor network, its communication details and various hardware components from the applications built on top of it. OGC's SWE initiative defines the term "sensor web" as an infrastructure enabling access to sensor networks and archived[12] sensor data that can be discovered and accessed using standard protocols and application programming interfaces. Through this abstraction from sensor details, their usage in applications is facilitated.

[5] [pɔd]
n. 密集小群
[6] ['ɔ:bitl]
adj. 轨道的，（道路）环城的，绕城的，外环的
[7] [ti'restriəl]
adj. 陆地的
[8] [ˌɔmnidi'rekʃənl]
adj. 全方向的，全向
[9] [ˌbaidi'rekʃənəl]
adj. 双向的

[10] 开放地理信息联盟

[11] [ˌhetəroudʒi'ni:iti]
n. 异质性，不均匀性，不纯一性

[12] ['ɑ:kaiv]
vt. 存档

2. Characteristics of Delin's sensor web architecture

Delin designed a sensor web as a web of interconnected[13] pods. All pods in a sensor web are equivalent in hardware (there are no special "gateway" or "slave[14]" pods). Nevertheless, there are additional functions that pods can perform besides participating in the general sensor web function. Any pod of a sensor web can be a portal pod and provides users access to the sensor web (both input and output). Access can be provided by RF modem, cell phone connections, laptop connections, or even an Internet Server. In some cases, a pod will have an attached removable memory unit[15] (such as a USB stick or a laptop) that stores collected data.

The term of mother pod refers to the pod that contains the master clock[16] of the synchronous sensor web system. The mother pod has no special hardware associated with it, its designation[17] as a mother is merely based on the ID number associated with the pod. Often the mother pod serves as a primary portal point to the Internet, but this is done only for deployment convenience. Early papers referenced the mother pod as "a prime node" if it additionally contained special hardware for a particular type of input/output device (say an RF modem).

Because of the inherent hopping of data within a sensor web, a pod with no attached sensors can be deployed as a relay[18] with the single purpose of[19] facilitating communication between the other pods and to expand the communication range to a particular end-point (such as a mother pod). Sensors can be attached to relay pods at a later time and relays can also serve as portal pods.

Each pod usually contains:
- one or more sensor leading to one or more data channel,
- a processing unit such as a micro-controller or microprocessor[20],
- a two-way communication component such as a radio and antenna (radio ranges are typically limited by government spectrum requirements; unlicensed bands will allow for communication of a few hundred yards in unobstructed[21] areas, although line of sight is not a requirement),
- an energy source such as a battery coupled with a solar cell[22],
- a package to protect components against sometimes harsh

[13] [ˌintə(:)kəˈnektid] adj. 互相连接的

[14] [sleiv] adj. 从属的

[15] removable memory unit：移动存储装置

[16] master clock：主时钟

[17] [ˌdezigˈneiʃən] n. 指定，分配

[18] [ˈriːlei] v. 转播，转发

[19] with the purpose of：以……为目的

[20] [maikrəuˈprəusesə] n. 微处理器

[21] [ˈʌnəbˈstrʌktid] adj. 没有障碍的

[22] solar cell：太阳能电池

environment. 　　Each pod also typically requires a support such as a pole or tripod. The number of pods may vary, with examples of sensor webs with 12 to 30 pods. The shape of a sensor web may impact its usefulness[23], for instance a particular deployment makes sure each pod is in range to communicate with at least two other pods. Sensor web measurement cycles have typically been between 30 seconds and 15 minutes for deployed systems thus far.	[23]['ju:sfulnis] n. 有效性
Sensor webs consisting of pods have been deployed for years. Sensor webs have been fielded in harsh[24] environments (including deserts, mountain snowpacks, and Antarctica) for the purposes of environmental science and have also proved valuable in urban search and rescue[25] and infrastructure protection. The technology is not only monitoring the environment but sometimes also controlling the environment by actuating devices[26].	[24][hɑ:ʃ] adj. 荒芜的，苛刻的 [25] search and rescue 搜救 [26]actuating device: 启动装置；调节装置

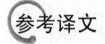

Text A 无线传感器网络

　　无线传感器网络由不同位置的自治传感器组成，这些传感器监控物理或环境状况（如温度、声音及压力等）并把其数据通过网络传给主位置。更现代的网络是双向的，它们也能控制传感器的行为。无线传感器网络最早用于像战场监控这样的军事活动；当今这类网络也在许多行业得以应用，如工业过程监控、机器健康监控等。

　　无线传感器网络由"节点"构成——从数个到成百上千的节点，每个节点连接一个（有时几个）传感器。这种传感器网络节点通常有几个部分：带有内置天线或连接了外置天线的无线收发器、一个微型处理器、与传感器连接的电路以及能源。能源常常是电池或内嵌的能量收集器。传感器节点也有多种大小，从鞋盒到粉尘不等，尽管必须制造出"尘埃"大小的功能部件。传感器节点的成本也有多种，从几美元到几百美元，这取决于每个节点的复杂性。传感器节点的尺寸和成本限制了资源，如能量、内存、计算速度和通信带宽。无线传感器网络的拓扑结构也不尽相同，从简单的星状网络到高级的多跳无线网状网络。网络之间切换的传输技术可以使用路由法或者泛洪法。

　　在计算机科学和通信学中，无线传感器网络是活跃的研究领域，每年都有许多研讨会。

1. 特点

无线传感器网络的主要特点包括：
- 能源消耗约束了使用电池或能源收集器的节点；
- 能够应付节点故障；

- 节点具有可移动性；
- 通信故障；
- 异种节点；
- 可扩展到大规模部署；
- 能够抵御严酷的环境条件；
- 易用；
- 能源消耗。

可以把传感器节点想象为小计算机，具有非常简单的接口和部件。通常它由以下部分组成：计算能力有限的处理器、有限的内存、传感器和 MEMS（包括特制电路）、通信设备（通常是无线或光学收发器）以及电池形式的电源。它也可能包括能源收集模块、辅助 ASIC 和可能的辅助通信设备（如 RS-232 或 USB）。

基站是一个或多个 WSN 部件，带有更多的计算、能源和通信资源。它们作为传感器节点和终端用户之间的通道，通常把数据从 WSN 转发给服务器。另外的特定部件是基于网络路径的路由器，供运算、计算和分布路由表使用。

2. 平台

2.1 标准和规范

WSN 当前的几个标准都是由包括 WAVE2M 这样的组织发布和开发的。在 WSN 领域有许多标准组织。IEEE 着重于物理和 MAC 层；因特网工程工作小组注重第三层及以上层。除此之外，还有像国际自动化学会这样的团体提供了垂直解决方案，覆盖了各层协议。最终，还有一些非标准的私有机制和规范。

可以用于 WSN 的标准远远少于其他计算系统，这使得大多数系统无法在不同系统之间直接通信。WSN 通信中使用的主要标准包括：

- WirelessHART；
- IEEE 1451；
- ZigBee / 802.15.4；
- ZigBee IP；
- 6LoWPAN。

2.2 硬件

WSN 的一个主要挑战是生产低成本和微小传感器节点。生产 WSN 硬件的小公司日益增多，这与 20 世纪 70 年代家庭计算的商业境况颇为相似。许多节点仍然处于研发期，软件尤为明显。传感器网络固有地使用极低功率的方式收集数据。

2.3 软件

能量是 WSN 节点最稀缺的资源，决定了 WSN 的寿命。要打算在各种环境（包括远程和野外）中部署 WSN，通信是关键。因此，算法和协议必须解决以下问题：寿命最长、稳健性、容错和自配置。

因为有限的能源决定了寿命，所以敏感元件的能源消耗必须最小并且传感器更有能效。在节点不工作时必须关闭无线电源以便节能。

在 WSN 软件研究中一些重要的话题是操作系统、安全性和移动性。

用于无线传感器网络节点的操作系统通常比一般的操作系统简单。有两个理由使其更像嵌入式系统。首先，无线传感器网络通常为特定应用而部署，而不是在普通平台上；其次，低成本和低功率需求使得大多数无线传感器节点都有低功率微控制器，这就使这些装置（如虚拟内存），要么不必要安装，要么安装成本太高。

因此，传感器网络可能使用像 eCos 或 uC/OS 这样的嵌入式操作系统。但是，这样的操作系统通常具有实时操作的特点。

TinyOS 或许是第一个专门为无线传感器网络设计的操作系统。TinyOS 基于事件驱动编程模型而不是多线程模型。TinyOS 程序由事件处理器和执行到底的任务组成。当一个外部事件发生时，如进来一个数据包或传感器读入了数据，TinyOS 就发送信号给适当的事件处理器来处理该事件。随后，事件处理器可以由 TinyOS 内核预先安排任务。

LiteOS 是一个新开发的无线传感器网络操作系统，它提供类似 UNIX 的概念并支持 C 编程语言。

Contiki 是使用 C 语言编程风格比较简单的操作系统，同时也提供像 6LoWPAN 和 Protothreads 这样的先进技术。

3. 其他概念

3.1 分布式传感器网络

如果在传感器网络中使用集中结构并且中心节点出了故障，那么整个网络就会崩溃，但是可以使用分布式控制结构来增加这种传感器网络的可靠性。

在 WSN 中使用分布式控制的理由如下：
- 传感器节点容易出故障；
- 更好地收集数据；
- 在中心节点出故障时提供备份；
- 没有核心的实体来分配资源并且它们必须是自组织的。

3.2 数据集成和传感器网络

从无线传感器网络收集的数据通常以数字格式存储在中心基站。另外，OGC 指定了专门用于互用接口和元数据编码的标准，能够实时地把异种传感器网络整合到因特网中，允许任何人通过网络浏览器监控无线传感器网络。

3.3 网内进程

为减少通信成本，有些算法删除或减少节点冗余传感器信息并避免转发无用信息。因为节点可以检查转发的信息，所以可以测量来自其他节点读数的平均值或方向。例如，在感知和监控应用中，监控环境的相邻的传感器节点通常注册类似的数值。这种数据冗余来自传感器的空间关系，激发了网内数据收集和挖掘技术。

Unit 7

Text A

How Wireless Networks Work

A wireless network or Wireless Local Area Network (WLAN) serves the same purpose as a wired one -- to link a group of computers. Because "wireless" doesn't require costly wiring, the main benefit is that it's generally easier, faster and cheaper to set up.

By comparison, creating a network by pulling wires throughout the walls and ceilings of an office can be labor-intensive and thus expensive. But even when you have a wired network already in place, a wireless network can be a cost-effective way to expand or augment it. In fact, there's really no such thing as a purely wireless network, because most link back to a wired network at some point.

1. The Basics

Wireless networks operate using radio frequency (RF) technology, a frequency within the electromagnetic spectrum associated with radio wave propagation. When an RF current is supplied to an antenna, an electromagnetic field is created that then is able to propagate through space.

The cornerstone of a wireless network is a device known as an access point (AP[1]). The primary job of an access point is to broadcast a wireless signal that computers can detect and "tune" into. Since wireless networks are usually connected to wired ones, an access point also often serves as a link to the resources available on a wired network, such as an Internet connection.

In order to connect to an access point and join a wireless network, computers must be equipped with wireless network adapters[2]. These are often built right into the computer, but if

---

[1] Short for Access Point, a hardware device or a computer's software that acts as a communication hub for users of a wireless device to connect to a wired LAN. APs are important for providing heightened wireless security and for extending the physical range of service a wireless user has access to.

[2] Often abbreviated as NIC, an expansion board you insert into a computer so the computer can be connected to a network. Most NICs are designed for a particular type of network, protocol, and media, although some can serve multiple networks.

not, just about any computer or notebook can be made wireless-capable through the use of an add-on adapter[1] plugged into an empty expansion slot, USB port, or in the case of notebooks, a PC Card slot.

2. Wireless Technology Standards

Because there are multiple technology standards for wireless networking, it pays to do your homework before buying any equipment. The most common wireless technology standards include the following:

- 802.11b: The first widely used wireless networking technology, known as 802.11b (more commonly called WiFi), first debuted almost a decade ago, but is still in use.
- 802.11g: In 2003, a follow-on version called 802.11g appeared offering greater performance (that is, speed and range) and remains today's most common wireless networking technology.
- 802.11n: Another improved standard called 802.11n is currently under development. But even though the 802.11n standard has yet to be finalized, you can still buy products based on the draft 802.11n standard, which you will be able to upgrade later to the final standard.

All the WiFi variants (802.11b, g and n products) use the same 2.4 GHz radio frequency, and as a result are designed to be compatible with each other, so you can usually use devices based on the different standards within the same wireless network. The catch is that doing so often requires special configuration to accommodate the earlier devices, which in turn can reduce the overall performance of the network. In an ideal scenario you'll want all your wireless devices, the access point and all wireless-capable computers to be using the same technology standard and to be from the same vendor whenever possible.

3. Wireless Speed & Range

When you buy a piece of wireless network hardware, it will often quote performance figures (i.e., how fast it can transmit data) based on the type of wireless networking standard it uses, plus any added technological enhancements. In truth, these performance figures are almost always wildly optimistic.

While the official speeds of 802.11b, 802.11g, and 802.11n networks are 11, 54, and 270 megabits per second (Mbps) respectively, these figures represent a scenario that is simply not attainable in the real world. As a general rule, you should assume that in a best-case scenario you'll get roughly one-third of the advertised performance.

It's also worth noting that a wireless network is by definition a shared network, so the more computers you have connected to a wireless access point, the less data each will be able to send and receive. Just as a wireless network's speed can vary greatly, the range can change too. For

---

[1] The circuitry required to support a particular device. For example, video adapters enable the computer to support graphics monitors, and network adapters enable a computer to attach to a network. Adapters can be built into the main circuitry of a computer or they can be separate add-ons that come in the form of expansion boards.

example, 802.11b and g officially work over a distance of up to 328 feet indoors or 1,312 feet outdoors, but the key term there is "up to". Chances are you won't see anywhere close to those numbers.

As you might expect, the closer you are to an access point, the stronger the signal and the faster the connection speed. The range and speed you get out of wireless network will also depend on the kind of environment in which it operates. And that brings us to the subject of interference.

4. Wireless Interference

Interference is an issue with any form of radio communication, and a wireless network is no exception. The potential for interference is especially great indoors, where different types of building materials (concrete, wood, drywall, metal, glass and so on) can absorb or reflect radio waves, affecting the strength and consistency of a wireless network's signal. Similarly, devices like microwave ovens and some cordless phones can cause interference because they operate in the same 2.4 frequency range as 802.11b/g/n networks. You can't avoid interference entirely, but in most cases it's not significant enough to affect the usability of the network. When it does, you can usually minimize the interference by relocating wireless networking hardware or using specialized antennas[1].

5. Data Security on Wireless Networks

In the same way that all you need to pick up a local radio station is a radio, all anyone needs to detect a wireless network within nearby range is a wireless-equipped computer. There's no way to selectively hide the presence of your network from strangers, but you can prevent unauthorized people from connecting to it, and you can protect the data traveling across the network from prying eyes. By turning on a wireless network's encryption feature, you can scramble the data and control access to the network.

Wireless network hardware supports several standard encryption schemes, but the most common are Wired Equivalent Privacy (WEP)[2], WiFi Protected Access (WPA)[3], and WiFi Protected Access 2 (WPA2)[4]. WEP is the oldest and least secure method and should be avoided.

---

[1] Also called an aerial (['ɛəriəl] n. 天线), an antenna is a conductor that can transmit, send and receive signals such as microwave, radio or satellite signals. A high-gain antenna increases signal strength, where a low-gain antenna receives or transmits over a wide angle.

[2] A security protocol for wireless local area networks (WLANs) defined in the 802.11b standard. WEP is designed to provide the same level of security as that of a wired LAN. LANs are inherently more secure than WLANs because LANs are somewhat protected, having some or all part of the network inside a building that can be protected from unauthorized access (未授权的访问).

[3] A WiFi standard that was designed to improve upon the security features of WEP. The technology is designed to work with existing WiFi products that have been enabled with WEP (i.e., as a software upgrade to existing hardware).

[4] Short for Wi-Fi Protected Access 2, the follow on security method to WPA for wireless networks that provides stronger data protection and network access control. It provides enterprise and consumer WiFi users with a high level of assurance that only authorized users can access their wireless networks. Based on the IEEE 802.11i standard, WPA2 provides government grade security by implementing the National Institute of Standards and Technology (NIST,美国国家技术和标准署) FIPS (Federal Information Processing Standards, 美国联邦信息处理标准) 140-2 compliant AES (Advanced Encryption Standard,高级加密标准) encryption algorithm and 802.1x-based authentication.

WPA and WPA2 are good choices, but provide better protection when you use longer and more complex passwords (all devices on a wireless network must use the same kind of encryption and be configured with the same password).

Unless you intend to provide public access to your wireless network -- and put your business data or your own personal data at risk -- you should consider encryption mandatory.

New Words

ceiling	['siːlɪŋ]	n. 天花板，最高限度
labor-intensive	['leibə-inˈtensiv]	adj. 劳动密集型的
cost-effective	[kɔst-iˈfektiv]	adj. 有成本效益的，划算的
augment	[ɔːgˈment]	v. 增加，增大
		n. 增加
electromagnetic	[ilektrəuˈmægnitik]	adj. 电磁的
spectrum	[ˈspektrəm]	n. 光谱，频谱
cornerstone	[ˈkɔːnəstəun]	n. 墙角石，基础
tune	[tjuːn]	vt. 收听
adapter	[əˈdæptə]	n. 适配器
debut	[ˈdebju]	v. 出现，亮相
finalize	[ˈfainəlaiz]	v. 把（计划，稿件等）最后定下来，定案
draft	[drɑːft]	n. 草稿，草案
upgrade	[ˈʌpgreid]	n. 升级
		vt. 使升级
catch	[kætʃ]	n. 捕捉
		v. 捕获
		vi. 抓住
accommodate	[əˈkɔmədeit]	vt. 供给，使适应，调节，调和
		vi. 适应
reduce	[riˈdjuːs]	vt. 减少，缩小，简化，还原
scenario	[siˈnɑːriəu]	n. 情景
quote	[kwəut]	vt. 提供，提出，报（价）
figure	[ˈfigə]	n. 外形，轮廓，图形，画像，数字，形状
		vt. 描绘，表示，象征
optimistic	[ˌɔptiˈmistik]	adj. 乐观的
respectively	[riˈspektivli]	adv. 分别地，各个地
attainable	[əˈteinəbl]	adj. 可到达的，可得到的
assume	[əˈsjuːm]	vt. 假定，设想

roughly	['rʌfli]	adv.	概略地，粗糙地
potential	[pə'tenʃəl]	adj.	潜在的，可能的
concrete	['kɔnkri:t]	n.	混凝土
drywall	['draiwɔ:l]	n.	（不抹灰的）板墙，干墙，石膏板预制件
reflect	[ri'flekt]	v.	反射
consistency	[kən'sistənsi]	n.	密度，一致性，连贯性
cordless	['kɔ:dlis]	n.	不用电线的
entirely	[in'taiəli]	adv.	完全地，全然地，一概地
usability	[,ju:zə'biləti]	n.	可用性
relocate	[,ri:ləu'keit]	v.	重新部署
prying	['praiiŋ]	adj.	爱打听的
		v.	打听，刺探（他人的私事）
encryption	[in'kripʃən]	n.	编密码，加密
mandatory	['mændətəri]	adj.	命令的，强制的，托管的

Phrases

by comparison	比较起来
pull wire	拉线
wired network	有线网络
be associated with	与……有联系，与……有关
electromagnetic field	电磁场
electromagnetic spectrum	电磁波频谱
be equipped with	装备
network adapter	网络适配器，网卡
just about	几乎
plug into	把(电器)插头插入，接通
expansion slot	扩充插槽
in the case of	在……的情况
be compatible with	适合，一致
overall performance	总性能，全部工作特性
a piece of	一套，一件
in truth	实际上
performance figure	性能指标
cordless phone	无绳电话
prevent sb. from doing sth.	阻止某人做某事

Abbreviations

WLAN (Wireless Local Area Network)　　无线局域网
RF (Radio Frequency)　　无线电频率
AP (Access Point)　　访问接入点
Mbps (Megabits per second)　　兆位每秒
WEP (Wired Equivalent Privacy)　　有线等效加密
WPA (WiFi Protected Access)　　WiFi 保护访问

Exercises

【EX.1】Answer the following questions according to the text.

1. What is the purpose of a wireless network?
2. What is the cornerstone of a wireless network? What is its primary job?
3. What must computers be equipped with in order to connect to an access point and join a wireless network?
4. What do the most common wireless technology standards include?
5. What radio frequency do all the WiFi variants (802.11b, g and n products) use?
6. What are the official speeds of 802.11b, 802.11g, and 802.11n networks?
7. What do the range and speed you get out of wireless network depend on?
8. Why can devices like microwave ovens and some cordless phones cause interference?
9. What are the most common standard encryption schemes wireless network hardware supports?
10. Is there really such thing as a purely wireless network in fact? Why?

【EX.2】Translate the following terms or phrases from English into Chinese and vice versa.

1. wired network　　　　　　　1. _____
2. electromagnetic field　　　　2. _____
3. electromagnetic spectrum　　3. _____
4. network adapter　　　　　　4. _____
5. be equipped with　　　　　　5. _____
6. overall performance　　　　　6. _____
7. performance figure　　　　　7. _____
8. expansion slot　　　　　　　8. _____
9. spectrum　　　　　　　　　　9. _____

10.	adapter	10.	
11.	n. 升级 vt. 使升级	11.	
12.	v. 反射	12.	
13.	v. 重新部署	13.	
14.	n. 可用性	14.	
15.	n. 编密码，加密	15.	

【EX.3】**Translate the following sentences into Chinese.**

1. Electromagnetic waves travel at the same speed as light.

2. An example of a physical interface is a network adapter.

3. Engineers will test the performance of the computer.

4. The internet is sometimes described as a cloud -- a big cordless (borderless) area of computing power.

5. The database security involves data secret, integrity and usability.

6. Key management is a critical technic of realizing database encryption.

7. It mainly includes symmetric encryption algorithms and asymmetric cryptographic algorithms and protocols.

8. The authorities are considering implementing a mandatory electronic recycling program.

9. You may not connect your laptop to the wired network in the computer labs.

10. Select this option to provide authenticated network access for wired and wireless Ethernet networks.

【EX.4】**Complete the following passage with appropriate words in the box.**

close	reader	simultaneously	indoor	operate
require	single	positioned	attached	needed

RFID chips are quite similar to bar code labels in that they typically work with a corresponding scanner or reader. However, RFID chips have significant advantages. Because an RFID chip communicates with a __1__ through radio waves (not infrared, which is being used by bar code technology), the chip doesn't have to be __2__ right in front of the reader. That is, line-of-sight is not __3__.

Also, unlike a bar code reader/label pair, which have to be really __4__ (about a few centimeters), some RFID reader/chip pairs can function even if they are a few meters apart. Furthermore, while a bar code label can only be read by a __5__ reader at a time, an RFID chip can transmit data to multiple readers __6__.

There are different kinds of RFID chips. Some __7__ batteries, known as 'active' chips, while others don't, known as 'passive'. Others are designed for __8__ use, while others are built for rugged, outdoor applications. The most common applications include object tracking and identification.

Chips can also differ in the kind of radio frequencies they __9__ on. Some communicate via UHF (Ultra High Frequency), others HF (High Frequency), and still others LF (Low

Frequency).

RFID chips can be ___10___ just about anywhere: clothes, shoes, vehicles, containers, and even plants, animals, and human beings (as implants). Miniaturized chips have even been attached to insects.

【EX.5】 Translate the following passage into Chinese.

Radio Frequency Identification Tag (RFID Tag)

Although RFID tags have similar applications to barcodes, they are far more advanced. For instance, reading information from an RFID tag does not require line-of-sight and can be performed over a distance of a few meters., This also means that a single tag can serve multiple readers at a time, compared to only one for a bar code tag.

In the context of RFID technology, the term "tag" is also meant to include labels and cards. The kind of tag depends on the body or object on which the tag will be attached to. RFID systems can operate either in UHF (Ultra High Frequency), HF (High Frequency), or LF (Low Frequency). Thus, tags can also vary in terms of the frequencies on which they will operate.

These tags can be attached to almost any object. Although the usual target objects are apparel, baggage, containers, construction materials, laundry, and bottles, they have also been attached to animals, humans, and vehicles.

Some RFID tags are designed for rugged, outdoor-based applications. These are built to endure natural and incandescent light, vibration, shock, rain, dust, oil, and other harsh conditions. They are normally passive, i.e., they don't require batteries to function. Thus, they can operate 24/7 without risk of losing power. Such heavy-duty tags are usually attached to trucks, cargo containers, and light rail cars for cargo tracking, fleet management, vehicle tracking, and vehicle identification, among others.

RFID

Radio frequency identification (RFID) is the use of a wireless noncontact system that uses radio-frequency electromagnetic fields to transfer data from a tag attached to an object for the purposes of automatic identification and tracking. Some tags require no battery and are powered by the electromagnetic fields used to read them. Others use a local power source and emit radio waves (electromagnetic radiation[1] at radio frequencies). The tag contains electronically stored information which can be read from up to several meters (yards) away. Unlike a bar code, the tag does not need to be within line of sight of the reader and may be embedded in the tracked object.

---

[1] Electromagnetic radiation (EM radiation or EMR) is a form of energy emitted and absorbed by charged particles, which exhibits wave-like behavior as it travels through space.

RFID tags are used in many industries. An RFID tag attached to an automobile during production can be used to track its progress through the assembly line. Pharmaceuticals can be tracked through warehouses. Livestock and pets may have tags injected[1], allowing positive identification of the animal.

Since RFID tags can be attached to clothing, possessions, or even implanted within people[2], the possibility of reading personally-linked information without consent has raised privacy concerns.

1. Design of RFID

A radio frequency identification system uses tags, or labels attached to the objects to be identified. Two-way radio transmitter-receivers called interrogators or readers send a signal to the tag and read its response. The readers generally transmit their observations to a computer system running RFID software or RFID middleware.

The tag's information is stored electronically in a nonvolatile memory. The RFID tag includes a small RF transmitter and receiver. An RFID reader transmits an encoded radio signal to interrogate the tag. The tag receives the message and responds with its identification information. This may be only a unique tag serial number, or may be product-related information such as a stock number, lot or batch number, production date, or other specific information.

RFID tags can be either passive, active or battery assisted passive. An active tag has an on-board battery and periodically transmits its ID signal. A battery assisted passive (BAP) has a small battery on board and is activated when in the presence of a RFID reader. A passive tag is cheaper and smaller because it has no battery. Instead, the tag uses the radio energy transmitted by the reader as its energy source. The interrogator must be close for RF field to be strong enough to transfer sufficient power to the tag. Since tags have individual serial numbers, the RFID system design can discriminate several tags that might be within the range of the RFID reader and read them simultaneously.

Tags may either be read only, having a factory-assigned serial number that is used as a key into a database, or may be read/write, where object-specific data can be written into the tag by the system user. Field programmable tags may be write-once, read-multiple; "blank" tags may be written with an electronic product code by the user.

RFID tags contain at least two parts: an integrated circuit for storing and processing information,

---

[1] A microchip implant is an identifying integrated circuit placed under the skin of a dog, cat, horse, parrot or other animal. The chip, about the size of a large grain of rice, uses passive RFID (Radio Frequency Identification) technology.

[2] A human microchip implant is an integrated circuit device or RFID transponder encased in <u>silicate glass</u> (硅酸盐玻璃) and implanted in the body of a human being. A subdermal implant typically contains a unique ID number that can be linked to information contained in an external database, such as personal identification, medical history, medications, <u>allergies</u> (['ælədʒi] n. 敏感症,), and contact information.

modulating[1] and demodulating[2] a radio-frequency (RF) signal, collecting DC power from the incident reader signal, and other specialized functions; and an antenna for receiving and transmitting the signal.

Fixed readers are set up to create a specific interrogation zone which can be tightly controlled. This allows a highly defined reading area for when tags go in and out of the interrogation zone. Mobile readers may be hand-held or mounted on carts or vehicles.

Signaling between the reader and the tag is done in several different incompatible ways, depending on the frequency band used by the tag. Tags operating on LF and HF frequencies are, in terms of radio wavelength, very close to the reader antenna, only a small percentage of a wavelength away. In this near field[3] region, the tag is closely coupled electrically with the transmitter in the reader. The tag can modulate the field produced by the reader by changing the electrical loading the tag represents. By switching between lower and higher relative loads, the tag produces a change that the reader can detect. At UHF and higher frequencies, the tag is more than one radio wavelength away from the reader, requiring a different approach. The tag can backscatter[4] a signal. Active tags may contain functionally separated transmitters and receivers, and the tag need not respond on a frequency related to the reader's interrogation signal.

An Electronic Product Code (EPC) is one common type of data stored in a tag. When written into the tag by an RFID printer, the tag contains a 96-bit string of data. The first eight bits are a header which identifies the version of the protocol. The next 28 bits identify the organization that manages the data for this tag; the organization number is assigned by the EPCGlobal consortium. The next 24 bits are an object class, identifying the kind of product; the last 36 bits are a unique serial number for a particular tag. These last two fields are set by the organization that issued the tag. Rather like a URL, the total electronic product code number can be used as a key into a global database to uniquely identify a particular product.

Often more than one tag will respond to a tag reader, for example, many individual products with tags may be shipped in a common box or on a common pallet. Collision detection is important to allow reading of data. Two different types of protocols are used to "singulate" a particular tag, allowing its data to be read in the midst of many similar tags. In a slotted Aloha system, the reader broadcasts an initialization command and a parameter that the tags individually use to pseudorandomly delay their responses. When using an "adaptive binary tree" protocol, the reader sends an initialization symbol and then transmits one bit of ID data at a time; only tags with matching bits respond, and eventually only one tag matches the complete ID string.

---

[1] In electronics and telecommunications, modulation is the process of varying one or more properties of a high-frequency periodic <u>waveform</u> (['weɪvfɔːm]n. 波形), called the <u>carrier signal</u> (载波信号), with a modulating signal which typically contains information to be transmitted.

[2] Demodulation is the act of extracting the original information-bearing signal from a modulated carrier wave.

[3] The near field (or near-field) and far field (or far-field) and the transition zone are regions of time varying electromagnetic field around any object that serves as a source for the field.

[4] In physics, backscatter (or backscattering) is the reflection of waves, <u>particles</u> (['pɑːtɪkl]n. 粒子), or signals back to the direction from which they came. It is a diffuse reflection due to scattering, as opposed to <u>specular reflection</u> (镜面反射) like a mirror.

Both methods have drawbacks when used with many tags or with multiple overlapping readers.

2. Miniaturization

RFIDs are easy to conceal or incorporate in other items. For example, in 2009 researchers at Bristol University successfully glued RFID micro-transponders to live ants in order to study their behavior. This trend towards increasingly miniaturized RFIDs is likely to continue as technology advances.

Hitachi holds the record for the smallest RFID chip, at 0.05mm × 0.05mm. This is 1/64th the size of the previous record holder, the mu-chip. Manufacture is enabled by using the silicon-on-insulator[1] (SOI) process. These dust-sized chips can store 38-digit numbers using 128-bit Read Only Memory (ROM[2]). A major challenge is the attachment of the antennas, thus limiting read range to only millimeters.

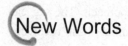

New Words

noncontact	[ˈnɔnˈkɔntækt]	adj. 没有接触的，非接触的
tag	[tæg]	n. 标签
		vt. 加标签于
track	[træk]	n. 轨迹，跟踪
		vt. 追踪
emit	[iˈmit]	vt. 发出，放射
yard	[jɑːd]	n. 码（长度单位）
reader	[ˈriːdə]	n. 阅读器，读卡机
livestock	[ˈlaivstɔk]	n. 家畜，牲畜
inject	[inˈdʒekt]	vt. 引入，插入，注入
implant	[imˈplɑːnt]	v. 植入，插入
label	[ˈleibl]	n. 标签，签条，标志
		vt. 贴标签于
identify	[aiˈdentifai]	vt. 识别，鉴别
interrogator	[inˈterəgeitə]	n. 询问器，询问机，侦测器
middleware	[ˈmidlwɛə]	n. 中间设备，中间件

[1] Silicon on insulator (SOI) technology refers to the use of a layered silicon-insulator-silicon substrate ([ˈsʌbstreit]n. 底层,下层,[) in place of conventional silicon substrates in semiconductor manufacturing, especially microelectronics ([ˈmaikrəui,lekˈtrɔniks]n.微电子学), to reduce parasitic ([,pærəˈsitik]adj.寄生的) device capacitance, thereby improving performance.

[2] Read-only memory (ROM) is a class of storage medium used in computers and other electronic devices. Data stored in ROM cannot be modified, or can be modified only slowly or with difficulty, so it is mainly used to distribute firmware (software that is very closely tied to specific hardware, and unlikely to need frequent updates).

nonvolatile	[ˈnɔnˈvɔlətail]	adj. 非易失性的
memory	[ˈmeməri]	n. 存储器，内存
encode	[inˈkəud]	vt. 编码，把（电文.情报等）译成电码（或密码）
interrogate	[inˈterəgeit]	vt. 询问
active	[ˈæktiv]	adj. 有源的
periodically	[ˌpiəriˈɔdikəli]	adv. 周期性地，定时性地
discriminate	[disˈkrimineit]	v. 区别，区别待遇
programmable	[ˈprəugræməbl]	adj. 可设计的，可编程的
modulate	[ˈmɔdjuleit]	vt.（信号）调制
demodulate	[diːˈmɔdjuːleit]	vt. 解调
incident	[ˈinsidənt]	n. 入射
tightly	[ˈtaitli]	adv. 紧紧地，坚固地
hand-held	[hænd-held]	adj. 手持的
incompatible	[ˌinkəmˈpætəbl]	adj. 不兼容的
band	[bænd]	n. 波段
wavelength	[ˈweivleŋθ]	n. 波长
approach	[əˈprəutʃ]	n. 方法，步骤，途径
backscatter	[bækˈskætə]	n. 反向散射，背反射
pallet	[ˈpælit]	n. 货盘
singulate	[ˈsiŋgjuleit]	vt. 挑出
pseudorandom	[ˌpsjuːdəuˈrændəm]	adj. 伪随机的
initialization	[iˌniʃəlaiˈzeiʃən]	n. 设定初值，初始化
miniaturization	[ˌminiətʃəraizeiʃən]	n. 小型化
transponder	[trænˈspɔndə]	n. 发射机应答器，询问机，转发器
miniaturize	[ˈminiətʃəraiz]	vt. 使小型化

Phrases

local power source	本地电源
electromagnetic radiation	电磁辐射
radio frequency	无线电频率
bar code	条形码
line of sight	视线，瞄准线
assembly line	（工厂产品的）装配线
radio signal	无线电信号
serial number	序号，序列号

stock number	物料编号
batch number	批号，批数
on-board battery	板载电池
in the presence of	在面前
read only	只读
write-once, read-multiple	单次写入多次读取（WORM）
integrated circuit	集成电路
interrogation zone	读取器询问区，侦测区
near field	近场
in the midst of	在……之中，在……的中途
binary tree	二叉树

Abbreviations

ID (IDentification, IDentity)	身份
BAP (Battery Assisted Passive)	电池辅助无源
DC (Direct Current)	直流电
LF (Low Frequency)	低频
HF (High Frequency)	高频
EPC (Electronic Product Code)	电子产品代码
EPCGlobal	国际物品编码协会（EAN）和美国统一代码委员会（UCC）的一个合资公司
SOI (Silicon-On-Insulator)	绝缘衬底上的硅
ROM (Read Only Memory)	只读存储器

Exercises

【EX.1】 **Fill in the blanks according to the text.**

1. Radio frequency identification (RFID) uses _____ that uses radio-frequency electromagnetic fields to transfer data from a tag attached to an object for the purposes of _____.

2. A radio frequency identification system uses _____ or _____ attached to the objects to be identified.

3. The tag's information is stored electronically in a _____. The RFID tag includes _____.

4. RFID tags can be either _____, _____ or _____. An active tag has _____ and periodically transmits its ID signal.

5. A passive tag is cheaper and smaller because _____. Instead, the tag uses the radio energy transmitted by _____ as its energy source.

6. RFID tags contain at least two parts: _____ for storing and processing information, modulating and demodulating a radio-frequency (RF) signal, collecting DC power from the incident reader signal, and other specialized functions; and _____ for receiving and transmitting the signal.

7. An Electronic Product Code (EPC) is _____ stored in a tag. When written into the tag by an RFID printer, the tag contains _____.

8. _____ can be used as a key into a global database to uniquely identify a particular product.

9. In a slotted Aloha system, the reader broadcasts _____ and _____ that the tags individually use to pseudorandomly delay their responses.

10. _____ holds the record for the smallest RFID chip, _____. This is 1/64th the size of the previous record holder, _____.

【EX.2】Translate the following terms or phrases from English into Chinese and vice versa.

1. bar code   1. _____
2. radio frequency   2. _____
3. local power source   3. _____
4. integrated circuit   4. _____
5. electromagnetic radiation   5. _____
6. near field   6. _____
7. noncontact   7. _____
8. radio signal   8. _____
9. track   9. _____
10. label   10. _____
11. vt. 识别，鉴别   11. _____
12. n. 中间设备，中间件   12. _____
13. adj. 非易失性的   13. _____
14. adj. 无源的   14. _____
15. adj. 有源的   15. _____

【EX.3】Translate the following sentences into Chinese.

1. Bar codes have replaced the traditional price tag in big stores.

2. Most often, the IBM disk-track format is used, sometimes with minor variations.

3. They also emit UHF waves of 225-400 MHz.

4. The photo-electric reader is capable of scanning characters at the rate of two thousand a second.

5. The development of data warehouse technology provides advantage for accomplishing

6. Label is a fixed length of 24 characters and contains standard information.

7. The middleware technology is effectively developed for resolving the distributed computing problems.

8. The ROM chip retains instructions in a permanently accessible, nonvolatile form.

9. The programmable controller (PLC) is used at abroad due to its higher reliability and convenient application.

10. This will also change according to the wavelength of the laser light.

Text C

What is Wireless Internet Service?

Broadband internet service is a form of high speed internet access. In fact, the name "broadband" has come to be synonymous[1] with high speed internet use in general. Since speed is measured by bit rate[2], the number of bits processed per unit of time, broadband internet service is defined as being 256 kbit/s (kilobits per second) or faster. Broadband typically downloads at a much faster speed than that, however. As a result, broadband internet service is categorized into two different connection groups: Tier 1 (T1) broadband connections range from 1.544 Mbit/s to 2.048 Mbit/s, and Tier 3 (T3) broadband connections range from 44.736 Mbit/s to 159.2 Gbit/s. With these rates of data transmission[3], broadband represents an evolution from the original high speed internet service, Integrated Services Digital Network (ISDN), and is by far a significant improvement upon the original internet service, dial-up.

The latest development in broadband internet service is the incorporation of wireless capabilities. Wireless broadband internet service is exactly what the name implies[4]: it is your high speed internet access without cables or wires. The versatility[5] of wireless internet and its potential for increasing productivity by users make consumers demand the service at an increasing rate. They want it in their home, at their office, even at their local coffee shop or bistro[6]. Hence the development of wireless broadband internet service: it is a packaged internet service deal that provides the ability to access the internet wirelessly from any location within the service's coverage

[1] [si'nɔniməs]
adj. 同义的

[2] bit rate：比特率

[3] data transmission：数据传输

[4] [im'plai]
vt. 暗示，意味

[5] [,və:sə'tiləti]
n. 多功能性

[6] ['bistrəu]
n. 小酒馆，小咖啡店

area[7].

1. Wireless Broadband Network

A term you may recognize in association with wireless broadband internet service includes wireless network. A wireless network is a single broadband internet arrangement established for your home or office. It requires several pieces of equipment that are all one-time cost items: a wireless transceiver, such as a wireless card or antenna, and a wireless router. In addition, you will have to purchase the broadband service, which is a continual[8] expense. You cannot utilize your wireless broadband tools without an ongoing broadband service. Together, the wireless devices and the broadband internet service make up your wireless broadband network. When employed, the network will send data to your broadband internet connection via these wireless tools that utilize a special wireless technology (known as WiFi). As a result you will be able to access the internet from anywhere inside the coverage area, as determined by the location of your wireless router.

2. Wireless Broadband Service

Wireless broadband internet service is growing in popularity[9] for locations outside the home or office as well. When considering broadband, another term you may recognize is wireless internet service. Although often used interchangeably[10] with wireless network, the two do not mean the same thing. Wireless broadband internet service generally refers to a package deal[11] that combines both the wireless technology and broadband service, and to which you can subscribe to. It differs from the wireless network in two ways: 1) it includes both technology and service, whereas having a wireless network necessitates your having to buy both, and 2) it is generally used in larger locations outside the home or office, such as the downtown area of a city or a college campus.

Areas that provide wireless broadband internet service are known as hotspots[12]. Starbucks Coffee and Borders Books are two common retailers that feature internet hotspots. Downtown areas in larger cities and major airports are two common public areas that also feature internet hotspots. They all provide wireless broadband internet service. The service is mostly utilized by laptop computers and handheld devices that are "wireless ready", meaning they are capable of connecting to the internet via internal or external wireless devices or cards. However, they require a paid subscription to the broadband

---

[7] coverage area:
有效区域

[8] [kən'tinjuəl]
adj. 连续的,频繁的

[9] [ˌpɔpju'læriti]
n. 普及,流行

[10] [ˌintə'tʃeindʒəbli]
adv. 可交地,可替交地

[11] package deal:
一揽子业务

[12] ['hɔtspɔt]
n. 热点,热区

service intended especially for this wireless use.

3. Wireless Broadband Mobile

Wireless internet connectivity[13] in cell phones is growing in popularity as well. Cell phones, and other devices featuring windows mobile applications, are now all being designed with advanced wireless technology. This offers them the ability to connect to a wireless broadband internet service, or to the internet via their own cellular phone network. EDGE and EVDO are two of the more popular next-generation mobile system technologies utilized by cellular phone developers.

EDGE[14] (Enhanced Data rates for GSM Evolution) was introduced into the North American via GSM[15] (Global Systems Mobile) networks in 2003 and is now available worldwide. EDGE increases data transmission rates and improves transmission reliability[16] in mobile devices that use it. More importantly, it allows the mobile device to connect to the Internet wirelessly, but its download speed is significantly slower than other mobile wireless technologies. EDGE transmits data at approximately 236.8 kbit/s, which is below the standard for a broadband connection. However, its theoretical maximum speed is 473.6 kbit/s, so it is still considered a wireless broadband technology.

EVDO[17] (Evolution-Data Optimized) is significantly faster than EDGE. It transmits data via radio signals, and for this reason is classified as a wireless broadband technology. It is employed in mobile devices around the world via CDMA[18] (Code Division Multiple Access) networks: cellular networks that achieve high data transmission speeds and support a vast number of users.

WiMAX is an emerging wireless broadband technology whose download speeds are approximately 10 Mb/s. It is expected to be within the 40 Mb/s range by next year. There is currently only one major WiMAX provider due to the fact that it must be run on its own network: it cannot utilize GSM or CDMA networks as EDGE and EVDO do. However there are plans for widespread WiMax commercial deployment by 2010, and will be marketed as a significantly advanced wireless alternative to Cable and DSL internet services.

---

[13][kənek'tiviti]
n. 连通性

[14] 增强型数据速率 GSM 演进技术
[15] 全球通
[16] transmission reliability:
传输可靠性

[17] 演进数据最优化

[18] 码分多址

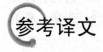

Text A 无线网络如何工作

无线网络或无线局域网与有线网络的用途一样——把一组计算机连接起来。因为"无线"不需要昂贵的布线，所以其主要优点在于更容易、更快速和更廉价地组建网络。

相比而言，通过在办公室天花板和墙壁布线来组建网络更费人力，因此也花费更大。即使在某个地方已经布置了有线网络，无线网络也是扩展网络的有效方法。实际上，也不存在纯粹的无线网络，因为大多数无线网络都在某一点连回有线网络。

1. 基础

无线网络使用 RF（无线频率）技术，RF 是与无线电波传播相关的电磁频谱中的频率。当一个 RF 电流提供给天线时，一个电磁场就产生了，随后能通过空间传播。

无线网络的基础是一个叫作访问接入点（AP）的设备。访问接入点的主要任务是广播可以被计算机发现和"收听"到的无线信号。因为无线网络通常连到有线网络，访问接入点通常也起连接到有线网络的有效资源的作用，如连接到因特网。

要连接到访问接入点并与无线网络连接，计算机必须配置无线网络适配器。这些适配器通常内置于计算机中。如果没有内置，也可以在计算机的空扩展槽或 USB 接口插入适配器，或在笔记本计算机的 PC 卡槽加上它。这样几乎所有的计算机或笔记本都可以无线联网了。

2. 无线技术标准

因为无线网络有多个技术标准，因此在购买计算机之前一定要做足功课。最常见的无线技术标准包括以下几种：

- 802.11b：第一个广泛使用的无线组网技术，叫作 802.11b（更普遍地叫作 WiFi），已经出现了十余年了，但仍还在用。
- 802.11g：2003 年出现了叫作 802.11g 的后续版本，它提供了更好的性能（即速度和范围），依然是如今最常用的无线组网技术。
- 802.11n：另一个改进的标准叫作 802.11n，目前还在开发中。但即使 802.11n 标准还在完善，仍然可以购买基于 802.11n 标准草案的产品，在标准完成后可以升级。

各种 WiFi（802.11b、g 和 n）都使用 2.4 GHz 的无线电频率，因此它们都被设计成相互兼容，所以可以在同一无线网络中使用不同标准的产品。如此一来，通常为了适应早期的设备要进行专门的配置，这也会相应地降低网络的整体性能。理想的情况是，全部无线网络设备、访问接入点和具有无线联网能力的全部计算机都使用相同的技术标准，并尽可能从一个销售商处购买。

3. 无线速度和范围

当购买一些无线网络硬件时，通常会提供基于所用无线组网标准的性能配置（传输数据的速率），还加上一些增强的技术。实际上，这些性能几乎总是被严重地夸大了。

802.11b、802.11g 和 802.11n 网络的官方速度分别是 11、54 和 270Mb/s，而这种速度在现实中简直无法实现。作为一般规律，可以认为在最理想的情况下，实现广告所宣称的三分之一性能。

还有一个值得重视的问题是无线网络被定义为共享网络，因此连入无线访问接入点的计算机越多，每个计算机能够收发的数据就越少。正如无线网络的速度可以有很多变化一样，其范围也可以改变。例如，802.11b 和 g 正式的工作距离高达室内 328 英尺或室外 1312 英尺，但关键术语是"高达"，在现实中可能永远都接近不了这个数。

如所希望的，离访问接入点越近，信号就越强而且连接速度也更快。得到的无线网络范围和速度也取决于运行的环境，而这就带来干扰问题。

4．无线干扰

在所有无线电通信中都存在干扰问题，无线网络也不例外。潜在的干涉在室内尤其严重，各种建筑材料（如混凝土、木头、纸面石膏板、金属、玻璃等）都可以吸收和反射无线电波，从而影响无线网络信号的强度和连续性。同样，像微波炉和无绳电话这样的设备也能产生干扰，因为它们运行在 2.4 频段，与 802.11b/g/n 网络一样。你不能完全避免干扰，但大多数情况下这不足以影响网络的可用性。如果有影响，通常可以通过重新部署无线组网硬件和使用特制天线使干扰最小化。

5．无线网络的数据安全

有一台收音机才能接收当地无线电台，同样，要检测附近的无线网络也需要一台装备了无线设备的计算机。无法把网络对陌生人隐藏起来，但可以阻止未经授权的人连接到网络，并保护在网络中传输的数据不被偷窥。通过打开无线网络的加密功能，可以搅乱数据并控制对网络的访问。

无线网络硬件支持几种标准加密方案，但最常用的是 WEP、WPA 和 WPA2。WEP 最老并且安全性最差，应尽量不用。WPA 和 WPA2 是一个好的选择，当使用更长的和更复杂的密码时可以提供很好的保护（同一无线网络中的全部设备必须使用相同的加密方法并配置相同的密码）。

除非打算让公众访问你的无线网络——把你的业务数据或个人数据置于危险中——否则你应该考虑强制使用加密技术。

Unit 8

Text A

WiFi

WiFi is a popular technology that allows an electronic device to exchange data wirelessly (using radio waves[1]) over a computer network, including high-speed Internet connections. The WiFi Alliance defines WiFi as any "wireless local area network (WLAN) products that are based on the Institute of Electrical and Electronics Engineers'(IEEE) 802.11 standards". However, since most modern WLANs are based on these standards, the term "WiFi" is used in general English as a synonym for "WLAN".

A device that can use WiFi (such as a personal computer, video-game console, smartphone, tablet, or digital audio player) can connect to a network resource such as the Internet via a wireless network access point. Such an access point (or hotspot[2]) has a range of about 20 meters (65 feet) indoors and a greater range outdoors. Hotspot coverage can comprise an area as small as a single room with walls that block radio waves or as large as many square miles -- this is achieved by using multiple overlapping access points.

1. Uses

To connect to a WiFi LAN, a computer has to be equipped with a wireless network interface controller[3]. The combination of computer and interface controller is called a station. All stations share a single radio frequency communication channel. Transmissions on this channel are received by all stations within range. The hardware does not signal the user that the

---

[1] Radio waves are a type of <u>electromagnetic radiation</u> (电磁辐射) with <u>wavelengths</u> (['weivleŋθ] n. 波长) in the <u>electromagnetic spectrum</u> (电磁波频谱) longer than infrared light.

[2] A hotspot is a site that offers Internet access over a wireless local area network through the use of a router connected to a link to an Internet service provider. Hotspots typically use WiFi technology.

[3] A wireless network interface controller (WNIC) is a network interface controller which connects to a radio-based computer network rather than a wire-based network such as Token Ring or Ethernet. A WNIC, just like other NICs, works on the Layer 1 and Layer 2 of the OSI Model.

transmission was delivered and is therefore called a best-effort delivery mechanism. A carrier wave is used to transmit the data in packets, referred to as "Ethernet frames[1]". Each station is constantly tuned in on the radio frequency communication channel to pick up available transmissions.

1.1 Internet Access

A WiFi-enabled device can connect to the Internet when within range of a wireless network. The coverage of one or more (interconnected) access points -- called hotspots -- can extend from an area as small as a few rooms to as large as many square miles. Coverage in the larger area may require a group of access points with overlapping coverage. Outdoor public WiFi technology has been used successfully in wireless mesh networks in London, UK.

WiFi provides service in private homes, high street chains and independent businesses, as well as in public spaces. Organizations and businesses, such as airports, hotels, and restaurants, often provide free-use hotspots to attract customers. Enthusiasts or authorities who wish to provide services or even to promote business in selected areas sometimes provide free WiFi access.

Routers that incorporate a digital subscriber line modem or a cable modem and a WiFi access point often set up in homes and other buildings, provide Internet access and internetworking to all devices connected to them, wirelessly or via cable.

Similarly, there are battery-powered routers that include a cellular mobile Internet radio modem and WiFi access point. When subscribed to a cellular phone carrier, they allow nearby WiFi stations to access the Internet over 2G, 3G, or 4G networks. Many smartphones have a built-in capability of this sort, including those based on Android, Bada, iOS (iPhone), and Symbian, though carriers often disable the feature, or charge a separate fee to enable it, especially for customers with unlimited data plans. "Internet pucks" provide standalone facilities of this type as well, without use of a smartphone; examples include the MiFi[2]- and WiBro-branded devices. Some laptops that have a cellular modem card can also act as mobile Internet WiFi access points.

An outdoor WiFi access point

WiFi also connects places that normally don't

---

[1] A <u>data packet</u> (数据包) on an Ethernet link is called an Ethernet frame. A frame begins with preamble and start frame <u>delimiter</u> ([diːˈlimitə]n.定界符，分隔符). Following which, each Ethernet frame continues with an Ethernet header featuring destination and source MAC addresses. The middle section of the frame is <u>payload</u> ([ˈpeiˌləud]n.有效载荷) data including any headers for other protocols (e.g. Internet Protocol) carried in the frame. The frame ends with a 32-bit <u>cyclic redundancy check</u> (循环冗余码校验) which is used to detect any <u>corruption</u> ([kəˈrʌpʃən]n.错误) of data in transit.

[2] MiFi used as a name for wireless routers that act as mobile WiFi hotspots.

have network access, such as kitchens and garden sheds.

1.1.1 City-wide WiFi

In the early 2000s, many cities around the world announced plans to construct city-wide WiFi networks. There are many successful examples; in 2004, Mysore became India's first WiFi-enabled city and second in the world after Jerusalem. A company called WiFiyNet has set up hotspots in Mysore, covering the complete city and a few nearby villages.

In 2005, Sunnyvale, California, became the first city in the United States to offer city-wide free WiFi, and Minneapolis has generated $1.2 million in profit annually for its provider.

In May 2010, London, UK, Mayor Boris Johnson pledged to have London-wide WiFi by 2012. Several boroughs including Westminster and Islington already have extensive outdoor WiFi coverage.

Officials in Korea's capital are moving to provide free Internet access at more than 10,000 locations around the city, including outdoor public spaces, major streets and densely populated residential areas. Seoul will grant leases to KT, LG Telecom and SK Telecom. The companies will invest $44 million in the project, which will be completed in 2015.

1.1.2 Campus-wide WiFi

Many traditional college campuses in the United States provide at least partial wireless WiFi Internet coverage. Carnegie Mellon University built the first campus-wide wireless Internet network, called Wireless Andrew at its Pittsburgh campus in 1993 before WiFi branding originated.

In 2000, Drexel University in Philadelphia became the United States' first major university to offer completely wireless Internet access across its entire campus.

The Far Eastern University in Manila is the first university in the Philippines to implement a campus-wide WiFi coverage for its students, faculty, and staff. St Xavier's College in Calcutta, India has recently implemented WiFi coverage at its campus.

1.2 Direct Computer-to-computer Communications

WiFi also allows communications directly from one computer to another without an access point intermediary. This is called ad hoc WiFi transmission. This wireless ad hoc network mode has proven popular with multiplayer handheld game consoles, such as the Nintendo DS, PlayStation Portable, digital cameras, and other consumer electronics devices. Some devices can also share their Internet connection using ad-hoc, becoming hotspots or "virtual routers".

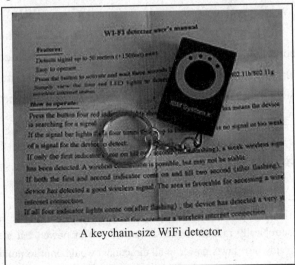

A keychain-size WiFi detector

2. Advantages and Limitations

2.1 Advantages

WiFi allows cheaper deployment of local area networks (LANs). Also spaces where cables cannot be run, such as outdoor areas and historical buildings, can host wireless LANs.

Manufacturers are building wireless network adapters into most laptops. The price of chipsets for WiFi continues to drop, making it an economical networking option included in even more devices.

Different competitive brands of access points and client network-interfaces can inter-operate at a basic level of service. Products designated as "WiFi Certified" by the WiFi Alliance are backwards compatible. Unlike mobile phones, any standard WiFi device will work anywhere in the world.

WiFi Protected Access encryption (WPA[1]) is considered secure, provided a strong passphrase is used. New protocols for quality of service (WMM) make WiFi more suitable for latency-sensitive applications (such as voice and video). Power saving mechanisms (WMM Power Save) extend battery life.

2.2 Limitations

Spectrum assignments and operational limitations are not consistent worldwide: most of Europe allows for an additional two channels beyond those permitted in the US for the 2.4 GHz band (1-13 vs. 1-11), while Japan has one more on top of that (1-14). As of 2007, Europe is essentially homogeneous in this respect.

A WiFi signal occupies five channels in the 2.4 GHz band. Any two channels numbers that differ by five or more, such as 2 and 7, do not overlap. The oft-repeated adage that channels 1, 6, and 11 are the only non-overlapping channels is, therefore, not accurate. Channels 1, 6, and 11 are the only group of three non-overlapping channels in the U.S. In Europe and Japan using Channels 1, 5, 9, and 13 for 802.11g and n is recommended.

Equivalent isotropically radiated power (EIRP[2]) in the EU is limited to 20 dBm (100 mW).

The current 'fastest' norm, 802.11n, uses double the radio spectrum/bandwidth (40 MHz) compared to 802.11a or 802.11g (20 MHz). This means there can be only one 802.11n network on the 2.4 GHz band at a given location, without interference to/from other WLAN traffic. 802.11n can also be set to use 20 MHz bandwidth only to prevent interference in dense

---

[1] WiFi Protected Access (WPA) and Wi-Fi Protected Access II (WPA2) are two security protocols and security certification programs developed by the WiFi Alliance to secure wireless computer networks. The Alliance defined these in response to serious weaknesses researchers had found in the previous system, WEP (Wired Equivalent Privacy).

[2] In radio communication systems, equivalent isotropically radiated power (EIRP) or, alternatively, effective isotropically radiated power is the amount of power that a theoretical isotropic antenna (全向天线) (which evenly distributes power in all directions) would emit to produce the peak power (峰值功率) density observed in the direction of maximum antenna gain ([geɪn]n. 增益). EIRP can take into account the losses in transmission line (传输线) and connectors and includes the gain of the antenna.

community.

2.3 Range

WiFi networks have limited range. A typical wireless access point using 802.11b or 802.11g with a stock antenna might have a range of 32 m (120 ft) indoors and 95 m (300 ft) outdoors. IEEE 802.11n, however, can more than double the range. Range also varies with frequency band. WiFi in the 2.4 GHz frequency block has slightly better range than WiFi in the 5 GHz frequency block which is used by 802.11a and optionally by 802.11n. On wireless routers with detachable antennas, it is possible to improve range by fitting upgraded antennas which have higher gain in particular directions. Outdoor ranges can be improved to many kilometers through the use of high gain directional antennas at the router and remote device(s). In general, the maximum amount of power that a WiFi device can transmit is limited by local regulations, such as FCC Part 15 in the US.

Due to reach requirements for wireless LAN applications, WiFi has fairly high power consumption compared to some other standards. Technologies such as Bluetooth (designed to support wireless PAN[1] applications) provide a much shorter propagation range of <10m and so in general have a lower power consumption. Other low-power technologies such as ZigBee have fairly long range, but much lower data rate. The high power consumption of WiFi makes battery life in mobile devices a concern.

Researchers have developed a number of "no new wires" technologies to provide alternatives to WiFi for applications in which WiFi's indoor range is not adequate and where installing new wires (such as CAT-5[2]) is not possible or cost-effective. For example, the ITU-T G.hn standard for high speed local area networks uses existing home wiring (coaxial cables, phone lines and power lines). Although G.hn does not provide some of the advantages of WiFi (such as mobility or outdoor use), it's designed for applications (such as IPTV[3] distribution) where indoor range is more important than mobility.

Due to the complex nature of radio propagation at typical WiFi frequencies, particularly the

---

[1] A personal area network (PAN) is a computer network used for communication among computerized ([kəm'pju:təraiz] vt. 用计算机处理，使计算机化) devices, including telephones and personal digital assistants (个人数字助理). PANs can be used for communication among the personal devices themselves (intrapersonal communication), or for connecting to a higher level network and the Internet (an uplink (['ʌp,liŋk] n. 向上传输,上行线)).

[2] Category 5 cable (Cat 5) is a twisted pair (双绞线) cable for carrying signals. This type of cable is used in structured cabling for computer networks such as Ethernet. The cable standard provides performance of up to 100 MHz and is suitable for 10BASE-T, 100BASE-TX (Fast Ethernet.快速以太网), and 1000BASE-T (Gigabit Ethernet). Cat 5 is also used to carry other signals such as telephony and video. In some cases, multiple signals can be carried on a single cable; Cat 5 can carry two conventional telephone lines as well as a single 100BASE-TX channel in a single cable or two 100BASE-TX channels in a single cable.

[3] IPTV is a system through which television services are delivered using the Internet protocol suite over a packet-switched network such as the Internet, instead of being delivered through traditional terrestrial ([ti'restriəl] adj. 陆地的), satellite signal, and cable television formats.

effects of signal reflection off trees and buildings, algorithms can only approximately predict WiFi signal strength for any given area in relation to a transmitter. This effect does not apply equally to long-range WiFi, since longer links typically operate from towers that transmit above the surrounding foliage.

The practical range of WiFi essentially confines mobile use to such applications as inventory-taking machines in warehouses or in retail spaces, barcode-reading devices at check-out stands, or receiving/shipping stations. Mobile use of WiFi over wider ranges is limited, for instance, to uses such as in an automobile moving from one hotspot to another. Other wireless technologies are more suitable for communicating with moving vehicles.

2.4 Data Security Risks

The most common wireless encryption-standard, Wired Equivalent Privacy (WEP), has been shown to be easily breakable even when correctly configured. WiFi Protected Access (WPA and WPA2) encryption, which became available in devices in 2003, aimed to solve this problem. WiFi access points typically default to an encryption-free (open) mode. Novice users benefit from a zero-configuration device that works out of the box, but this default does not enable any wireless security, providing open wireless access to a LAN. To turn security on requires the user to configure the device, usually via a software graphical user interface (GUI). On unencrypted WiFi networks connecting devices can monitor and record data (including personal information). Such networks can only be secured by using other means of protection, such as a VPN or secure Hypertext Transfer Protocol (HTTP) over Transport Layer Security.

2.5 Interference

WiFi connections can be disrupted or the internet speed lowered by having other devices in the same area. Many 2.4 GHz 802.11b and 802.11g access-points default to the same channel on initial startup, contributing to congestion on certain channels. WiFi pollution, or an excessive number of access points in the area, especially on the neighboring channel, can prevent access and interfere with other devices' use of other access points. This can become a problem in high-density areas, such as large apartment complexes or office buildings with many WiFi access points.

Additionally, other devices use the 2.4 GHz band: microwave ovens, ISM band[1] devices, security cameras, ZigBee devices, Bluetooth devices, video senders, cordless phones, baby monitors, and (in some countries) Amateur radio, all of which can cause significant additional interference. It is also an issue when municipalities or other large entities (such as universities) seek to provide large area coverage.

---

[1] The industrial, scientific and medical (ISM) radio bands are radio bands (portions of the radio spectrum) reserved internationally for the use of radio frequency energy for industrial, scientific and medical purposes other than communications.

New Words

alliance	[əˈlaiəns]	n. 联盟，联合
tablet	[ˈtæblit]	n. 平板计算机
block	[blɔk]	vt. 妨碍，阻塞
overlap	[ˈəuvəˈlæp]	v.（与……）交迭
interface	[ˈintə(:),feis]	n. 界面，接口
controller	[kənˈtrəulə]	n. 控制器
channel	[ˈtʃænl]	n. 信道，频道
hardware	[ˈhɑ:dwɛə]	n.（计算机的）硬件，（电子仪器的）部件
Ethernet	[ˈi:θənet]	n. 以太网
frame	[freim]	n. 帧，框架
constantly	[ˈkɔnstəntli]	adv. 不变地，经常地
interconnect	[,intə(:)kəˈnekt]	vt. 使互相连接
enthusiast	[inˈθju:ziæst]	n. 热心者，狂热者
authority	[ɔ:ˈθɔriti]	n. 权威，威信，权威人士
cable	[ˈkeibl]	n. 电缆
disable	[disˈeibl]	v. 使失去能力
puck	[pʌk]	n. 恶作剧的小妖精
pledge	[pledʒ]	vt. 保证，发誓
grant	[grɑ:nt]	vt. 同意，准予
faculty	[ˈfækəlti]	n. 全体教员
campus	[ˈkæmpəs]	n. 校园
intermediary	[,intəˈmi:diəri]	n. 中间物 adj. 中间的，媒介的
multiplayer	[ˈmʌltiˈpleiə]	n. 多玩家
virtual	[ˈvə:tjuəl]	adj. 虚的，虚拟的
manufacturer	[,mænjuˈfæktʃərə]	n. 制造业者，厂商
chipset	[ˈtʃipset]	n. 芯片集
passphrase	[ˈpɑ:sfreiz]	n. 密码短语口令
homogeneous	[,hɔməuˈdʒi:njəs]	adj. 同类的，相似的，均一的，均匀的
adage	[ˈædidʒ]	n. 格言，谚语
norm	[nɔ:m]	n. 标准，规范
interference	[,intəˈfiərəns]	n. 冲突，干涉
stock	[stɔk]	adj. 普通的，常备的
detachable	[diˈtætʃəbl]	adj. 可分开的，可分离的
fitting	[ˈfitiŋ]	n. 装配，装置

adequate	[ˈædikwit]	adj.	适当的，足够的
reflection	[riˈflekʃən]	n.	反射
algorithm	[ˈælgəriðəm]	n.	算法
surrounding	[səˈraundiŋ]	n.	围绕物，环境
		adj.	周围的
foliage	[ˈfəuliidʒ]	n.	植物
confine	[ˈkɔnfain]	vt.	限制，禁闭
		n.	界限，边界
breakable	[ˈbreikəbəl]	adj.	易攻破的
default	[diˈfɔːlt]	n.	默认（值），缺省（值）
disrupt	[disˈrʌpt]	v.	使中断，使分裂，破坏
congestion	[kənˈdʒestʃən]	n.	拥塞
pollution	[pəˈluːʃən]	n.	污染

Phrases

video-game console	视频游戏控制台
digital audio player	数字音频播放机
wireless network access point	无线网络接入点
communication channel	通信电路，信道
best-effort delivery mechanism	尽力传输机制
carrier wave	载波
tune in	收听
pick up	捡起，获得
digital subscriber line	数字用户线
densely populated residential areas	人口稠密居民区
digital camera	数码相机
backwards compatible	向后兼容
quality of service	服务质量
Latency-Sensitive Application	传输延迟的网路应用
differ by	相差
limited range	有限范围
vary with …	随……而变化
directional antenna	指向天线，定向天线
local regulation	局部调节
coaxial cable	同轴电缆
power line	电力线，输电线
signal strength	信号强度

in relation to	关于，涉及，与……相比
out of the box	开箱即用
microwave oven	微波炉
video sender	视频传输装置

Abbreviations

WiFi (WIreless FIdelity)	无线保真
WME (Wireless Multimedia Extension)	无线多媒体扩展
EIRP (Equivalent isotropically radiated power)	等效全向辐射功率
EU (Energy Unit)	能量单位
FCC (Federal Communications Commission)	（美国）通信委员会
IPTV (Internet Protocol television)	网络电视
GUI (Graphical User Interface)	图形用户界面
VPN (Virtual Private Network)	虚拟个人网络
HTTP (Hypertext Transfer Protocol)	超文本传输协议
ISM (Industrial, Scientific and Medical)	工业，科学和医学

Exercises

【EX.1】Answer the following questions according to the text.

1. What does the WiFi Alliance define WiFi as?

2. What does a computer have to be equipped with in order to connect to a WiFi LAN?

3. What do the routers allow nearby WiFi stations to do when subscribed to a cellular phone carrier?

4. Which city in the United States was the first city which offered city-wide free WiFi? When?

5. Who built the first campus-wide wireless Internet network? What was it called?

6. Which university is the first in the Philippines to implement a campus-wide WiFi coverage for its students, faculty, and staff?

7. WiFi Certified products only work in certain places, don't they?

8. How many channels does a WiFi signal occupy in the 2.4 GHz band? What range does a typical wireless access point using 802.11b or 802.11g with a stock antenna might have?

9. What is the most common wireless encryption-standard?

10. What can disrupt WiFi connections or lower the internet speed?

【EX.2】 Translate the following terms or phrases from English into Chinese and vice versa.

1. wireless network access point
2. carrier wave
3. backwards compatible
4. communication channel
5. latency-sensitive application
6. directional antenna
7. block
8. interface
9. coaxial cable
10. frame
11. n. 装置，设备
12. vt. 使互相连接
13. v. 使失去能力
14. n. 芯片集
15. n. 算法

【EX.3】 Translate the following sentences into Chinese.

1. Notebook and Tablet PC batteries are usually of the Smart Lithium-Ion type.
2. The result of experiment embodied the fine control property of the controller.
3. Ethernet adapters allow users to share files and printing capabilities over a network at high transfers rates.
4. Users say these developmental tools transform interconnect operations into standard data programming.
5. PCI bus can interconnect peripheral components with CPU.
6. The masses of Java virtual machines (JVM) are implemented in software.
7. Motherboard chipset cannot cache the whole system memory.
8. Numeric simulation indicates that this algorithm is effective and feasible.
9. How to change the default port number for FTP Server?
10. Into increase the capacity of channel, the frequency of carrier wave moved to higher endlessly.

【EX.4】 Complete the following passage with appropriate words or expressions in the box.

| configurations | compatible | ensure | spectrum | plug |
| broadcasting | regulation | modem | marketing | center |

"WiFi" stands for "wireless fidelity". This is a __1__ name and bares no relation particularly to the technology. WiFi networks use the 2.4 GHz radio __2__ to transmit data. For comparison's sake your mobile phone operates at around 800 Mhz and FM radio operates at up to 100 MHz.

At the __3__ of a WiFi network is the WiFi router. Although routers come in many __4__, one of the most flexible arrangements is an ADSL __5__, Ethernet router and WiFi base station all rolled into one device.

This gives you the fall back position of Ethernet or the ability to __6__ in a non WiFi network printer. For security reasons you should __7__ your WiFi router is capable of NAT, WPA and the ability to turn off SSID __8__.

There are a number of standards in WiFi; a, b & g. G is the current standard. Many g devices are backwardly __9__ with b devices. WiFi is a global standard and now there are many manufacturers of WiFi products; thus the price has come down in recent years.

Different countries have different supervision systems concerning WiFi. There are more __10__ in Australia than in the United States.

【EX.5】 Translate the following passage into Chinese.

What is WiFi?

WiFi (short for "wireless fidelity") is a term for certain types of wireless local area network (WLAN) that use specifications in the 802.11 family. The term WiFi was created by an organization called the WiFi Alliance, which oversees tests that certify product interoperability. A product that passes the alliance tests is given the label "WiFi certified" (a registered trademark).

Originally, WiFi certification was applicable only to products using the 802.11b standard. Today, WiFi can apply to products that use any 802.11 standard. The 802.11 specifications are part of an evolving set of wireless network standards known as the 802.11 family. WiFi has gained acceptance in many businesses, agencies, schools, and homes as an alternative to a wired LAN. Many airports, hotels, and fast-food facilities offer public access to WiFi networks. These locations are known as hot spots. Many charge a daily or hourly rate for access, but some are free. An interconnected area of hot spots and network access points is known as a hot zone.

Unless adequately protected, a WiFi network can be susceptible to access by unauthorized users who use the access as a free Internet connection. Any entity that has a wireless LAN should use security safeguards such as the Wired Equivalent Privacy (WEP) encryption standard, the more recent WiFi Protected Access (WPA), Internet Protocol Security (IPSec), or a virtual private network (VPN).

How Bluetooth Works

When you use computers, entertainment systems or telephones, the various pieces and parts of the systems make up a community of electronic devices. These devices communicate with each other using a variety of wires, cables, radio signals and infrared light beams, and an even greater variety of connectors, plugs and protocols.

There are lots of different ways that electronic devices can connect to one another. For example:

- Component cables
- Electrical wires
- Ethernet cables
- WiFi
- Infrared signals

The art of connecting things is becoming more and more complex every day. In this passage, we will look at a method of connecting devices, called Bluetooth, which can streamline the process. A Bluetooth connection is wireless and automatic, and it has a number of interesting features that can simplify our daily lives.

1. The Problem

When any two devices need to talk to each other, they have to agree on a number of points before the conversation can begin. The first point of agreement is physical: Will they talk over wires, or through some form of wireless signals? If they use wires, how many are required--one, two, eight, 25? Once the physical attributes are decided, several more questions arise:

- How much data will be sent at a time? For instance, serial ports send data 1 bit at a time, while parallel ports send several bits at once.

- How will they speak to each other? All the parties in an electronic discussion need to know what the bits mean and whether the message they receive is the same message that was sent. This means developing a set of commands and responses known as a protocol.

Bluetooth offers a solution to the problem.

2. How Bluetooth Creates a Connection

Bluetooth takes small-area networking to the next level by removing the need for user intervention and keeping transmission power extremely low to save battery power. Picture this: You're on your Bluetooth-enabled cell phone, standing outside the door to your house. You tell the person on the other end of the line to call you back in five minutes so you can get in the house and put your stuff away. As soon as you walk in the house, the map you received on your cell phone from your car's Bluetooth-enabled GPS[1] system is automatically sent to your

---

[1] The Global Positioning System (GPS) is a space-based satellite navigation system that provides location and time information in all weather (全天候) conditions, anywhere on or near the Earth where there is an unobstructed (['ʌnəb'strʌktid] adj. 没有障碍的，畅通无阻的) line of sight to four or more GPS satellites.

Bluetooth-enabled comphuter, because your cell phone picked up a Bluetooth signal from your PC and automatically sent the data you designated for transfer. Five minutes later, when your friend calls you back, your Bluetooth-enabled home phone rings instead of your cell phone. The person calls the same number, but your home phone picks up the Bluetooth signal from your cell phone and automatically rerouted the call because it realizes you are home. And each transmission signal to and from your cell phone consumes just 1 milliwatt of power, so your cell phone charge is virtually unaffected by all of this activity.

Bluetooth is essentially a networking standard that works at two levels:

- It provides agreement at the physical level--Bluetooth is a radio-frequency standard.
- It provides agreement at the protocol level, where products have to agree on when bits are sent, how many will be sent at a time, and how the parties in a conversation can be sure that the message received is the same as the message sent.

The big draws of Bluetooth are that it is wireless, inexpensive and automatic. The older Bluetooth 1.0 standard has a maximum transfer speed of 1 megabit per second (Mbps), while Bluetooth 2.0 can manage up to 3 Mbps. Bluetooth 2.0 is backward compatible with 1.0 devices.

3. How Bluetooth Operates

Bluetooth networking transmits data via low-power radio waves. It communicates on a frequency of 2.45 gigahertz (actually between 2.402 GHz and 2.480 GHz, to be exact). This frequency band has been set aside by international agreement for the use of industrial, scientific and medical devices(ISM).

A number of devices that you may already use take advantage of this same radio-frequency band. Baby monitors, garage-door openers and the newest generation of cordless phones all make use of frequencies in the ISM band. Making sure that Bluetooth and these other devices don't interfere with one another has been a crucial part of the design process.

One of the ways Bluetooth devices avoid interfering with other systems is by sending out very weak signals of about 1 milliwatt. By comparison, the most powerful cell phones can transmit a signal of 3 watts. The low power limits the range of a Bluetooth device to about 10 meters, cutting the chances of interference between your computer system and your portable telephone or television. Even with the low power, Bluetooth does not require line of sight between communicating devices. The walls in your house won't stop a Bluetooth signal, making the standard useful for controlling several devices in different rooms.

Bluetooth can connect up to eight devices simultaneously. With all of those devices in the same 10-meter radius, you might think they'd interfere with one another, but it's unlikely. Bluetooth uses a technique called spread-spectrum frequency hopping that makes it rare for more than one device to be transmitting on the same frequency at the same time. In this technique, a device will use 79 individual, randomly chosen frequencies within a designated range, changing from one to another on a regular basis. In the case of Bluetooth, the transmitters change frequencies 1,600 times every second, meaning that more devices can make full use of a limited slice of the radio spectrum[1]. Since every Bluetooth transmitter uses spread-spectrum transmitting automatically, it's unlikely that two transmitters will be on the same frequency at the same time. This same technique minimizes the risk that portable phones or baby monitors will disrupt Bluetooth devices, since any interference on a particular frequency will last only a tiny fraction of a second.

When Bluetooth-capable devices come within range of one another, an electronic conversation takes place to determine whether they have data to share or whether one needs to control the other. The user doesn't have to press a button or give a command -- the electronic conversation happens automatically. Once the conversation has occurred, the devices -- whether they're part of a computer system or a stereo -- form a network. Bluetooth systems create a personal-area network (PAN), or piconet, that may fill a room or may encompass no more distance than that between the cell phone on a belt-clip and the headset on your head. Once a piconet is established, the members randomly hop frequencies in unison so they stay in touch with one another and avoid other piconets that may be operating in the same room.

4. Bluetooth Piconets[2]

Let's say you have a typical modern living room with typical modern stuff inside. There's an entertainment system with a stereo, a DVD player, a satellite TV receiver and a television; there's also a cordless telephone and a personal computer. Each of these systems uses Bluetooth, and each forms its own piconet to talk between the main unit and peripheral.

The cordless telephone has one Bluetooth transmitter in the base and the other in the handset. The manufacturer has programmed each unit with an address that falls into a range of addresses it has established for a particular type of device. When the base is first turned on, it sends radio signals asking for a response from any units with an address in a particular range. Since the handset has an address in the range, it responds, and a tiny network is formed. Now, even if one of these devices should receive a signal from another system, it will ignore it since it's not from within the network. The computer and entertainment system go through similar routines, establishing networks among addresses in ranges established by manufacturers. Once the networks are established, the systems begin talking among themselves. Each piconet hops randomly through the available frequencies, so all of the piconets are completely separated from one another.

Now the living room has three separate networks established, each one made up of devices that know the address of transmitters it should listen to and the address of receivers it should talk

---

[1] Radio spectrum refers to the part of the electromagnetic spectrum corresponding to radio frequencies -- that is, frequencies lower than around 300 GHz (or, equivalently, wavelengths longer than about 1 mm).Different parts of the radio spectrum are used for different radio transmission technologies and applications.

[2] A piconet is an ad-hoc computer network linking a wireless user group of devices using Bluetooth technology protocols. It allows one master device (主设备) to interconnect with up to seven active slave devices (从设备). Up to 255 further slave devices can be inactive ([in'æktiv]adj.停止的, 非活动的), or parked, which the master device can bring into active status at any time.

to. Since each network is changing the frequency of its operation thousands of times a second, it's unlikely that any two networks will be on the same frequency at the same time. If it turns out that they are, then the resulting confusion will only cover a tiny fraction of a second, and software designed to correct for such errors weeds out the confusing information and gets on with the network's business.

New Words

Bluetooth	[ˈbluːtuːθ]	n. 蓝牙
infrared	[ˈinfrəˈred]	adj. 红外线的
		n. 红外线
plug	[plʌg]	vt. 插上，插栓
		n. 插头，插销
streamline	[ˈstriːmlain]	v. 使现代化，使简单化
automatic	[ˌɔːtəˈmætik]	adj. 自动的，机械的
simplify	[ˈsimplifai]	vt. 单一化，简单化
conversation	[ˌkɔnvəˈseiʃən]	n. 会话，交谈
attribute	[əˈtribju(ː)t]	n. 属性，品质，特征
reroute	[riˈruːt]	vt. 变更路径，更改路由
arise	[əˈraiz]	vi. 出现，发生，起因于
solution	[səˈljuːʃən]	n. 解答，解决办法，解决方案
consume	[kənˈsjuːm]	vt. 消耗
milliwatt	[ˈmiliwɔt]	n. 毫瓦
virtually	[ˈvəːtjuəli]	adv. 事实上，实质上
unaffected	[ˌʌnəˈfektid]	adj. 未受影响的，自然的
megabit	[ˈmegəbit]	n. 百万位，兆位
gigahertz	[ˈgigəhəːts]	n. 千兆赫
garage	[ˈgærɑːʒ]	n. 汽车间，修车厂，车库
radius	[ˈreidjəs]	n. 半径，范围，界限
unlikely	[ʌnˈlaikli]	adj. 未必的，不太可能的，靠不住的
randomly	[ˈrændəmli]	adv. 随即地，随便地
minimize	[ˈminimaiz]	vt. 将……减到最少，最小化
risk	[risk]	n. 冒险，风险
		vt. 冒……的危险
disrupt	[disˈrʌpt]	vt. 使中断，使分裂，使瓦解，破坏
stereo	[ˈstiəriəu]	n. 立体声
		adj. 立体的
encompass	[inˈkʌmpəs]	v. 包围，环绕
piconet	[ˈpikənet]	n. 微微网
base	[beis]	n. 机座，主机

ignore	[ɪgˈnɔː]	vt. 忽略
routine	[ruːˈtiːn]	n. 常规，日常事务，程序
confusion	[kənˈfjuːʒən]	n. 混乱，混淆

Phrases

entertainment system	家庭影院
make up	构成
a community of	许多的，一群
a variety of	多种的
infrared light beam	红外线光束
component cable	色差线
electrical wire	电线
infrared signal	红外线信号
agree on	对……达成协议，对……取得一致意见
user intervention	用户干涉，用户介入，用户干预
transmission power	发射功率，传输功率
manage to	达成，设法
set aside	留出
make sure	确信，证实，确保
interfere with	妨碍，干涉，干扰
cordless telephone	无绳电话
make use of	使用，利用
connect up	连起来，接上
spread-spectrum frequency hopping	扩频跳频，展频跳频
on a regular basis	经常，例行的，有规律的
portable phone	手提电话
baby monitor	婴儿监控器
a fraction of	一小部分
in unison	一致地
stay in touch	保持联系
Bluetooth piconet	蓝牙微微网
DVD player	DVD 播放机
satellite TV receiver	卫星电视接收机
turn on	开启，开始
be separated from …	和……分离开，和……分散
turn out	结果
weed out	清除

confusing information 混乱信息，容易混淆的信息
get on with 继续做

Abbreviations

PC (Personal Computer) 个人计算机
PAN (Personal Area Network) 个人局域网

Exercises

【EX.1】Answer the following questions according to the text.

1. What are the different ways that electronic devices can connect to one another mentioned in the passage?
2. When any two devices need to talk to each other, what do they have to do?
3. What are the two levels Bluetooth works at?
4. What are the big draws of Bluetooth?
5. How does Bluetooth networking transmit data? On what frequency does it communicate?
6. What is one of the ways Bluetooth devices avoid interfering with other systems?
7. Why can several devices in different rooms be controlled?
8. What is the technique that makes it rare for more than one device to be transmitting on the same frequency at the same time?
9. What happens when Bluetooth-capable devices come within range of one another?
10. How many Bluetooth transmitter does the cordless telephone have? What happens when the base is first turned on?

【EX.2】Translate the following terms or phrases from English into Chinese and vice versa.

1. infrared signal   1. _____
2. transmission power   2. _____
3. make sure   3. _____
4. interfere with   4. _____
5. spread-spectrum frequency hopping   5. _____
6. Bluetooth piconet   6. _____
7. plug   7. _____
8. confusing information   8. _____
9. conversation   9. _____
10. Bluetooth   10. _____

11.	n. 属性，品质，特征 _____	11. _____
12.	vt. 消耗 _____	12. _____
13.	n. 微微网 _____	13. _____
14.	n. 混乱，混淆 _____	14. _____
15.	adj. 红外线的 n. 红外线 _____	15. _____

【EX.3】 **Translate the following sentences into Chinese.**

1. Bluetooth is the newest technical standard for short range radio at present.
2. In infrared imaging system, all false and unnecessary signal are called noise.
3. Plug in the AC adapter and restart your notebook.
4. The session object represents a single conversation between a consumer and provider.
5. The new computer has a debug routine that sorts out any errors in the program.
6. If you ignore this error, you may render your device inoperable.
7. The user can monitor the system from an external PC through the serial port.
8. Configuring devices attached to a parallel port can be more complex.
9. With the increasing transmission rate requirements, more and more devices support parallel port communication.
10. This company designed a kind of virtual instrument based on parallel port of computer.

Text C

Electronic Product Code (EPC)

1. What are the Electronic Product Code (EPC) and EPCglobal?

Designed to be stored on an RFID tag, the Electronic Product Code (EPC) is a unique number that identifies a specific item in the supply chain[1]. The EPC can be associated with dynamic data such as the origination point of an item or the date of its production. Much like a Global Trade Item Number (GTIN[2]) or Vehicle Identification Number (VIN[3]), the EPC is key to unlocking the power of the information systems that are part of the EPCglobal Network™.

EPCglobal Inc™ has the responsibility for oversight of the EPC and the standards, specifications, and guidelines for the Auto-ID infrastructure[4] to support its use. EPCglobal is a not-for-profit joint venture between GS1 (formerly EAN[5] International) and GS1 US (formerly the Uniform Code Council). GS1 is a leading global

[1] supply chain: 供应链
[2] 全球贸易项目代码
[3] 车辆识别号码，车架号码
[4] [ˈinfrəˈstrʌktʃə] n. 基础
[5] European Article Number: 欧洲商品码

organization dedicated to the design and implementation of global standards and solutions to improve efficiency and visibility in supply and demand chains. GS1 US is a not-for-profit member organization of GS1 and is dedicated to the development and implementation of standards-based, global supply chain solutions. For more information about EPCglobal, visit www.epcglobalinc.org.

2. Will the EPC number be the same as the current UPC number?

From a data perspective, the UPC is the foundation of the EPC. EPCglobal has published definitions that outline the EPC structure and its relationship to the UPC. The way the data structures exist should allow for easy migration[6] from the UPC into the EPC environment with a one-to-one correlation. EPCglobal fosters technical standards development through Action Groups, composed of end users and solution providers working together to advance RFID technologies and ensure the needs of the community are met. All standards, specifications, and guidelines are continually being reviewed by these Action Groups and it is a good idea to revisit the site regularly[7] to see new developments.

3. What is the EPCglobal Network?

The EPCglobal Network is a framework that enables immediate, automatic identification and sharing of information on items in the supply chain. The network consists of the ID System (EPC tags and EPC readers), EPC Middleware, EPC Information Services (which enable trading partners to exchange information), and Discovery Services, which is a suite of services to enable users to find data related to a specific EPC.

4. Where do you see the EPCglobal Network going, and will we truly have end-to-end visibility[8] of our shipments to these retailers someday?

The stated intent for the EPCglobal Network is to facilitate end-to-end visibility of goods and assets in an n-tier supply chain. The system, if widely adopted, could eliminate[9] human error from data collection, reduce inventories, keep products in stock, reduce loss and waste, and improve safety and security. Much of the framework and many of the components to support this network have been developed, and there are no technological barriers[10] to creating

[6] [mai'greiʃən]
n. 移植，移往

[7] ['regjuləli]
adv. 有规律地，有规则地

[8] [,vizi'biliti]
n. 可见度，可见性

[9] [i'limineit]
vt. 排除，消除

[10] ['bæriə]
n. 障碍物，栅栏，屏障

end-to-end visibility.

5. What is the difference between EPC's Gen 1 tags and Gen 2 tags?

With regard to[11] Generation 1, there are Class 0 and Class 1 specifications for tags in the UHF band. Class 0 was originated as a protocol by Matrics Technology Systems (acquired by Symbol Technologies) and Class 1 was originated as a protocol by Alien Technologies. Class 0 has been defined by EPCglobal as a read-only device. Class 1 is defined in the EPCglobal specification as a tag that is one-time programmable. In practice, the products that are available from Alien Technologies are reprogrammable. And Matrics/Symbol has released "Class 0+" products, which are based on the same protocol as the Class 0 device, but are, in fact, fully rewriteable[12].

With regard to Generation 2, Class 1 (Class 0 was dropped) standards were ratified[13] at the end of 2004 as a response to the limitations of the Generation 1 standards. Gen 2 provides expanded data functionality and better performance. It is designed to support EPC codes up to 256 bits long, and has the provision for extra data to be carried in the tag based on a single RFID protocol. In addition, G2 tags should be comparable with regard to radio frequencies (from 860 MHz to 960 MHz) globally, allowing tags to work consistently in different countries under differing emissions standards. Tags must be able to understand three different approved modulation schemes as well as be able to transmit at several different speeds or data rates. In addition, Gen 2 includes a method to support "dense-interrogator channelized signaling[14]" (also called "dense reader mode[15]"), which attempts to reduce interference among readers to make it less likely that reader signals will impede tag signals. An in-depth analysis of the differences between Generation 1 and Generation 2 protocols is discussed in Zebra's white papers Managing the EPC Generation Gap and Gen 2 Implications for Smart Label Printing.

6. Is it better to start my RFID pilot with Gen 1 or Gen 2 tags? Does it matter?

Gen 2 protocols offer significant performance enhancements over the first generation of EPCglobal UHF protocols, including superior tag throughput[16], improved accuracy[17], and compliance with global spectrum regulations. In addition, many new vendors have committed to supporting EPC Generation 2 and have brought

[11] with regard to: 关于

[12] [riːˈraitˈeibl] adj. 可重写的

[13] [ˈrætifai] vt. 批准,认可

[14] dense-interrogator channelized signaling: 密集询问器信道化信令

[15] dense reader mode: 密集阅读器模式

[16] [ˈθruːput] n. 吞吐量

[17] [ˈækjurəsi] n. 精确性,正确度

new designs to market. This allows users to find the best tags for their applications; leverage standards-based interoperability[18] among tags, interrogators, printer/encoders[19], etc.; as well as gain from aggressive pricing spawned by competition. If you are starting your RFID pilot now, it is best to go to Gen 2 right from the start.

7. Does "dense reader mode" mean I don't need to worry about how close readers are to other RFID equipment?

No. While the enhancements in Gen 2 represent a major leap forward in RFID technology improvements, it does not mean that users can bypass[20] the learning curve[21] associated with an RFID pilot. They will still need to understand the physical requirements of laying out[22] an RFID environment to minimize RF interference from hardware and to optimize read rates. Ideally, users should identify where RFID data is generated, transmitted, and utilized, so business process and operational improvements--such as better real-time visibility of products and inventories in the supply chain--can be achieved. Issues such as training personnel and establishing metrics and milestones to determine progress will also need to be addressed. To be sure that you are going to have as smooth and seamless[23] an RFID implementation as possible, it is still wise to turn to seasoned[24], trusted RFID specialists who have a solid track record in the technology.

8. With the improved interoperability and performance of Gen 2 tags, does it matter very much which hardware we choose? Won't all products that meet the standards work with each other seamlessly?

Not necessarily, and it is still a good idea to conduct due diligence and proper research before investing in Gen 2 products. Gen 2 is a flexible standard that can be implemented in many ways by different vendors. With dozens of[25] variations of Gen 2-compliant tags and hundreds more likely on the horizon, chips may vary in memory size, programming speed, and other characteristics. In addition, different antenna designs can perform better or worse when distance or orientation to interrogators is changed. Also consider that the amount of power the printer/encoder requires to write data to the RFID chip is a complex function of the inlay's[26] chip type, antenna design, and antenna size. Users may need to use different tag designs to provide optimal read performance on a

[18] [ˌɪntərˌɔpərəˈbɪləti]
n. 互用性
[19] [ɪnˈkoʊdə]
n. 译码器，编码器

[20] [ˈbaɪpɑːs]
vt. 绕过，迂回
[21] learning curve:
学习曲线
[22] lay out:
布置，安排

[23] [ˈsiːmlɪs]
adj. 无缝的
[24] [ˈsiːznd]
adj. 经验丰富的，老练的

[25] dozens of:
许多的

[26] [ˈɪnleɪ]
n. 镶嵌

variety of items. Each set of tags may require different encoding power levels, making it important for printer/encoder settings to be changed easily without requiring extensive IT support or reprogramming[27]. It is very wise to thoroughly test Gen 2 media to ensure tags selected truly support a given application. Consult experienced solution providers, like Zebra, to ensure the proper smart label media is compatible with your printer/encoder and optimized for your application.

[27] [ˈriːprəʊɡræm] v. 改编，重新编程

9. Will Class 1 Gen 2 become the dominant EPC UHF standard?

The arrival of Gen 2 does not signal the retirement or obsolescence[28] of other RFID protocols. Gen 1 tags will likely be used through 2007 until existing supplies are exhausted[29]. And RFID technologies are very likely to rapidly evolve into future generations in the coming years. In addition, different protocol standards can be used for different applications, just as numerous bar code symbologies are used today. Organizations should build their RFID infrastructure with multi-protocol printer/encoders and interrogators. Multi-protocol equipment provides investment protection and simplifies upgrades because it can simultaneously support different RFID standards and tag types.

[28] [ˌɔbsəˈlesns] n. 荒废，退化
[29] [iɡˈzɔːstid] adj. 耗尽的，疲惫的

10. With all the recent and ongoing changes in RFID, how can I ensure that what I choose today will support my RFID initiative in the coming years?

A flexible, configurable, and upgradeable RFID infrastructure is required to support Gen 2 and beyond as well as allow users to reap[30] the business benefits of improved operations. Features like multi-protocol support, software-defined radios, and adjustable[31] power settings provide long-term investment protection and lower the total cost of ownership of your RFID infrastructure as it matures and evolves. When evaluating RFID investments, determine if the products:

[30] [riːp] v. 收获
[31] [əˈdʒʌstəbl] adj. 可调整的

- meet your current needs for protocols, options, and features;
- include simultaneous support for multiple RFID protocols; and
- offer a low-cost, clear, easy, and efficient upgrade path that can sustain operations with minimal disruption.

Text A WiFi

WiFi 是一种流行技术，允许电子设备（使用无线电波）通过计算机网络，包括高速因特网，无线地交换数据。WiFi 联盟把 WiFi 定义为任何"基于 IEEE802.11 标准的无线局域网（WLAN）产品"。但是，因为大多数现代的 WLAN 都是基于这些标准的，术语 WiFi 在英语中与 WLAN 的意思一样。

一个能够使用 WiFi 的设备（如个人计算机、视频游戏台、智能电话、平板电脑或数字音频播放机）可以通过无线网络访问接入点连接到像因特网这样的网络资源。这样的访问点（或热区）在室内是大约 20 米（65 英尺）的范围，在室外更大。热区覆盖的地域小到墙壁围成的单人间，大到数平方英里——这要通过多个访问点衔接实现。

1. 使用

要连接到 WiFi 局域网，计算机必须配置无线网络接口控制器。计算机与接口控制器组合起来叫作站点。所有站点共享一个无线电频率通信通道。该通道上传输的信号可以被有效范围内的全部站点接收。硬件并不给用户发出传输完成的信号，因此被称为尽力传输机制。用载波来传输打包的数据，这种数据叫作"以太网帧"。每个站点一直收听无线电频率通信通道以便拾取有效的传输信息。

1.1 因特网访问

在有效范围中活动的 WiFi 设备可以连接到因特网。一个或多个（互连的）访问接入点叫作热区，热区覆盖范围可以小到几间房大到数平方英里。要覆盖较大的范围需要相互衔接的一组访问接入点。在英国伦敦已经成功使用了室外公共 WiFi 技术。

WiFi 可以在私人住宅、繁华大街、独立商业机构和公共空间提供服务。组织和商业机构（如机场、旅馆和娱乐场所）通常提供免费的热区来吸引顾客。那些希望在特定区域提供服务或扩展业务的热心人士或权威人士有时也提供免费的 WiFi 服务。

带有数字用户线路调制解调器或电缆调制解调器的路由器和一个 WiFi 访问接入点通常设置在房间里或大楼内，给以有线或无线方式连接到它们之上的所有设备提供联网和因特网访问服务。

类似地，也有电池供电的路由器，包括蜂窝移动因特网无线调制解调器和 WiFi 访问接入点。与手机运营商签约后，它们会允许附近的 WiFi 站点通过 2G、3G 或 4G 网络访问因特网。许多智能手机都内置了这类功能，包括基于 Android、Bada、iOS（iPhone）和 Symbian 的手机，虽然携带者常常关闭这个功能，或为激活这个功能单独付费，客户使用受限制的数据套餐时更是如此。"因特网精灵"为非智能手机提供这类功能，如包括品牌为 MiFi 和 WiBro 的设备。有些带有蜂窝调制解调器卡的笔记本计算机也可以作为移动 WiFi 访问接入点。

WiFi 也可以用在平常无法联网的地方，如厨房和花棚。

1.1.1 城域 WiFi

早在 21 世纪之年初，许多城市就宣布要建设城域 WiFi 网络，也有许多成功的范例。2004 年，迈索尔成为印度第一个、全世界第二个启用 WiFi 的城市。耶路撒冷是世界第一个使用 WiFi 的城市。一个叫作 WiFiyNet 公司在迈索尔建立了覆盖全市和附近少数村庄的热区。

2005 年，加利福尼亚州的桑尼维尔成为美国第一个提供城域免费 WiFi 的城市，明尼阿波利斯每年为其提供者产生一百二十万的利润。

2010 年 5 月，英国伦敦市长鲍里斯•约翰逊誓言到 2012 年建成全市的 WiFi。几个区域，包括威斯敏斯特和伊斯灵顿，已经实现室外 WiFi 覆盖。

韩国官方正致力于在该市超过 10000 处提供免费因特网接入，包括室外公共场所、主要大街和人口稠密区域。汉城同意该项目由 KT、LG Telecom 和 SK Telecom 承担。这些公司将为此项目投资 4400 万美元，将于 2015 年完成。

1.1.2 校园网

美国许多传统大学的校园内至少有部分区域被无线 WiFi 因特网覆盖。卡内基梅隆大学于 1993 年在匹兹堡校区建了第一个校园无线因特网，叫作无线安德鲁，那时 WiFi 还没有出现。

2000 年，费城的德雷克塞尔大学实现了校园无线因特网的全覆盖，为美国名牌大学之先。

马尼拉的远东大学在菲律宾率先实现了校园 WiFi 覆盖，以供学生、教师和员工使用。印度加尔各答圣泽维尔学院最近用 WiFi 覆盖了整个校园。

1.2 引导计算机对计算机通信

WiFi 也允许从一个计算机到另一计算机的直接通信，而无须经过访问接入点。这叫作点对点 WiFi 传输。这种无线点对点网络模式广泛用于多人手持游戏机（如任天堂 DS、便携游戏机、数码相机）和其他消费电子设备。某些设备可以使用点对点方式共享其因特网连接，变成热区或"虚拟路由器"。

2. 优点和局限性

2.1 优点

WiFi 使部署局域网更廉价。在不能布线的地方，如室外或历史建筑，都可以使用无线局域网。

厂家已在给大多数便携机内置无线网络适配器。WiFi 芯片组的价格持续下降，使其成为更多设备经济组网的选择。

具有竞争力的不同品牌的访问接入点和客户网络接口可以交互运行在基本服务层面。通过 WiFi 联盟得到"WiFi 认证"的产品是向后兼容的。与移动电话不同，任一标准的 WiFi 设备都可以在世界各地工作。

只要使用了坚固的密码短语口令，WiFi 安全访问加密就是可信赖的。用于服务质量（WMM）的新协议使 WiFi 更适应传输延迟的网络应用（如语音和视频）。省电机制（WMM Power Save）延长了电池寿命。

2.2 限制

频谱分配和运营限制并非全球一致：欧洲大多数国家增加了两个通道，即 1-13。美国在 2.4 GHz 波段使用 1-13 通道，而日本使用的是 1-14，比欧洲国家还多一个通道。2007

年，欧洲基本上实现了统一。

一个 WiFi 信号占用 2.4 A GHz 波段的 5 个通道。任何两个通道数相差 5 或更多，（如 2 和 7）都不重叠。因此，"只有通道 1、6 和 11 才是非重叠的通道"这一人们常常重复的说法并不精确。通道 1、6 和 11 只是美国非重叠的三个通道中一组。欧洲和日本推荐对 802.11g 和 n 使用通道 1、5、9 和 13。

欧盟的等效全向辐射功率限制为 20dBm (100 毫瓦)。

当前"最快"的 802.11n 使用的无线电频谱和带宽 (40MHz) 是 802.11a 或 802.11g（20 MHz）的两倍。这意味着在特定场合在 2.4GHz 波段只有一个 802.11n 网络，且不会与其他 WLAN 流量冲突。802.11n 也可设定为只用 20MHz 带宽以防止在密集人群中产生冲突。

2.3 范围

WiFi 网络范围有限。使用 802.11b 或 802.11g 带有伸缩天线的无线访问接入点在室内的范围通常是 32 米（120 英尺）在室外是 95 米（300 英尺）。然而，IEEE 802.11n 的范围能够扩大一倍。范围也随频率波段而变。在 2.4GHz 频段的 WiFi 比 5GHz 频段的 WiFi 范围稍微大些。802.11a 使用 5GHz，802.11n 选择使用 5GHz。在带有可分离天线的无线路由器上，通过安装更高增益的定向天线可以增大范围。通过在路由器或远程设备中使用高增益定向天线室外范围可以扩大到若干千米。一般来说，WiFi 设备可以传输的最大功率受当地规章的限制，如在美国受 FCC Part 15 的限制。

由于延伸无线局域网应用的需要，WiFi 的功耗比其他标准明显要高。例如，蓝牙（用于支持无线 PAN 应用）这样的技术提供小于 10 米范围的传播，因此功耗更小。另外如 ZigBee 这样的技术，范围相对较大但数据传输率低得多。高功耗的 WiFi 使得移动设备中的电池寿命至关重要。

研究人员已经开发了许多"不用敷设新线路"的技术，当 WiFi 技术不满足室外要求或无法敷设新线（如 CAT-5）或布线成本太高时，用其替代 WiFi。例如，用于高速局域网的 ITU-T G.hn 使用家中现有线路（同轴电缆、电话线和电力线）。虽然 G.hn 没有 WiFi 的一些优点（如移动性或可用于室外），但它适用于室内范围比移动性更重要的应用（如 IPTV 传输）。

由于在特定 WiFi 频率无线电传输的复杂性，尤其是树木和建筑反射信号的影响，算法只能大概预测任一发射器相关区域 WiFi 信号的强度。这不会影响大范围 WiFi，因为更长的连接通常建在高塔上，可以避开周围植物的影响。

WiFi 的实际范围主要限定了一些设备应用的移动性，如库房或零售场所中的取货机、收款台的条码阅读设备或收货/送货站。更大范围的 WiFi 移动应用是受限的，如在从一个热区移动到另一热区的汽车上使用。其他无线技术更适应与移动车辆通信。

2.4 数据安全风险

已经表明，最常用的无线加密标准 WEP 即使配置正确也很容易攻破。WPA 和 WPA2 加密法在 2003 年已经应用到设备中，目的是解决这些问题。通常 WiFi 访问接入点默认是无加密的（开放）模式。新手受益于开箱即用的零配置设备，但这个默认设置没有任何无线安全，提供对 LAN 的开放式无线访问。用户通常通过软件图形用户界面（GUI）配置设备以满足安全需求。连接在未加密网络上的设备可以监控和记录数据（包括个人信息）。只有采用其他防护措施实现此类网络的安全，如 VPN 或在传输层安全上的安全超文本传输协议（HTTP）。

2.5 冲突

同一区域的其他设备可能使 WiFi 连接中断或速度下降。许多 2.4GHz 802.11b 和 802.11g 访问接入点默认初始的那个通道，这会造成某些通道的堵塞。WiFi 污染或该区域访问接入点（尤其是邻近通道）太多可能阻止访问并对使用其他访问接入点的其他设备造成相互干扰。在高密集区域也可能有这个问题，这些区域包括有许多 WiFi 访问接入点的大综合住宅区或办公楼。

另外，还有一些设备使用 2.4GHz 波段：微波炉、ISM 波段设备、安全照相机、ZigBee 设备、蓝牙设备、视频传输装置、无绳电话、婴儿监控器和有些国家的业余无线电，所有这些都可以引起其他的严重冲突。当市政当局或其他大的实体（如大学）寻求大区域覆盖时也有这个问题。

Unit 9

Text A

Barcode

1. Introduction

The last 25 years have seen phenomenal growth in the use of barcodes. We are all familiar with the use of barcodes in retail stores, but that is only one very visible aspect to the world of automatic identification.

The wider use of computers in business has increased the demand for and usefulness of data. Data of all kinds is transmitted day and night between companies, from the stock levels and reorder requirements of the neighbourhood supermarket to the movement of vast sums between the world money markets.

With this data explosion comes the need for fast, automated data input. Barcodes can satisfy this demand. Within a fraction of a second the sophisticated equipment on a supermarket checkout can read a barcode from a grocery item, decode it into an article number, look up that number on the main computer, and record the price and item title on the bill receipt. At the same time the main computer logs the decrease in stock and when it has fallen to a predetermined level, sends an electronic message down the telephone line to the main warehouse. The same computer network carries the automatic reorder information to the individual suppliers and so on down the chain of supply.

The barcode image is an ideal way of automatically identifying an article. Unlike magnetic stripes or radio frequency tags it is cheap to produce, requiring only ink and paper. Unlike text or graphics it can be read quickly and in any orientation by a relatively inexpensive machine. All that is needed is an accurate and reliable way of producing the barcode image.

2. Barcode Uses

Although the first commercial implementation of barcoding was for grocery distribution in 1970, the use of barcodes has grown enormously ever since.

We now see many stores across the world using barcodes at the checkout, and also throughout their distribution chain. Inter-company and intra-company distribution outside of the retail arena also uses bar coding. Barcodes are used in vehicle manufacture, document tracking, data input for domestic video recorders, time control, security access, in some hospitals even human beings are being automatically identified by a barcoded tag worn around the wrist.

Many standards have been developed for the use and control of numbering systems applied to barcodes. Some standards may be international. Some may only apply to one industry or just one company or office.

Barcode users may be split into two groups; those who are using barcodes within a controlled system where they must adhere to the coding standards laid down by an outside body and those who wish to originate barcodes for purely their own use and therefore have free rein to choose the most suitable barcode type.

Dependent on the type of system which is being operated, the user may wish to produce the same barcode on all items of a particular type or may wish to uniquely identify each individual item (such as a legal file or document).

3. Barcode Structure

All barcodes are constructed from a series of bars and intervening spaces. The relative size of these bars and spaces and the number of them is decided by the specification for the symbology (or barcode type) which is being used. There are a number of symbologies in common use. Each symbology differs in the way data is encoded and often also in the type or amount of data. Generally speaking, only one symbology is chosen for a particular application.

To ensure compatibility of systems, it is important that all users of a barcode agree on the way in which it is used and how data is encoded. In a small system such as the tracking of documents within a single office, it is easy to control the type of barcode that is used. However, in a large and complex system such as that for retail products in the U.K., the agreement and control is much more problematical.

For this reason the use of barcodes within certain fields is administered and controlled by official (or semi-official) bodies. Such bodies will publish specifications stating which barcode symbology is to be used for a particular application, what limits are applied to size and quality, and the numbering system that is used. In the case of barcodes which identify an article, the official body will issue the numbers that are used so that conflicts do not occur.

Here are just a few of the official bodies and the areas they administer:

GS1(Associations in most countries)

   EAN 8[1] & 13 for retail items

   Interleaved 2 of 5 (ITF)[2] for outer cases

---

[1] An EAN-8 is a barcode and is derived from the longer European Article Number (EAN-13) code. It was introduced for use on small packages where an EAN-13 barcode would be too large; for example on cigarettes, pencils (though it is rarely used for pencils), and <u>chewing gum</u> (口香糖) packets.

[2] Interleaved 2 of 5 is a continuous two-width barcode symbology encoding digits. It is used commercially on 135 film, for ITF-14 barcodes, and on <u>cartons</u> (['kɑːtən] n. 硬纸盒, 纸板箱) of some products, while the products inside are labeled with UPC or EAN. I2/5 encodes pairs of digits; the first digit is encoded in the five bars (or black lines), while the second digit is encoded in the five spaces (or white lines) interleaved with them. Two out of every five bars or spaces are wide (hence exactly 2 of 5).

  Code 128 for supplementary coding
The Publishers Association
  ISBN coding for books
The British Library/Periodicals Barcoding Association
  ISSN coding for magazines and periodicals
Uniform Code Council USA
  UPC coding for retail items in the U.S. and Canada

There are many other bodies covering such fields as transport, blood banking, pharmaceuticals and the automotive industry.

Those involved in bar coding should understand the relationship between the Barcode Symbology and its Application Specification.

A symbology is not specific to a particular application or numbering system. It is simply the rules that govern the construction of the barcode and its operational limits.

The Application Specification adopts a particular symbology and defines how articles will be numbered. Certain Application Specifications administer the coding of items within a particular area but adopt the symbology and application spec of another larger sector.

For example, book coding in the U.K falls under the ISBN (International Standard Book Numbering) system, but has been incorporated into the EAN-13 implementation administered by the GS1.

Most barcode symbologies have certain common features.

3.1 Human Readable Characters

Many newcomers to barcoding have misconceptions about the information a barcode contains. They are familiar with the use of barcodes in retail stores and assume that the barcode contains the price of the item. This is hardly ever the case. The barcode will carry only the unique number which identifies that item. At the supermarket checkout the number is read by the scanner and the price is extracted from a "look-up" table on the stores main computer.

In almost all cases all of the useful information is printed in "human-readable" form, usually at the base of the code. A standard font is recommended for the Human Readable Characters (HRC's) in most symbologies. While this font is usually OCR-B or OCR-A, both fonts were designed to be readable by a machine. In practice, the HRC's are not machine read and a standard font is used simply for uniformity of appearance.

3.2 Light Margins

All barcode types require a certain amount of light space to the left and right of the barcode. This enables the scanner to differentiate between the barcode and surrounding graphics. Should the wrong type of graphic image intrude on the light margin, there is a risk that the barcode will not decode, or worse, will decode incorrectly.

One of the most common causes of bad reads is light margin incursion. For this reason, some symbologies employ a method of protecting the quiet zone. For example, an unbroken rule or box may be defined around the code. As UPC codes have human readable characters left and right of the main code, the quiet zones are generally well protected. With the EAN13 code a human readable character appears to the left of the code but not on the right. The specifications recommend that a light margin indicator be placed on the right of the code to dissuade designers from placing graphics within the quiet zone.

3.3 Barcode Dimensions

The method of describing barcode size varies between symbologies. Code types such as UPC and EAN use a magnification factor based around the standard size (100% magnification). All dimensions are scaled proportionally as the magnification factor changes. Although there is a recommended height for each magnification factor, this is sometimes adjusted in practice. Excessive reduction (truncation) should be avoided as it may impede scanning.

Other symbologies employ a size definition based on the width of the narrowest bar in the code.

Many symbol types are modular, that is the width of all bars and spaces is derived from the narrow bar (or X dimension). In such codes the wide bars and spaces are constructed from 2, 3 or more narrow bars according to the encodation rules which apply. Therefore, to describe the size of the barcode it is only necessary to define the narrow bar width and the height of the code.

Code 39 differs from the above in that while it defines narrow bar width, it also defines the ratio between wide and narrow bars (between 2:1 and 3:1). As there are many possible combinations of narrow bar width and wide/narrow ratio, users of Code39 find it convenient to talk in terms of characters per inch (CPI), that is the number of digits which could be encoded by a code of 1" width.

- One complication to the above rule is the adjustment of 1/13 of a narrow bar to certain parts of UPC and EAN codes. This is undertaken to give an even distribution of bar width tolerances and improve the scanability of the code.

3.4 Start and Stop Characters

It is usual for a symbology to have a start and stop pattern at each end of the barcode symbol. This special bar/space arrangement may simply tell the scanner that the read was complete. In the case of variable length barcodes if a start/stop pattern is not used it will be possible for a scanner to read part of the code and assume it has read the complete code.

A start and stop pattern may also indicate the orientation of the barcode. By having a differing pattern on the left from the right the scanner can detect if the code was read upside-down.

4. Getting a Good Scan

The data contained within the barcode is read by moving a spot of light across the barcode, starting in the white space before the first bar and moving through all the bars and spaces to the white area at the other end of the code.

If the spot of light moves off the edge of the code during the sweep, the code will not scan correctly. Therefore, when printing a barcode, the method of scanning must be considered when choosing the barcode dimensions. In applications where the barcode is scanned using a wand (a pen shaped barcode reader) a code which has been shortened (or truncated) will still read so long as the wand can easily be passed over the full width of the code without going off the edge.

Most supermarket checkouts use moving beam scanners, where a beam of light moves over the code. There is no way of controlling the items path over the beam sufficiently to ensure that the beam will move horizontally across the code. The wider the code is the greater the chance of the beam going off the top or bottom before scanning the entire width. It is obvious that by increasing the height, the chances of a good scan are improved.

For this reason, most barcoding specifications use a magnification factor which is expressed in percentage terms. For each magnification factor there is a nominal height so as the width of the barcode increases so does the height, maintaining the scanability. In working practice truncation (the reduction in height of the code without a reduction in width) is used. Care should be taken when truncating as scanning may be impaired.

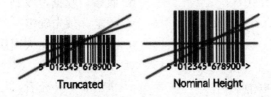

The two examples above show the same three scans over a nominal height code and a truncated code. While all three would give good scans on the nominal code, only one would scan on the truncated barcode.

Contrast:

Another area of possible danger is that of the contrast between the bars and spaces. For the best possible scan, all the bars should reflect no light at all and all the spaces should reflect 100%. In practice this never happens, but barcodes will still read providing the lightness of the bars and the darkness of the spaces do not exceed certain limits.

As mentioned above, black bars and white spaces are best, but some colour combinations produce good scans, others definitely do not. Most scanners use red light, therefore any colour which reflects red light is suitable for spaces and any colour absorbing red light is needed for bars.

Shades and hues can vary, but here is a general guide on what can be used:

Good Bar Colours: Black, Green, Blue, Dark Brown

Good Space Colours: White, Red, Yellow, Orange

New Words

phenomenal	[fi'nɔminl]	adj. 显著的，现象的
visible	['vizəbl]	adj. 看得见的，明显的

		n. 可见物
identification	[aiˌdentifiˈkeiʃən]	n. 辨认，识别，鉴定，证明
usefulness	[ˈjuːsfulnis]	n. 有用，有效性
reorder	[riːˈɔːdə]	v. 再订购，重新安排
		n. 再订购
neighbourhood	[ˈneibəhud]	n. 邻近，邻居关系
explosion	[iksˈpləuʒən]	n. 爆发，发出
satisfy	[ˈsætisfai]	v. 满意，确保
checkout	[ˈtʃekaut]	n. (超级市场中的)付款处，结账；检验,校验
grocery	[ˈgrəusəri]	n. 食品，杂货
article	[ˈɑːtikl]	n. 物品，商品
record	[ˈrekɔːd]	vt. 记录
receipt	[riˈsiːt]	n. 收条，收据，收到
predetermine	[ˈpriːdiˈtəːmin]	v. 预定，预先确定
warehouse	[ˈwɛəhaus]	n. 仓库，货栈，大商店
		vt. 贮入仓库
supplier	[səˈplaiə]	n. 供应者，补充者，厂商
reliable	[riˈlaiəbl]	adj. 可靠的，可信赖的
implementation	[ˌimplimenˈteiʃən]	n. 执行
standard	[ˈstændəd]	n. 标准，规格
international	[ˌintə(ː)ˈnæʃənəl]	adj. 国际的，世界的
construct	[kənˈstrʌkt]	vt. 建造，构造，创立
intervene	[ˌintəˈviːn]	vi. 插入，介入，（指时间）介于其间
compatibility	[kəmˌpætiˈbiliti]	n. 兼容性
agreement	[əˈgriːmənt]	n. 协定，协议
body	[ˈbɔdi]	n. 团体
conflict	[ˈkɔnflikt]	n. 冲突
		vi. 抵触，冲突
supplementary	[ˌsʌpliˈmentəri]	adj. 附加的
pharmaceuticals	[ˌfɑːməˈsjuːtikəlz]	n. 医药品
symbology	[simˈbɔlədʒi]	n. 符号系统，符号学
adopt	[əˈdɔpt]	vt. 采用
define	[diˈfain]	vt. 定义，详细说明
spec	[spek]	n. 说明，规格
readable	[ˈriːdəbəl]	adj. 可读的，易读的
misconception	[ˈmiskənˈsepʃən]	n. 误解
font	[fɔnt]	n. 字体，字形
uniformity	[ˌjuːniˈfɔːmiti]	n. 同样，一式，一致，均匀
appearance	[əˈpiərəns]	n. 出现，露面，外貌，外观

employ	[im'plɔi]	v. 使用
dimension	[di'menʃən]	n. 尺寸，尺度；维（数），度（数），元
magnification	[,mægnifi'keiʃən]	n. 扩大，放大倍率
adjust	[ə'dʒʌst]	vt. 调整，调节
impede	[im'pi:d]	v. 妨害，阻止
narrow	['nærəu]	n. 狭窄部分
		adj. 狭窄的
		v. 变窄
complication	[,kɔmpli'keiʃən]	n. 复杂化，（使复杂的）因素
adjustment	[ə'dʒʌstmənt]	n. 调整，调节
undertake	[,ʌndə'teik]	vt. 承担，保证
tolerance	['tɔlərəns]	n. 偏差，容差
upside-down	[ʌpsaid-'daun]	adv. 颠倒
truncate	['trʌŋkeit]	v. 把……截短
		adj. 截短的
sufficiently	[sə'fiʃəntli]	adv. 十分地，充分地
truncation	[trʌŋ'keiʃən]	n. 切断
lightness	['laitnis]	n. 亮度
darkness	['dɑ:knis]	n. 暗度
definitely	['definitli]	adv. 明确地，干脆地
absorb	[əb'sɔ:b]	vt. 吸收
hue	[hju:]	n. 颜色，色彩；色度

Phrases

retail store	零售店
stock level	库存水平
money market	金融市场，货币市场
a fraction of a second	一秒钟的若干分之几，一转眼的工夫
magnetic stripe	（卡片或文件上的）磁条
ever since	从那时到现在
distribution chain	配送链
video recorder	录影机
be split into …	被分为……
adhere to	粘附，粘着，追随，拥护
free rein	完全的行动自由
baked beans	（加番茄酱等制的）烘豆
relative size	相对大小，相对值

numbering system	编号系统
publishers association	出版者协会
blood bank	血库
fall under	受到（影响等），被归入
be familiar with	熟悉
hardly ever	难得，几乎从来不
light margin	空白区
quiet zone	静止区
unbroken rule	完整的破折号
dissuade from	劝止某人做
magnification factor	扩大因数，放大倍数，放大系数
in practice	在实践中，实际上
move off	离开
go off	离开，消失
beam of light	光束
be suitable for	合适的
dark brown	茶褐色，咖啡色

Abbreviations

GS1 (Globe standard 1)	国际物品编码协会
EAN (European Article Number)	欧洲商品编码
ITF (Interleaved Two and Five)	交插二五
ISBN (International Standard Book Numbering)	国际标准图书编号
ISSN (International Standard Serial Number)	国际标准连续出版物编号
HRC (Human Readable Characters)	人类可读的字符
OCR-B (Optical Character Recognition-International Standard)	光字符识别-国际标准
OCR-A (Optical Character Recognition-ANSI Standard)	光字符识别-美国标准协会标准
CPI (Characters Per Inch)	每英寸字符数

Exercises

【EX.1】Answer the following questions according to the text.

1. What has the last 25 years seen?
2. What was the first commercial implementation of barcoding for?

3. How many groups may Barcode users be split into? What are they?

4. What are all barcodes constructed from?

5. What is important to ensure compatibility of systems?

6. What do OCR-A and OCR-B stand for? And what are they?

7. What is one of the most common causes of bad reads?

8. How is Code 39 differ from others mentioned in the passage?

9. What kind of scanners do most supermarket checkouts use?

10. What light do most scanners use? What are good bar colours and good space colours?

【EX.2】 Translate the following terms or phrases from English into Chinese and vice versa.

1. distribution chain
2. light margin
3. quiet zone
4. magnification factor
5. usefulness
6. visible
7. record
8. predetermine
9. implementation
10. compatibility
11. n. 说明，规格
12. n. 维(数)，度(数)
13. vt. 调整，调节
14. n. 偏差，容差
15. n. 复杂化

【EX.3】 Translate the following sentences into Chinese.

1. I was persuaded of the usefulness of his new device.

2. Therefore, the safety stock is included in the reorder level.

3. Don't make me reenter that information at the time of checkout.

4. This is the procedure for adding data or information to an existing record.

5. We will need to call on our supplier to get more inventory.

6. The technical standard was not substantially exceeded.

7. For added security, our systems offer compatibility with advanced encryption devices.

8. Do you know how to adjust this new machine?

9. Many programmers want their own procedures embedded OCR recognition module.

10. A well-run supply chain compresses time, reduces expensive distribution processes as well as costly buffer inventories.

【EX.4】Complete the following passage with appropriate words in the box.

constraints	update	inventor	basic	symbol
interactive	mainstream	descriptions	scan	equal

Barcodes are a pretty big deal -- and not just at the grocery store. 2D barcodes are the ___1___ of recognition technologies used for mobile marketing. You'll be hearing more about newcomers such as NFC, but for now, the majority of folks are sticking with 2D.

In mobile tagging, the barcode is a printed ___2___ that connects a physical object (a magazine ad) to a digital experience on a smartphone (a cool video). Why should you care? Because a 2D barcode like a Microsoft Tag barcode adds a whole new dimension to your marketing campaigns, making them more engaging and ___3___.

You can put a 2D barcode on just about anything -- printed materials, packaging, posters, signs, websites, clothing. When people can ___4___ the barcode with their smartphones, they instantly see the online content you've created -- from a product video to a sweepstakes to a custom mobile site.

But not all barcodes are created ___5___. The type of barcode you use is important, because features and ease of use vary. There are three types of barcodes in common use: Microsoft Tag barcodes, QR Codes, and traditional linear barcodes.

1. Tag Barcodes

Tag barcodes are the newest edition of 2D barcodes. They offer more flexibility than older formats both in the barcode design and the content behind it. Because Tag barcodes are linked to data stored on a server, you can deliver a more robust online experience -- including entire mobile sites -- and ___6___ the content any time without having to change the Tag. So, if you link a Tag on your business card to your résumé, it will still be valid after you get that big promotion. Tags can be black-and-white or full-color, including custom images (e.g., a company logo).

2. QR Code

The Quick Response (QR) Code was the earliest 2D barcode. It was designed to be a bump up from its predecessor, the 1D barcode, because it can contain more information. While not technically open source, the ___7___ of the QR Code and owner of the QR Code trademark, DENSO, has allowed the patents for the code to be freely available to the public. QR Codes have a variety of disparate formats and reader apps, and can be black-and-white or basic colors. Because of these ___8___, QR Codes are best suited for simple designs that don't require integration with your branding.

3. Traditional Barcodes

It's not likely, but it's possible the 1D barcode on your loaf of bread carries a little something extra. Some marketers provide ___9___ product information using the 1D barcodes you've known for years. Some services use mobile apps to scan these barcodes and display data such as prices, ___10___, and user reviews.

【EX.5】 **Translate the following passage into Chinese.**

What is 2D barcode?

A 2D (two-dimensional) barcode is a graphical image that stores information both horizontally and vertically. As a result, 2D codes can store up to 7,089 characters, significantly greater storage than is possible with the 20-character capacity of a unidimensional barcode.

2D barcodes are also known as quick response codes because they enable fast data access. 2D barcodes are often used in conjunction with smart phones. The user simply photographs a 2D barcode with the camera on a phone equipped with a barcode reader. The reader interprets the encoded URL, which directs the browser to the relevant information on a Web site. This capability has made 2D barcodes useful for mobile marketing. Some 2D barcode systems also deliver information in a message for users without Web access.

Here are some examples how 2D barcodes are being used:
- Nike used 2D barcodes on posters along the route of an extreme sports competition. Mobile users captured barcodes to access sponsored pictures, video and data.
- Some newspapers include 2D barcodes on stories that link mobile users to developing coverage.
- 2D barcodes on products in stores link to product reviews.
- Some people post 2D barcodes that link to their blogs or Facebook pages.

Text B

QR Code

QR Code (abbreviated from Quick Response Code) is the trademark for a type of matrix barcode (or two-dimensional code) first designed for the automotive industry. More recently, the system has become popular outside the industry due to its fast readability and large storage capacity compared to standard UPC barcodes[1]. The code consists of black modules (square dots) arranged in a square pattern on a white background. The information encoded can be made up of four standardized kinds ("modes") of data (numeric, alphanumeric, byte/binary, Kanji).

1. Invention

The QR Code was invented in Japan by the Toyota subsidiary Denso Wave in 1994 to track

---

[1] The Universal Product Code (UPC) is a barcode symbology (i.e., a specific type of barcode) that is widely used in North America, the United Kingdom, Australia, New Zealand and in other countries for tracking trade items in stores. Its most common form, the UPC-A, consists of 12 numerical digits, which are uniquely assigned to each trade item. Along with the related EAN barcode, the UPC is the only barcode allowed for scanning trade items at the point of sale, per GS1 standards. UPC data structures are a component of <u>GTINs</u> (Global Trade Item Numbers, 全球贸易项目代码). All of these data structures <u>follow</u> (['fɔləu]vt.遵循) the global GS1 standards.

vehicles during the manufacturing process, and was originally designed to allow components to be scanned at high speed. It has since become one of the most popular types of two-dimensional barcodes.

Unlike the older one-dimensional barcode that was designed to be mechanically scanned by a narrow beam of light, the QR code is detected as a 2-dimensional digital image by a semiconductor image sensor[1] and is then digitally analyzed by a programmed processor. The processor locates the three distinctive squares at the corners of the image, and uses a smaller square near the fourth corner to normalize the image for size, orientation, and angle of viewing. The small dots are then converted to binary numbers and validity checked with an error-correcting code.

2. Standards

There are several standards in documents covering the physical encoding of QR Codes:

- October 1997 -- AIM (Association for Automatic Identification and Mobility) International.
- January 1999 -- JIS X 0510.
- June 2000 -- ISO/IEC 18004:2000 Information technology -- Automatic identification and data capture techniques -- Barcode symbology -- QR code (now withdrawn). Defines QR code models 1 and 2 symbols.
- 1 September 2006 -- ISO/IEC 18004:2006 Information technology -- Automatic identification and data capture techniques -- QR Code 2005 barcode symbology specification. Defines QR code 2005 symbols, an extension of QR Code model 2. Does not specify how to read QR Code model 1 symbols, or require this for compliance.

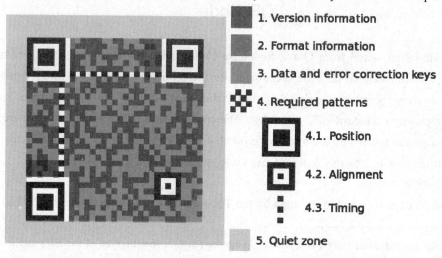

---

[1] An image sensor is a device that converts an optical image into an electronic signal. It is used mostly in digital cameras, camera modules and other imaging devices. Early analog sensors were video camera tubes, most currently used are digital <u>charge-coupled device</u> (CCD，电荷耦合器件) or <u>complementary metal–oxide–semiconductor</u> (CMOS，互补金属氧化物半导体) active pixel ([5piksEl] n. 像素) sensors.

At the application layer, there is some variation between most of the implementations. Japan's NTT DoCoMo has established de facto standards for the encoding of URLs, contact information, and several other data types. The open-source "ZXing" project maintains a list of QR Code data types.

3. Uses

Formerly only for industrial uses, they have in recent years become common in consumer advertising and packaging, because the popularity of smartphones "has put a barcode reader in everyone's pocket" for the first time. As a result, the QR Code has become a focus of advertising strategy, since it provides quick and effortless access to the brand's website. Besides the convenience brought to the consumer, the importance of this capability is that it increases the conversion rate[1] (that is, it increase the chance that contact with the advertisement will convert to a sale), by coaxing qualified prospects further down the conversion funnel[2] without any delay or effort, bringing the viewer to the advertiser's site immediately, where a longer and more targeted sales pitch may continue. Although initially used to track parts in vehicle manufacturing, QR Codes are now (as of 2012) used over a much wider range of applications, including commercial tracking, entertainment and transport ticketing, product/loyalty marketing and in-store product labeling. It can also be used in storing personal information for the use of the government. An example of this is Philippines National Bureau of Investigation (NBI) where NBI clearances now come with a QR Code. Many of these applications target mobile-phone users (via mobile tagging[3]). Users may receive text, add a vCard[4] contact to their device, open a Uniform Resource Identifier (URI[5]), or compose an e-mail or text message after scanning QR Codes. They can generate and print their own QR Codes for others to scan and use by visiting

---

[1] In internet marketing, the conversion rate is the proportion of visitors to a website who take action to go beyond a casual content view or website visit, as a result of subtle or direct requests from marketers, advertisers, and content creators.

[2] Conversion funnel is a technical term used in e-commerce operations to describe the track a consumer takes through an Internet advertising or search system, navigating an e-commerce website and finally converting to a sale.

[3] Mobile tagging is the process of providing data read from tags for display on mobile devices, commonly encoded in a two-dimensional barcode, using the camera of a camera phone as the reader device. The contents of the tag code is usually a URL for information addressed and accessible through Internet.

[4] vCard is a file format standard for electronic business cards. vCards are often attached to E-mail messages, but can be exchanged in other ways, such as on the World Wide Web or instant messaging. They can contain name and address information, phone numbers, e-mail addresses, URLs, logos, photographs, and <u>audio clips</u> (音频片断，音频剪辑).

[5] In computing, a uniform resource identifier (URI) is a string of characters used to identify a name or a resource. Such identification enables interaction with representations of the resource over a network (typically the World Wide Web) using specific protocols. Schemes specifying a <u>concrete</u> (['kɔnkri:t] adj.具体的) syntax and associated protocols define each URI.

one of several pay or free QR Code-generating sites or apps. Google has a popular API[1] to generate QR Codes, and apps for scanning QR Codes can be found on nearly all smartphone devices.

QR Codes storing addresses and Uniform Resource Locators (URLs[2]) may appear in magazines, on signs, on buses, on business cards, or on almost any object about which users might need information. Users with a camera phone equipped with the correct reader application can scan the image of the QR Code to display text, contact information, connect to a wireless network, or open a web page in the telephone's browser. This act of linking from physical world objects is termed hardlinking[3] or object hyperlinking[4]. QR Codes may also be linked to a location to track where a code has been scanned. Either the application that scans the QR Code retrieves the geo information by using GPS and cell tower triangulation (aGPS) or the URL encoded in the QR Code itself is associated with a location.

In June 2011, the Royal Dutch Mint (Koninklijke Nederlandse Munt) issued the world's first official coin with a QR Code to celebrate the centennial of its current building and premises. The coin was able to be scanned by a smartphone and link to a special website with contents about the historical event and design of the coin. This was the first time of a QR code used on currency.

3.1 Use in Mobile Operating Systems

QR Codes can be used in Google's mobile Android operating system using Google Goggles or 3rd party barcode scanners. QR Codes can be used in iOS devices [iPhone/iPod/iPad] via 3rd party barcode scanners. The browser supports URI redirection[5], which allows QR Codes to send metadata to existing applications on the device. The new iPhone 5 has QR code folders to manage your QR codes. Nokia's Symbian operating system features a barcode scanner which

---

[1] An application programming interface (API) is a protocol intended to be used as an interface by software components to communicate with each other. An API may include specifications for routines, data structures, object classes, and variables ([ˈvɛəriəbl] n. 变量).

[2] In computing, a uniform resource locator (URL) (originally called universal resource locator) is a specific character string that constitutes a reference to an Internet resource. A URL is technically a type of uniform resource identifier (URI), but in many technical documents and verbal discussions, URL is often used as a synonym for URI.

[3] A hardlink (one word) is one of several methods of object hyperlinking including graphical tags (2D barcodes), SMS tags and RFID tags. The hardlink method establishes a reference link between a physical world object and a .mobi web page just as a traditional hyperlink establishes an electronic reference to information on a Web page.

[4] Object hyperlinking is a neologism ([niːˈɒlədʒizəm] n. 新语) that usually refers to extending the Internet to objects and locations in the real world. The current Internet does not extend beyond the electronic world. Object hyperlinking aims to extend the Internet to the real world by attaching object tags with URLs as meta-objects to tangible ([ˈtændʒəbl] adj. 切实的) objects or locations. These object tags can then be read by a wireless mobile device and information about objects and locations retrieved and displayed.

[5] URL redirection, also called URL forwarding, is a World Wide Web technique for making a web page available under more than one URL address.

can read QR Codes, while mbarcode is a QR Code reader for the Maemo[1] operating system. In the Apple iOS, a QR Code reader is not natively included, but more than fifty paid and free apps are available with both scanning capabilities and hard-linking to URI. Google Goggles is also available for iOS. With BlackBerry devices, the App World application can natively scan QR Codes and load any recognized Web URLs on the device's Web browser. Windows Phone 7.5 is able to scan QR Codes through the Bing search app. They can also be used on the Nintendo 3DS.

3.2 Uses in Retail

Recently there has been a move away from traditional magnetic card, stamp or punchcard based schemes to QR code based loyalty programs.

3.3 QR Code Virtual Stores

According to one study, in June 2011, 14 million mobile users scanned a QR Code or a barcode. Some 58% of those users scanned a QR or barcode from their home, while 39% scanned from retail stores; 53% of the 14 million users were men between the ages of 18 and 34.

4. Design

4.1 Storage

The amount of data that can be stored in the QR Code symbol depends on the data type (mode, or input character set), version (1···40, indicating the overall dimensions of the symbol), and error correction level. The maximum storage capacities occur for 40-L symbols (version 40, error correction level L):

Maximum character storage capacity (40-L)			
character refers to individual values of the input mode/data type			
Input mode	max. characters	bit/byte	possible characters, default encoding
Numeric only	7,089	3⅓	0, 1, 2, 3, 4, 5, 6, 7, 8, 9
Alphanumeric	4,296	5½	0–9, A–Z (upper-case only), space, $, %, *, +, -, ., /, :
Binary/byte	2,953	8	ISO 8859-1
Kanji/kana	1,817	13	Shift JIS X 0208

4.2 Encryption

Encrypted QR Codes, which are not very common, have a few implementations. An Android app, for example, manages encryption and decryption of QR codes using the DES algorithm[2] (56 bits). Japanese immigration use encrypted QR Codes when placing visas in

---

[1] Maemo is a software platform developed by Nokia and improved upon by the Maemo community for smartphones and Internet tablets. It is based on the Debian Linux distribution, but has no relation to it. The platform comprises the Maemo operating system and the Maemo SDK (Software Development Kit, 软件开发工具包).

[2] The Data Encryption Standard (DES) is a previously predominant ([pri'dɔminənt] adj. 卓越的, 支配的, 主要的) algorithm for the encryption of electronic data. It was highly influential ([,influ'enʃəl] adj. 有影响的) in the advancement of modern cryptography in the academic world (学术界).

passports.

4.3 Error Correction

Codewords are 8 bits long and use the Reed–Solomon error correction[1] algorithm with four error correction levels. The higher the error correction level is, the less the storage capacity. The following table lists the approximate error correction capability at each of the four levels:

Level L (Low)	7% of codewords can be restored.
Level M (Medium)	15% of codewords can be restored.
Level Q (Quartile)	25% of codewords can be restored.
Level H (High)	30% of codewords can be restored.

Due to the design of Reed–Solomon codes and the use of 8-bit codewords, an individual code block cannot be more than 255 codewords in length. Since the larger QR symbols contain much more data than that, it is necessary to break the message up into multiple blocks. The QR specification does not use the largest possible block size, though; instead, it defines the block sizes so that no more than 30 error-correction symbols appear in each block. This means that 15 errors per block can be corrected at most, which limits the complexity of certain steps in the decoding algorithm. The code blocks are then interleaved together, making it less likely that localized damage to a QR symbol will overwhelm the capacity of any single block.

Damaged but still decodable QR code

Thanks to error correction, it is possible to create artistic QR Codes that still scan correctly, but contain intentional errors to make them more readable or attractive to the human eye, as well as to incorporate colors, logos and other features into the QR Code block.

4.4 Encoding

The format information records two things: the error correction level and the mask pattern used for the symbol. Masking is used to break up patterns in the data area that might confuse a scanner, such as large blank areas or misleading features that look like the locator marks. The mask patterns are defined on a 6×6 grid that is repeated as necessary to cover the whole symbol. Modules corresponding to the dark areas of the mask are inverted. The format information is protected from errors with a BCH code[2], and two complete copies are included in each QR symbol.

The message data is placed from right to left in a zigzag pattern, as shown below. In larger

---

[1] In coding theory, Reed–Solomon (RS) codes are non-binary cyclic error-correcting codes invented by Irving S. Reed and Gustave Solomon. They described a systematic way of building codes that could detect and correct multiple random (['rændəm] adj. 随机的) symbol errors.

[2] In coding theory, the BCH codes form a class of cyclic error-correcting codes that are constructed using finite fields (有限的领域). BCH codes were invented in 1959 by Hocquenghem, and independently in 1960 by Bose and Ray-Chaudhuri.The abbreviation BCH comprises the initials of these inventors' names.

symbols, this is complicated by the presence of the alignment patterns and the use of multiple interleaved error-correction blocks.

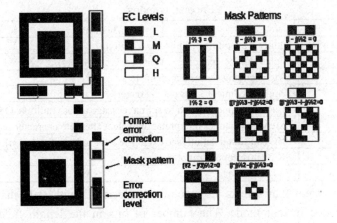

Meaning of format information

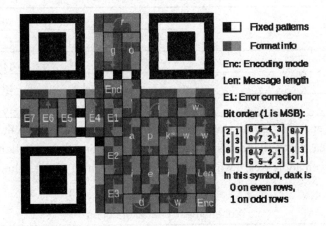

Message placement within a QR symbol

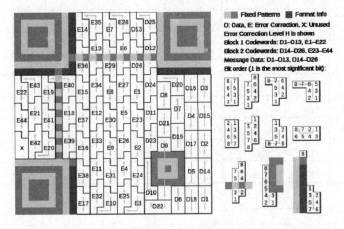

Larger symbol illustrating interleaved blocks

Four-bit indicators are used to select the encoding mode and convey other information. Encoding modes can be mixed as needed within a QR symbol.

Encoding modes

Indicator	Meaning
0001	Numeric encoding (10 bits per 3 digits)
0010	Alphanumeric encoding (11 bits per 2 characters)
0100	Byte encoding (8 bits per character)
1000	Kanji encoding (13 bits per character)
0011	Structured append (used to split a message across multiple QR symbols)
0111	Extended Channel Interpretation (select alternate character set or encoding)
0101	FNC1 in first position (see Code 128[1] for more information)
1001	FNC1 in second position
0000	End of message

After every indicator that selects an encoding mode is a length field that tells how many characters are encoded in that mode. The number of bits in the length field depends on the encoding and the symbol version.

Number of bits per length field

Encoding	Ver. 1–9	10–26	27–40
Numeric	10	12	14
Alphanumeric	9	11	13
Byte	8	16	16
Kanji	8	10	12

Alphanumeric encoding mode stores a message more compactly than the byte mode, but it cannot store lower-case letters and has only a limited selection of punctuation marks, which are sufficient for most web addresses. Two characters are coded in an 11-bit value by this formula:

$$V = 45 \times C_1 + C_2$$

Alphanumeric character codes

Code	Character	Code	Character	Code	Character	Code	Character	Code	Character
00	0	09	9	18	I	27	R	36	SP
01	1	10	A	19	J	28	S	37	$
02	2	11	B	20	K	29	T	38	%
03	3	12	C	21	L	30	U	39	*
04	4	13	D	22	M	31	V	40	+
05	5	14	E	23	N	32	W	41	-
06	6	15	F	24	O	33	X	42	.
07	7	16	G	25	P	34	Y	43	/
08	8	17	H	26	Q	35	Z	44	:

---

[1] Cōde 128 is a very high-density (高密度的) barcode symbology. It is used for alphanumeric or numeric-only barcodes. It can encode all 128 characters of ASCII.

5. Risks

Malicious QR Codes combined with a permissive reader can put a computer's contents and user's privacy at risk. This practice is known as "attagging", a portmanteau of "attack tagging". They are easily created and can be affixed over legitimate QR Codes. On a smartphone, the reader's many permissions allow use of the camera, full Internet access, read/write contact data, GPS, read browser history, read/write local storage, and global system changes.

Risks include linking to dangerous web sites with browser exploits, enabling the microphone/camera/GPS, and then streaming those feeds to a remote server, analysis of sensitive data (passwords, files, contacts, transactions), and sending email/SMS/IM messages or DDOS[1] packets as part of a botnet[2], corrupting privacy settings, stealing identity, and even containing malicious logic themselves such as JavaScript[3] or a virus. These actions could occur in the background while the user is only seeing the reader opening a seemingly harmless web page. In Russia, a malicious QR Code caused phones that scanned it to send premium texts at a fee of US$6 each.

New Words

matrix	[ˈmeitriks]	n. 矩阵
readability	[ˌriːdəˈbiliti]	n. 易读，可读性
kanji	[ˈkɑːndʒi]	n. 日本汉字
subsidiary	[səbˈsidjəri]	adj. 辅助的，补充的
semiconductor	[ˈsemikənˈdʌktə]	n. 半导体
processor	[ˈprəusesə]	n. 处理机，处理器
distinctive	[disˈtiŋktiv]	adj. 与众不同的，有特色的
normalize	[ˈnɔːməlaiz]	v. 使标准化，规格化
validity	[vəˈliditi]	n. 有效性，合法性，正确性
withdraw	[wiðˈdrɔː]	v. 撤销
compliance	[kəmˈplaiəns]	n. 依从，顺从
effortless	[ˈefətlis]	adj. 容易的，不费力气的

---

[1] In computing, a denial-of-service attack (DoS attack) or distributed denial-of-service attack (DDoS attack) is an attempt to make a machine or network resource <u>unavailable</u> ([ˌʌnəˈveiləbl] adj. 难以获得的) to its intended users. Although the means to carry out, motives for, and targets of a DoS attack may vary, it generally consists of the efforts of one or more people to temporarily or indefinitely interrupt or suspend services of a host connected to the Internet.

[2] Botnets are groups of computers connected to the Internet that have been taken over by a hacker. The hacker controls all the computers and they behave like a "robot network" (a.k.a. "botnet").

[3] JavaScript (sometimes abbreviated as JS) is a <u>scripting language</u> (脚本语言) commonly implemented as part of a web browser in order to create enhanced <u>user interfaces</u> (用户界面) and dynamic websites.

website	[ˈwebsait]	n.	网站
pitch	[pitʃ]	n.	投放
		vt.	投，掷，定位于
browser	[ˈbrauzə]	n.	浏览器
currency	[ˈkʌrənsi]	n.	流通
folder	[ˈfəuldə]	n.	文件夹
blackberry	[ˈblækbəri]	n.	黑莓
search	[səːtʃ]	n.	搜寻，查究
		v.	搜索，搜寻
Nintendo	[ninˈtendəu]	n.	任天堂
alphanumeric	[ˌælfənjuːˈmerik]	adj.	字母数字的
binary	[ˈbainəri]	adj.	二进位的，二元的
kana	[ˈkɑːnə]	n.	<日>假名
decryption	[diːˈkripʃən]	n.	解密
approximate	[əˈprɔksimeit]	adj.	近似的，大约的
		v.	近似，接近
codeword	[kəudwəːd]	n.	码字
restore	[risˈtɔː]	vt.	恢复，修复
overwhelm	[ˌəuvəˈwelm]	vt.	覆没，压倒
intentional	[inˈtenʃənəl]	adj.	有意图的，故意的
logo	[ˈlɔgɔ]	n.	徽标
mask	[mɑːsk]	v.	掩膜
mark	[mɑːk]	n.	标志，记号
		v.	做标记
zigzag	[ˈzigzæg]	n.	Z字形，锯齿形
		adj.	曲折的，锯齿形的，Z字形的
convey	[kənˈvei]	vt.	传达
compactly	[ˈkɔmpæktli]	adv.	紧凑地，紧密地，简洁地
malicious	[məˈliʃəs]	adj.	怀恶意的
permissive	[pə(ː)ˈmisiv]	adj.	许可的
portmanteau	[pɔːtˈmæntəu]	n.	合成词
affix	[əˈfiks]	vt.	使附于，粘贴
exploit	[iksˈplɔit]	v.	使用，利用
sensitive	[ˈsensitiv]	adj.	敏感的
corrupt	[kəˈrʌpt]	vt.	破坏
virus	[ˈvaiərəs]	n.	病毒
harmless	[ˈhɑːmlis]	adj.	无害的
botnet	[bɔtnet]	n.	僵尸网

Phrases

two-dimensional code	二维码
be made up of …	由……组成
angle of view	视角
binary number	二进制数码
validity check	有效性检查
error-correcting code	纠错码
automatic identification and data capture	自动识别和数据捕捉
in recent years	最近几年中
conversion rate	转化率
conversion funnel	转化漏斗
in-store product labeling	在库产品标签
business card	名片
geo information	位置信息，地理信息
3rd party	第三方
move away	离开
magnetic card	磁卡片，磁性卡片
character set	字符集
error correction	纠错，数据纠正
Reed–Solomon error correction algorithm	里德-所罗门纠错算法
block size	字区大小
code block	码组
format information	格式信息
mask pattern	掩模图案
lower-case letter	小写字母
be sufficient for	足够
web address	网址
sensitive data	敏感数据
in the background	在背后，在幕后，作为后果

Abbreviations

QR Code (Quick Response Code)	快速响应码
AIM (Automatic Identification and Mobility)	自动识别和移动
JIS (Japanese Industrial Standard)	日本工业标准

NTT (Nippon Telegraph and Telephone Public Corporation)　日本电报电话公共公司
NBI (Philippines National Bureau of Investigation)　菲律宾国家调查局
URI (Uniform Resource Identifier)　统一资源标识符
app (application)　应用
API (Application Programming Interface)　应用编程接口
DES (Data Encryption Standard)　数据加密标准
IM（Instant Messenger）　即时消息，即时通信
DDoS (Distributed Denial of Service)　分布式拒绝服务

Exercises

【EX.1】 Answer the following questions according to the text.

1. What is QR Code abbreviated from? When and where was the QR Code invented?
2. What are the several standards in documents covering the physical encoding of QR Codes?
3. What has Japan's NTT DoCoMo established?
4. Why has the QR Code become a focus of advertising strategy?
5. Who and when issued the world's first official coin with a QR Code? What for?
6. How many mobile users scanned a QR Code or a barcode in June 2011 according to one study?
7. What does the amount of data that can be stored in the QR Code symbol depend on?
8. What does an Android app do?
9. What is the relationship between the error correction level and the storage capacity?
10. What are the two things the format information records? How is the message data placed?

【EX.2】 Translate the following terms or phrases from English into Chinese and vice versa.

1. two-dimensional code　　　　1. _____
2. be made up of …　　　　　　2. _____
3. error-correcting code　　　　3. _____
4. geo information　　　　　　　4. _____
5. validity check　　　　　　　　5. _____
6. character set　　　　　　　　6. _____
7. code block　　　　　　　　　7. _____
8. error correction　　　　　　　8. _____
9. mask pattern　　　　　　　　9. _____

10.	Web address	10. _____
11.	敏感数据	11. _____
12.	n. 矩阵	12. _____
13.	n. 有效性，合法性，正确性	13. _____
14.	n. 浏览器	14. _____
15.	n. 解密	15. _____

【EX.3】Translate the following sentences into Chinese.

1. Conversely, some applications represent data as a matrix of many small contiguous pieces of data.

2. Semiconductor devices can perform a variety of control functions in electronic equipment.

3. Today, the semiconductor industry is in a dramatically changing market environment.

4. Simulation result indicated the validity and efficiency of the proposed algorithm.

5. HTML forced the browser to display data a certain way.

6. The data can be accessed by remote client via Web browser.

7. This folder's path has unsupported characters.

8. Data logging uses file formats of common computer platforms, which can be accessed without special software.

9. Hardware encrypting resists decryption intensely, but it is very inconvenient for users.

10. Symmetric encryption requires the same key for both encryption and decryption.

Text C

Choosing the Right Barcode Scanner

Barcode scanners[1] have become easier to use than ever before. Long gone are the days of dealing with decoder boxes and multiple cables going everywhere. Simply plug the cable into the scanner and PC and you're up and running!

While their operation has become easier, there are now more options and varieties of scanners to choose from. Picking the right one can be a challenge without understanding the various types and options.

The first step in finding the right scanner is identifying your specific needs:

- Where will the scanner be used? Is it a rugged[2] environment?
- How often will it be used?
- What kind of barcodes will you be reading?

[1]['skænə]
n. 扫描器，扫描仪

[2]['rʌgid]
adj. 恶劣的

- How will the scanner be used?
- Can you stay connected to a PC?

Knowing how you'll be using the scanner will help you decide what scanner type, form factor, and other options you'll need. Understanding each of these factors will help you find the right scanner for your needs.

1. Barcode Scanner Types

One of the most important concerns when choosing a suitable scanner is the type of scan engine[3] it has. This is ultimately dependent on the type of barcodes that you will be reading and how aggressive a unit you'll need. There are 3 main types of scan engines.

1.1 Laser

This is the most well known scanner type. It uses a red diode laser[4] to read the reflectance[5] of the black and white spaces in a barcode. Laser scanners are only able to read standard linear (1D) barcodes but are also the most cost effective option. Standard laser scanners can read from a few inches to a foot or two away depending on the size of the barcode. There are also extended range laser scanners, like the Motorola LS3408ER, which can read up to 35ft away when using large reflective[6] labels.

1.2 Linear Imager

Linear imager scanners are similar to lasers in that they also only read 1D barcodes. But instead of reading reflected light from the laser, they take a picture[7] of the barcode. It then analyzes this image to extract the information from the code. Linear imagers, like the Honeywell 1300g, have become a very good replacement for laser scanner as their read ranges and costs have become similar. A linear imager also does a better job reading poorly printed or damaged codes compared to lasers. For applications that need a more aggressive scanner, a linear imager will be a great fit for the same cost.

1.3 2D Area Imagers

Like linear imagers, full 2D imagers also capture an image to analyze. But compared to the linear only devices, these scanners can read any type of barcode. 1D, stacked, and 2D barcodes are all supported by a 2D imager. Another advantage these imagers have is that the orientation of the barcode isn't important when reading. With lasers and linear imagers, you have to line up[8] the indicator horizontally across the barcode. A 2D imager is taking a more detailed

[3]['endʒin]
n. 引擎，发动机

[4]diode laser:
二极管激光器
[5][ri'flektəns]
n. 反射比，反射系数

[6][ri'flektiv]
adj. 沉思的

[7]take a picture:
摄影，照相

[8]line up:
v. 整队，排列

image and is more intelligent, so you can read a code in any direction. This results in faster reads with less aiming[9]. 2D imagers, like the Honeywell 1900, can also read barcodes off of any surface including a monitor or phone screen. With their added abilities and very aggressive reading, 2D imagers are becoming more popular in all industries to speed up[10] scanning applications and expand the ways in which barcodes are used.

2. Form Factors

Once you know what type of scanner you'll need, the next big question is what form factor[11] the scanner will be. Most of us are familiar with the basic gun-style and in-counter scanners from retail and grocery stores. There are 5 main form factors for scanners, and each has advantages depending on your application and how you'll use the scanner.

2.1 Handheld

These are by far the most common form that scanners come in and are very easy to operate. Simply aim the scanner at the barcode and pull the trigger[12]. Most models, like the Motorola LS2208, will also offer a stand for hands-free operation. Handheld scanners[13] are also available in cordless form to avoid cable clutter[14] and increase your mobility.

2.2 Presentation

Presentation scanners[15], like the Metrologic MS7580, are designed to sit on a countertop[16] and don't need to be picked-up or held. These scanners are made for[17] hands-free scanning and will not require triggering[18] read. Likewise, instead of a single aimer like handheld scanners, presentation scanners have wide reading areas to reduce the need for aiming. You'll find these types of scanners at retail check-outs since it is easy to scan many items quickly. Just present the barcode in front of the scanner and it will read it automatically.

2.3 Mobile Computer

While they also do more than what basic scanners do, mobile computers provide complete freedom since both the PC and scanner are in a single device. Where other scanners need to be connected to a PC, mobile computers like the Motorola MC75A can move around freely while storing information into their internal memory or communicate via WiFi and Cellular (WAN) networks. Mobile computers are ideal for applications that require true mobility like inventory management[19] and asset tracking.

2.4 In-counter

In-counter scanners[20] are similar to presentation scanners in that

[9]['eim] v. 瞄准，对准

[10]speed up: 加速

[11]form factor: 物理尺寸和形状，产品规格

[12]pull the trigger: 扣动扳机
[13]handheld scanner: 手持式扫描器
[14]['klʌtə] n. 混乱

[15]presentation scanner: 固定式影像扫描器
[16]['kaʊntətɒp] n. 工作台面，柜台
[17]be made for: 最理想的，最适宜的
[18]['trigə] vt. 触发

[19]inventory management: 库存管理
[20]in-counter scanner: 台面式扫描器

you just present the barcode in front of the reader -- however, these are made to be embedded into a countertop. You have probably come across these types of scanners at grocery stores and self check-out lines. Units like the Datalogic Magellan 8300, are easy to operate for any user. Many models also have integrated scales to completely serve a POS[21] lane.

2.5 Fixed Mount[22]

A fixed scanner is a bit more specialized compared to the other types since it is really meant to be integrated with a larger automated system. These scanners are made to be mounted on a conveyor line[23] or in a kiosk and do not have a typical trigger or button to scan. Often, these scanners will always be on or get triggered by external sensors or controllers. Fixed scanners come in a wide range of speeds, like the Microscan MS-9, to accommodate even very high speed assembly lines[24] without any user intervention.

3. Connectivity -- Corded vs. Cordless

Every scanner has to communicate with a PC to transmit the barcode information into the software that you are using. Historically, there were only corded scanners that connected directly to the PC through a cable. These are still the most common scanner type and normally interface with a PC through a USB connection. Serial (RS232), PS/2, and proprietary terminal connections are also available for many models. Corded scanners are easy to get running and will be your least expensive option.

Cordless[25] scanners have become more common today as their costs have become much more affordable. These handheld scanners function the same way a corded scanner works except that the scanner communicates to a base station wirelessly. This base station is then connected to your PC through a cable. Your PC does not need to have any wireless support since the cradle[26] and scanner handle all of this. Just plug in the cradle, pair the scanner to the base, and you are ready to start scanning. It is very easy to replace a corded scanner with a cordless one since it has no effect on your PC or software.

Most cordless scanners use Bluetooth to communicate, which normally gives you a range of 33ft[27]. There are some specialized Bluetooth and proprietary wireless units that can transmit beyond 200ft. Some models also offer additional features that corded scanners don't, such as batch memory modes and direct pairing. The Motorola LS4278,

---

[21] POS(Point of Sale) 销售终端

[22] fixed mount: 固定架，支架

[23] conveyor line: 输送线

[24] assembly lines: 组装线，装配线

[25] ['kɔːdlis] adj. 不用电线的

[26] ['kreidl] n. 支架，托架

[27] 英尺（foot, feet）

for example, can pair directly to a device without using its cradle. This makes it a perfect match to use with a laptop, tablet, or smartphone that has built-in Bluetooth capabilities. Cordless scanners can provide greater mobility and freedom from cable clutter in any application.

4. Ruggedness[28]

Regardless of the environment that you'll be using your scanner in, ruggedness is always something to consider. Environment is a big factor, though you should also consider how the scanner will be used. You may be in a standard environment but if the scanners are mistreated, a more rugged option will help save time and money down the road.

Most scanners are designed for daily use in an office or retail environment. An accidental[29] drop once in a while will be ok. But if you are using your scanners in a warehouse or outdoor environment, you will want to consider a ruggedized unit like the Motorola LS3408FZ. The differences between a ruggedized and standard model are quite drastic[30]. Rugged units are completely sealed against dust and can handle repeated 6ft drops on concrete. With a rubberized[31] case, they can handle severe mistreatment. Some of them can even be used as a hammer without any problems!

You can always tell a ruggedized scanner by their bright yellow or red cases. They may be more expensive, but the time lost when a scanner breaks and the cost of replacing it quickly balances out the initial extra cost[32].

5. Finding the Right Scanner

With all the options available for barcode scanners today, it's important to find the right device for your business needs. Determining how you will use the scanner and what features you need will make the decision process easier.

[28]['rʌgidnis] n. 坚固性，耐久性

[29][,æksi'dentl] adj. 意外的

[30]['dræstik] adj. 极端的

[31]['rʌbəraiz] vt. 涂橡胶，用橡胶处理

[32]extra cost: 额外成本，额外费用

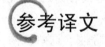

参考译文

Text A 条形码

1. 说明

过去的25年见证了条形码应用的迅猛增长。大家都熟悉条形码在零售店的应用，但那只是自动识别技术的一个显见的应用而已。

计算机在商业中的广泛应用增加了对数据的需求和数据的效用。各种数据在公司之间日夜传输，从附近超市的库存水平和再订货需求到世界金融市场巨量资金的流动。

这种数据爆炸要求数据输入更快、更自动化。条形码能够满足这些需求。在眨眼间超市结账台的精确设备就可以读取货物标签上条形码、解码为一个商品号、在主计算机中查找该号并在账单上打印定价和商品名称。同时，主计算机记录库存的减少，并且，当库存降到预设水平之下时，用电话线发送电子信息给主库。该计算机网络就自动把重新订货信息发送给某个供应商，并沿着供应链传递信息。

条形码图像是自动识别商品的理想方法。与磁条或无线射频标签不同，它的产生更廉价，只需要一点墨水和纸张。与文本或图形不同，它可以用相对便宜的机器快速并全方位地阅读。所有这些都需要一个精确而可靠的方法来产生条形码图像。

2. 条形码的使用

虽然1970年条形码首次商业应用于杂货店的货物配送，但从那以后得到了巨大的发展。

我们现在看到世界各地的商店都在结账台和配送链使用条形码，除了零售场所之外，公司内部和公司之间也使用条形码。在车辆制造、文档跟踪、家庭录像机的数据输入、时间控制和安全访问中使用条形码。在某些医院，甚至可以通过佩戴在手腕上的条形码标签来自动识别病人。

现在已经开发出来了许多标准供条形码编码系统使用并对其控制。有些是国际化的，有些只能用于某一行业或某一公司或部门。

条形码用户可分为两大类，一类是在一个被控系统中使用条形码的人，他们必须遵守由其他组织制定的编码标准；另一类是希望制作出完全供自己使用的条形码，并可以自由地选择最适合自己的条形码类型。

根据所运行系统的类型，用户也许希望在某一特定类型的所有物品上使用同样的条形码，也希望可以唯一地标识每个物品（如法律文件或文档）。

3. 条形码结构

所有的条形码都由一系列的黑条和介于其间的白条构成。黑条与白条的相对尺寸及其数目由所用的符号系统（或条形码类型）规范确定。常用的符号系统有多个。每个符号系统数据编码的方法不同，类型或数据量也不同。一般而言，对一种特定的应用只能选一种符号系统。

要确保系统的兼容性，所有的条形码用户应该遵循同样的用法和数据编码方法，这很重要。在类似办公室内文档跟踪这样的小系统中，要控制所用的条形码类型很容易。但是，对像英国零售产品这样大而复杂的系统，协作与控制要复杂得多。

因此，在特定领域条形码的使用由一个官方（或半官方）机构管理与控制。这些机构发布规范来规定特定应用中所要用的条形码符号系统、应用尺寸和质量有何限制以及所用的编号系统。在使用条形码识别物体时，官方机构将发布所用的号码以便不会发生冲突。

以下列出一些官方机构及其所管辖的领域：

（1）GS1（大多数国家的协会）。
- EAN 8 & 13 用于零售商品；
- ITF 交错码用于外壳；

- Code 128 用于补充编码。

（2）出版商协会。

ISBN 用于图书编码。

（3）英国图书馆期刊条码技术协会。

ISSN 用于期刊杂志的编码。

（4）美国统一代码委员会。

UPC 用于美国和加拿大零售商品的编码。

有许多其他的机构负责如运输、血库、药物和汽车工业这样的领域。

那些涉及条形码编码的人应该懂得条形码符号与其应用规范之间的关系。

一个符号系统并不针对特定的应用或编码系统，它只是一些简单的条形码的构造及其运作限制的规则。

应用规范采用特定符号系统并定义了物品编号的方法。某些应用规范管理特定领域内物品的编码方法，但采用其他更大范围的符号系统和应用规范。

例如，英国的书籍编码属于 ISBN（国际标准图书编号）系统，但也与由 GS1 管理的 EAN-13 相结合。

大多数条形码符号系统有一些共同的特点。

3.1 人可读字符

许多条形码编码新手对条形码包含的信息都有误解。他们熟悉零售店中条形码的使用并认为条形码中包括了商品的定价，但情况并非如此。条形码只携带标识该商品的唯一识别号码。在超市的结账台扫描仪读取该号码，从存放在主机中的"查询表"中提取价格。

在几乎所有情况下，所有有用的信息都以"人可读"的形式印刷，通常位于条形码底部。在大多数符号中推荐使用 HRC's（人可读字符）标准字型。这些字型通常用 OCR-B（光字符识别-国际标准）或 OCR-A（光字符识别-美国标准协会标准），这两种字型都是为机器读取设计的。在实际应用中，HRC's 不是机器读取并且只是使用标准字型，以便外观一致。

3.2 光边

所有种类的条形码都需要在条形码左侧和右侧留空。这让扫描仪可以区分条形码和周围的图像。如果在光边出现错误类型的图像，就会有条形码不能解码或解码错误的风险。

造成阅读错误的最常见原因之一是侵入光边。因此，一些符号系统采用了一个保护该静区的方法。例如，在该码的周围放置连续的破折号或方框。由于 UPC 编码在主码的左右有人可读的字符，该静区通常会受到很好的保护。EAN13 代码中人可读字符出现在代码的左侧，而右侧没有。规范推荐把光边指示符放在代码右侧以便规劝设计者不要在静区放置图片。

3.3 条形码维度

不同符号系统描述条形码的尺寸的方法不同，如 UPC 和 EAN 这类编码使用基于标准尺寸（100%放大率）的放大系数。各个维度都按照放大系数按比例进行相应改变。虽然每个放大系数都有推荐的高度，但在实际应用中有时会调整。要避免过度降低高度（截短），因为这会造成扫描障碍。

其他符号系统使用基于代码中最窄黑条的宽度定义尺寸。

许多符号类型是模块化的，也就是全部黑条和白条宽度来自于窄黑条（或 X 维度）。在这种编码中，宽黑条和白条由 2、3 个或者更多的窄黑条构成，这取决于其所用的编码规则。因此，要描述条形码尺寸只需定义窄黑条的宽度和代码的高度即可。

代码 39 与此不同，因为它在定义窄黑条宽度的同时，也定义宽黑与窄黑条的比率（在 2:1 和 3:1 之间）。因为可能有多种窄黑条宽度和宽/窄比率组合，所以代码 39 用户发现用"每英寸字符数 CPI"（也就是 1 英寸内可以编码的字符数）表达很方便。

以上规则的一个复杂之处在于对 UPC 和 EAN 代码的某些部分调整为窄黑条的 1/13，这可以保证条宽容错的平均分布并增加代码的可扫描性。

3.4 起止符

一个符号系统通常在条形码的每一端都要有起止符。这个特殊的黑条/白条布局可以简明地告诉扫描仪读取已经完成。对长度不一的条形码，如果不使用起止符有可能造成扫描仪只读了部分代码却认为已经读完了整个代码。

起止符也可以指明条形码的方向。通过在条形码左右放置不同的符号，扫描仪可以检测代码是否被读颠倒了。

4. 得到好的扫描

条形码中的数据通过光点扫过来获得，从第一个黑条前的那个空白区域开始，扫过全部黑条和白条直到代码的另一端的空白区域。

如果在扫描期间光点移出代码边界之外，代码就无法正确扫描。因此，在印制代码时，选择代码维度必须要考虑扫描的方法。在应用中，在用扫描棒（一个笔形条形码阅读器）扫描时，一个缩短的（或截短的）代码也可以容易地读出，只要阅读棒可以扫过代码的全部长度而不出界。

大多数超市结账台使用移动光束扫描仪，光束移过代码。要控制光束经过商品的路径，以便光束可以垂直地经过代码，这是无法实现的。代码越宽，在扫过整个宽度之前，光束离开顶部或底部的可能性越大。显而易见，增加高度可以增加扫描质量。

因此，大多数条形码规范都使用以百分比表示的放大系数。对于每个放大系数都有一个标称的高度，以便条形码宽度增加时高度也相应地增加，以保持其可扫描性。在工作实际中会截短代码（减少代码的高度而不减少其宽度）。当截短时要小心，因为也许会扫错。

以上两例表明在正常高度代码和截短代码上相同的三次扫描。在正常代码上的三次扫描良好，但在截短代码上只有一次扫描成功。

对比度：

另一个可能出现的危险在于黑条与白条的对比度。最理想的情况是，所有的黑条都不反射光而所有的白条都百分之百地反射光。在实际中这绝无可能，在符合限制的条件内，还是可以读取有点亮的黑条和有点暗的白条的条形码。

如上所述，纯黑的黑条和纯白的白条最佳，但有些彩色组合也可以实现好的扫描效果，也有些不行。大多数扫描仪用红光，因此，任何可以反射红光的颜色都可以做白条，另外一些吸收红光的颜色可以做黑条。

阴影和色调也可改变，以下是可用颜色的简要指南：

好的黑条颜色：黑、绿、蓝、咖啡色。

好的白条颜色：白、红、黄、橙色。

Unit 10

Text A

What is ZigBee?

ZigBee is an open WPAN (Wireless Personal Area Networks) standard based on the IEEE 802.15.4 protocol. While IEEE 802.15.4 defines PHY(physical) and MAC (Medium Access Control) layers, ZigBee takes care of higher layers (e.g., network, application profiles, …). The development of ZigBee/IEEE 802.15.4 is motivated to address those applications in which only low transfer data rate is involved. Compared to other wireless communication techniques, ZigBee/IEEE 802.15.4 possesses the following advantages:
- Low power consumption;
- Low cost;
- Flexible, reliable and self-healing network;
- Large number of nodes;
- Fast, easy deployment;
- Security;
- Ability to be used globally;
- Product interoperability;
- Vendor independence.

The term "ZigBee" originates from honeybees' method of communicating newfound food sources. This silent-but-powerful communication system is known as the "ZigBee Principle." By dancing in a zig-zag pattern, the bee is able to share critical information, such as the location, distance, and direction of a newly discovered food source to its fellow hive members.

1. What is IEEE 802.15.4?

IEEE 802.15.4 is a standard defined by the IEEE (Institute of Electrical and Electronics Engineers, Inc.) for low-rate WPAN[1]. This standard defines the "physical layer" and the

---

[1] A WPAN (wireless personal area network) is a personal area network--a network for interconnecting devices centered around an individual person's workspace--in which the connections are wireless. Typically, a wireless personal area network uses some technology that permits communication within about 10 meters--in other words, a very short range. One such technology is Bluetooth, which was used as the basis for a new standard, IEEE 802.15.

"medium access layer." The specification for the physical layer, or PHY, defines a low-power spread spectrum radio operating at 2.4 GHz with a basic bit rate of 250 kilobits per second. There are also PHY specifications for 915 MHz and 868 MHz that operate at lower data rates.

2. How is ZigBee different from other wireless standards (e.g. Bluetooth)?

There are a multitude of standards that address mid to high data rates for voice, PC LANs, video, etc. However, ZigBee here has been a wireless network standard that meets the unique needs of sensors and control devices. Sensors and control devices don't need high bandwidth, but they do need low latency and very low energy consumption for long battery lives and for large device arrays.

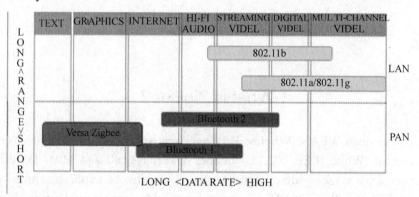

3. What are the real-lift applications of ZigBee?

ZigBee is well suited for a wide range of building automation, industrial, medical and residential control and monitoring applications. Examples include the following:

- Lighting controls;
- Automatic Meter Reading;
- Wireless smoke and CO_2 detectors;
- HVAC control;
- Heating control;
- Home control, including units such as intrusion sensors, motion detectors, glass break detectors, standing water sensors, loud sound detectors, etc;
- Environmental controls;
- Blind, drapery and shade controls;
- Medical sensing and monitoring;
- Universal Remote Control to a Set-Top Box[1] which includes Home Control;
- Industrial and building automation;
- Asset management.

---

[1] A set-top box (STB) or set-top unit (STU) is an information appliance device that generally contains a tuner (['tjuːnə] n. 调谐器) and connects to a television set and an external source of signal, turning the source signal into content in a form that can then be displayed on the television screen or other display device. Set-top boxes can also enhance source signal quality. They are used in cable television (有线电视) and satellite television systems, as well as other uses.

For example, wireless sensors (temperature, humidity, shock, etc.) are installed into containers, where they form a mesh network. Multiple containers in a ship form a mesh to report sensor data to the ship control center, and further to a port control center.

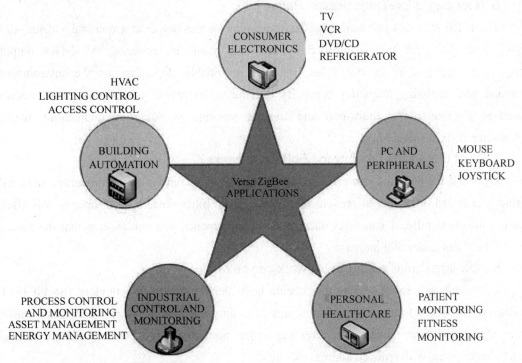

4. How reliable is the data delivery?

Reliable data delivery is critical to ZigBee applications. The underlying IEEE 802.15.4 standard provides strong reliability through several mechanisms at multiple layers. For example, it uses 27 channels in three separate frequency bands.

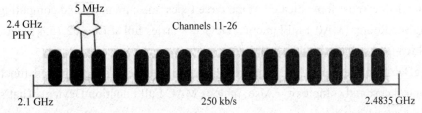

5. How long is the battery life?

The basic IEEE 802.15.4 node is fundamentally efficient in terms of battery performance. You can expect battery lifetimes from a few months to many years as a result of the system's power-saving modes and battery-optimized network parameters, such as a selection of beacon intervals, guaranteed time slots, and enablement / disablement options. Consider a typical security application, such as a magnetic reed switch door sensor. The sensor itself consumes almost no electricity; it's the radio that uses the bulk of the power. The sensor is configured to have a "heartbeat" at one-minute intervals and to immediately send a message when an event occurs. Assuming dozens of events per day, analysis shows that the sensor can still outlast an alkaline AAA battery. The configuration allows the network to update the sensor parameters remotely, change its reporting interval, or perform other remote functions and still have (theoretical) battery longevity well beyond the shelf life.

6. How long is the Transmission Range?

The IEEE 802.15.4 standard specifies transmitter output power at a nominal -3dBm[1] (0.5 mW), with the upper limit controlled by the local regulatory agencies. At -3dBm output, single-hop ranges of 10 to more than 100m are reasonable, depending on the environment, antenna, and operating frequency band. By introducing extensible and sophisticated network function, ZigBee allows multi-hop and flexible routing, providing communication ranges exceeding the basic single-hop.

7. What is the Data Latency for ZigBee Networks?

ZigBee/IEEE 802.15.4 can provide latencies as low as 16ms in a beacon-centric network, using guaranteed time slots to prevent interference from other sensors. Data latency will affect battery life. Generally, if you relax data-latency requirements, you can assume that the battery life of the client nodes will increase.

8. How large/small a ZigBee Network can be?

The addressing space allows of extreme node density--up to 264 devices (64 bit IEEE address), which may form different topologies depending on customer needs: star, mesh, cluster tree. At the same time, using local addressing, simple networks of more than 65,000 (2^{16}) nodes can be configured, with reduced address overhead.

9. What types of ZigBee Devices exist in a network?

IEEE MAC[2] specification introduces three device types. ZigBee specifies the following ZigBee Devices:

- ZigBee Coordinator (MAC Network Coordinator[3]). Maintains overall network knowledge; most sophisticated of the three types; most memory and computing power.
- ZigBee Router (MAC Full Function Device: Carries full IEEE 802.15.4 functionality and all features specified by the standard).
- ZigBee End Device (MAC Reduced Function Device: Carries limited functionality to control cost and complexity. Also, may be MAC Full Function Device). That's where the physical devices reside.

10. What Topologies are supported by ZigBee?

The figure below illustrates the possible network configurations and the roles of the

---

[1] dBm (sometimes dBmW) is an abbreviation for the power ratio in decibels (['desibel]n.分贝) (dB) of the measured power referenced to one milliwatt (['miliwɔt] n. 毫瓦) (mW).

[2] A Media Access Control address (MAC address) is a unique identifier ([ai'dentifaiə] n. 标识符) assigned to network interfaces for communications on the physical network segment.

[3] The network coordinator manages signals between end devices, high power repeaters and the application controller ([kən'trəulə] n. 控制器) in directed network systems.

devices.

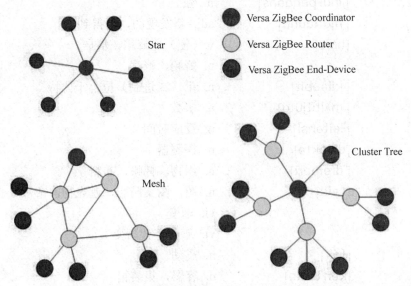

As shown above, there are three different network topologies that are supported by ZigBee, namely the star, mesh and cluster tree or hybrid networks. Each has its own advantages and can be used to advantage in different situations. The star network is commonly used, having the advantage of simplicity. As the name suggests it is formed in a star configuration with outlying nodes communicating with a central node. Mesh or peer-to-peer networks enable high degrees of reliability. They consist of a variety of nodes placed as needed, and nodes within range being able to communicate with each other to form a mesh. Messages may be routed across the network using the different stations as relays. There is usually a choice of routes that can be used and this makes the network very robust. If interference is present on one section of a network, then another can be used instead. Finally there is what is known as a cluster tree network. This is essentially a combination of star and mesh topologies.

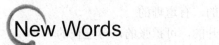

New Words

protocol	[ˈprəutəkɔl]	n. 协议
profile	[ˈprəufail]	n. 剖面，侧面，外形，轮廓
motivate	[ˈməutiveit]	v. 激发，促进
address	[əˈdres]	vt. 解决，处理
involve	[inˈvɔlv]	vt. 涉及
possess	[pəˈzes]	vt. 占有，拥有，持有
self-heal	[ˈselfˈhiːl]	n. 自体愈合植物
deployment	[diˈplɔimənt]	n. 部署

interoperability	[ˈintərˌɔpərəˈbiləti]	n. 互用性，协同工作的能力
independence	[ˌindiˈpendəns]	n. 独立
newfound	[ˈnjuːfaund]	adj. 新发现的，新得到的
hive	[haiv]	v. (使)入蜂箱，群居 n. 蜂箱，蜂房
kilobit	[ˈkiləubit]	n. 千（二进制）位，千比特
multitude	[ˈmʌltitjuːd]	n. 多数
latency	[ˈleitənsi]	n. 反应时间
detector	[diˈtektə]	n. 探测器
drapery	[ˈdreipəri]	n. 织物，帏帐，布料
shade	[ʃeid]	n. 荫，图案阴影，遮光物，帘 vi. 渐变 vt. 遮蔽，使渐变
shock	[ʃɔk]	n. 震动
container	[kənˈteinə]	n. 容器，集装箱
mechanism	[ˈmekənizəm]	n. 机械装置，机构，机制
fundamentally	[fʌndəˈmentəli]	adv. 基础地，根本地
guarantee	[ˌgærənˈtiː]	n. & vt. 保证，担保
beacon	[ˈbiːkən]	n. 信标
interval	[ˈintəvəl]	n. 时间间隔
enablement	[iˈneiblmənt]	n. 启动，允许
disablement	[diˈseiblmənt]	n. 无力化，无能力
heartbeat	[ˈhɑːtbiːt]	n. 心跳
outlast	[autˈlɑːst]	vt. 比……长久，比……活得长
alkaline	[ˈælkəlain]	adj. 碱性的
longevity	[lɔnˈdʒeviti]	n. 寿命
nominal	[ˈnɔminl]	adj. 名义上的
reasonable	[ˈriːznəbl]	adj. 合理的，有道理的
extensible	[ikˈstensibəl]	adj. 可展开的，可扩张的，可延长的
sophisticated	[səˈfistikeitid]	adj. 先进的
density	[ˈdensiti]	n.密度
overhead	[ˈəuvəhed]	n. 开销，管理费用
coordinator	[kəuˈɔːdineitə]	n. 协调器
functionality	[ˌfʌŋkʃəˈnæliti]	n. 功能性
complexity	[kəmˈpleksiti]	n. 复杂性
illustrate	[ˈiləstreit]	vt. 举例说明，图解
outlying	[ˈautlaiiŋ]	adj. 边远的，偏僻的
essentially	[iˈsenʃəli]	adv. 本质上，本来
combination	[ˌkɔmbiˈneiʃən]	n. 结合，联合，合并

Phrases

low transfer data rate	低传输数据率
originate from	发源于
kilobits per second	每秒千比特
a multitude of	许多
battery live	电池寿命
be well suited for	很适合
Universal Remote Control	通用远程控制
set-top box	置顶盒
asset management	资产管理
ship control center	船舶控制中心
port control center	港口管理中心
in terms of …	根据，按照，用……的话，在……方面
as a result of	作为结果
power-saving mode	省电模式
guaranteed time slot	有保证时隙
shelf life	保质期
magnetic reed switch	磁簧开关
the bulk of	大半，大部分的
output power	输出功率
regulatory agency	管理机构
allow of	允许
control cost	控制成本
hybrid network	混合网络
peer-to-peer network	点对点网络

Abbreviations

WPAN (Wireless Personal Area Networks)	无线个人局域网
MAC (Medium Access Control)	媒体访问控制
dBm	分贝毫瓦

Exercises

【EX.1】**Answer the following questions according to the text.**

1. What is ZigBee? Where does the term "ZigBee" originate from?
2. What is IEEE 802.15.4?

3. What is ZigBee well suited for?

4. What is critical to ZigBee applications? What does the underlying IEEE 802.15.4 standard provide?

5. How long can you expect battery lifetimes?

6. The sensor is configured to have a "heartbeat" at one-minute intervals and to immediately send a message when an event occurs. What does the configuration allow the network to do?

7. What does ZigBee allow by introducing extensible and sophisticated network function?

8. What can you assume generally if you relax data-latency requirements?

9. What ZigBee Devices does ZigBee specify?

10. How many topologies are supported by ZigBee? What are they?

【EX.2】 Translate the following terms or phrases from English into Chinese and vice versa.

1. low transfer data rate   1. _____
2. kilobits per second   2. _____
3. universal remote control   3. _____
4. power-saving mode   4. _____
5. set-top box   5. _____
6. output power   6. _____
7. peer-to-peer network   7. _____
8. hybrid network   8. _____
9. protocol   9. _____
10. address   10. _____
11. vt. 涉及   11. _____
12. vt. 占有，拥有，持有   12. _____
13. n. 反应时间   13. _____
14. n. 部署   14. _____
15. n. 信标   15. _____

【EX.3】 Translate the following sentences into Chinese.

1. The cross - layer protocol has been a hot topic in WSN research.

2. File transfer protocol can help users transfer files between computers on internet.

3. Distributed object management is important in implementing distributed object interoperability.

4. This detector can acquire multiple signals.

5. Since the overhead cost is high, professional services are also relatively expensive.

6. ZigBee Home Automation delivers a standard that can make every home a smarter, safer and more energy efficient environment for consumers and families.

7. In a mesh network, packets are forwarded wirelessly from node to node.

8. The wide use of Peer - to - Peer networks causes network congestion.

9. In recent years, Peer - to - Peer is one of the research hot spot in network technology.

10. Hybrid networks are combinations of star, ring, and bus networks.

【EX.4】 **Complete the following passage with appropriate words in the box.**

| incorporate | surf | networking | super-fast | mobile |
| connectivity | send | low-power | conform | cabling |

Bluetooth and WiFi are both wireless networking standards that provide connectivity via radio waves. The main difference: Bluetooth's primary use is to replace cables, while WiFi is largely used to provide wireless, high-speed access to the Internet or a local area network.

1. Bluetooth

First developed in 1994, Bluetooth is a __1__, short-range (30 feet) networking specification with moderately fast transmission speeds of 800 kilobits per second. Bluetooth provides a wireless, point-to-point, "personal area network" for PDAs, notebooks, printers, __2__ phones, audio components, and other devices. The wireless technology can be used anywhere you have two or more devices that are Bluetooth enabled. For example, you could __3__ files from a notebook to a printer without having to physically connect the two devices with a cable.

A few notebooks, such as the IBM ThinkPad T30, now include built-in Bluetooth __4__. And $129 will buy you a Bluetooth card for expansion-slot Palm PDAs, allowing you to connect to printers, notebooks, mobile phones, and other devices without cables.

Despite the promises of Bluetooth, however, hardware makers have been slow to __5__ it into their products. Some experts believe it could be eight years before Bluetooth is commonly used. They attribute the technology's lagging adoption rate to poor usability and confusion about what Bluetooth is and does.

2. WiFi

Short for Wireless Fidelity, WiFi is a user-friendly name for devices that have been certified by the Wireless Ethernet Compatibility Alliance to __6__ to the industry-standard wireless networking specification IEEE 802.11b. WiFi began appearing in products in late 1998. The standard currently provides access to Ethernet networks such as a corporate LAN or the Internet at __7__ speeds of up to 11 megabits per second.

WiFi connections can be made up to about 300 feet away from a "hot spot" (slang for a WiFi networking node). When your notebook or PDA has a WiFi networking card or built-in chip, you can __8__ the Internet at broadband speeds wirelessly. WiFi networking nodes are proliferating globally; many Starbucks locations, for instance, offer access to WiFi hot spots for a fee.

Many notebooks today have IEEE 802.11b built-in; those that don't can be adapted via WiFi connectivity PC Cards. WiFi is also the basis for some home networking products, allowing you to share high-speed Internet connections without __9__. Late last year, products featuring a newer wireless networking specification, IEEE 802.11a (called WiFi5 by WECA), debuted. This standard provides transmission speeds of up to 54 mbps. Wireless __10__ is expected to grow in popularity as a practical, flexible way to replace some LANs. With wireless networking, for instance, workers can carry their notebooks from cubicle to conference room and stay connected to the corporate network.

【EX.5】 **Translate the following passage into Chinese.**

ZigBee

Pioneered by Philips Semiconductors, ZigBee is a low data rate, two-way standard for home automation and data networks. The standard originates from the Firefly Working Group and provides a specification for up to 254 nodes including one master managed from a single remote control. Real usage examples of ZigBee includes home automation tasks such as turning lights on, turning up the heat, setting the home security system, or starting the VCR. With ZigBee all these tasks can be done from anywhere in the home at the touch of a button. ZigBee also allows for dial-in access via the Internet for automation control.

The ZigBee standard uses small and very low-power devices to connect together to form a wireless control web. A ZigBee network is capable of supporting up to 254 client nodes plus one full functional device (master). ZigBee protocol is optimized for very long battery life measured in months to years from inexpensive, off-the-shelf non-rechargeable batteries, and can control lighting, air conditioning and heating, smoke and fire alarms, and other security devices. The standard supports 2.4 GHz (worldwide), 868 MHz (Europe) and 915 MHz (Americas) unlicensed radio bands with range up to 75 meters.

Text B

3G and 4G

1. 3G Technology

1.1 Definition of 3G

3G is the third generation of wireless technologies. It comes with enhancements over previous wireless technologies, like high-speed transmission, advanced multimedia access and global roaming. 3G is mostly used with mobile phones and handsets as a means to connect the phone to the Internet or other IP networks in order to make voice and video calls, to download and upload data and to surf the net.

1.2 How is 3G Better?

3G has the following enhancements over 2.5G and the previous networks:
- Several times higher data speed;
- Enhanced audio and video streaming;
- Videoconferencing support;
- Web and WAP browsing at higher speeds;

- IPTV (TV through the Internet) support.

1.3 3G Technical Specifications

The transfer rate for 3G networks is between 128 and 144 kbps (kilobits per second) for devices that are moving fast and 384 kbps for slow ones (like for pedestrians). For fixed wireless LANs, the speed goes beyond 2 Mbps.

3G is a set of technologies and standards that include WCDMA[1], WLAN and cellular radio, among others.

3G follows a pattern of G's that started in the early 1990's by the ITU. The pattern is actually a wireless initiative called the IMT-2000 (International Mobile Communications 2000). 3G therefore comes just after 2G and 2.5G, the second generation technologies. 2G technologies include, among others, the Global System for Mobile (GSM[2])--the famous mobile phone technology we use today. 2.5G brings standards that are midway between 2G and 3G, including the General Packet Radio Service (GPRS[3]), Enhanced Data rates for GSM Evolution (EDGE[4]), Universal Mobile Telecommunications System (UMTS) etc.

1.4 What is Required for Using 3G?

The first thing you require is a device (e.g. a mobile phone) that is 3G compatible. This is where the name 3G phone comes from - a phone that has 3G functionality; nothing to do with the number of cameras or the memory it has. An example is the iPhone 3G.

3G phones commonly have two cameras since the technology allows the user to have video calls, for which a user-facing camera is required for capturing him/her.

Unlike with WiFi which you can get for free in hotspots, you need to be subscribed to a service provider to get 3G network connectivity. We often call this kind of service a data plan or network plan.

Your device is connected to the 3G network through its SIM card (in the case of a mobile phone) or its 3G data card (which can be of different types: USB[5], PCMCIA[6] etc.), which are

---

[1] WCDMA stands for Wideband Code Division Multiple Access. It is one of the main systems used for third generation, or 3G, mobile communication networks. The term is often used interchangeably with UMTS, which stands for Universal Mobile Telecommunications Systems. Technically WCDMA is merely (['miəli]adv.仅仅, 只，不过) one example of UMTS technology.

[2] GSM is a standard set developed by the European Telecommunications Standards Institute (ETSI, 欧洲通信标准协会) to describe protocols for second generation (2G) digital cellular networks used by mobile phones.

[3] GPRS is a cellular networking service that supports WAP, SMS (Short Messaging Service,短消息服务) text messaging, and other data communications. GPRS technology is integrated into so-called 2.5G mobile phones designed to provide faster data transfer speeds than older 2G cellular networks.

[4] Enhanced Data rates for GSM Evolution (EDGE) is a radio based high-speed mobile data standard which acts as an enhancement for General Packet Radio Service (GPRS) networks. EDGE (also known as EGPRS) is a superset to GPRS and can function on any network with GPRS deployed on it, provided the carrier implements the necessary upgrades.

[5] Universal Serial Bus (USB) is an industry standard developed in the mid-1990s that defines the cables, connectors ([kə'nəktə] n. 连接器) and communications protocols used in a bus for connection, communication and power supply (供电) between computers and electronic devices.

[6] A PCMCIA card is a credit card-size memory or I/O device that connects to a personal computer, usually a notebook or laptop computer.

both generally provided/sold by the service provider. Through that, you get connected to the Internet whenever you are within a 3G network. Even if you are not in one, you can still use 2G or 2.5G services provided by the service provider.

1.5 What does 3G Cost?

3G is not very cheap, but it is worthwhile for users that need connectivity on the move. Some providers offer it within a somewhat costly package, but most of them have plans where the user pays for the amount of data transferred. This is because the technology is packet-based. For example, there are service plans where there is a flat rate for the first Gigabyte of data transferred, and a per minute cost for each additional Megabyte.

1.6 3G and Voice

Wireless technologies are a way for mobile users to make free or cheap calls worldwide and save a lot of money due to the latest telephony applications and services. 3G networks have the advantage of being available on the move, unlike WiFi, which is limited to a few meters around the emitting router. So, a user with a 3G phone and a 3G data plan is well-equipped for making free mobile calls. She will only have to download one of the free applications and install on her mobile phone and start making calls.

2. How will 4G Networks Change Business?

2.1 4G

Today's cell phones are generally great at what they were originally intended to do -- make calls, send text messages[1], that sort of thing. But with an ever-growing amount of Internet-related activity taking place on modern mobile phones, the current networks can't keep up. They have a knack for becoming completely swamped whenever too many people try to update their Twitter account, download music, watch videos, check traffic reports or do whatever other online activities they're burning to do while away from their traditional computers.

Just as mainstream cell-users have started to get more comfortable with the term 3G, the third-generation technology that supports "smartphones," whispers of a mythical 4G on the horizon have already started to spread. In a basic sense, 4G (fourth generation wireless communications) will involve settling mobile communications firmly and fully into the realm of Voice over Internet Protocol (VoIP). Although 4G technology will eventually be implemented in a variety of mobile gadgets, such as laptops and gaming devices, it will have the most noticeable impact in the case of mobile phones since they still deal with voice data differently.

In essence, cell phones will use the same basic VoIP system that computer softphone software programs and many long-distance carriers do now. They'll transfer all the information they have to send over a wireless Internet connection in a manner conforming to various Internet Protocols (IP). This will enable them to more completely maximize packet switching, which is a great way to send information quickly from one destination to another, and at a much lower cost.

When 4G networks become standard, users should notice a difference. 4G technology has

---

[1] SMS stands for short message service. Simply put, it is a method of communication that sends text between cell phones, or from a PC or handheld to a cell phone. The "short" part refers to the maximum size of the text messages: 160 characters (['kærɪktə] n. 字符) (letters, numbers or symbols in the Latin alphabet). For other alphabets, such as Chinese, the maximum SMS size is 70 characters.

some persuasive benefits, which are helping accelerate the industry's push in its direction. Peak times might still be a little pokey, but overall, it should be a step up from the service most cell phone users are familiar with today.

2.2 Benefits to the Bottom Line

There are several ways a business could benefit from upgrading to 4G-friendly technology. With all its data being transmitted by VoIP[1] -- that is, without any voice data still hitting the airwaves through a separate, dedicated transmission line -- the business could save money and benefit from enhanced security.

Just as important, the service will generally be quite a bit faster than what's available now. This improved performance and reliability will push cell phones more fully into the realm of mobile PCs like laptops in terms of overall capabilities. 3G got people part of the way there, but because the networks aren't 100 percent VoIP, they still get a little choppy when everyone's active on their phones at the same time; the goal for 4G networks is to increase the bandwidth and throughput capabilities so that more customers will feel secure trusting their cell phones to perform whenever necessary.

Having a phone that can fulfill every Internet role normally performed by a PC lets employees maximize their time without being chained to a computer, both at home and on the go. Plus, they can easily keep on top of work matters during all those little moments of downtime that are sprinkled throughout the average day, like time spent waiting in lines at grocery stores, sitting through advertisements before movie previews or riding in carpools during commutes.

One trend that's likely to become more common is phones designed to be ideal for videoconferencing[2]. That way, colleagues working from remote locations can transmit streaming videos -- whether they're out sick or out on safari-- with just the cameras on their cells. (Although in the case of under-the-weather employees, they might want to still stick with simple teleconferencing depending on how they're looking.)

All in all, lots more applications and devices geared toward the business side of life are sure to become available as 4G moves from the planning stages into practical utilization.

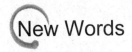

New Words

definition	[ˌdefiˈniʃən]	n. 定义，解说
generation	[ˌdʒenəˈreiʃən]	n. 产生，发生

---

[1] VoIP (voice over IP) is an IP telephony term for a set of facilities used to manage the delivery of voice information over the Internet. VoIP involves sending voice information in digital form (数字形式) in discrete packets rather than by using the traditional circuit-committed protocols of the public switched telephone network (PSTN, 公用电话交换网络).

[2] Videoconferencing is the conduct of a videoconference (also known as a video conference or videoteleconference ([ˈtelikɔnfərəns]n.远程电信会议)) by a set of telecommunication technologies which allow two or more locations to communicate by simultaneous two-way video and audio transmissions. It has also been called 'visual collaboration (虚拟协作)' and is a type of groupware ([ˈgruːpwɛə] n. 组件,群件).

enhancement	[in'hɑːnsmənt]	n. 增进，增加
previous	['priːvjəs]	adj. 在前的，早先的
		adv. 在……以前
multimedia	['mʌlti'miːdjə]	n. 多媒体
roam	[rəum]	v. & n. 漫游
handset	['hændset]	n. 电话听筒，手机，手持机
call	[kɔːl]	v. 调用
download	[daunləud]	v. 下载
upload	['ʌp,ləud]	v. 上传
video	['vidiəu]	n. 视频
videoconference	[,vidiəu'kɔnfərəns]	n. 视频会议
pedestrian	[pe'destriən]	n. 步行者
cellular	['seljulə]	adj. 细胞的
midway	['mid'wei]	n. 中途，半路
worthwhile	['wəːθ'wail]	adj. 值得做的，值得出力的
megabyte	['megəbait]	n. 兆字节
knack	[næk]	n. 诀窍
swamp	[swɔmp]	v. 陷入沼泽，淹没，覆没
mainstream	['meinstriːm]	n. 主流
whisper	['wispə]	n. 耳语，私语，密谈
mythical	['miθikəl]	adj. 神话的，虚构的
noticeable	['nəutisəbl]	adj. 显而易见的，值得注意的
softphone	['sɔftfəun]	n. 软件电话
carrier	['kæriə]	n. 载波（信号）
persuasive	[pə'sweisiv]	adj. 有说服力的
accelerate	[æk'seləreit]	v. 加速，促进
push	[puʃ]	n. 推，推动
pokey	['pəuki]	adj. 迟钝的，狭小的
airwave	['ɛəweiv]	n. 电视广播
realm	[relm]	n. 领域
choppy	['tʃɔpi]	adj. 波浪起伏的
throughput	['θruːput]	n. 吞吐量
fulfill	[ful'fil]	vt. 履行，实现，完成
sprinkle	['spriŋkl]	v. 洒，喷撒
preview	['priːvjuː]	n. 事先查看，预览
carpool	['kɑːpuːl]	n. 合用汽车
		v. 拼车

commute	[kəˈmjuːt]	n.	通勤来往，乘车上下班
under-the-weather	[ˈʌndə-ðə-ˈweðə]	adj.	身体不适，生病
teleconferencing	[teliˈkɔnfərənsiŋ]	n.	电信会议
utilization	[ˌjuːtilaiˈzeiʃən]	n.	利用

Phrases

global roaming	全球漫游
surf the net	网上冲浪
technical specification	技术规范
transfer rate	传输率
go beyond	超出
a set of	一组，一套
mobile phone	移动电话，手机
data plan	数据套餐
network plan	网络套餐
data card	数据卡
flat rate	统一费用
text message	文字信息
keep up	维持，继续
deal with	安排，处理，涉及
in essence	实际上
in a manner	在某种意义上
conform to	符合，遵照
low cost	低成本
bottom line	概要；底线
wait in lines	排队等候
dedicated transmission line	专用传输线
benefit from	受益于
quite a bit	相当多
sit through	一直挺到结束，耐着性子看完（或听完）
streaming video	流视频
on safari	外去远足，远行狩猎
stick with	[口]坚持做（某事）
all in all	总而言之
be geared toward	使适合于

Abbreviations

3G (Third Generation)   第三代通信
IP (Internet Protocol)   网际协议
WAP (Wireless Application Protocol)   无线应用协议
kbps (kilobits per second)   每秒千字节
WCDMA (Wideband Code Division Multiple Access)   宽带码分多址
IMT (International Mobile Communication)   国际移动通信
GPRS (General Packet Radio Service)   通用分组无线业务
EDGE (Enhanced Data rates for GSM Evolution)   GSM 增强数据率演进
UMTS (Universal Mobile Telecommunications System)   通用移动通信系统
SIM (Subscriber Identity Module)   用户身份识别模块
4G (Fourth Generation)   第四代通信
VoIP (Voice over Internet Protocol)   网络语音，网络电话

Exercises

【EX.1】Fill in the blanks according to the text.

1. 3G is the third generation of _____. It is mostly used with mobile phones and handsets as a means to connect the phone _____.

2. The transfer rate for 3G networks is _____ for devices that are moving fast and _____ for slow ones (like for pedestrians).

3. The first thing you require for using 3G is a device (e.g. a mobile phone) that is _____.

4. 3G phones commonly have _____. You need to be subscribed to a service provider to _____.

5. Your mobile phone is connected to the 3G network through _____. 3G is not very cheap, but it is worthwhile for _____.

6. Wireless technologies are a way for mobile users to _____ and save a lot of money due to _____.

7. Although 4G technology will eventually be implemented in a variety of mobile gadgets, such as _____, it will have the most noticeable impact in the case of _____ since they still deal with voice data differently.

8. 4G technology has some persuasive benefits, which _____.

9. The goal for 4G networks is to _____ so that more customers will feel secure trusting their cell phones _____.

10. Having a phone that can fulfill every Internet role normally performed by _____ lets employees _____ without being chained to a computer, both at home and _____.

【EX.2】Translate the following terms or phrases from English into Chinese and vice versa.

1. technical specification _____   1. _____
2. network plan _____   2. _____
3. transfer rate _____   3. _____
4. deal with _____   4. _____
5. conform to _____   5. _____
6. streaming video _____   6. _____
7. enhancement _____   7. _____
8. dedicated transmission line _____   8. _____
9. videoconference _____   9. _____
10. throughput _____   10. _____
11. n. 多媒体 _____   11. _____
12. n. 电信会议 _____   12. _____
13. n. 利用 _____   13. _____
14. n. 载波（信号）_____   14. _____
15. v. 下载 _____   15. _____

【EX.3】Translate the following sentences into Chinese.

1. This definition will be used for any pair of operators.
2. Multimedia is the combination of computer and video technology.
3. Data compression is one of key techniques in multimedia.
4. For delivering multimedia data correctly at the user interface, synchronization is essential.
5. PDA (personal digital assistant) can send email, download information and play music.
6. Not surprisingly, free apps are often the hottest type of download.
7. Why am I not able to upload the customized face?
8. This printer is of low power consumption, fine safety and high reliability.
9. How much downtime did we log last month?
10. The more network nodes, the larger network throughput.

Text C

NFC
Everyone in the smartphone world has been talking about NFC,

but what exactly is it and how is it significant to you, the end user? NFC stands for Near Field Communication and is all set to change the way we exchange information while on the go. NFC is a short-range[1] communication technology that enables devices to exchange information with other NFC-enabled devices or certain NFC supporting cards, much like the way a card reader scans and reads a credit card. This has several obvious practical applications already developed and in use in some countries, most notably Japan. Furthermore, NFC is an open standard and therefore, there is plenty[2] of room for innovation of further applications.

1. How NFC Works

Before we move on to its applications, let's take a look at how NFC works, without getting into[3] technical details. You basically put the back of an NFC-enabled device against either the back of another NFC-enabled device or an NFC-supported card, and the device automatically recognizes it, showing a prompt on screen to read or write information to the device -- it really is that simple.

2. Technical Specifications

NFC is an ISO 18000-3 RFID compatible short-range point-to-point communication standard governed under IEC[4] and ISO specification 13157, amongst others. It operates on a frequency of 13.56 MHz and supports data transfer at a relatively slow rate of 424 kbps, though future improvements will most likely increase this. It has an operating range of under 20 cm and takes less than 0.2 second to establish the connection. Power consumption during reading the data is under 15 mA, though it can be more when writing data.

3. Benefits over Other Wireless Communication Standards

Why use a whole new technology when we already have WiFi and Bluetooth etc. that we can utilize for the purpose? One might ask. The answer is for convenience and security.

Bluetooth and WiFi communication has a broader coverage than NFC, often ranging from 1 meter to 100 meters. This can lead to two problems. If the devices are set to accept connections without authentication, anyone within this range can connect to them and access the information stored on the other device, creating a major security issue. While this security concern[5] can be addressed by requiring a password[6] for establishing the connection, this leads to another problem: pairing the devices securely using Bluetooth or

[1][ʃɔːtˈreindʒ]
adj. 短射程的

[2][ˈplenti]
n. 丰富，大量

[3]get into:
进入，陷入

[4]International Electrotechnical Commission:
国际电工委员会

[5][kənˈsəːn]
vt. 涉及，关系到
n. 关系，关注
[6][ˈpɑːswəːd]
n. 密码，口令

establishing a secure connection over WiFi involves navigating through the device settings and entering passwords, which takes away the convenience[7].

NFC addresses both these issues by requiring close contact[8] between the devices to allow information exchange, and automatically presenting the available options on the screen for the user to select. Thus, a dozen people with NFC-enabled devices can be in the same room with no password set for NFC communication, yet none of them would run the risk of any unauthorized information access via NFC.

4. Current Practical Applications

We have seen what NFC is about, how it works and what benefits it carries over other short-range wireless communication technologies, but what in what practical scenarios can NFC be used? There are plenty, to be sure!

4.1 As an RFID Tag Scanner

An NFC device can act as an RFID tag scanner, reading information embedded in form of RFID tags in media such as posters, billboards, brochures[9], leaflets[10], menus and other similar promotional or informative material. An example of this would be when you visit a restaurant, you can scan the menu card by touching your phone or tablet connected to the device, then an interactive, animated[11] menu will be presented on your phone, with detailed descriptions of menu items, their reviews by other users and perhaps even videos of their preparation.

4.2 As a Debit/Credit Card Substitute

NFC makes it possible to replace your plastic money[12] with your phone. Once the information that is usually carried in your credit card has been stored in your phone and made accessible via NFC, you can simply touch your phone to a terminal the way you scan your credit card, and make payments[13] accordingly. This can make mobile ticketing and payments a breeze[14].

4.3 For Data Exchange

Two NFC-enabled phones can be made to exchange data after establishing a connection by bringing them within NFC's operation range. This can replace visiting cards[15], as you'll only need to touch your phone to that of someone else and your virtual business card can then be transferred to their device with one tap on the screen. Sharing photos and other media on your phone with others gets similarly easy.

---

[7][kən'viːnjəns]
n. 便利，方便

[8]['kɔntækt]
n. & vt. 接触，联系

[9][brəʊ'ʃjʊə]
n. 小册子

[10]['liːflit]
n. 传单

[11]['ænimeitid]
adj. 活生生的，动画的

[12]plastic money：
n. 信用卡

[13]['peimənt]
n. 付款，支付

[14][briːz]
n. 轻而易举的事

[15]visiting card：
n. 名片

4.4 For Bluetooth Pairing or WiFi Authentication

Pairing two Bluetooth devices to establish a connection involves navigating menus to enable Bluetooth, scan for a device, initiate pairing and enter the pass code[16] on each device. With NFC, you will just need to bring the devices together to be automatically prompted to initiate Bluetooth pairing by a tap on each screen. The same can also apply to establishing a secure WiFi connection.

5. Future Prospects[17]

Apart from the above-mentioned applications of NFC which are already implemented and in use in certain regions of the world, the future prospects of this communication standard are also bright. Let's take a look at some of the roles NFC is bound to play in our lives in the years to come.

5.1 Personal Payments

In the near future, NFC will enable you to give your daughter her pocket money[18] simply by touching your smartphone to hers, choosing to transfer money and selecting an amount, which she can spend by using her phone as her debit/credit card substitute[19] at the cafe, as explained above.

5.2 Keyless Security

Your NFC-enabled mobile device will act as the key to the locks on your car, your safe and your house. Though to ensure no one else can use your phone to gain access, NFC will only act as initiating the unlocking mechanism, which will have to be verified by facial, iris[20] or retina[21] recognition by your phone's camera, voice recognition by its microphone, fingerprint[22] scan by its touch screen or a combination of these. The result would be secure, keyless access to your vehicles, safes, workplace and dwellings.

5.3 National, International and Corporate Identification

NFC-enabled devices will be used to store to replace your social security[23]/national identity card, drivers license, employer card and passport, with added security measures in form of biometric scanning.

5.4 Social Networking

People will use NFC to exchange personal information with others in social interactions[24], as well as form personal social networks to share location-based information such as opinions and reviews of others on a business or recreational venue. You can leave your opinion of a place at an RFID tag and other visitors can read it. You can also

---

[16]pass code：一次性密码，临时密码

[17]['prɔspekt] n. 前景，前途，期望

[18]pocket money n. 零用钱

[19]['sʌbstitjuːt] n. 代用品，代替者 v. 代替，替换

[20]['aiəris] n. 虹膜

[21]['retinə] n. 视网膜

[22]['fiŋgərint] n. 指纹，手印 vt. 采指纹

[23]social security：n. 社会保障，社会保险

[24]social interaction：社交

read those left by others with their NFC-enabled device. NFC-based check-ins at locations can also be used to reward people and offer them services accordingly.

5.5 Entertainment

NFC will make playing multiplayer games with someone a breeze, as you will be able to initiate the game simply by bringing the devices close together.

5.6 Health and Public Safety

Doctors will be able to use NFC to scan their patient's phones for live health statistics such as pulse, blood pressure, body temperature etc., which will be gathered by the patient's device using certain censors. Thus, without directly scanning the bodies of patients and having to keep records of hundreds of patients in their devices, doctors will have quick access to such vital statistics in order to treat[25] them better. This can become especially handy under medical emergencies. Furthermore, patients will be able to use their devices to convey their medical situation at hospital receptions, to be more efficiently and quickly directed to the appropriate department.

[25][tri:t]vt. 治疗

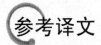

参考译文

Text A ZigBee 是什么？

ZigBee 是一个基于 IEEE 802.15.4 协议的 WPAN 开放标准。IEEE 802.15.4 定义了物理层和 MAC 层，而 ZigBee 主要处理更高层（如网络、应用方面等）。ZigBee/ IEEE 802.15.4 的开发主要解决了与低传输速率相关的应用。与其他无线通信技术相比，ZigBee/IEEE 802.15.4 具有以下优点：

- 低功耗；
- 低成本；
- 灵活的、可靠的和自愈合网络；
- 节点众多；
- 容易快速部署；
- 安全；
- 能用于全球；
- 产品可互用；
- 与经销商无关。

术语 ZigBee 来自蜜蜂找到食物源的沟通方法。这种无声但有效的沟通方法叫作

"ZigBee 法则"。通过多变的舞蹈,蜜蜂能够与其他伙伴分享重要信息,如新发现的食品源的位置、距离和方向。

1. IEEE 802.15.4 是什么

IEEE 802.15.4 是由 IEEE 为低速率 WPAN 定义的标准。该标准定义了"物理层"和"介质访问层"。物理层(PHY)规范定义了以 2.4 GHz 运行的低功耗无线扩频。其基本位率是 250kbps,也有在 915 MHz 和 868 MHz 低速率运行的物理层规范。

2. ZigBee 与其他无线标准(如蓝牙)的异同

ZigBee 用于语音、PC 局域网、视频等的中高速率标准众多。但是,这里的 ZigBee 一直是能够满足传感器和控制设备特殊需求的无线网络标准。传感器和控制设备不需要大带宽,但的确需要低延迟和极低功耗以便延长电池寿命和实现大设备部署。

3. ZigBee 的现实应用

ZigBee 非常适用于楼宇自动化、工业、医学、住宅控制与监控。例如:
- 控制照明;
- 自动读取仪表;
- 无线烟尘和 CO_2 探测器;
- HVAC 控制;
- 取暖控制;
- 家庭控制,包括闯入传感器、移动探测器、玻璃破碎探测器、积水探测器、声音探测器;
- 环境控制;
- 帘幕和光线控制;
- 医疗监测与监控;
- 对包括家居控制的机顶盒实现全球远程控制;
- 工业和楼宇自动化;
- 资产管理。

例如,把无线传感器(温度、适度、震动等)安装到集装箱中,构成一个网状网络。船上的多个集装箱组成一个网络,把传感器数据报告给船舶控制中心,并进一步报告给港口控制中心。

4. 数据传输的可靠性

可靠地传输数据对 ZigBee 十分重要。通过多层中的数种机制,IEEE 802.15.4 标准提供了坚固的可靠性。例如,在三个分开的频段使用 27 个通道。

5. 电池寿命

就电池性能来说,基本的 IEEE 802.15.4 节点实现基础效用。由于该系统具有节能模式和电池优化网络参数(如选择信标间隔、保证时隙和启用/关闭选项),电池寿命可能是从几个月到许多年。考虑一个特定的安全应用,如磁力开关门传感器。传感器本身几乎不耗电,是接收器用电。该传感器被设定为每分钟"心跳"一次,并且当发生意外时立即发送消息。假定每天开门多次,分析表明传感器仍然比碱性 AAA 电池寿命长。这种配置允许网络远程更新传感器参数、改变报告间隔或执行其他远程任务,理论上电池寿命可以远远超过保质期。

6. 传输距离

IEEE 802.15.4 标准规定正常的传输输出功率为-3dBm（0.5 毫瓦），上限由当地管理机构规定。以-3dBm 输出，单跳的范围从 10 到 100 多米是合适的，这取决于环境、天线和运行频段。通过引进可扩展的和成熟的网络功能，ZigBee 允许使用多跳和柔性路由，提供远远超过基本单跳的通信距离。

7. ZigBee 网络的数据延迟

在信标—中心网络中，ZigBee/IEEE 802.15.4 可以提供最短 16 毫秒的延迟，使用保证时隙可以防止来自其他传感器的干扰。数据延迟会影响电池寿命。通常，如果放宽对数据延迟的要求，就可以认为会增加客户节点的电池寿命。

8. ZigBee 网络的规模

寻址空间允许最大的节点密度高达 264 个设备（64 位 IEEE 地址），可以根据用户需求组成不同的拓扑结构：星状、网状、树状。同时，使用本地寻址，可以配置超过 65 000（2^{16}）个节点的简单网络，减少地址开销。

9. 网络中的 ZigBee 设备

IEEE MAC 规范介绍了三种设备。ZigBee 规范列出了以下设备：

- ZigBee 协调器（MAC 网络协调器）：维护整个网络知识；三类中最成熟设备；大内存和计算能力强。
- ZigBee 路由器（MAC 全功能设备：支持 IEEE 802.15.4 全部功能和该标准规定的所有特点）。
- ZigBee 端设备（MAC 精简功能设备：支持有限功能以控制成本和复杂性，也可是 MAC 全功能设备）。这是物理设备所处的位置。

10. ZigBee 支持的拓扑结构

图中表明了可能的网络配置和设备的角色。

如上图所示，ZigBee 支持三种不同的拓扑结构，即星状、网状和树状或混合网络。每种结构都有自己的优点并可以用于不同的情况以体现优势。星状网络很常用，优点是简单，如其名称所示，其组成如星，远处的节点与中心节点通信。网状或点对点网络可靠性高，由按需放置的多个节点组成，其中的每个节点都可与组成网络的其他节点相互通信。消息可以在网络的不同节点间接力传输。通常可以选择路由，这使得网络很健壮。如果在网络中的一个站点发送了冲突，可以用其他站点替代。最后是树状网络，它实际上是星状网络和网状网络的组合。

参考答案

Unit 1

Text A

【EX.1】Answer the following questions according to the text.

1. It stands for Internet of Things.
2. Smartphone apps are likely to provide an important window on the world of IoT.
3. In the future your alarm clock will let you sleep in if your train is delayed, rearrange a taxi, and even email your boss if you're stuck on a motorway.
4. According to Grant Notman, the IoT is removing mundane repetitive tasks or creating things that just weren't possible before, enabling more people to do more rewarding tasks and leaving the machines to do the repetitive jobs.
5. The IoT on its own is nothing more than back-office admin.
6. According to Jean-Paul Edwards, the consumer won't be interested in the Internet of Things. They will be interested in what the IoT allows them to do or what it saves them from doing.
7. The Internet of Things is based around embedded RFID chips, barcodes and sensors.
8. Someone can do so by stick a RFID chip on the handlebars.
9. It is New Songdo City. It is 40 miles south of Seoul in South Korea.
10. A Cisco-powered concept called U.Life is based on a city wide wired broadband network. Its aim is to build a low energy, incredibly efficient city with private investment.

【EX.2】Translate the following terms or phrases from English into Chinese and vice versa.

1.	interaction	1.	n. 交互
2.	network	2.	n. 网络
3.	template (=templet)	3.	n. 模板
4.	broadband	4.	n. 宽带
5.	barcode	5.	n. 条形码
6.	motion sensor	6.	运动传感器

7. self repair	7. 自修复
8. wired broadband network	8. 有线宽带网络
9. smart city	9. 智慧城市
10. device	10. n. 装置，设备
11. vt. 感知	11. sense
12. n. 同时，同步	12. sync
13. adj. 智能的，敏捷的	13. smart
14. adj. 无线的	14. wireless
15. adv. 自动地，机械地	15. automatically

【EX.3】Translate the following sentences into Chinese.

1. 打印机是除显示器外最常用的输出设备。
2. 通信系统采用有线和无线相结合的方式。
3. 蓝牙技术是一种短距离无线数据与语音通信的开放性标准。
4. 本文介绍了传感器节点的软件与硬件设计。
5. 你可以在网上搜索各种显示器的信息。
6. 随着技术力量不断增强，计算机硬件的便携性和灵活性也不断增加。
7. 芯片是计算机中最有价值的部分。
8. 最近，该公司发布了业内第一款组合了 RFID 和条码的产品。
9. 我的计算机有网络接口，可以与其他计算机连在一起。
10. 总体而言，宽带接入技术正朝着高带宽、光纤化、无线化方向发展。

【EX.4】Complete the following passage with appropriate words in the box.

1. technologies 2. applications 3. tagged 4. network 5. computing
6. embedded 7. concept 8. development 9. tracked 10. check

【EX.5】Translate the following passage into Chinese.

物联网（IoT）究竟意味着什么？

物联网（IoT）是一个计算的概念，描述了未来的日常物体将被连接到互联网并能被其他设备识别。作为通信方式，这个词与 RFID 一样，也可以包含其他的传感器技术、其他无线技术及 QR 码等。

物联网重要的原因在于，一个可以表示为数字形式的物体比该物体存在还要重要。该物体不仅仅与你有关，现在也与周围物体相关，与一个数据库中的数据相关，如此等等。当许多物体统一行动，它们就被称为具有"环境智能"。

我们中的大多数人想到了与计算机、平板计算机和智能手机的连接。物联网描述如此的世界：任何的东西都可以连接并智能化通信。换句话说，有了物联网，这个物质世界将成为一个大的信息系统。

Text B

【EX.1】Answer the following questions according to the text.

1. The Internet of Things came into being in 2008.
2. The technical utopians think of the Internet of Things as a good thing that will bring

untold benefits.

3. The sceptics warn us of the dangers inherent in not only having an ever growing Internet of Things, but our increasing reliance on it.

4. By 2020, there will be 24 billion devices connected to the internet.

5. Sparked has developed a sensor that measures a cow's vital signs as well as movement and interactions with other cows.

6. Tied in with real-time artificial intelligence, the car's network could be providing the driver with feedback and advice, and interacting with the internet for route information.

7. There will be about 400 million wearable wireless sensors by 2014.

8. Everybody has experienced that moment when a computer or phone has defeated all your attempts to do something basic such as connecting to a wireless network.

9. The most pressing concern Schumpeter raises is that who will end up owning and controlling the data from the Internet of Things.

10. The Internet of Things can ultimately be used for the benefit or detriment of individuals and society as a whole.

【EX.2】 Translate the following terms or phrases from English into Chinese and vice versa.

1. media player
2. connectedness
3. parallel
4. traffic
5. spyware
6. infrastructure
7. message
8. robust
9. environment
10. social media
11. 灾难性故障，突变失效
12. 容错
13. 人工智能
14. v. 连接，联合
15. v. 收集，聚集，集中，搜集

1. 媒体播放器
2. n. 连通性
3. adj. 并行的，平行的，并联的
4. n. 通信量；流量
5. n. 间谍软件
6. n. 基础
7. n. 消息，通信，信息 vt. 通知
8. adj. 健壮的
9. n. 环境，外界
10. 社交媒介
11. catastrophic failure
12. fault tolerant
13. artificial intelligence
14. connect
15. collect

【EX.3】 Translate the following sentences into Chinese.

1. 你必须把这条电线和那条接起来。
2. 变量是一个标识符，其值在运行时可以改变。
3. 无处不在的因特网将使每台计算机都成为您的办公室。
4. 该信号处理系统实现了有效的信号检测。
5. 你需要利用反馈信息来监控进展。
6. 实现链路的无缝切换是支持移动网络的关键技术。

7. 为了确保安全，我们应该对信息进行编码。
8. 探测器必须操作方便，可靠而牢固。
9. 最后，好的标准能够降低维护费用，提高设计和代码的重复利用。
10. 这就是 Internet 装置隐藏的成本：基础结构的成本。

Unit 2

Text A

【EX.1】Answer the following questions according to the text.

1. M2M refers to data communications between two or more machines.
2. M2M systems are task-specific. It means that a given system is purpose-built for just one specific device, or a very restricted class of devices in an industry.
3. Wireless M2M is machine to machine communication through wireless technologies such as CDMA.
4. M2M can be used in nine fields.
5. Yes, it can offer centralized service support and data management.
6. No, they are not. You can move them should you need to.
7. Wireless networks deliver real time information to mobile devices.
8. A wireless network can be deployed much more quickly than a fixed network as no cabling is needed between devices.
9. PSTN/fixed line is less cost effective.
10. CDMA airtime/data usage is billed according to the amount of data used.

【EX.2】Translate the following terms or phrases from English into Chinese and vice versa.

1.	centralize	1.	vt. 集聚，集中
2.	modem	2.	n. 调制解调器
3.	mobility	3.	n. 活动性，移动性，机动性.
4.	server	4.	n. 服务器
5.	logistic	5.	adj. 物流的，后勤的
6.	ensure	6.	v. 确保，保证
7.	automation	7.	n. 自动控制，自动操作
8.	remote access control	8.	远程访问控制
9.	building automation	9.	楼宇自动化
10.	product lifecycle	10.	产品生命周期
11.	移动设备	11.	mobile device
12.	n. 功能，作用	12.	function
13.	n. 信息通信业务，远程信息处理	13.	telematics

14.	n. 停工期	14.	downtime
15.	v. 部署，展开，配置	15.	deploy

【EX.3】Translate the following sentences into Chinese.

1. 电子学、声学和激光技术的发展为增加准确性和及时采取管理提供了遥测技术。
2. 是否具有 VLAN 功能是衡量局域网交换机的一项重要指标。
3. 无线局域网是计算机网络的重要组成部分。
4. 该厂的自动化大大提高了它的生产力。
5. 物流和供应链管理有什么区别？
6. 逻辑模拟是数字电路自动设计的重要组成部分。
7. 在数据库中，字段包含某个实体的信息。
8. 然后可以分发定制组件，或者把它们从测试环境转移到生产环境中。
9. 通过 10Mbps 的有线电视调制解调器，同样的文件只要 8 秒钟就能下载完。
10. 当远程访问控制失败时就会出现这些错误信息。

【EX.4】Complete the following passage with appropriate words in the box.

1. services　　2. urban　　3. adapted to　　4. security　　5. transportation
6. waste　　7. changed　　8. public　　9. free　　10. optimize

【EX.5】Translate the following passage into Chinese.

数字城市

术语"数字城市"或"数字社区"（也使用智能社区、信息城市和电子城市）指的是连接的社区，结合了宽带通信基础设施，基于开放的工业标准的灵活的、面向服务的计算基础架构，以及创新的服务，以满足政府及其雇员、公民和企业的需求。数字社区的地理维度（空间）的变化多端：它们可以从一个城区扩展到数百万都市。

尽管无线基础设施是数字城市的基础设施的一个关键因素，但它只是第一步。数字城市可能需要有线宽带基础设施，它不仅仅只是个网络。数字城市提供可互操作的、基于因特网的政府服务，使无处不在的连接转变关键的政府的工作流程，包括政府内部部门与员工间的流程以及外部的公民和企业间的流程。数字城市服务可以通过无线移动设备实现，也可通过面向服务的企业架构实现，包括 Web 服务、可扩展标记语言（XML）以及移动化的软件应用。

Text B

【EX.1】Answer the following questions according to the text.

1. A car's microchip tells the engine how to operate under various conditions so that the car can achieve the best fuel economy.

2. They "talk" in a language known as "telemetry".

3. The three very common technologies that are coming together to create Machine to Machine communications are wireless sensors, the Internet and personal computers.

4. Because it relies on common technology, it could help a homeowner maintain the perfect lawn or create a shopping list at a button's touch.

5. They both transmit data through a sensor.

6. The major difference between the two is that telemetry communication use a random radio signal while M2M communications uses existing networks, such as wireless networks used by the public, to transmit the data.

7. The sensors in older telemetry communications were highly specialized and often needed strong power sources to transmit data.

8. The explosive growth of public wireless networks is probably the biggest change that has opened M2M communications to many more sectors.

9. It shows how M2M works.

10. The sectors M2M is applied in are utility companies, traffic control, telemedicine and businesses.

【EX.2】Translate the following terms or phrases from English into Chinese and vice versa.

1.	break up	1.	打碎，破碎，分裂，结束
2.	dedicated line	2.	专用线
3.	result in	3.	引起，导致，以……为结局
4.	personal computer	4.	个人计算机，缩写为 PC
5.	at a button's touch	5.	只按一键，一触即成
6.	microchip	6.	n. 微芯片
7.	maximize	7.	vt. 取……最大值，最佳化
8.	parameter	8.	n. 参数，参量
9.	facility	9.	n. 设备，工具
10.	sensitivity	10.	n. 敏感，灵敏（度），灵敏性
11.	n. 精确性，正确度	11.	accuracy
12.	n. 流出	12.	outflow
13.	vt.（熟练地）操作，巧妙地处理	13.	manipulate
14.	n. 性能，容量	14.	capability
15.	n. 覆盖	15.	coverage

【EX.3】Translate the following sentences into Chinese.

1. 一般的微型芯片像大米颗粒大小。
2. 处理器本身通常需要一块或几块逻辑板。
3. 未来电子计算机的发展在很大程度上决定于软件。
4. 函数的一个声明包含变量参数列表。
5. 远程存取控制失败时会出现这些错误信息。
6. 计算机直接向生产过程发出控制动作而无须进行人工干预。
7. 这种传感器灵敏度高，响应时间快且稳定性好。
8. 信号会被转为数字代码。
9. 这台计算机处理数据有多快？
10. 大多数商用路由器都有某种内置的包过滤功能。

Unit 3

Text A

【EX.1】Answer the following questions according to the text.

1. Smart home technology was developed in 1975.
2. A message in numerical code includes the following:
   - An alert to the system that it's issuing a command,
   - An identifying unit number for the device that should receive the command and
   - A code that contains the actual command, such as "turn off."
3. Two most prominent radio networks in home automation are ZigBee and Z-Wave.
4. ZigBee's platform is based on the standard set by the Institute for IEEE (Electrical and Electronics Engineers) for wireless personal networks.
5. Motion sensors will send an alert when there's motion around your house, and they can even tell the difference between pets and burglars.
6. When joining up an X10 and a Z-Wave product, it requires a bridging device.
7. First, smart homes obviously have the ability to make life easier and more convenient. Then, they provide some energy efficiency savings. Last, smart home technology promises tremendous benefits for an elderly person living alone.
8. A smart home probably sounds like a nightmare to those people not comfortable with computers.
9. One of the challenges of installing a smart home system is balancing the complexity of the system against the usability of the system.
10. Smart homes come with some security concerns, ethical questions about privacy and the question of whether an individual needs all this technology.

【EX.2】Translate the following terms or phrases from English into Chinese and vice versa.

	English		Chinese
1.	home network	1.	家庭网络
2.	security alarm	2.	安全警报器
3.	remote control	3.	遥控，遥控装置，遥控操作
4.	radio wave	4.	无线电波
5.	mesh network	5.	网状网络
6.	Source Routing Algorithm	6.	源路由算法
7.	crowd	7.	v. 群集，拥挤，挤满
8.	regulation	8.	n. 调节，校准
9.	web server	9.	网络服务器

10.	网络服务器	10.	Web server
11.	关掉，切断	11.	shut off
12.	adj. 兼容的，一致的	12.	compatible
13.	n. 调节器	13.	modulator
14.	n. 节点	14.	node

【EX.3】Translate the following sentences into Chinese.

1. 在命令行和基于字符的菜单时代，界面通常间接地为用户提供服务。
2. 这个系统和这台计算机的硬件不兼容。
3. 我们的接收器不够灵敏，未能收到这个信号。
4. 您想不用鼠标，而使用数字键盘吗？
5. 发射机电路由脉冲信号产生电路、带通滤波器和功率放大器组成。
6. 根据统计学分析，在这两种不均衡的衡量标准之间仅有些许的关联。
7. 比如，有的网站中嵌入视频播放器，游戏和其他交互体验上的网页。
8. 在传输过程中音频和视频信号可能被压缩，或并未被压缩。
9. 新版程序的用户界面比原来程序的好得多。
10. 请检查用户名是否正确，然后再输入一次密码。

【EX.4】Complete the following passage with appropriate words in the box.

1. switch   2. entertainment   3. coded   4. convey   5. transmitter
6. receive   7. plugged   8. smart   9. installed 10. standardize

【EX.5】Translate the following passage into Chinese.

什么是"智能家居"？

一个智能家居是这样一所房屋：它具有高度先进的自动化系统，可以控制照明、温度、多媒体、安全、实现窗和门的自动操作以及许多其他功能。

智能家居中呈现"智能"的原因在于其计算机系统可以监控日常生活的许多方面。例如，冰箱可以列出所存内容的清单、建议菜单、推荐健康的替代品以及和订购食品。智能家居系统甚至可能清洁猫砂盒和给植物浇水。

智能家居技术是真实的，它越来越先进。编码信号通过家中的线路发送到开关和插座，每一个房间的电器和电子设备的运行都可以用程序控制。家庭自动化对那些以往独立生活的老年人和残疾人特别有用。

Text B

【EX.1】Fill in the blanks according to the text.

1. Global Positioning System, 24 satellites, the U.S. Department of Defense
2. twice a day, signal information
3. at least three satellites, track movement
4. their parallel multichannel design
5. the U.S. Coast Guard, a network of towers, beacon transmitters
6. solar energy, roughly 7,000 miles an hour

7. 1978

8. L1 and L2, the L1 frequency of 1575.42 MHz

9. three, a pseudorandom code, ephemeris data and almanac data.

10. the relative position of the satellites, at wide angles, in a line, in a tight grouping

【EX.2】Translate the following terms or phrases from English into Chinese and vice versa.

1.	distance measurement	1.	距离测量，远距测量
2.	backup battery	2.	备用电源，备份电源
3.	take advantage of	3.	利用
4.	timing error	4.	同步误差，定时误差
5.	solar panel	5.	太阳电池板，太阳能电池板
6.	navigation	6.	n. 导航，领航
7.	charge	7.	n. 电荷，充电 v. 充电
8.	transmit	8.	vt. 传输，发射 vi. 发射信号
9.	factor	9.	n. 因素，要素，因数
10.	onboard	10.	adj. 随带的，板载的
11.	vt. 做备份 adj. 备份的，支持性的	11.	backup
12.	n. 频率，周率	12.	frequency
13.	n. 替换，复位，交换，代替者	13.	replacement
14.	n. 签署，同意	14.	subscription
15.	信标发送机	15.	beacon transmitter

【EX.3】Translate the following sentences into Chinese.

1. 导航设备的质量极为重要，不容忽视。
2. 这是目前传送电子邮件等某些类型数据的最高效方式。
3. 将天线安置在底部意味着传感器会探测到更少的电磁波。
4. 当主系统不能工作时，后备系统立即投入工作代替之。
5. 为每个数据库创建一个子目录以便存储备份文件。
6. 本文首先介绍了射频识别技术的基本原理。
7. 这样的能量转化也被看作能量衰减。
8. 浏览器是一个计算机软件，用来在因特网上搜索信息。
9. 这些电流能够大大降低弱电流测量的准确度。
10. 电功率以瓦特为测量单位，它是以著名的英国工程师詹姆斯·瓦特命名的。

Unit 4

Text A

【EX.1】Answer the following questions according to the text.

1. The Open Systems Interconnection model (OSI model) is a product of the Open Systems

Interconnection effort at the International Organization for Standardization.

2. A layer is a collection of similar functions that provide services to the layer above it and receives services from the layer below it.

3. The Physical Layer defines the electrical and physical specifications for devices. In particular, it defines the relationship between a device and a transmission medium, such as a copper or optical cable.

4. The Data Link Layer provides the functional and procedural means to transfer data between network entities and to detect and possibly correct errors that may occur in the Physical Layer.

5. The Network Layer provides the functional and procedural means of transferring variable length data sequences from a source host on one network to a destination host on a different network, while maintaining the quality of service requested by the Transport Layer.

6. The Transport Layer controls the reliability of a given link through flow control, segmentation/desegmentation, and error control.

7. Binding is the operation of setting up a session between two processes.

8. The Presentation Layer establishes context between Application Layer entities, in which the higher-layer entities may use different syntax and semantics if the presentation service provides a mapping between them.

9. Application layer functions typically include identifying communication partners, determining resource availability, and synchronizing communication.

10. In distinct usage in distributed computing, the term network architecture often describes the structure and classification of distributed application architecture, as the participating nodes in a distributed application are often referred to as a network.

【EX.2】Translate the following terms or phrases from English into Chinese and vice versa.

1.	data link layer	1.	数据链路层
2.	Point-to-Point Protocol (PPP)	2.	点对点协议
3.	transport layer	3.	传输层
4.	logical addressing scheme	4.	逻辑寻址方案
5.	Local area network	5.	局域网
6.	session layer	6.	会话层
7.	distributed computing	7.	分布式计算
8.	virtual circuit	8.	虚拟线路，虚拟电路
9.	presentation layer	9.	表示层
10.	data link layer	10.	数据链路层
11.	n. 构架，框架，结构	11.	framework
12.	adj. 功能的	12.	functional
13.	n. 转发器，中继器	13.	repeater

14.	n. 进程，程序	14.	procedure
15.	n. 路由器	15.	router

【EX.3】Translate the following sentences into Chinese.

1. 实践证明该软件结构具有通用性和可扩展性。
2. 在面向对象环境中，框架由抽象类和具体类组成。
3. 软件做了产品需求规格说明书中规定不应该做的事情。
4. 在这台计算机上配置家用网路期间出现了错误。
5. 网络集线器是连接一个局域网内的多个节点的设备。
6. 从一个端设备发送的信号由中继站转发到另一个端设备。
7. 因为选定的网络适配器已经用于网络连接，所以无法禁用它。
8. 只有以太网便于与来自不同厂家的产品组合。
9. 在路由器上配置默认路由的指令是哪个？
10. 对局域网上的数据报进行分类可为网络入侵检测提供重要依据。

【EX.4】Complete the following passage with appropriate words in the box.

1. system　　2. node　　3. same　　4. collision　　5. delay
6. token-passing　　7. logical　　8. workstation　　9. captured　　10. decreased

【EX.5】Translate the following passage into Chinese.

网络

网络是由两个或多个相互连接的计算机系统组成的整体。计算机网络有多种类型，包括：

- 局域网（LAN）：这些计算机在地理上非常接近。
- 广域网（WAN）：这些计算机相隔较远并通过电话线或无线电波连接。
- 园区网（CAN）：这些计算机在限定的地理区域内，如大学校园或军事基地。
- 城域网（MAN）：为一个城镇或城市而设计的数据网络。
- 家庭网（HAN）：一个包含在用户家庭中的网络，可以连接个人数字设备。

除了这些类型外，也可以根据以下特点来区分网络类型：

- 拓扑：计算机系统的地理布局。常见拓扑包括总线状、星状和环状。
- 协议：协议定义了网络中计算机通信的常用规则集和信号。用于 LAN 的最流行的协议之一叫作以太网；另一个用于 PC 的 LAN 协议是 IBM 令牌网。
- 体系结构：网络大体上可以分为点对点结构或客户/服务器结构。

网络中的计算机有时叫作节点。用于分配网络资源的计算机和设备叫作服务器。

Text B

【EX.1】Fill in the blanks according to the text.

1. the arrangement of the various elements (links, nodes, etc.)
2. physical topologies, logical topologies
3. the placement of the network's various components, how data flows within a network

4. unimpeded communications between the two endpoints, proportional to the number of potential pairs of subscribers

5. all of the nodes of the network, a terminator

6. a common transmission medium, the main section of the transmission medium

7. the hub or the switch, the simplicity of adding additional nodes, the hub represents a single point of failure

8. three levels, the physical topology of a star

9. star ring network, star bus network

10. linear and ring.

【EX.2】Translate the following terms or phrases from English into Chinese and vice versa.

1. physical topology
2. circuit switching
3. daisy chain
4. packet switching
5. topology
6. placement
7. telecommunication
8. reconfigure
9. backbone
10. proportional
11. n. 终结器
12. n. 端口
13. adj. 外围的 n. 外围设备
14. n. 网络集线器，网络中心
15. n. 终结器

1. 物理拓扑
2. 线路交换，线路转接
3. 串式链接，链接式
4. 包交换技术
5. n. 拓扑，布局
6. n. 放置，布置
7. n. 电信，无线电通信，电信学
8. v. 重新装配，改装
9. n. 骨干，支柱
10. adj. 相称的，均衡的
11. terminator
12. port
13. peripheral
14. hub
15. logical topology

【EX.3】Translate the following sentences into Chinese.

1. 结构拓扑优化设计方法是近几年发展起来的新方法，并取得了瞩目的进展。
2. 通信技术实际上是指设备与设备之间的互通互联。
3. 在一个规模宏大的电信网络中，运行着众多不同厂商的设备。
4. 网络传输终结点已有与其关联的地址。
5. 今天的以太网——特别是主干网——采用交换式而不是共享式以太网。
6. 此工作站没有足够的资源来打开另一网络会话。
7. PCI总线实现了周边设备与中央处理器的互连。
8. 要在众多电子设备中脱颖而出的一个办法就是把硬件设计得新颖一些。
9. 线缆是不对称的：下行速度远远快于上行速度。
10. 它是信息技术与管理知识相结合的产物。

Unit 5

Text A

【EX.1】 Answer the following questions according to the text.

1. Networking hardware includes all computers, peripherals, interface cards and other equipment needed to perform data processing and communications within the network.

2. A file server is a very fast computer with a large amount of RAM and storage space, along with a fast network interface card.

3. The file server controls the communication of information between the nodes on a network.

4. A typical workstation is a computer that is configured with a network interface card, networking software, and the appropriate cables.

5. The Network Interface Card (NIC) provides the physical connection between the network and the workstation.

6. The three most common network interface connections are Ethernet cards, LocalTalk connectors, and Token Ring cards.

7. A concentrator is a device that provides a central connection point for cables from workstations, servers, and peripherals.

8. The repeater does this by electrically amplifying the signal it receives and rebroadcasting it.

9. A bridge monitors the information traffic on both sides of the network so that it can pass packets of information to the correct location. It manages the traffic to maintain optimum performance on both sides of the network.

10. If you have a school LAN that you want to connect to the Internet, you will need to buy a router.

【EX.2】 Translate the following terms or phrases from English into Chinese and vice versa.

1.	network operating system	1.	网络操作系统
2.	serial port	2.	串行端口
3.	hard drive	3.	硬盘驱动器
4.	fiber optics cable	4.	光导纤维电缆
5.	unshielded twisted-pair	5.	非屏蔽双绞线
6.	parallel port	6.	并行端口
7.	bridge	7.	n. 桥接器
8.	microprocessor	8.	n. 微处理器
9.	preinstall	9.	v. 预设,预安装

10.	connector	10.	n. 连接器
11.	n. 收发器	11.	transceiver
12.	n. 地址	12.	address
13.	n. 碰撞，冲突	13.	collision
14.	v. 分割 n. 段，节，片断	14.	segment
15.	vi. 配置，设定	15.	configure

【EX.3】**Translate the following sentences into Chinese.**

1. 集中器到采集器之间采用无线自组织网络进行数据传输。
2. 解调频率通常在几兆赫兹至几百兆赫兹的范围内。
3. 第2种选择具有技术优越性，但需要性能更高的设备。
4. 同轴电缆也用于海底电话线。
5. 我们正在使用这种晶体管来放大电话信号。
6. 它可以重新恢复存储单元中因读取数据而破坏的数据。
7. 在安装和启动之前，请检查所有的部件是否有损坏。
8. 微软公司采用了非常聪明的方法来解决这个问题。
9. 你要用哪个函数重定向浏览器到一个新的页面？
10. 过滤路由为防火墙的连通性建立了基本规则。

【EX.4】**Complete the following passage with appropriate words in the box.**

1. devices   2. signals   3. carrier   4. random   5. provides
6. amplify   7. designed   8. host   9. surrounded   10. electricity

【EX.5】**Translate the following passage into Chinese.**

网关

网关是一个网络互连系统，能够相连两个使用不同协议的网络。网关可以完全由软件实现，也可以完全由硬件实现，或由软、硬件组合实现。根据其所支持的协议类型，网关可以运行在OSI模型的任何一层。

因为按照定义网关可以出现在网络的边界，可以把类似防火墙这样的功能整合到其中。在家庭网络中，一个宽带路由器通常可以起网关的作用，虽然普通的计算机也可配置执行相同的功能。

Text B

【EX.1】**Answer the following questions according to the text.**

1. A network switch is a computer networking device that links network segments or network devices. The term commonly refers to a multi-port network bridge that processes and routes data at the data link layer (layer 2) of the OSI model.

2. A switch is more intelligent than a hub. Because a switch is receives a message from any device connected to it and then transmits the message only to the device for which the message is meant while a hub receives a message and then transmits it to all the other devices on its

network.

3. An Ethernet switch operates at the data link layer of the OSI model.

4. A device that operates simultaneously at more than one of these layers is a multilayer switch.

5. Because most switch port mirroring provides only one mirrored stream, network hubs can be useful for fanning out data to several read-only analyzers.

6. Because switches can have redundant power circuits connected to uninterruptible power supplies, the connected device can continue operating even when regular office power fails.

7. Because every packet is repeated on every other port, packet collisions affect the entire network, limiting its capacity.

8. They are store and forward, cut through, fragment free and adaptive switching.

9. The two sub-classes of managed switches marketed today are smart (or intelligent) switches and enterprise Managed (or fully managed) switches.

10. Two popular methods that are specifically designed to allow a network analyst to monitor traffic are port mirroring and SMON (Switch Monitoring).

【EX.2】Translate the following terms or phrases from English into Chinese and vice versa.

1.	network segment	1.	网段
2.	multilayer switch	2.	多层交换
3.	network bridge	3.	网桥
4.	full duplex	4.	全双工
5.	half duplex	5.	半双工
6.	fan out	6.	扇出
7.	wireless access point	7.	无线接入点
8.	port mirroring	8.	端口镜像，端口映射
9.	error checking	9.	误差校验，错误校验
10.	adaptive switching	10.	自适应交换
11.	即插即用	11.	plug and play
12.	智能交换机	12.	smart switch
13.	adj. 模块化的，组合的	13.	modular
14.	n. 闯入，侵扰	14.	intrusion
15.	n. 防火墙	15.	firewall

【EX.3】Translate the following sentences into Chinese.

1. 多层交换机的生命力取决于所支持的协议。
2. 大部分电缆网络已经升级为宽带。
3. 它把用户名和域名分开。
4. 在默认情况下，这意味着自动重传有效。
5. 该平台使用模块化方法构建，具有良好复用性。

6. 防火墙类似于一个虚拟的网络安全守卫。
7. 存储器的组织与内部容量及结构有关。
8. 下面的字符串缓冲区初始容量是多少?
9. 一些 UNIX 系统的操作必须要在控制台运行。
10. 通常,无线局域网是由带无线网卡的站点和接入点构成。

Unit 6

Text A

【EX.1】Answer the following questions according to the text.

1. A wireless sensor network (WSN) consists of spatially distributed autonomous sensors to monitor physical or environmental conditions, such as temperature, sound, pressure, etc. and to cooperatively pass their data through the network to a main location.

2. Sensor nodes can be imagined as small computers, extremely basic in terms of their interfaces and their components.

3. They act as a gateway between sensor nodes and the end user as they typically forward data from the WSN on to a server.

4. Predominant standards commonly used in WSN communications include WirelessHART, IEEE 1451, ZigBee / 802.15.4, ZigBee IP and 6LoWPAN.

5. One major challenge in a WSN is to produce low cost and tiny sensor nodes.

6. Energy is the scarcest resource of WSN nodes.

7. Some of the important topics in WSN software research are operating systems, security and mobility.

8. TinyOS is perhaps the first operating system specifically designed for wireless sensor networks. TinyOS is based on an event-driven programming model.

9. Distributed control is used in WSNs for the following reasons:
- Sensor nodes are prone to failure
- For better collection of data
- To provide nodes with backup in case of failure of the central node
- There is also no centralized body to allocate the resources and they have to be self organized.

10. The data gathered from wireless sensor networks is usually saved in the form of numerical data in a central base station.

【EX.2】Translate the following terms or phrases from English into Chinese and vice versa.

1. sensor node   1. 传感器节点
2. communication bandwidth   2. 通信带宽

3.	multihop wireless mesh network	3.	多跳无线网状网络
4.	star network	4.	星状网络
5.	fault tolerance	5.	容错
6.	base station	6.	基站，基地
7.	sensing device	7.	灵敏元件，传感器
8.	embedded operating system	8.	嵌入式操作系统
9.	microcontroller	9.	n. 微控制器
10.	computational	10.	adj. 计算的
11.	n. 平台	11.	platform
12.	n. 坚固性，健壮性，鲁棒性	12.	robustness
13.	n. 多线程	13.	multithreading
14.	n. 元数据	14.	metadata
15.	n. 处理者，处理器	15.	handler

【EX.3】Translate the following sentences into Chinese.

1. 边界网关协议在自治系统之间提供无环路的路由。
2. 在众多的数据通信方式中，同轴电缆是一个理想的双向因特网访问技术。
3. 计算网格是一种新兴的高性能计算技术。
4. 该算法同样适用于普通的关系数据库。
5. 近年来，鲁棒性分析引起了越来越多的关注。
6. 事件处理程序是为响应事件而编写的代码。
7. 元数据是数据仓库的灵魂。
8. 异构数据库互操作的核心思想是数据共享和透明访问。
9. Web 服务标准的出现解决了异构信息系统之间的互操作问题。
10. 如今设计移动设备时，要考虑系统层面的功率消耗，这很重要。

【EX.4】Complete the following passage with appropriate words in the box.

1. converts   2. liquid   3. voltmeter   4. touching   5. aware
6. responds   7. indicates   8. measure   9. sensitivities 10. manufactured

【EX.5】Translate the following passage into Chinese.

传感器网络

传感器网络由特定的带有通信设施的传感器组成，以便监控和记录各个位置的情况。通常可监控的参数为温度、湿度、压力、风向和速度、照度、振动强度、声音强度、电源电压、化学物质浓度、污染等级和重要身体机能。

传感器网络由多个称为传感器节点的检测站组成，每个都小、轻并便携。每个传感器节点都带有传感器、微型计算机、收发器和电源。传感器根据感知的物理效应和现象产生电信号。微型计算机处理并存储传感器输出的信号。收发器（有线或无线的）从中心计算机接受命令并把数据传输到该计算机。每个传感器节点都由电力设备或电池供电。

传感器网络的潜在应用包括：
- 工业自动化；
- 自动化和智能住宅；

- 视频监控；
- 交通监控；
- 医疗设备监控；
- 天气情况的监测；
- 空中交通管制；
- 机器人控制。

Text B

【EX.1】Fill in the blanks according to the text.

1. to detect enemy intrusion, the geo-fencing of gas or oil pipelines
2. measure the levels of pollutants in the air
3. the use of accurate sensors
4. A network of Sensor Nodes
5. analyzing water properties
6. natural disasters
7. the "live" data feed that is possible
8. surface or underground water, a country's water infrastructure
9. maintenance of wiring in a difficult environment, more efficient water use and reduces waste
10. wireless sensor networks, loads, fatigue, vibration, crack evolution

【EX.2】Translate the following terms or phrases from English into Chinese and vice versa.

1.	data retrieval	1.	数据检索
2.	data transmission	2.	信息传输，数据传输
3.	intrusion	3.	n. 闯入，侵扰
4.	utmost	4.	n. 极限，最大可能 adj. 极度的，最远的
5.	magnitude	5.	n. 数量，量级
6.	autonomy	6.	n. 自治
7.	ambient	7.	adj. 周围的 n. 周围环境
8.	retrieval	8.	n. 取回，恢复，修补，重获，挽救
9.	feed	9.	n.&v. 输入，馈送
10.	reliability	10.	n. 可靠性
11.	电池组	11.	battery pack
12.	n. 检查，视察	12.	inspection
13.	完成，实现，执行	13.	carry out
14.	adj. 可信赖的	14.	trustworthy
15.	n. 手册，指南	15.	manual

【EX.3】Translate the following sentences into Chinese.
1. 网络监控是网络领域的关键技术之一。
2. 在线自动监测是信息技术在环境监测领域的应用。
3. 无线传感器网络的应用十分广泛，能够实时监测、采集和处理环境信息。
4. 无线传感器网络能够实时收集、处理环境信息，然后把结果发送给其用户。
5. 数据挖掘一般分为描述数据挖掘和预测数据挖掘。
6. 数据挖掘是一种用于决策支持系统的新兴技术。
7. 数据挖掘就是从大量的数据中提取或挖掘知识。
8. 存储数据的爆炸性增长激起对数据挖掘技术的更多需求。
9. 遗传算法在数据挖掘中有着重要的地位。
10. 聚类是一种有效的数据挖掘和文本挖掘方法。

Unit 7

Text A

【EX.1】Answer the following questions according to the text.

1. The purpose of a wireless network is to link a group of computers.

2. The cornerstone of a wireless network is a device known as an access point (AP). The primary job of an access point is to broadcast a wireless signal that computers can detect and "tune" into.

3. In order to connect to an access point and join a wireless network, computers must be equipped with wireless network adapters.

4. The most common wireless technology standards include 802.11b，802.11g，802.11n.

5. All the WiFi variants (802.11b, g and n products) use the same 2.4 GHz radio frequency.

6. The official speeds of 802.11b, 802.11g, and 802.11n networks are 11, 54, and 270 megabits per second (Mbps) respectively.

7. The range and speed you get out of wireless network depend on how close you are to an access point and the kind of environment in which it operates.

8. Devices like microwave ovens and some cordless phones can cause interference because they operate in the same 2.4 frequency range as 802.11b/g/n networks.

9. The most common standard encryption schemes wireless network hardware supports are Wired Equivalent Privacy (WEP), WiFi Protected Access (WPA), and WiFi Protected Access 2 (WPA2).

10. In fact, there's really no such thing as a purely wireless network, because most link back to a wired network at some point.

【EX.2】Translate the following terms or phrases from English into Chinese and vice versa.

1. wired network   1. 有线网络

2. electromagnetic field 2. 电磁场
3. electromagnetic spectrum 3. 电磁波频谱
4. network adapter 4. 网络适配器，网卡
5. be equipped with 5. 装备
6. overall performance 6. 总性能，全部工作特性
7. performance figure 7. 性能指标
8. expansion slot 8. 扩充插槽
9. spectrum 9. n. 光谱，频谱
10. adapter 10. n. 适配器
11. n. 升级 vt. 使升级 11. upgrade
12. v. 反射 12. reflect
13. v. 重新部署 13. relocate
14. n. 可用性 14. usability
15. n. 编密码，加密 15. encryption

【EX.3】Translate the following sentences into Chinese.
1. 电磁波传送的速度和光速相同。
2. 物理接口的一个示例是网络适配器。
3. 工程师们将测试这台计算机的性能。
4. 互联网有时候被描述成一朵巨大的、拥有无边际计算能力的云。
5. 数据库安全涉及数据库中数据的机密性、完整性及可用性。
6. 密钥管理是实现数据库加密的关键技术。
7. 它主要包括对称密码算法和非对称密码算法及协议。
8. 当局正考虑采取强制性的电子器材回收计划。
9. 你不可以将你的笔记本连接到计算机实验室的有线网络上。
10. 选择此选项来为有线和无线以太网络提供经过身份验证的网络访问。

【EX.4】Complete the following passage with appropriate words in the box.
1. reader 2. positioned 3. needed 4. close 5. single
6. simultaneously 7. require 8. indoor 9. operate 10. attached

【EX.5】Translate the following passage into Chinese.

射频识别标签

虽然 RFID 的应用与条形码类似，但要先进得多。例如，读取 RFID 标签的信息时，标签无须在视线之内，数米之外也可以读取。这也意味着，一个标签可以同时为多个阅读器服务，而条形码标签只能被一个阅读器读取。

在 RFID 技术领域，术语"标签"也意味着包括标记和卡片。标签的类型取决于标签所贴的人体或物体。RFID 系统可以工作在 UHF（超高频）、HF（高频）或 LF（低频）。因此，工作频率不同标签也不同。

这些标签几乎可以贴到任何物体上。虽然常用的目标对象是服装、行李、容器、建筑材料、要洗的衣物和瓶子，但也可以贴到动物、人和车辆之上。

有些 RFID 标签专为野外和户外应用而设计。这些都是为了适应大自然的强烈光线、振动、冲击、雨水、灰尘、油和其他恶劣的环境条件。它们通常是无源的，即不需要电池。因此，它们可以全天候工作，不怕断电。这种耐用标签通常用于卡车、集装箱、货物跟踪轻轨车、车队管理、车辆跟踪和车辆识别等。

Text B

【EX.1】Fill in the blanks according to the text.

1. a wireless noncontact system, automatic identification and tracking
2. tags, labels
3. nonvolatile memory, a small RF transmitter and receiver
4. passive, active, battery assisted passive, an on-board battery
5. it has no battery, the reader
6. an integrated circuit, an antenna
7. one common type of data, a 96-bit string of data
8. The total electronic product code number
9. an initialization command, a parameter
10. Hitachi, at 0.05mm × 0.05mm, the mu-chip

【EX.2】Translate the following terms or phrases from English into Chinese and vice versa.

1.	bar code	1.	条形码
2.	radio frequency	2.	无线电频率
3.	local power source	3.	本地电源
4.	integrated circuit	4.	集成电路
5.	electromagnetic radiation	5.	电磁辐射
6.	near field	6.	近场
7.	noncontact	7.	adj. 没有接触的，非接触的
8.	radio signal	8.	无线电信号
9.	track	9.	n. 轨迹，跟踪 vt. 追踪
10.	label	10.	n. 标签，签条，标志 vt. 贴标签于
11.	vt. 识别，鉴别	11.	identify
12.	n. 中间设备，中间件	12.	middleware
13.	adj. 非易失性的	13.	nonvolatile
14.	adj. 无源的	14.	passive
15.	adj. 有源的	15.	active

【EX.3】Translate the following sentences into Chinese.

1. 在大商店里条形码已经取代了传统的价目标签。
2. 在大多数情况下，使用 IBM 的磁盘磁道格式，有时需要有少许变化。

3. 它们也发射 225～400MHz 之间的超高频波。
4. 光电阅读器每秒钟能扫描两千字符。
5. 数据仓库技术的发展为实现这一目标提供了有利条件。
6. 标签的固定长度是 24 个字符并包括一些标准信息。
7. 中间件技术是解决分布式计算问题的有效方案。
8. ROM 芯片以可以长期读取的、不会丢失的形式保存指令。
9. 由于可靠性较高且应用方便，可编程控制器得到了广泛应用。
10. 这也会随着激光波长的改变而改变。

Unit 8

Text A

【EX.1】Answer the following questions according to the text.

1. The WiFi Alliance defines WiFi as any "wireless local area network (WLAN) products that are based on the Institute of Electrical and Electronics Engineers' (IEEE) 802.11 standards".

2. In order to connect to a WiFi LAN, a computer has to be equipped with a wireless network interface controller.

3. When subscribed to a cellular phone carrier, they allow nearby WiFi stations to access the Internet over 2G, 3G, or 4G networks.

4. In 2005, Sunnyvale, California, was the first city in the United States to offer city-wide free WiFi.

5. Carnegie Mellon University built the first campus-wide wireless Internet network. It was called Wireless Andrew.

6. The Far Eastern University in Manila is the first university in the Philippines to implement a campus-wide WiFi coverage for its students, faculty, and staff.

7. No, any standard WiFi device will work anywhere in the world.

8. A WiFi signal occupies five channels in the 2.4 GHz band. A typical wireless access point using 802.11b or 802.11g with a stock antenna might have a range of 32 m (120 ft) indoors and 95 m (300 ft) outdoors.

9. The most common wireless encryption-standard is Wired Equivalent Privacy (WEP).

10. Having other devices in the same area can be disrupt WiFi connections or lower the internet speed.

【EX.2】Translate the following terms or phrases from English into Chinese and vice versa.

1. wireless network access point　　1. 无线网络接入点
2. carrier wave　　　　　　　　　　2. 载波
3. backwards compatible　　　　　　3. 向后兼容

4.	communication channel	4.	通信电路，信道
5.	latency-sensitive application	5.	传输延迟的网路应用
6.	directional antenna	6.	指向天线，定向天线
7.	block	7.	vt. 妨碍，阻塞
8.	interface	8.	n. 界面，接口
9.	coaxial cable	9.	同轴电缆
10.	frame	10.	n. 帧，框架
11.	n. 装置，设备	11.	device
12.	vt. 使互相连接	12.	interconnect
13.	v. 使失去能力	13.	disable
14.	n. 芯片集	14.	chipset
15.	n. 算法	15.	algorithm

【EX.3】Translate the following sentences into Chinese.

1. 笔记本及掌上计算机的电池通常属于智能锂离子电池。
2. 实验结果表明，该控制器有优良的控制性能。
3. 以太网络适配器允许用户在网络上高速共享文件和打印性能。
4. 用户们称这些开发工具把互连操作转变成标准的数据编程。
5. PCI 局部总线实现了周边设备与中央处理器的高速互连。
6. 目前的 Java 虚拟机大多由软件实现。
7. 主板芯片组无法缓存所有系统内存。
8. 数字模拟表明此种算法有效可行。
9. 如何改变 FTP 服务器的默认端口号？
10. 为了增加信道容量，载波频段不断地向高频方向移动。

【EX.4】Complete the following passage with appropriate words or expressions in the box.

1. marketing   2. spectrum   3. center   4. configurations   5. modem
6. plug   7. ensure   8. broadcasting 9. compatible   10. regulation

【EX.5】Translate the following passage into Chinese.

什么是 WiFi

WiFi（简称"无线保真"）是用于某些类型的无线局域网（WLAN）的术语，这些 WLAN 使用 802.11 系列规格。WiFi 这个词由一个叫作无线 WiFi 联盟的组织创造的。该组织负责测试以证明产品的互操作性。通过了联盟测试的产品给"WiFi 认证"标签（注册商标）。

原来，WiFi 认证是只适用于使用 802.11b 标准的产品。今天，WiFi 可以适用任何使用 802.11 标准的产品。802.11 规范是一个不断发展的无线网络标准，被称为 802.11 系列。WiFi 已经被许多公司、代理商、学校和家庭认可，取代了有线局域网。许多机场、酒店、快餐店提供公共接入 WiFi。这些地方被称为热点。许多地方按日或小时收费，但有些是免费的。热点和网络接入点相互连接的区域被称为热区。

除非有充分的保护，WiFi 网络容易受到未经授权用户的访问，他们用它免费访问互联网。任何一个使用无线局域网的实体都应该使用安全措施，如有线等效保密（WEP）加密标准、最近的 WiFi 保护接入（WPA）、互联网协议安全（IPSec）或一个虚拟专用网络（VPN）。

Text B

【EX.1】Answer the following questions according to the text.

1. The different ways that electronic devices can connect to one another mentioned in the passage are component cables, electrical wires, Ethernet cables, WiFi and Infrared signals.

2. When any two devices need to talk to each other, they have to agree on a number of points before the conversation can begin.

3. The two levels Bluetooth works at are:
- The physical level -- Bluetooth is a radio-frequency standard.
- The protocol level, where products have to agree on when bits are sent, how many will be sent at a time, and how the parties in a conversation can be sure that the message received is the same as the message sent.

4. The big draws of Bluetooth are that it is wireless, inexpensive and automatic.

5. Bluetooth networking transmits data via low-power radio waves. It communicates on a frequency of 2.45 gigahertz (actually between 2.402 GHz and 2.480 GHz, to be exact).

6. One of the ways Bluetooth devices avoid interfering with other systems is by sending out very weak signals of about 1 milliwatt.

7. Because the walls in your house won't stop a Bluetooth signal, which makes the standard useful for controlling several devices in different rooms.

8. The technique which is called spread-spectrum frequency hopping.

9. When Bluetooth-capable devices come within range of one another, an electronic conversation takes place to determine whether they have data to share or whether one needs to control the other.

10. The cordless telephone has two Bluetooth transmitters, one in the base and the other in the handset. When the base is first turned on, it sends radio signals asking for a response from any units with an address in a particular range.

【EX.2】Translate the following terms or phrases from English into Chinese and vice versa.

1.	infrared signal	1.	红外线信号
2.	transmission power	2.	发射功率，传输功率
3.	make sure	3.	确信，证实，确保
4.	interfere with	4.	妨碍，干涉，干扰
5.	spread-spectrum frequency hopping	5.	扩频跳频，展频跳频
6.	Bluetooth piconet	6.	蓝牙微微网
7.	plug	7.	vt. 插上，插栓 n. 插头，插销

8.	confusing information	8.	混乱信息，扰乱信息
9.	conversation	9.	n. 会话，交谈
10.	Bluetooth	10.	n. 蓝牙
11.	n. 属性，品质，特征	11.	attribute
12.	vt. 消耗	12.	consume
13.	n. 微微网	13.	piconet
14.	n. 混乱，混淆	14.	confusion
15.	adj. 红外线的 n. 红外线	15.	infrared

【EX.3】Translate the following sentences into Chinese.

1. 蓝牙技术是目前最新的短距离无线通信技术标准。
2. 在红外成像系统中，任何虚假和不需要的信号统称为噪声。
3. 插入交流电源适配器并重新启动笔记本计算机。
4. 会话对象表示使用者和提供程序之间的单个对话。
5. 这台新的计算机有一个解决程序中任何差错的调试程序。
6. 如果忽略此错误，可能会导致设备无法使用。
7. 用户能够通过串行接口从外部计算机监视系统。
8. 配置连接到并口的装置可能更复杂。
9. 随着对传输速率要求的日益提高，越来越多的设备都支持并口通信。
10. 这家公司设计了一种基于计算机并行接口的虚拟仪器。

Unit 9

Text A

【EX.1】Answer the following questions according to the text.

1. The last 25 years has seen phenomenal growth in the use of barcodes.
2. The first commercial implementation of barcoding was for grocery distribution in 1970.
3. Barcode users may be split into two groups; those who are using barcodes within a controlled system where they must adhere to the coding standards laid down by an outside body and those who wish to originate barcodes for purely their own use and therefore have free rein to choose the most suitable barcode type.
4. All barcodes are constructed from a series of bars and intervening spaces.
5. To ensure compatibility of systems, it is important that all users of a barcode agree on the way in which it is used and how data is encoded.
6. OCR-B stands for Optical Character Recognition-International Standard. OCR-A stands for Optical Character Recognition-ANSI Standard. They are both fonts designed to be readable by a machine.
7. One of the most common causes of bad reads is light margin incursion.

8. Code 39 differs from others in that while it defines narrow bar width, it also defines the ratio between wide and narrow bars (between 2∶1 and 3∶1).

9. Most supermarket checkouts use moving beam scanners.

10. Most scanners use red light. Good Bar Colours are Black, Green, Blue, Dark Brown. Good Space Colours are White, Red, Yellow, Orange.

【EX.2】Translate the following terms or phrases from English into Chinese and vice versa.

1.	distribution chain	1.	配送链
2.	light margin	2.	空白区
3.	quiet zone	3.	静止区
4.	magnification factor	4.	扩大因数，放大倍数，放大系数
5.	usefulness	5.	n. 有用，有效性
6.	visible	6.	adj. 看得见的，明显的 n. 可见物
7.	record	7.	vt. 记录
8.	predetermine	8.	v. 预定，预先确定
9.	implementation	9.	n. 执行
10.	compatibility	10.	n. 兼容性
11.	n. 说明，规格	11.	spec
12.	n. 维（数），度（数）	12.	dimension
13.	vt. 调整，调节	13.	adjust
14.	n. 偏差，容差	14.	tolerance
15.	n. 复杂化	15.	complication

【EX.3】Translate the following sentences into Chinese.

1. 我相信了其新装置的实用性。
2. 因此，在重订购水平中包括安全库存。
3. 别让我在结账的时候重新输入那个信息。
4. 这就是把数据或信息加到现存的记录中去的过程。
5. 我们必须请供应商送来更多存货。
6. 技术标准没有根本性地超越。
7. 为了增加安全性，我们的系统提供与先进加密设备的兼容性。
8. 你知道如何调整这台新机器吗？
9. 许多程序员都想在自己的程序嵌入OCR的识别模块中。
10. 一个经营良好的供应链能压缩时间、减少昂贵的配送过程及安全库存成本。

【EX.4】Complete the following passage with appropriate words in the box.

1. mainstream   2. symbol   3. interactive   4. scan   5. equal
6. update   7. inventor   8. constraints   9. basic   10. descriptions

【EX.5】Translate the following passage into Chinese.

什么是2D码

2D（二维）码是在水平和垂直方向存储信息的图形图像。因此，二维码可以存储多达

7089 个字符，存储能力比存储 20 个字符的一维码明显大得多。

二维码也被称为快速响应码，因为它们能够快速实现数据访问。二维码常常与智能手机联合使用。用户只需用配备条码阅读器的手机拍照二维码。阅读器就对 URL 解码，把浏览器引导到网站的相关信息。这种能力使得二维码可用于移动营销。一些二维码系统用短信给用户提供信息，而无须接入网络。

下面举例说明 2D 码的使用方法：

- 耐克公司把二维条码用于极限运动比赛路途的海报上，移动用户可通过捕获条码来访问赞助商的照片、视频和数据。
- 一些报纸在故事中包括二维条码，以便把移动用户连接到故事的后续进展中。
- 商店中产品的二维码链接到产品的评论。
- 一些人发布链接到他们的博客或脸书网页的二维码。

Text B

【EX.1】 Answer the following questions according to the text.

1. QR Code is abbreviated from Quick Response Code. It was invented in Japan by the Toyota subsidiary Denso Wave in 1994.

2. The several standards in documents covering the physical encoding of QR Codes are AIM (Association for Automatic Identification and Mobility) International, JIS X 0510, ISO/IEC 18004:2000 and ISO/IEC 18004:2006.

3. Japan's NTT DoCoMo has established de facto standards for the encoding of URLs, contact information, and several other data types.

4. The QR Code has become a focus of advertising strategy, since it provides quick and effortless access to the brand's website.

5. In June 2011, the Royal Dutch Mint (Koninklijke Nederlandse Munt) issued the world's first official coin with a QR Code to celebrate the centennial of its current building and premises.

6. According to one study, in June 2011, 14 million mobile users scanned a QR Code or a barcode.

7. The amount of data that can be stored in the QR Code symbol depends on the data type (mode, or input character set), version (1, …, 40, indicating the overall dimensions of the symbol), and error correction level.

8. An Android app manages encryption and decryption of QR codes using the DES algorithm (56 bits).

9. The higher the error correction level is, the less the storage capacity.

10. The two things the format information records are the error correction level and the mask pattern used for the symbol. The message data is placed from right to left in a zigzag pattern.

【EX.2】 Translate the following terms or phrases from English into Chinese and vice versa.

1. two-dimensional code   1. 二维码

2.	be made up of …	2.	由……组成
3.	error-correcting code	3.	纠错码
4.	geo information	4.	位置信息，地理信息
5.	validity check	5.	有效性检查
6.	character set	6.	字符集
7.	code block	7.	码组
8.	error correction	8.	纠错，数据纠正
9.	mask pattern	9.	掩模图案
10.	web address	10.	网址
11.	敏感数据	11.	sensitive data
12.	n. 矩阵	12.	matrix
13.	n. 有效性，合法性，正确性	13.	validity
14.	n. 浏览器	14.	browser
15.	n. 解密	15.	decryption

【EX.3】Translate the following sentences into Chinese.

1. 与之相反，有些程序把数据表示为由许多连续的小片数据组成的矩阵。
2. 半导体器件在电子设备中能起各种各样的控制作用。
3. 当今，半导体产业处于一个风云变幻的市场环境。
4. 仿真结果表明了该算法的快速性和有效性。
5. HTML 迫使浏览器以一种特定的方式显示数据。
6. 远程客户可以通过网络浏览器访问数据。
7. 该文件夹路径中包含不支持的字符。
8. 数据记录使用普通计算机平台的文件格式，它无需特殊的软件便可以被访问。
9. 硬件加密方法有较强的抗解密性，但用户使用不方便。
10. 对称加密要求加密与解密使用同样的密钥。

Unit 10

Text A

【EX.1】Answer the following questions according to the text.

1. ZigBee is an open WPAN (Wireless Personal Area Networks) standard based on the IEEE 802.15.4 protocol. The term "ZigBee" originates from honeybees' method of communicating newly found food sources.

2. IEEE 802.15.4 is a standard defined by the IEEE (Institute of Electrical and Electronics Engineers, Inc.) for low-rate WPAN. This standard defines the "physical layer" and the "medium access layer."

3. ZigBee is well suited for a wide range of building automation, industrial, medical and residential control and monitoring applications.

4. Reliable data delivery is critical to ZigBee applications. The underlying IEEE 802.15.4 standard provides strong reliability through several mechanisms at multiple layers.

5. You can expect battery lifetimes from a few months to many years as a result of the system's power-saving modes and battery-optimized network parameters.

6. The configuration allows the network to update the sensor parameters remotely, change its reporting interval, or perform other remote functions and still have (theoretical) battery longevity well beyond the shelf life.

7. By introducing extensible and sophisticated network function, ZigBee allows multi-hop and flexible routing, providing communication ranges exceeding the basic single-hop.

8. Generally, if you relax data-latency requirements, you can assume that the battery life of the client nodes will increase.

9. ZigBee specifies the following ZigBee Devices: ZigBee Coordinator, ZigBee Router and ZigBee End Device.

10. Three different network topologies are supported by Zigbee. They are the star, mesh and cluster tree or hybrid networks.

【EX.2】Translate the following terms or phrases from English into Chinese and vice versa.

1.	low transfer data rate	1.	低传输数据率
2.	kilobits per second	2.	每秒千比特
3.	universal remote control	3.	通用远程控制
4.	power-saving mode	4.	省电模式
5.	set-top box	5.	置顶盒
6.	output power	6.	输出功率
7.	peer-to-peer network	7.	点对点网络
8.	hybrid network	8.	混合网络
9.	protocol	9.	n. 协议
10.	address	10.	vt. 解决，处理
11.	vt. 涉及	11.	involve
12.	vt. 占有，拥有，持有	12.	possess
13.	n. 反应时间	13.	latency
14.	n. 部署	14.	deployment
15.	n. 信标	15.	beacon

【EX.3】Translate the following sentences into Chinese.

1. 无线传感器网络中，跨层协议的设计已成为热点话题。
2. 文件传输协议使用户能在两个联网的计算机之间传输文件。
3. 分布对象管理对实现分布对象互操作很重要。

4. 这个探测器能捕捉多种信号。

5. 由于管理费用高，专业服务也相对昂贵。

6. ZigBee 家庭自动化提供了一个标准，可以为消费者和家人建立一个更智能、更安全、更节能的家庭环境。

7. 在网状网络当中，信息包在节点之间以无线的方式传送。

8. 对等网络的普遍应用带来了网络拥塞。

9. 对等网（P2P）是近年来互联网技术研究的一个热点。

10. 混合型网络是星状、环状和总线状网络的组合。

【EX.4】Complete the following passage with appropriate words in the box.

1. low-power   2. mobile   3. send   4. connectivity   5. incorporate
6. conform   7. super-fast   8. surf   9. cabling   10. networking

【EX.5】Translate the following passage into Chinese.

ZigBee

ZigBee 由飞利浦半导体公司率先推出，它是一个用于家庭自动化和数据网络的低数据速率、双向标准。该标准来源于萤火虫工作组，提供了多达 254 个节点的规范，包括一个主设备，由单个远程控制管理。实际使用 ZigBee 的例子包括家庭自动化任务，如开灯、打开暖气、设置家庭安全系统或启动录像机。有了 ZigBee，这些任务可以通过在家中任何地方触摸一个按钮完成。ZigBee 也允许通过因特网接入访问以便实现自动控制。

ZigBee 标准采用小和非常低功耗设备连接在一起形成一个无线控制网络。一个 ZigBee 网络能够支持多达 254 客户节点和一个全功能设备（主设备）。利用 ZigBee 协议可以延长便宜的现有的非充电电池寿命（从几个月到几年），可以控制照明、空调和暖气、火灾烟雾警报器和其他安全设备。该标准支持 2.4 GHz 的（全球）、868MHz（欧洲）和 915MHz（美洲）和无执照的无线电波段，范围可达 75m。

Text B

【EX.1】Fill in the blanks according to the text.

1. wireless technologies, to the Internet or other IP networks
2. between 128 and 144 kbps (kilobits per second), 384 kbps
3. 3G compatible
4. two cameras, get 3G network connectivity
5. its SIM card or its 3G data card, users that need connectivity on the move
6. make free or cheap calls worldwide, the latest telephony applications and services
7. laptops and gaming devices, mobile phones
8. are helping accelerate the industry's push in its direction
9. increase the bandwidth and throughput capabilities, to perform whenever necessary
10. a PC, maximize their time, on the go

【EX.2】Translate the following terms or phrases from English into Chinese and vice versa.

1.   technical specification   1.   技术规范

2.	network plan	2.	网络套餐
3.	transfer rate	3.	传输率
4.	deal with	4.	安排，处理，涉及
5.	conform to	5.	符合，遵照
6.	streaming video	6.	流视频
7.	enhancement	7.	n. 增进，增加
8.	dedicated transmission line	8.	专用传输线
9.	videoconference	9.	n. 视频会议
10.	throughput	10.	n. 吞吐量
11.	n. 多媒体	11.	multimedia
12.	n. 电信会议	12.	teleconferencing
13.	n. 利用	13.	utilization
14.	n. 载波（信号）	14.	carrier
15.	v. 下载	15.	download

【EX.3】Translate the following sentences into Chinese.

1. 这个定义适用于任何一对运算符。
2. 多媒体是计算机和视频技术的结合。
3. 数据压缩是多媒体中的关键技术。
4. 要把多媒体数据正确地发送到用户界面，同步很关键。
5. PDA（个人数字助理）能够收发邮件、下载资料和播放音乐。
6. 毫不奇怪，免费软件经常是最热门的下载类型。
7. 为什么不能上传自定义头像？
8. 该打印机具有功耗低、安全性好、可靠性高的特点.
9. 我们上个月的故障停机时间有多长？
10. 网络节点数目越多，网络的吞吐率也越大。

词汇总表

说明：课次表明了该词汇在本书中所在的单元。例如，1A 标识该词在第一单元的 Text A 中出现，1B 标识该词在第一单元的 Text B 中出现。

单词表

单 词	音 标	意 义	课次
abode	[ə'bəud]	n. 住所，住处	3A
absorb	[əb'sɔ:b]	vt. 吸收	9A
abstraction	[æb'strækʃən]	n. 提取	6A
accelerate	[æk'seləreit]	v. 加速，促进	10B
accept	[ək'sept]	v. 接受，认可，承认	4A
accommodate	[ə'kɔmədeit]	vt. 供给，使适应，调节，调和 vi. 适应	7A
accomplish	[ə'kɔmpliʃ]	vt. 完成，达到，实现	2A
accuracy	['ækjurəsi]	n. 精确性，正确度	2B
accurate	['ækjurit]	adj. 精确的，正确的	3B
achieve	[ə'tʃi:v]	vt. 得到，获得	2B
acknowledgment	[ək'nɔlidʒmənt]	n. 确认，承认	4A
active	['æktiv]	adj. 主动的，活动的	5A
active	['æktiv]	adj. 有源的	7B
activity	[æk'tiviti]	n. 活动，行动	6A
ad-hoc	['æd'hɔk]	adj. 特别	6A
adage	['ædidʒ]	n. 格言，谚语	8A
adapter	[ə'dæptə]	n. 适配器	7A
address	[ə'dres]	n. 地址	5A
address	[ə'dres]	vt. 解决，处理	10A
adequate	['ædikwit]	adj. 适当的，足够的	8A
adjust	[ə'dʒʌst]	vt. 调整，调节	9A
adjustment	[ə'dʒʌstmənt]	n. 调整，调节	9A
adopt	[ə'dɔpt]	vt. 采用	9A
adversary	['ædvəsəri]	n. 敌手，对手	3B
aerospace	['ɛərəuspeis]	n. 航空航天学	2B
affix	[ə'fiks]	vt. 使附于，粘贴	9B
aftermarket	['ɑ:ftə,mɑ:kit]	n. 贩卖修理用零件的市场	2A
agent	['eidʒnt]	n. 代理	5B

续表

单词	音标	意义	课次
agreement	[əˈgriːmənt]	n. 协定，协议	9A
airwave	[ˈɛəweiv]	n. 电视广播	10B
albeit	[ɔːlˈbiːit]	conj. 尽管；即使	1A
alert	[əˈləːt]	n. 警惕，警报	2B
algorithm	[ˈælgəriðəm]	n. 算法	8A
alkaline	[ˈælkəlain]	adj. 碱性的	10A
alleviate	[əˈliːvieit]	vt. 使（痛苦等）易于忍受，减轻	1B
alliance	[əˈlaiəns]	n. 联盟，联合	8A
allocate	[ˈæləukeit]	vt. 分派，分配	6A
almanac	[ˈɔːlmənæk]	n. 历书，年鉴	3B
alphanumeric	[ˌælfənjuːˈmerik]	adj. 字母数字的	9B
altitude	[ˈæltitjuːd]	n.（尤指海拔）高度	3B
ambient	[ˈæmbiənt]	adj. 周围的 n. 周围环境	6B
amplify	[ˈæmplifai]	vt. 放大，增强	5A
analyse	[ˈænəlaiz]	vt. 分析，分解 n. 分析	1B
analysis	[əˈnælisis]	n. 分析，分解	5B
analytic	[ˌænəˈlitik]	adj. 分析的，解析的	5B
analyzer	[ˈænəlaizə]	n. 分析者，分析器	5B
angle	[ˈæŋgl]	n. 角度	3B
antenna	[ænˈtenə]	n. 天线	6A
antiquated	[ˈæntikweitid]	adj. 老式的，陈旧的	2B
app (=application)	[ˌæpliˈkeiʃən]	n. 应用	1A
appearance	[əˈpiərəns]	n. 出现，露面，外貌，外观	9A
appliance	[əˈplaiəns]	n. 用具，器具	3A
approach	[əˈprəutʃ]	n. 方法，步骤，途径	7B
approximate	[əˈprɔksimeit]	adj. 近似的，大约的 v. 近似，接近	9B
approximately	[əprɔksiˈmətli]	adv. 近似地，大约	3B
architecture	[ˈɑːkitektʃə]	n. 体系机构	4A
arise	[əˈraiz]	vi. 出现，发生，起因于	8B
arrangement	[əˈreindʒmənt]	n. 排列，安排	4B
article	[ˈɑːtikl]	n. 物品，商品	9A
aspect	[ˈæspekt]	n. 方面	6B
assume	[əˈsjuːm]	vt. 假定，设想	7A
atmosphere	[ˈætməsfiə]	n. 大气，空气	3B
atmospheric	[ˌætməsˈferik]	adj. 大气的	3B
attach	[əˈtætʃ]	vt. 缚上，系上，贴上	2A
attainable	[əˈteinəbl]	adj. 可到达的，可得到的	7A
attempt	[əˈtempt]	n. 努力，尝试，企图 vt. 尝试，企图	1B
attribute	[əˈtribjuː(ː)t]	n. 属性，品质，特征	8B
audio	[ˈɔːdiəu]	adj. 音频的，声频的，声音的	3A
augment	[ɔːgˈment]	v. 增加，增大 n. 增加	7A
authority	[ɔːˈθɔriti]	n. 权威，威信，权威人士	8A
automatic	[ˌɔːtəˈmætik]	adj. 自动的，机械的	8B

续表

单 词	音 标	意 义	课次
automatically	[ɔ:tə'mætikli]	adv. 自动地，机械地	1A
automation	[ɔ:tə'meiʃən]	n. 自动控制，自动操作	2A
autonomous	[ɔ:'tɔnəməs]	adj. 自治的	6A
autonomy	[ɔ:'tɔnəmi]	n. 自治	6B
available	[ə'veiəbl]	adj. 可用到的，可利用的，有用的	1B
avoid	[ə'vɔid]	vt. 避免，消除	2B
backbone	['bækbəun]	n. 骨干，支柱	4B
backscatter	[bæk'skætə]	n. 反向散射，背反射	7B
backup	['bækʌp]	n. 后援，支持 vt. 做备份 adj. 备份的，支持性的	3B
balance	['bæləns]	vt. 平衡	1B
band	[bænd]	n. 波段	7B
barcode	['bɑ:kəud]	n. 条形码	1A
base	[beis]	n. 机座，主机	8B
battery	['bætəri]	n. 电池	6A
battlefield	['bæt(ə)lfi:ld]	n. 战场，沙场	6A
beacon	['bi:kən]	n. 信标	10A
bearing	['bɛəriŋ]	n. 方位	3B
bidirectional	[,baidi'rekʃənəl]	adj. 双向的	6A
binary	['bainəri]	adj. 二进位的，二元的	9B
binding	['baindiŋ]	n. 绑定	4A
blackberry	['blækbəri]	n. 黑莓	9B
blind	[blaind]	adj. 瞎的，盲目的 vt. 使失明，缺乏眼光或判断力	1A
block	[blɔk]	vt. 妨碍，阻塞	8A
blockage	['blɔkidʒ]	n. 妨碍，封锁	1A
blog	[blɔk]	n. 博客	1B
Bluetooth	['blu:tu:θ]	n. 蓝牙	8B
body	['bɔdi]	n. 团体	9A
boost	[bu:st]	v. 推进	5A
botnet	[bɔtnet]	n. 僵尸网	9B
branching	['brɑ:ntʃiŋ]	n. 分歧 adj. 发枝的	4B
breakable	['breikəbəl]	adj. 易攻破的	8A
bridge	[bridʒ]	n. 桥接器	5A
Brisbane	['brizbən]	n. 布里斯班（澳大利亚东部港市）	6B
broadband	['brɔ:dbænd]	n. 宽带	1A
broadcast	['brɔ:dkɑ:st]	n. & v. 广播	4A
browser	['brauzə]	n. 浏览器	9B
buffer	['bʌfə]	n. 缓冲器	5B
built-in	['bilt'in]	adj. 内置的，固定的，嵌入的 n. 内置	3B
bulldozer	['buldəuzə]	n. 推土机	2B
burglar	['bə:glə]	n. 夜贼	3A
bus	[bʌs]	n. 总线	4B

续表

单　　词	音　　标	意　　义	课次
cable	['keibl]	n. 电缆	8A
calendar	['kælində]	n. 日历	1A
call	[kɔ:l]	v. 调用	10B
campus	['kæmpəs]	n. 校园	8A
capability	[,keipə'biliti]	n. 性能，容量	2B
capacity	[kə'pæsiti]	n. 容量，才能	5B
carpool	['kɑ:pu:l]	n. 合用汽车　v. 拼车	10B
carrier	['kæriə]	n. 载波（信号）	10B
casualty	['kæʒjuəlti]	n. 损坏，事故	5A
catch	[kætʃ]	n. 捕捉　v. 捕获　vi. 抓住	7A
ceiling	['si:liŋ]	n. 天花板，最高限度	7A
cellular	['seljulə]	adj. 细胞的	10B
centralize	['sentrəlaiz]	vt. 集聚，集中	2A
cereal	['siəriəl]	n. 麦片	1B
channel	['tʃænl]	n. 信道，频道	8A
characteristic	[,kæriktə'ristik]	adj. 特有的，表示特性的，典型的　n. 特性，特征	4A
charge	[tʃɑ:dʒ]	n. 电荷，充电　v. 充电	3B
chassis	['ʃæsi]	n. 底盘	5B
checkout	['tʃekaut]	n.（超级市场中的）付款处，结账；检验，校验	9A
chip	[tʃip]	n. 芯片	1A
chipset	['tʃipset]	n. 芯片集	8A
choppy	['tʃɔpi]	adj. 波浪起伏的	10B
chore	[tʃɔ:]	n. 家务杂事	1A
civilian	[si'viljən]	adj. 民间的，民用的	3B
cliché	['kli:ʃei]	n. 口头禅，陈词滥调	1A
coaxial	[kəu'æksəl]	adj. 同轴的，共轴的	5A
codeword	[kəudwə:d]	n. 码字	9B
collect	[kə'lekt]	v. 收集，聚集，集中，搜集	1B
collection	[kə'lekʃən]	n. 集	4A
collision	[kə'liʒən]	n. 碰撞，冲突	5A
combination	[,kɔmbi'neiʃən]	n. 结合，联合，合并	10A
combine	[kəm'bain]	v. 组合，（使）联合，（使）结合	5B
comfortable	['kʌmfətəbl]	adj. 舒适的	3A
command	[kə'mɑ:nd]	n. 命令，掌握 v. 命令，支配	3A
commute	[kə'mju:t]	n. 通勤来往，乘车上下班	10B
compactly	['kɔmpæktli]	adv. 紧凑地，紧密地，简洁地	9B
compatibility	[kəm,pæti'biliti]	n. 兼容性	9A
compatible	[kəm'pætəbl]	adj. 兼容的，一致的	3A
complex	['kɔmpleks]	adj. 复杂的，合成的，综合的　n. 联合体	1A
complexity	[kəm'pleksiti]	n. 复杂性	10A
compliance	[kəm'plaiəns]	n. 依从，顺从	9B

续表

单词	音标	意义	课次
complication	[ˌkɔmpliˈkeiʃən]	n. 复杂化，（使复杂的）因素	9A
component	[kəmˈpəunənt]	n. 成分　adj. 组成的，构成的	2A
comprise	[kəmˈpraiz]	vt. 包含，包括；由……组成；由……构成	1A
computational	[ˌkɔmpju(ː)ˈteiʃənəl]	adj. 计算的	6A
concentration	[ˌkɔnsenˈtreiʃən]	n. 浓度	6B
concentrator	[ˈkɔnsentreitə]	n. 集中器	5A
concern	[kənˈsəːn]	vt. 涉及，关系到　n. (利害)关系，关心，关注	1B
concrete	[ˈkɔnkriːt]	n. 混凝土	7A
conference	[ˈkɔnfərəns]	n. 会议，讨论会，协商会	6A
configuration	[kənˌfigjuˈreiʃən]	n. 构造，结构，配置	4A
configure	[kənˈfigə]	vi. 配置，设定	5A
confine	[ˈkɔnfain]	vt. 限制，禁闭　n. 界限，边界	8A
conflict	[ˈkɔnflikt]	n. 冲突　vi. 抵触，冲突	9A
confusion	[kənˈfjuːʒən]	n. 混乱，混淆	8B
congestion	[kənˈdʒestʃən]	n. 拥塞	8A
connect	[kəˈnekt]	v. 连接，联合	1B
connectedness	[kəˈnektidnes]	n. 连通性	1B
connection	[kəˈnekʃən]	n. 连接，接线，线路	4A
connectivity	[kənekˈtiviti]	n. 连通性	2A
connector	[kəˈnektə]	n. 连接器	5A
consequence	[ˈkɔnsikwəns]	n. 结果	6B
conserve	[kənˈsəːv]	vt. 保存，保藏	6A
consistency	[kənˈsistənsi]	n. 密度，一致性，连贯性	7A
console	[kənˈsəul]	n. 控制台	5B
constantly	[ˈkɔnstəntli]	adv. 不变地，经常地	8A
constellation	[ˌkɔnstəˈleiʃən]	n. [天]星群，星座，灿烂的一群	3B
construct	[kənˈstrʌkt]	vt. 建造，构造，创立	9A
consume	[kənˈsjuːm]	vt. 消耗	8B
consumer	[kənˈsjuːmə]	n. 消费者，客户	1B
consumption	[kənˈsʌmpʃən]	n. 消费，消耗	6A
contact	[ˈkɔntækt]	vt. 联系	2B
container	[kənˈteinə]	n. 容器，集装箱	10A
contaminant	[kənˈtæminənt]	n. 致污物，污染物	2B
content	[ˈkɔntent]	n. 内容	1A
continuum	[kənˈtinjuəm]	n. 连续统一体，闭联集	4A
control	[kənˈtrəul]	n. & vt. 控制，支配，管理	1A
controller	[kənˈtrəulə]	n. 控制器	8A
converge	[kənˈvəːdʒ]	v. 聚合，聚集	5B
convergence	[kənˈvəːdʒəns]	n. 集中，集合	5B
conversation	[ˌkɔnvəˈseiʃən]	n. 会话，交谈	8B
convert	[kənˈvəːt]	vt. 使转变，转换……	4A

续表

单　　词	音　　标	意　　义	课次
convey	[kən'vei]	vt. 传达	9B
cooperatively	[kəu'ɔpərətivli]	adv. 合作地，协力地	6A
coordinator	[kəu'ɔ:dineitə]	n. 协调器	10A
cordless	['kɔ:dlis]	n. 不用电线的	7A
cornerstone	['kɔ:nəstəun]	n. 墙角石，基础	7A
correlation	[,kɔri'leiʃən]	n. 相互关系，相关性	6A
correspond	[kɔris'pɔnd]	vi. 符合，协调，通信，相应	6A
corrupt	[kə'rʌpt]	vt. 破坏	9B
cost-effective	[kɔst-i'fektiv]	adj. 有成本效益的，划算的	7A
coverage	['kʌvəridʒ]	n. 覆盖	2B
critical	['kritikəl]	adj. 评论的，危急的，临界的	1A
crowd	[kraud]	v. 群集，拥挤，挤满	3A
currency	['kʌrənsi]	n. 流通	9B
customize	['kʌstəmaiz]	v. 定制，用户化	5B
dam	[dæm]	n. 水坝	6B
darkness	['dɑ:knis]	n. 暗度	9B
database	['deitəbeis]	n. 数据库，资料库	2A
datagram	['deitəgræm]	n. 数据报	4A
debut	['debju]	v. 出现，亮相	7A
decryption	[di:'kripʃən]	n. 解密	9B
dedicated	['dedikeitid]	adj. 专门的，专注的	5B
default	[di'fɔ:lt]	n. 默认（值），缺省（值）	8A
defeat	[di'fi:t]	n. & v. 击败	1B
define	[di'fain]	vt. 定义，详细说明	9A
definitely	['definitli]	adv. 明确地，干脆地	9A
definition	[,defi'niʃən]	n. 定义，解说	10B
degradation	[,degrə'deiʃən]	n. 降级，降格，退化	3B
degrade	[di'greid]	v.（使）降级，（使）退化	3B
delay	[di'lei]	v. & n. 耽搁，延迟，迟滞	1A
deliver	[di'livə]	vt. 递送，交付	2A
delivery	[di'livəri]	n. 递送，交付，交货	1A
demodulate	[di:'mɔdju:leit]	vt. 解调	7B
dense	[dens]	adj. 密集的，浓厚的	3B
density	['densiti]	n. 密度	10A
depict	[di'pikt]	vt. 描述，描写	4B
deploy	[di'plɔi]	v. 部署，展开，配置	2A
deployment	[di'plɔimənt]	n. 部署	10A
detachable	[di'tætʃəbl]	adj. 可分开的，可分离的	8A
detect	[di'tekt]	vt. 探测，发现	1B
detection	[di'tekʃən]	n. 侦查，探测	5B
detector	[di'tektə]	n. 探测器	10A
determine	[di'tə:min]	vt. 决定，断定	5A
detriment	['detrimənt]	n. 损害，损害物	1B

单词	音标	意义	课次
develop	[di'veləp]	vt. 发展，开发	1B
device	[di'vais]	n. 装置，设备	1A
dim	['dim]	adj. 暗淡的，模糊的，无光泽的 vt. 使暗淡，使失去光泽	3A
dimension	[di'menʃən]	n. 尺寸，尺度；维（数），度（数），元	9A
dimmer	['dimə]	n. 调光器	3A
disability	[,disə'biliti]	n. 无力，无能，残疾	3A
disable	[dis'eibl]	v. 使失去能力	8A
disablement	[di'seiblmənt]	n. 无力化，无能力	10A
discriminate	[dis'krimineit]	v. 区别，区别待遇	7B
disrupt	[dis'rʌpt]	v. 使中断，使分裂，破坏	8A
disrupt	[dis'rʌpt]	vt. 使中断，使分裂，使瓦解，破坏	8B
dissipate	['disipeit]	v. 驱散，消耗	4B
distinctive	[dis'tiŋktiv]	adj. 与众不同的，有特色的	9B
distribute	[dis'tribju(:)t]	vt. 分发，分配，分布，分类，分区	3A
ditto	['ditəu]	n. 同上，同上符号，很相似的东西 vt. 重复 adv. 与前同地	1A
domain	[dəu'mein]	n. 范围，区域，领域	5B
download	[daunləud]	v. 下载	10B
downtime	['dauntaim]	n. 停工期	2A
draft	[drɑ:ft]	n. 草稿，草案	7A
dramatically	[drə'mætikəli]	adv. 戏剧地，引人注目地	6B
drapery	['dreipəri]	n. 织物，帏帐，布料	10A
draw	[drɔ:]	n. 有吸引力的人（或事物）	3A
drywall	['draiwɔ:l]	n.（不抹灰的）板墙，干墙，石膏板预制件	7A
dual	['dju(:)əl]	adj. 双的，二重的，双重	3A
duplicate	['dju:plikeit]	vt. 使成双，使加倍；复制 n. 复制品；复印件 adj. 复制的，副本的；成对的，二倍的	2A
dwarf	[dwɔ:f]	vt. 使显得矮小；使相形见绌 n. 矮子；侏儒	1B
dynamical	[dai'næmikəl]	adj. 动态的	4B
economy	[i:'kɔnəmi]	n. 经济，节约，节约措施，经济实惠	2B
effective	[i'fektiv]	adj. 有效的，被实施的	2A
effortless	['efətlis]	adj. 容易的，不费力气的	9B
electromagnetic	[ilektrəu'mægnitik]	adj. 电磁的	7A
element	['elimənt]	n. 要素，元素，成分，元件	2B
elimination	[i,limi'neiʃən]	n. 排除，除去，消除	2A
embankment	[im'bæŋkmənt]	n. 堤防	6B
embed	[im'bed]	vt. 使插入，使嵌入，深留，嵌入	1A
embedded	[em'bedid]	adj. 嵌入的，嵌入式	1A
emergency	[i'mə:dʒənsi]	n. 紧急情况，突然事件，非常时刻，紧急事件	3A

续表

单 词	音 标	意 义	课次
emerging	[i'mə:dʒiŋ]	adj. 新兴的，不断出现的，涌现的	2A
emit	[i'mit]	vt. 发出，放射	7B
employ	[im'plɔi]	v. 使用	9A
enablement	[i'neiblmənt]	n. 启动，允许	10A
enable	[i'neibl]	vt. 使能够	6B
encapsulate	[in'kæpsjuleit]	v. 封装	4A
encode	[in'kəud]	vt. 编码，把（电文.情报等）译成电码（或密码）	7B
encompass	[in'kʌmpəs]	v. 包围，环绕	8B
encrypt	[in'kript]	v. 加密，将……译成密码	4A
encryption	[in'kripʃən]	n. 编密码，加密	7A
endless	['endlis]	adj. 无止境的，无穷的	1A
endpoint	['endpɔint]	n. 端点，终点	4B
engine	['endʒin]	n. 发动机；引擎	2B
enhance	[in'hɑ:ns]	vt. 提高，增强	6B
enhancement	[in'hɑ:nsmənt]	n. 增进，增加	10B
ensure	[in'ʃuə]	v. 确保，保证	2A
entertainment	[entə'teinmənt]	n. 娱乐	3A
enthusiast	[in'θju:ziæst]	n. 热心者，狂热者	8A
entirely	[in'taiəli]	adv. 完全地，全然地，一概地	7A
entity	['entiti]	n. 实体	4A
environment	[in'vaiərənmənt]	n. 环境，外界	1B
ephemeris	[i'feməris]	n. 历书	3B
errant	['erənt]	adj. 漂泊的；偏离正道的，错误的	2B
essentially	[i'senʃəli]	adv. 本质上，本来	10A
establish	[is'tæbliʃ]	vt. 建立，设立	4A
estimate	['estimeit]	v. & n. 估计，估价，评估	1B
Ethernet	['i:θənet]	n. 以太网	8A
eventually	[i'ventjuəli]	adv. 最后，终于	3A
evolve	[i'vɔlv]	v. （使）发展，（使）进展，（使）进化	2A
exceed	[ik'si:d]	vt. 超越，胜过 vi. 超过其他	5A
exchange	[iks'tʃeindʒ]	vt. 交换	2A
expand	[iks'pænd]	vt. 使膨胀，扩张 vi. 发展	2B
experience	[iks'piəriəns]	n. & vt. 经验，体验，经历	1B
exploit	[iks'plɔit]	v. 使用，利用	9B
explosion	[iks'pləuʒən]	n. 爆发，发出	9A
explosive	[iks'pləusiv]	adj. 爆炸（性）的，爆发（性）的	2B
extensible	[ik'stensibəl]	adj. 可展开的，可扩张的，可延长的	10A
exterior	[eks'tiəriə]	adj. 外部的，外在的，表面的 n. 外部，表面，外形	3A
external	[eks'tə:nl]	adj. 外部的	5A
facility	[fə'siliti]	n. 设备，工具	2B
factor	['fæktə]	n. 因素，要素，因数	3B

续表

单　　词	音　　标	意　　义	课次
faculty	['fækəlti]	n. 全体教员	8A
fatigue	[fə'ti:g]	n. 疲劳	6B
feed	[fi:d]	n. & v. 输入，馈送	6B
feedback	['fi:dbæk]	n. 反馈，反应	1B
figure	['figə]	n. 外形，轮廓，图形，画像，数字，形状 vt. 描绘，表示，象征	7A
finalize	['fainəlaiz]	v. 把（计划，稿件等）最后定下来，定案	7A
fingerprint	['fiŋgəprint]	n. 指纹，手印　vt. 采指纹	3A
firewall	['faiəwɔ:l]	n. 防火墙	5B
fit	[fit]	vt. 安装	2B
fitting	['fitiŋ]	n. 装配，装置	8A
flexibility	[,fleksə'biliti]	n. 弹性，适应性，灵活性	2A
flooding	['flʌdiŋ]	n. 涌入，流入	6B
flyover	['flaiəuvə]	n. 立交桥	6B
folder	['fəuldə]	n. 文件夹	9B
foliage	['fəuliidʒ]	n. 植物	8A
font	[fɔnt]	n. 字体，字形	9A
footfall	['futfɔ:l]	n. 客流量	2A
forerunner	['fɔ:,rʌnə]	n. 先驱（者）	2B
forest	['fɔrist]	n. 森林，林木　adj. 森林的　vt. 植树于	6B
format	['fɔ:mæt]	n. 形式，格式　vt. 安排……的格式	4A
fortnight	['fɔ:tnait]	n. 两星期	1A
forward	['fɔ:wəd]	vt. 转发，转寄，运送	5B
fragmentation	[,frægmen'teiʃən]	n. 分段	4A
frame	[freim]	n. 帧，框架	8A
framework	['freimwə:k]	n. 构架，框架，结构	4A
frequency	['fri:kwənsi]	n. 频率，周率	3B
fridge	[fridʒ]	n. 冰箱	
frustrate	[frʌs'treit]	v. 挫败，阻挠，阻止	
frustrating	[frʌs'treitiŋ]	adj. 令人灰心的；使人沮丧的；让人懊恼的	1A
fuel	[fjuəl]	n. 燃料	2B
fulfill	[ful'fil]	vt. 履行，实现，完成	10B
function	['fʌŋkʃən]	n. 功能，作用	2A
functional	['fʌŋkʃnl]	adj. 功能的	4A
functionality	[,fʌŋkʃə'næliti]	n. 功能性	10A
fundamentally	[fʌndə'mentəli]	adv. 基础地，根本地	10A
furore	[fju:'rɔ:ri]	n. 狂热	1B
futuristic	[fju:tʃə'ristik]	adj. 超现代化的，超时髦的，最先进的	3A
gadget	['gædʒit]	n. 小器具，小配件，小玩意	1A
gain	[gein]	vt. 获得，得到	2A
garage	['gærɑ:ʒ]	n. 汽车间，修车厂，车库	8B

续表

单词	音标	意义	课次
gather	[ˈgæðə]	n. 集合，聚集 vi. 集合，聚集 vt. 使聚集，搜集	2B
generation	[ˌdʒenəˈreiʃən]	n. 产生，发生	10B
genuine	[ˈdʒenjuin]	adj. 真实的，真正的	6A
geo-fencing	[gjəu-ˈfensiŋ]	n. 地理围栏	6B
geometry	[dʒiˈɔmitri]	n. 几何学，几何形状；几何图形	3B
giant	[ˈdʒaiənt]	n. 巨人 adj. 庞大的，巨大的	1B
gigabyte	[ˈgigəbait]	n. 十亿字节，吉字节	5A
gigahertz	[ˈgigəhə:ts]	n. 千兆赫	8B
glacier	[ˈglæsjə]	n. 冰河	6B
grant	[grɑ:nt]	vt. 同意，准予	8A
greenhouse	[ˈgri:nhaus]	n. 温室	6B
grocery	[ˈgrəusəri]	n. 食品，杂货	9A
guarantee	[ˌgærənˈti:]	n. & vt. 保证，担保	10A
hacker	[ˈhækə]	n. 黑客	3A
hand-held	[hænd-held]	adj. 手持的	7B
handlebar	[ˈhændlbɑ:]	n. 手把	1A
handler	[ˈhændlə]	n. 处理者，处理器	6A
handset	[ˈhændset]	n. 电话听筒，手机，手持机	10B
harbinger	[ˈhɑ:bindʒə]	n. 先驱，预兆 vt. 预告，做……的前驱	1B
hardware	[ˈhɑ:dwɛə]	n. （计算机的）硬件，（电子仪器的）部件	8A
harmless	[ˈhɑ:mlis]	adj. 无害的	9B
harsh	[hɑ:ʃ]	adj. 苛刻的，荒芜的	6A
hazardous	[ˈhæzədəs]	adj. 危险的，冒险的	6B
heartbeat	[ˈhɑ:tbi:t]	n. 心跳	10A
herd	[hə:d]	n. 兽群，牧群 v. 把……赶在一起放牧，成群	1B
heterogeneity	[ˌhetərəudʒiˈni:iti]	n. 异种，异质，不同成分	6A
heterogeneous	[ˌhetərəuˈdʒi:niəs]	adj. 不同种类的，异类的	6A
hierarchical	[ˌhaiəˈrɑ:kikəl]	adj. 分等级的	4A
hierarchy	[ˈhaiərɑ:ki]	n. 层次，层级	3A
highlight	[ˈhailait]	vt. 加亮，使显著，突出 n. 加亮区，最显著（重要）部分	1B
hive	[haiv]	v. （使）入蜂箱，群居 n. 蜂箱，蜂房	10A
homeowner	[ˈhəum,əunə]	n. 自己拥有住房者，（住自己房子的）私房屋主	2B
homogeneous	[ˌhɔməuˈdʒi:njəs]	adj. 同类的，相似的，均一的，均匀的	8A
hop	[hɔp]	v. 跳跃	6A
hormone	[ˈhɔ:məun]	荷尔蒙，激素	1B
hub	[hʌb]	n. 网络集线器，网络中心	4B
hue	[hju:]	n. 颜色，色彩；色度	9A
huge	[hju:dʒ]	adj. 巨大的，极大的，无限的	1A
humidity	[hju:ˈmiditi]	n. 湿度	6B

单 词	音 标	意 义	课次
identical	[aiˈdentikəl]	adj. 同一的，同样的	4B
identification	[ai,dentifiˈkeiʃən]	n. 辨认，识别，鉴定，证明	9A
identifier	[aiˈdentifaiə]	n. 标识符	1B
identify	[aiˈdentifai]	vt. 识别，鉴别	7B
ignore	[igˈnɔː]	vt. 不理睬，忽略	4B
illustrate	[ˈiləstreit]	vt. 举例说明，图解	10A
immaterial	[,iməˈtiəriəl]	adj. 非实质的	1A
immediately	[iˈmiːdjətli]	adv. 立即，马上，直接地	2A
immense	[iˈmens]	adj. 极广大的，无边的，<口>非常好的	3A
impedance	[imˈpiːdəns]	n. 阻抗，电阻	4B
impede	[imˈpiːd]	v. 妨害，阻止	9A
implant	[imˈplɑːnt]	v. 植入，插入	7B
implement	[ˈimplimənt]	v. 实施，实现	2A
implementation	[,implimenˈteiʃən]	n. 执行	9A
improvement	[imˈpruːvmənt]	n. 改进，进步	1B
inaccessible	[,inækˈsesəbl]	adj. 达不到的，难以接近	6B
inaccuracy	[inˈækjurəsi]	n. 错误	3B
incapable	[inˈkeipəbl]	adj. 无能力的，不能的	6A
incident	[ˈinsidənt]	n. 入射	7B
incompatible	[,inkəmˈpætəbl]	adj. 不兼容的	7B
increasingly	[inˈkriːsiŋli]	adv. 日益，愈加	1B
independence	[,indiˈpendəns]	n. 独立	10A
independent	[indiˈpendənt]	adj. 独立的，不受约束的	2A
indicator	[ˈindikeitə]	n. 指标，指示器	2A
individual	[,indiˈvidjuəl]	n. 个人 adj. 个人的	1B
induce	[inˈdjuːs]	vt. 促使，导致，引起	5B
industry	[ˈindəstri]	n. 行业	2A
infancy	[ˈinfənsi]	n. 幼年	2A
infrared	[ˈinfrəˈred]	adj. 红外线的 n. 红外线	8B
infrastructure	[ˈinfrəˈstrʌktʃə]	n. 基础	1B
inherent	[inˈhiərənt]	adj. 固有的，内在的，与生俱来的	1B
initialization	[i,niʃəlaiˈzeiʃən]	n. 设定初值，初始化	7B
initiate	[iˈniʃieit]	vt. 开始，发动 v. 开始，发起	3A
inject	[inˈdʒekt]	vt. 引入，插入，注入	7B
inspect	[inˈspekt]	v. 检查	5A
inspection	[inˈspekʃən]	n. 检查，视察	6B
inspire	[inˈspaiə]	vt. 激发，产生	6A
instance	[ˈinstəns]	n. 实例，要求 vt. 举……为例	4A
instantaneous	[,instənˈteinjəs]	adj. 瞬间的，即刻的，即时的	3A
instigator	[ˈinstigeitə]	n. 发动器	3A
intake	[ˈinteik]	n. （水管、煤气管等的）入口，进口	2B
integration	[,intiˈgreiʃən]	n. 综合，集成	2A
intelligent	[inˈtelidʒənt]	adj. 聪明的，智能的	5A

续表

单　　词	音　　标	意　　义	课次
intentional	[in'tenʃənəl]	adj. 有意图的，故意的	9B
interaction	[,intər'ækʃən]	n. 交互	1A
intercom	['intəkɔm]	n. 内部通信联络系统	1A
intercommunication	['intəkə,mju:ni'keiʃən]	n. 双向（或多向）通信	2A
interconnect	[,intə(:)kə'nekt]	vt. 使互相连接	8A
interconnection	[,intə(:)kə'nekʃən]	n. 互联	4B
interface	['intə(:)feis]	n. 界面，接口	8A
interference	[,intə'fiərəns]	n. 冲突，干涉	8A
intermediary	[,intə'mi:diəri]	n. 中间物　adj. 中间的，媒介的	8A
internal	[in'tə:nl]	adj. 内在的，内部的	5A
international	[,intə(:)'næʃənəl]	adj. 国际的，世界的	9A
interoperability	['intər,ɔpərə'biləti]	n. 互用性，协同工作的能力	10A
interrogate	[in'terəgeit]	vt. 询问	7B
interrogator	[in'terəgeitə]	n. 询问器，询问机，侦测器	7B
intersection	[,intə(:)'sekʃən]	n. 十字路口	5A
interval	['intəvəl]	n. 时间间隔	10A
intervene	[,intə'vi:n]	vi. 插入，介入，（指时间）介于其间	9A
intervention	[,intə(:)'venʃən]	n. 干涉	2B
intrusion	[in'tru:ʒən]	n. 闯入，侵扰	5B
investment	[in'vestmənt]	n. 投资	1A
involve	[in'vɔlv]	vt. 涉及	10A
ionosphere	[ai'ɔnəsfiə]	n. 电离层	3B
issue	['isju:]	n. 问题	1B
juice	[dʒu:s]	n. 电，动力来源	3A
kana	['kɑ:nə]	n. <日>假名	9B
kanji	['kɑ:ndʒi]	n. 日本汉字	9B
keypad	['ki:pæd]	n. 小键盘，键区	3A
kilobit	['kiləubit]	n. 千（二进制）位，千比特	10A
kiosk	['ki:ɔsk]	n. 亭子	2A
kit	[kit]	n. 成套工具，用具包，工具箱	3A
knack	[næk]	n. 诀窍	10B
label	['leibl]	n. 标签，签条，标志　vt. 贴标签于	7B
labor-intensive	['leibə-in'tensiv]	adj. 劳动密集型的	7A
landslide	['lændslaid]	n. 山崩，泥石流	6B
latency	['leitənsi]	n. 反应时间	10A
latitude	['lætitju:d]	n. 纬度，范围	3B
launch	[lɔ:ntʃ, lɑ:ntʃ]	vi. 发射，投放市场	3B
lawn	[lɔ:n]	n. 草地，草坪	2B
layer	['leiə]	n. 层	4A
lazy	['leizi]	adj. 懒惰的，懒散的	3A
leverage	['li:vəridʒ]	vt. 杠杆作用　n. 杠杆	2A
lightness	['laitnis]	n. 亮度	9A
limitation	[,limi'teiʃən]	n. 限制，局限性	3A

续表

单 词	音 标	意 义	课次
link	[liŋk]	n. & vt. 链接	4B
literally	['litərəli]	adv. 照字面意义，逐字地	1B、5B
live	[laiv]	adj. 活的，生动的，精力充沛的	2A
livestock	['laivstɔk]	n. 家畜，牲畜	7B
location	[ləu'keiʃən]	n. 位置，场所，特定区域	3B
logistic	[ləu'dʒistik]	adj. 物流的，后勤的	2A
logo	['lɔgəu]	n. 徽标	9B
longevity	[lɔn'dʒeviti]	n. 寿命	10A
longitude	['lɔndʒitju:d]	n. 经度，经线	3B
magnification	[,mægnifi'keiʃən]	n. 扩大，放大倍率	9A
magnitude	['mægnitju:d]	n. 数量，量级	6B
mainstream	['meinstri:m]	n. 主流	10B
maintenance	['meintinəns]	n. 维护，保持	1B
malicious	[mə'liʃəs]	adj. 怀恶意的	9B
mandatory	['mændətəri]	adj. 命令的，强制的，托管的	7A
manipulate	[mə'nipjuleit]	vt.（熟练地）操作，巧妙地处理	2B
manual	['mænjuəl]	n. 手册，指南 adj. 手的，手动的，手工的	6B
manufacture	[,mænju'fæktʃə]	vt. 制造，加工 n. 制造，制造业，产品	1A
manufacturer	[,mænju'fæktʃərə]	n. 制造业者，厂商	8A
map	[mæp]	vt. 映射	4A
mapping	['mæpiŋ]	n. 映射	4A
mark	[mɑ:k]	n. 标志，记号 v. 做标记	9B
mask	[mɑ:sk]	v. 掩膜	9B
matrix	['meitriks]	n. 矩阵	9B
maximization	[,mæksəmai'zeiʃən]	n. 最大值化，极大值化	6A
maximize	['mæksmaiz]	vt. 取……最大值，最佳化	2B
measure	['meʒə]	vt. 测量，测度，估量 n. 量度器，量度标准，测量，措施	1B
mechanism	['mekənizəm]	n. 机械装置，机构，机制	10A
megabit	['megəbit]	n. 百万位，兆位	8A
megabyte	['megəbait]	n. 兆字节	10B
megahertz	['megə,hə:ts]	n. 兆赫	5A
memory	['meməri]	n. 存储器，内存	7B
message	['mesidʒ]	n. 消息，通信，信息 vt. 通知	1B
metadata	['metə'deitə]	n. 元数据	6A
microchip	['maikrəutʃip]	n. 微芯片	2B
microcontroller	['maikrəukən'trəulə]	n. 微控制器	6A
microprocessor	[maikrəu'prəusesə]	n. 微处理器	5A
microscopic	[maikrə'skɔpik]	adj. 极小的，微小的	6A
microsegmentation	['maikrəj,segmən'teiʃən]	n. 微段	5B
middleware	['midlwɛə]	n. 中间设备，中间件	7B
midway	['mid'wei]	n. 中途，半路	10B

续表

单　　词	音　　标	意　　义	课次
military	[ˈmilitəri]	adj. 军事的，军用的	3B
milliwatt	[ˈmiliwɔt]	n. 毫瓦	8B
miniaturization	[ˌminiətʃəraizeiʃən]	n. 小型化	7B
miniaturize	[ˈminiətʃəraiz]	vt. 使小型化	7B
minimize	[ˈminimaiz]	vt. 将……减到最少，最小化	8B
minor	[ˈmainə]	adj. 较小的，次要的	5B
misconception	[ˌmiskənˈsepʃən]	n. 误解	9A
mobility	[məuˈbiliti]	n. 活动性，移动性，机动性	2A
modem	[ˈməudəm]	n. 调制解调器	2A
modular	[ˈmɔdjulə]	adj. 模块化的，组合的	5B
modulate	[ˈmɔdjuleit]	vt.（信号）调制	7B
modulator	[ˈmɔdjuleitə]	n. 调节器	3A
module	[ˈmɔdju:l]	n. 模块	5B
monitor	[ˈmɔnitə]	vt. 监控　n. 监视器，监控器	1A
mote	[məut]	n. 尘埃，微粒	6A
motivate	[ˈməutiveit]	v. 激发，促进	10A
motorway	[ˈməutəwei]	n. 汽车高速公路	1A
mount	[maunt]	v. 安装，放置	5B
multicast	[ˈmʌltikɑ:st]	n. 多点传送；多播，组播	5B
multichannel	[ˌmʌltiˈtʃænl]	adj. 多通话线路的，多通道的，多波段的	3B
multilayer	[ˈmʌltiˌleiə]	n. 多层	5B
multimedia	[ˈmʌltiˈmi:djə]	n. 多媒体	10B
multiplayer	[ˈmʌltiˈpleiə]	n. 多玩家	8B
multiplex	[ˈmʌltipleks]	v. 多路传输，多路复用；多重发信　adj. 多元的	4A
multipoint	[ˈmʌltipɔint]	adj. 多点（式）的，多位置的	4A
multi-port	[ˈmʌlti-pɔ:t]	n. 多口，多个端口	5B
multislot	[ˈmʌltislɔt]	n. 多插槽，多插座	5A
multithreading	[ˈmʌltiˈθrediŋ]	n. 多线程	6A
multitude	[ˈmʌltitju:d]	n. 多数	10A
mundane	[ˈmʌndein]	adj. 世界的，世俗的，平凡的	1A
mythical	[ˈmiθikəl]	adj. 神话的，虚构的	10B
nagging	[ˈnægiŋ]	adj. 唠叨的，挑剔的	3A
narrow	[ˈnærəu]	n. 狭窄部分　adj. 狭窄的　v. 变窄	9A
navigation	[ˌnæviˈgeiʃən]	n. 导航，领航	3B
necessitate	[niˈsesiteit]	v. 成为必要	5B
neighbourhood	[ˈneibəhud]	n. 邻近，邻居关系	9A
neighbouring	[ˈneibəriŋ]	adj. 附近的，毗邻的	6A
netmodem	[netˈməudəm]	n. 网络调制解调器	5A
network	[ˈnetwə:k]	n. 网络	1A
newfound	[ˈnju:faund]	adj. 新发现的，新得到的	10A
niche	[nitʃ]	n. 合适的位置，小生境	4A
nightmare	[ˈnaitmeə]	n. 梦魇，噩梦，可怕的事物	3A

单 词	音 标	意 义	课次
Nintendo	[nin'tendəu]	n. 任天堂	9B
node	[nəud]	n. 节点	3A
noisy	['nɔizi]	adj. 噪声的，嘈杂的	3A
nominal	['nɔminl]	adj. 名义上的	10A
noncontact	['nɔn'kɔntækt]	adj. 没有接触的，非接触的	7B
nonvolatile	['nɔn'vɔlətail]	adj. 非易失性的	7B
norm	[nɔ:m]	n. 标准，规范	8A
normalize	['nɔ:məlaiz]	v. 使标准化，规格化	9B
noticeable	['nəutisəbl]	adj. 显而易见的，值得注意的	10B
notification	[,nəutifi'keiʃən]	n. 通知，布告，告示	3A
notify	['nəutifai]	v. 通报	6B
ocean	['əuʃən]	n. 大海，海洋	6B
onboard	['ɔn'bɔ:d]	adj. 随带的，板载的	3B
optical	['ɔptikəl]	adj. 视力的，光学的	6A
optimistic	[,ɔpti'mistik]	adj. 乐观的	7A
optimize	['ɔptimaiz]	vt. 使最优化	5B
optimum	['ɔptiməm]	n. 最适宜 adj. 最佳的	5A
option	['ɔpʃən]	n. 选项，选择权	5A
orbit	['ɔ:bit]	n. 轨道 vt. 绕……轨道而行 vi. 进入轨道，沿轨道飞行	3B
orbital	['ɔ:bitl]	adj. 轨道的	3B
order	['ɔ:də]	n. 次序，顺序，命令，定购，订单 vt. 命令，定购，定制	1A
outage	['autidʒ]	n. 储运损耗	1B
outflow	['autfləu]	n. 流出	2B
outlast	[aut'lɑ:st]	vt. 比……长久，比……活得长	10A
outlying	['autlaiiŋ]	adj. 边远的，偏僻的	10A
overhead	['əuvəhed]	n. 开销，管理费用	10A
overlap	['əuvə'læp]	v. （与……）交迭	8A
overwhelm	['əuvə'welm]	vt. 覆没，压倒	9B
pacemaker	['peismeikə]	n. 领跑者，带头人	1A
pallet	['pælit]	n. 货盘	7B
panel	['pænl]	n. 面板，嵌板，仪表板	5B
parallel	['pærəlel]	adj. 并行的，平行的，并联的；相同的，类似的	1B
parameter	[pə'ræmitə]	n. 参数，参量	2B
particle	['pɑ:tikl]	n. 粒子，点，极小量	6B
particular	[pə'tikjulə]	n. 细节，详细 adj. 特殊的，特别的，独特的	6A
partway	['pɑ:twei]	v. 到中途，到达一半	4B
passive	['pæsiv]	adj. 被动的，无源的	5A
passphrase	['pɑ:sfreiz]	n. 密码短语口令	8A
password	['pɑ:swə:d]	n. 密码，口令	3A

续表

单　　词	音　　标	意　　义	课次
pattern	[ˈpætən]	n. 式样，模式，图案　vt. 模仿，仿造	1A
pedestrian	[peˈdestriən]	n. 步行者	10B
peer	[piə]	n. 同等的人　vt. 与……同等	3A
performance	[pəˈfɔ:məns]	n. 履行，执行，性能	4A
periodically	[ˌpiəriˈɔdikəli]	adv. 周期性地，定时性地	7B
peripheral	[pəˈrifərəl]	adj. 外围的　n. 外围设备	4B
permanent	[ˈpə:mənənt]	adj. 永久的，持久的	4B
permissive	[pə(ː)ˈmisiv]	adj. 许可的	9B
persuasive	[pəˈsweisiv]	adj. 有说服力的	10B
pharmaceuticals	[ˌfɑ:məˈsju:tikəlz]	n. 医药品	9A
pharmacy	[ˈfɑ:məsi]	n. 药剂学，配药业，制药业	1A
phenomenal	[fiˈnɔminl]	adj. 显著的，现象的	9A
phenomenon	[fiˈnɔminən]	n. 现象	6B
piconet	[ˈpikənet]	n. 微微网	8B
pipeline	[ˈpaipˌlain]	n. 管道，管线	6B
pitch	[pitʃ]	n. 投放　vt. 投，掷，定位于	9B
placement	[ˈpleismənt]	n. 放置，布置	4B
platform	[ˈplætfɔ:m]	n. 平台	6A
pledge	[pledʒ]	vt. 保证，发誓	8A
plot	[plɔt]	vt. 标绘出，绘制……的图表（或平面图）	1A
plug	[plʌg]	vt. 插上，插栓　n. 插头，插销	3A
pokey	[ˈpəuki]	adj. 迟钝的，狭小的	10B
pollutant	[pəˈlu:tənt]	n. 污染物质	6B
pollution	[pəˈlu:ʃən]	n. 污染	8A
population	[ˌpɔpjuˈleiʃən]	n. 人口	1A
port	[pɔ:t]	n. 端口	4B
portmanteau	[pɔ:tˈmæntəu]	n. 合成词	9B
portray	[pɔ:ˈtrei]	v. 描绘	1B
position	[pəˈziʃən]	n. 位置　vt. 安置，决定……的位置	3B
possess	[pəˈzes]	vt. 占有，拥有，持有	10A
potential	[pəˈtenʃəl]	adj. 潜在的，可能的	7A
poverty	[ˈpɔvəti]	n. 贫穷，贫困，贫乏，缺少	1B
precise	[priˈsais]	adj. 精确的，准确的　n. 精确	3B
predetermine	[ˈpri:diˈtə:min]	v. 预定，预先确定	9A
predict	[priˈdikt]	vt. 预言，预测	1A
predominant	[priˈdɔminənt]	adj. 支配的，主要的，有影响的	6A
preemptive	[priːˈemptiv]	adj. 有先买权的，有强制收购权的，抢先的	6B
pregnant	[ˈpregnənt]	adj. 怀孕	1A
preinstall	[ˈpri:inˈstɔ:l]	v. 预设，预安装	5A
prescription	[priˈskripʃən]	n. 指示，规定	1A
preserve	[priˈzə:v]	vt. 保护，保持，保存	5A
pressing	[ˈpresiŋ]	adj. 紧迫的　v. 挤压	1B

续表

单　词	音　标	意　义	课次
prevalent	[ˈprevələnt]	adj. 普遍的，流行的	1A
preventive	[priˈventiv]	adj. 预防性的	2A
preview	[ˈpriːvjuː]	n. 事先查看，预览	10B
previous	[ˈpriːvjəs]	adj. 在前的，早先的　adv. 在……以前	10B
primarily	[ˈpraimərili]	adv. 首先，起初；主要地，根本上	5B
principle	[ˈprinsəpl]	n. 法则，原则，原理	4A
privacy	[ˈpraivəsi]	n. 隐私	1B
probability	[ˌprɔbəˈbiliti]	n. 概率，或然性，可能性	5B
procedure	[prəˈsiːdʒə]	n. 进程，程序	4A
process	[prəˈses]	n. 过程，作用，方法，程序，步骤　vt. 加工，处理	2B
processor	[ˈprəusesə]	n. 处理机，处理器	9B
profile	[ˈprəufail]	n. 剖面，侧面，外形，轮廓	10A
programmable	[ˈprəugræməbl]	adj. 可设计的，可编程的	7B
progression	[prəˈgreʃən]	n. 行进，级数	5B
prominent	[ˈprɔminənt]	adj. 卓越的，显著的，突出的	3A
promote	[prəˈməut]	vt. 促进，发扬，提升	2B
propagate	[ˈprɔpəgeit]	v. 传播	4B
propagation	[ˌprɔpəˈgeiʃən]	n. （声波，电磁辐射等）传播	6A
property	[ˈprɔpəti]	n. 性质，特性；财产，所有权	6A
proportional	[prəˈpɔːʃənl]	adj. 相称的，均衡的	4B
proprietary	[prəˈpraiətəri]	adj. 所有的　n. 所有者，所有权	6A
protocol	[ˈprəutəkɔl]	n. 协议	10A
protothread	[ˈprəutəuθred]	n. 轻量级线程	6A
province	[ˈprɔvins]	n. 范围，职责	2B
prying	[ˈpraiiŋ]	adj. 爱打听的　v. 打听，刺探（他人的私事）	7A
pseudorandom	[ˌpsjuːdəuˈrændəm]	adj. 伪随机的	7B
puck	[pʌk]	n. 恶作剧的小妖精	8A
purify	[ˈpjuərifai]	v. 净化	2B
purpose-built	[ˈpəːpəsbilt]	adj. 为特定目的建造的	2A
pursuit	[pəˈsjuːt]	n. 追求，追赶；工作	3A
push	[puʃ]	n. 推，推动	10B
quiet	[ˈkwaiət]	vt. 使平静，使安心　vi. 平静下来	3A
quote	[kwəut]	vt. 提供，提出，报（价）	7A
rack	[ræk]	n. 架，设备架　vt. 放在架上	5A
radius	[ˈreidjəs]	n. 半径，范围，界限	8B
random	[ˈrændəm]	n. 随意，任意　adj. 随机的，任意的，随便的	2B
randomly	[ˈrændəmli]	adv. 随即地，随便地	8B
ratify	[ˈrætifai]	vt. 批准，认可	6A
readability	[ˌriːdəˈbiliti]	n. 易读，可读性	9B
readable	[ˈriːdəbl]	adj. 可读的，易读的	9A

续表

单　词	音　标	意　义	课次
reader	['ri:də]	n. 阅读器，读卡机	7B
reality	[ri(:)'æliti]	n. 真实，事实	1B
realm	[relm]	n. 领域	10B
rearrange	['ri:ə'reindʒ]	vt. 再排列，重新安排	1A
reasonable	['ri:znəbl]	adj. 合理的，有道理的	10A
reassembly	['ri:ə'sembli]	n. 重新装配	4A
rebroadcast	[ri:'brɔ:dkɑ:st]	v. & n. 转播，重播	5A
receipt	[ri'si:t]	n. 收条，收据，收到	9A
receiver	[ri'si:və]	n. 接受者，接收器	3A
reception	[ri'sepʃən]	n. 接收	3B
receptor	[ri'septə]	n. 接收器，感受器	3A
recipient	[ri'sipiənt]	n. 接收者	4B
recognize	['rekəgnaiz]	vt. 认可，承认，公认	3A
reconfigure	[,ri:kən'figə]	v. 重新装配，改装	4B
reconstruct	['ri:kən'strʌkt]	v. 重建；重造，修复	1B
reconverge	[rikən'və:dʒ]	v. 重新聚合	5A
record	['rekɔ:d]	vt. 记录	9A
redirect	['ri:di'rekt]	vt. 重寄，使改道，使改变方向	5A
reduce	[ri'dju:s]	vt. 减少，缩小，简化，还原	7A
reduction	[ri'dʌkʃən]	n. 减少，缩影，变形，缩减量	2A
redundancy	[ri'dʌndənsi]	n. 冗余	5B
redundant	[ri'dʌndənt]	adj. 多余的，冗余的	5B
reflect	[ri'flekt]	v. 反射	7A
reflection	[ri'flekʃən]	n. 反射	8A
regenerate	[ri'dʒenərit]	vt. 使新生，重建	5A
regulate	['regjuleit]	vt. 控制，调节，校准	1A
regulation	[regju'leiʃən]	n. 调节，校准	3A
relative	['relətiv]	n. 亲戚	1A
reliability	[ri,laiə'biliti]	n. 可靠性	6B
reliable	[ri'laiəbl]	adj. 可靠的，可信赖的	9A
reliance	[ri'laiəns]	n. 信任，信心，依靠	1B
relocate	['ri:ləu'keit]	v. 重新部署	7A
reminder	[ri'maində]	n. 提醒的人，暗示	1B
remote	[ri'məut]	adj. 遥远的，远程的	2B
remotely	[ri'məutli]	adv. 遥远地，偏僻地	1A
renovation	[,renəu'veiʃən]	n. 革新	3A
reorder	['ri:'ɔ:də]	v. 再订购，重新安排　n. 再订购	9A
repeater	[ri'pi:tə]	n. 转发器，中继器	4A
repetitive	[ri'petitiv]	adj. 重复的，反复性的	1A
replacement	[ri'pleismənt]	n. 替换，复位，交换，代替者	3B
request	[ri'kwest]	vt. & n. 请求，要求	4A
reroute	[ri'ru:t]	vt. 变更路径，更改路由	8B
resemble	[ri'zembl]	vt. 像，类似	6A

续表

单 词	音 标	意 义	课次
reside	[ri'zaid]	vi. 驻留	5A
resistor	[ri'zistə]	n. 电阻器	4B
respectively	[ri'spektivli]	adv. 分别地，各个地	7A
restore	[ris'tɔ:]	vt. 恢复，修复	9B
restrict	[ris'trikt]	vt. 限制，约束，限定	2A
retail	['ri:teil]	n. 零售 adj. 零售的 v. 零售	2A
retransmission	[,ri:trænz'miʃən]	n. 转播，中继，重发	5B
retransmit	[,ri:trænz'mit]	v. 转播，转发	4A
retrieval	[ri'tri:vəl]	n. 取回，恢复，修补，重获，挽救	6B
revenue	['revinju:]	n. 收入，税收	2A
revolutionary	['revə'lu:ʃənəri]	adj. 革命的	1B
rewire	[ri:'waiə]	vt. 再接电线，改电路	3A
rhythm	['riðəm]	n. 节奏，韵律	2B
risk	[risk]	n. 冒险，风险 vt. 冒……的危险	8B
roam	[rəum]	v. & n. 漫游	10B
robust	[rə'bʌst]	adj. 健壮的	1B
robustness	[rə'bʌstnes]	n. 坚固性，健壮性，鲁棒性	6B
roughly	['rʌfli]	adv. 概略地，粗糙地	7A
roundabout	['raundəbaut]	adj. 迂回的，转弯抹角的	1B
route	[ru:t]	v. 发送 n. 路线，路程，通道	5A
router	['ru:tə]	n. 路由器	4A
routine	[ru:'ti:n]	n. 常规，日常事务，程序	8B
runoff	['rʌnɔ:f]	流量，溢流	2B
safeguard	['seif,gɑ:d]	n. 保护，保卫；防护措施；安全设施 vt. 保护	1B
safety	['seifti]	n. 安全，保险，安全设备，保险装置	1B
satellite	['sætəlait]	n. 人造卫星	3B
satisfy	['sætisfai]	v. 满意，确保	9A
scalability	[,skeilə'biliti]	n. 可量测性	6A
scale	[skeil]	n. 刻度，衡量，比例	1A
scarce	[skɛəs]	adj. 缺乏的，不足的，稀有的	6A
scenario	[si'nɑ:riəu]	n. 情景	7A
sceptic	['skeptik]	n. 怀疑论者	1B
seamless	['si:mlis]	adj. 无缝的	1B
search	[sə:tʃ]	n. 搜寻，查究 v. 搜索，搜寻	9B
security	[si'kjuəriti]	n. 安全	1B
segment	['segmənt]	v. 分割 n. 段，节，片断	5A
segmentation	[,segmən'teiʃən]	n. 分割	4A
self-heal	['self'hi:l]	n. 自体愈合植物	10A
semantics	[si'mæntiks]	n. 语义	4A
semiconductor	['semikən'dʌktə]	n. 半导体	9B
sense	[sens]	vt. 感知	1A
sensitive	['sensitiv]	adj. 敏感的	9B

续表

单　　词	音　　标	意　　义	课次
sensitivity	[ˌsensiˈtiviti]	n. 敏感，灵敏（度），灵敏性	2B
sensor	[ˈsensə]	n. 传感器	6A
separate	[ˈsepəreit]	adj. 分开的，分离的，个别的，单独的　v. 分开，隔离，分散，分别	5B
sequence	[ˈsiːkwəns]	n. 次序，顺序，序列	4A
serialization	[ˌsiəriəlaiˈzeiʃən]	n. 序列化	4A
server	[ˈsəːvə]	n. 服务器	2A
session	[ˈseʃən]	n. 会话	4A
shade	[ʃeid]	n. 荫，图案阴影，遮光物，帘　vi. 渐变　vt. 遮蔽，使渐变	10A
share	[ʃεə]	n. & v. 分享，共享	5A
shock	[ʃɔk]	n. 震动	10A
shortcut	[ˈʃɔːtkʌt]	n. 捷径	5A
sign	[sain]	n. 标记，符号，记号　v. 签名（于），署名（于），签署	1B
signal	[ˈsignl]	n. 信号　adj. 信号的　v. 发信号	2B
significantly	[sigˈnifikəntli]	adv. 意味深长地，值得注目地	3B
similarly	[ˈsiməli]	adv. 同样地，类似于	2B
simplify	[ˈsimplifai]	vt. 单一化，简单化	8B
simultaneously	[siməlˈteiniəsly]	adv. 同时地	4B
singulate	[ˈsiŋgjuleit]	vt. 挑出	7B
slide	[slaid]	v.（使）滑动，（使）滑行	1A
smart	[smɑːt]	adj. 智能的，敏捷的	1A
smartphone	[ˈsmɑːtfəun]	n. 智能电话	1A
snoop	[snuːp]	vi. 探听，调查	5B
softphone	[ˈsɔftfəun]	n. 软件电话	10B
software	[ˈsɔftwεə]	n. 软件	2B
solution	[səˈljuːʃən]	n. 解答，解决办法，解决方案	8B
sophisticated	[səˈfistikeitid]	adj. 先进的	10A
spatial	[ˈspeiʃəl]	adj. 空间的	6A
spatially	[ˈspeiʃəli]	adv. 空间地	6A
spec	[spek]	n. 说明，规格	9A
specialized	[ˈspeʃəlaizd]	adj. 专门的	2B
specific	[spiˈsifik]	n. 细节　adj. 详细而精确的，明确的，特殊的	2A
specification	[ˌspesifiˈkeiʃən]	n. 规范，详述，规格，说明书	4A
spectrum	[ˈspektrəm]	n. 光谱，频谱	7A
split	[split]	v. 分开，分裂，分离	5B
spoke	[spəuk]	n. 轮辐	4B
sport	[spɔːt]	vt. 佩戴	1A
spotty	[ˈspɔti]	adj. 多污点的，质量不一的	2B
sprinkle	[ˈspriŋkl]	v. 洒，喷撒	10B
spyware	[ˈspaiwεə]	n. 间谍软件	1B

单　词	音　标	意　义	课次
stack	[stæk]	n. 堆栈　v. 堆叠	4A
stackable	['stækəbl]	adj. 可堆叠的，易叠起堆放的	5B
standard	['stændəd]	n. 标准，规格	9A
standardized	['stændə‚daizd]	adj. 标准的	5A
starter	['stɑ:tə]	n. 起动器，起动钮	3A
statistic	[stə'tistik]	n. 统计数字	1B
stereo	['stiəriəu]	n. 立体声　adj. 立体的	8B
stock	[stɔk]	adj. 普通的，常备的	8A
Stockholm	['stɔkhəum]	n. 斯德哥尔摩（瑞典首都）	6B
storage	['stɔridʒ]	n. 存储	4A
strategically	[strə'ti:dʒikəli]	adv. 战略上	3A
streamline	['stri:mlain]	v. 使现代化，使简单化	8B
subnet	['sʌb‚net]	n. 子网络，分支网络	4A
subscription	[sʌb'skripʃən]	n. 签署，同意	3B
subsidiary	[səb'sidjəri]	adj. 辅助的，补充的	9B
sufficiently	[sə'fiʃəntli]	adv. 十分地，充分地	9A
supermarket	['sju:pə‚mɑ:kit]	n. 超级市场	1A
supplementary	[‚sʌpli'mentəri]	adj. 附加的	9A
supplier	[sə'plaiə]	n. 供应者，补充者，厂商	9A
surpass	[sə:'pɑ:s]	vt. 远远超出	1A
surrounding	[sə'raundiŋ]	n. 围绕物，环境　adj. 周围的	8A
surveillance	[sə:'veiləns]	n. 监视，监督	2A
sustainability	[‚steinə'biləti]	n. 持续性，能维持性，永续性	1B
swamp	[swɔmp]	v. 陷入沼泽，淹没，覆没	10B
swappable	['swɔpəbl]	adj. 可替换的	5B
switch	[switʃ]	n. 交换机	5B
symbology	[sim'bɔlədʒi]	n. 符号系统，符号学	9A
symmetrical	[si'metrikəl]	adj. 对称的，均匀的	4B
sync	[siŋk]	n. 同时，同步	1A
synchronize	['siŋkrənaiz]	v. 同步	4A
synthesis	['sinθisis]	n. 综合，合成	4A
tablet	['tæblit]	n. 平板计算机	8A
tag	[tæg]	n. 标签　vt. 加标签于	7B
task	[tɑ:sk]	n. 任务，作业　v. 分派任务	6A
tasty	['teisti]	adj. 有品味的；有趣的	1A
technical	['teknikəl]	adj. 技术的，技术上的	1B
telecommunication	['telikəmju:ni'keiʃən]	n. 电信，长途通信，无线电通信，电信学	4B
teleconferencing	[teli'kɔnfərensiŋ]	n. 电信会议	10B
telematics	['telimə'ti:ks]	n. 信息通信业务，远程信息处理	2A
telemedicine	['teli‚medisin]	n.（通过遥测、电话、电视等手段求诊的）远距离医学	2B
telemetry	[ti'lemitri]	n. 遥感勘测，自动测量记录传导	2A
temperature	['tempritʃə]	n. 温度	6A

续表

单 词	音 标	意 义	课次
template	['templɪt]	n. 模板（=templet）	1A
term	[tə:m]	vt. 把……称为；把……叫做	1A
terminator	['tə:mineitə]	n. 终结器	4B
terrain	['terein]	n. 地形	3B
theoretically	[θiə'retikəli]	adv. 理论上，理论地	1B
thermostat	['θə:məstæt]	n. 自动调温器，温度调节装置	3A
throughput	['θru:put]	n. 吞吐量	10B
tightly	['taitli]	adv. 紧紧地，坚固地	7B
tiny	['taini]	adj. 很少的，微小的	6A
tolerance	['tɔlərəns]	n. 偏差，容差	9A
topology	[tə'pɔlədʒi]	n. 拓扑，布局	4B
touchscreen	['tʌtʃskri:n]	n. 触摸屏	1A
track	[træk]	n. 轨迹，跟踪 vt. 追踪	7B
traffic	['træfik]	n. 通信量；流量	1B
tramcar	['træmkɑ:]	n. 电车，矿车	6B
transaction	[træn'zækʃən]	n. 办理，处理，事务	5B
transceiver	[træn'si:və]	n. 收发器	5A
transmit	[trænz'mit]	vt. 传输，转送，传达，发射，传播 vi. 发射信号，发报	3B
transmitter	[trænz'mitə]	n. 发射机，转送者，变送器	3A
transparent	[træns'pɛərənt]	adj. 透明的，显然的，明晰的	4A
transponder	[træn'spɔndə]	n. 发射机应答器，询问机，转发器	7B
transport	[træns'pɔ:t]	vt. 传送，运输	1B
treatment	['tri:tmənt]	n. 处理	2B
tremendous	[tri'mendəs]	adj. 极大的，巨大的	3A
trend	[trend]	n. 倾向，趋势	2B
triangulation	[trai,æŋgju'leiʃən]	n. 三角测量，分成三角形	3B
trivial	['triviəl]	adj. 琐细的，价值不高的，微不足道的	1B
troposphere	['trɔpəusfiə]	n. 对流层	3B
truncate	['trʌŋkeit]	v. 把……截短 adj. 截短的	9A
truncation	[trʌŋ'keiʃən]	n. 切断	9A
trunk	[trʌŋk]	n. 干线，树干，主干	4B
trustworthy	['trʌst,wə:ði]	adj. 可信赖的	6B
tune	[tju:n]	vt. 收听	7A
tunnel	['tʌnl]	n. 隧道，地道	6B
ubiquitous	[ju:'bikwitəs]	adj. 到处存在的，（同时）普遍存在的	1B
ultimately	['ʌltimətli]	adv. 最后，终于，根本，基本上	1B
unaffected	[,ʌnə'fektid]	adj. 未受影响的，自然的	8B
undertake	[,ʌndə'teik]	vt. 承担，保证	9A
under-the-weather	['ʌndə-ðə-'weðə]	adj. 身体不适，生病	10B
uniformity	[,ju:ni'fɔ:miti]	n. 同样，一式，一致，均匀	9A
unimpeded	[,ʌnim'pi:did]	adj. 未受阻止的，没受到阻碍的	4B
uninterruptible	[ʌn,intə'rʌptibl]	adj. 不可打断的，不可中断的	5B

续表

单词	音标	意义	课次
universal	[ˌjuːniˈvəːsəl]	adj. 普遍的，全体的，通用的	1B
unlikely	[ʌnˈlaikli]	adj. 未必的，不太可能的，靠不住的	8B
unnecessary	[ʌnˈnesisəri]	adj. 不必要的，多余的	5A
unshielded	[ʌnˈʃiːldid]	adj. 无防护的，无铠装的，无屏蔽的	5A
untold	[ʌnˈtəuld]	adj. 未透露的，数不清的	1B
upgrade	[ˈʌpgreid]	n. 升级 vt. 使升级	7A
uplink	[ˈʌpˌliŋk]	n. 向上传输，上行线，卫星上行链路	5B
upload	[ˈʌpˌləud]	v. 上传	10B
upside-down	[ʌpsaid-ˈdaun]	adv. 颠倒	9A
urbanisation	[ˈəːbənaizeiʃən]	n. 都市化	1A
usability	[ˌjuːzəˈbiləti]	n. 可用性	7A
usefulness	[ˈjuːsfulnis]	n. 有用，有效性	9A
utility	[juːˈtiliti]	效用，有用	2A
utilization	[ˌjuːtilaiˈzeiʃən]	n. 利用	10B
utilize	[juːˈtilaiz]	vt. 利用	4B
utmost	[ˈʌtməust]	n. 极限，最大可能，极力 adj. 极度的，最远的	6B
utopian	[juːˈtəupjən]	n. 乌托邦，空想家，理想主义者 adj. 乌托邦的，理想化的，不切实际的	1B
validity	[vəˈliditi]	n. 有效性，合法性，正确性	9B
variable	[ˈvɛəriəbl]	adj. 可变的，不定的	6A
varied	[ˈvɛərid]	adj. 各式各样的	1A
vast	[vɑːst]	adj. 巨大的，大量的	1B
vegetation	[ˌvedʒiˈteiʃən]	n. 植物	6B
vent	[vent]	n. 通风孔	6B
verify	[ˈverifai]	vt. 检验，校验	5B
vibration	[vaiˈbreiʃən]	n. 振动，颤动，摇动，摆动	6B
video	[ˈvidiəu]	n. 视频	10B
videoconference	[ˌvidiəuˈkɔnfərəns]	n. 视频会议	10B
virtual	[ˈvəːtjuəl]	adj. 虚的，虚拟的	8A
virtually	[ˈvəːtjuəli]	adv. 事实上，实质上	8B
virus	[ˈvaiərəs]	n. 病毒	9B
visible	[ˈvizəbl]	adj. 看得见的，明显的 n. 可见物	9A
vital	[ˈvaitl]	adj. 生死攸关的，重大的，至关重要的	1B
volcano	[vɔlˈkeinəu]	n. 火山	6B
vulnerable	[ˈvʌlnərəb(ə)l]	adj. 易受攻击的	3A
warehouse	[ˈwɛəhaus]	n. 仓库，货栈，大商店 vt. 贮入仓库	9A
wastewater	[ˈweistwɔːtə]	n. 废水	6B
watt	[wɔt]	n. 瓦特	3B
wavelength	[ˈweivleŋθ]	n. 波长	7B
wearable	[ˈwɛərəbl]	adj. 可穿用的，可佩带的	1B
wearer	[ˈwɛərə]	n. 穿用者，佩戴者	1A
website	[ˈwebsait]	n. 网站	9B

续表

单词	音标	意义	课次
wellbeing	[wel'bi:iŋ]	n. 幸福，福利，安乐	1B
whisper	['wispə]	n. 耳语，私语，密谈	10B
wildlife	['waildlaif]	n. 野生动植物	2B
wireless	['waiəlis]	adj. 无线的	1A
withdraw	[wið'drɔ:]	v. 撤销	9B
withstand	[wið'stænd]	vt. 抵挡，经受住	6A
workshop	['wə:kʃɔp]	n. 车间，工场	6A
workstation	['wə:ksteiʃən]	n. 工作站	5A
worthwhile	['wə:ð'wail]	adj. 值得做的，值得出力的	10B
yard	[jɑ:d]	n. 码（长度单位）	7B
zigzag	['zigzæg]	n. Z字形，锯齿形 adj. 曲折的，锯齿形的，Z字形的	9B

词组表

词组	意义	课次
3rd party	第三方	9B
a community of	许多的，一群	8B
a fraction of	一小部分	8B
a fraction of a second	一秒钟的若干分之几，一转眼的工夫	9A
a grain of	一粒；一点点，一些	6A
a multitude of	许多	10A
a piece of	一套，一件	7A
a plume of	一股，一团，一缕	2B
a set of	一组，一套	10B
a variety of	多种的	8B
abstract syntax notation one	抽象语法表示法1，抽象语法符号1	4A
act on …	对……起作用，按……行动，作用于	4B
adaptive switching	自适应交换	5B
adhere to	粘附，粘着，追随，拥护	9A
administrative time	修理准备时间，管理实施时间	5B
advanced intelligent network	高级智能网	4A
agree on	对……达成协议，对……取得一致意见	8B
air conditioning	空调	1A
air pollution	空气污染	6B
air quality monitoring	空气质量监测	6B
all in all	总而言之	10B
allow of	容许	10A
almanac data	卫星年历	3B
along with …	连同……一起，随同……一起	5A
angle of view	视角	9B
application layer	应用层	4A
area monitoring	区域监测	6B
artificial intelligence	人工智能	1B

续表

词　　组	意　　义	课次
as a result of	作为结果	10A
as a whole	总体上	1B
assembly line	（工厂产品的）装配线	7B
asset management	资产管理	10A
asset tracking	资产跟踪	2A
at a button's touch	只按一键，一触即成	2B
at one's command	听某人指挥，在某人的掌握之中	3A
at the time	当时，在那个时候	2B
atmospheric pressure	大气压力	6B
atomic clock	原子钟	3B
attach... to	附在	5A
automatic identification and data capture	自动识别和数据捕捉	9B
baby monitor	婴儿监控器	8B
back and forth	来来往往地，来回地	5B
back-office admin	后台管理	1A
backup battery	备用电源，备份电源	3B
backwards compatible	向后兼容	8A
baked beans	（加番茄酱等制的）烘豆	9A
bar code	条形码	7B
base station	基站，基地	6A
base upon	根据，依据	4B
batch number	批号，批数	7B
battery live	电池寿命	10A
battery pack	电池组	6B
battlefield surveillance	战场侦察，战场监视	6A
be adequate for	适合，足够	5B
be associated with	与……有联系，与……有关	7A
be based on	基于	1A
be capable of	能够	1B
be compatible with	适合，一致	7A
be composed of	由……组成	6A
be equipped with	装备	7A
be familiar with	熟悉	9A
be geared toward	使适合于	10B
be incorporated into	融入	5A
be interested in	对……感兴趣	1A
be likely to	可能；倾向于	1A
be made up of ...	由……组成	9B
be prone to ...	有……的倾向，易于	6A
be responsible for	负责	2B
be saved on ...	被保存在……上	5A
be separated from ...	和……分离开，和……分散	8B
be similar to ...	与……相似	5A

续表

词　　组	意　　义	课次
be split into …	被分为……	9A
be stuck	卡住了，动不了；被困住了，被难住了	1A
be sufficient for	足够	9B
be suitable for	合适的	9A
be used for …	用作……	6B
be well suited for	很适合	10A
beacon antenna	信标天线	3B
beacon transmitter	信标发送机	3B
beam of light	光束	9A
benefit from	受益于	10B
best-effort delivery mechanism	尽力传输机制	8A
binary number	二进制数码	9B
binary tree	二叉树	7B
bit pattern	位组合格式，位的形式	4A
block size	字区大小	9B
blood bank	血库	9A
blood pressure	血压	1B
Bluetooth piconet	蓝牙微微网	8B
bottom line	概要；底线	10B
break up	打碎，破碎，分裂，结束	2B
bridging device	桥接设备	3A
bring about	使发生，致使	1B
building automation	楼宇自动化	2A
business card	名片	9B
by comparison	比较起来	7A
cable layout	电缆配线图，电缆敷设图	4B
carrier wave	载波	8A
carry out	完成，实现，贯彻，执行	6B
catastrophic failure	灾难性故障，突变失效	1B
catch on	流行；抓牢，理解	1A
cellular telephone	移动电话	
cellular tower	蜂窝塔	2B
cereal box	麦片盒子	1B
character set	字符集	9B
circuit switching	线路交换，线路转接	4B
civilian use	民用	3B
clear up	整理，消除	5A
coaxial cable	同轴电缆	8A
code block	码组	9B
coffee maker	咖啡壶	3A
collision probability	碰撞概率，冲突几率	5B
come into being	形成，产生	1B
commercial switch	商用交换机	5B

续表

词　　组	意　　义	课次
commercial use	商业用途	5B
communicate with …	与……通信，与……沟通	1A
communication bandwidth	通信带宽	6A
communication channel	通信电路，信道	8A
communication cost	通信成本	2A
communication network	通信网络	4A
component cable	色差线	8B
conduct research	进行研究	2B
conform to	符合，遵照	10B
confusing information	混乱信息，容易混淆的信息	8B
connect up	连起来，接上	8B
content delivery network	内容交付网络，内容分发网络.	5B
context aware network	情景感知网络	4A
control center	控制中心，调度室	6B
control cost	控制成本	10A
conversion funnel	转化漏斗	9B
conversion rate	转化率	9B
cope with	应付	6A
cordless phone	无绳电话	7A
cordless telephone	无绳电话	8B
cost saving	节约成本	2A
customer service	客户服务	1A
cut in half	切成两半	4B
daisy chain	串式链接，链接式	4B
dark brown	茶褐色，咖啡色	9A
data acquisition	数据获取	6A
data card	数据卡	10B
data file	数据文件	5A
data flow	数据流	4B
data link layer	数据链路层	4A
data logging	数据资料记录	6B
data management	数据管理	2A
data mining	数据挖掘	6B
data plan	数据套餐	10B
data retrieval	数据检索	6B
data transmission	信息传输，数据传输	6B
database file	数据库文件	5A
dead spot	哑点，死点，（接收机）盲点，非灵敏区	2B
deal with	安排，处理，涉及	10B
decision making	决策，判定	2A
dedicated line	专用线	2B
dedicated transmission line	专用传输线	10B
delivery slot	交货时间段；交货槽，输送槽	1A

续表

词　　组	意　　义	课次
densely populated residential areas	人口稠密居民区	8A
Department of Defense	国防部	3B
differ by	相差	8A
different from …	异于……	2B
differential beacon receiver	差分信标接收器，微分信标接收器	3B
digital audio player	数字音频播放机	8A
digital camera	数码相机	8A
digital content signage	数字标牌	2A
digital subscriber line	数字用户线	8A
directional antenna	指向天线，定向天线	8A
dispense with	免除，省却	1A
dissuade from	劝止某人做	9A
distance measurement	距离测量，远距测量	3B
distributed computing	分布式计算	4A
distribution chain	配送链	9A
double whammy	祸不单行，双重打击，双重灾难	1A
drinkable water	可饮用水	2B
drinking water	饮用水	2B
drought warning	旱情预报	6B
dual mesh network	对偶网格网络	3A
DVD player	DVD 播放机	8B
electrical wire	电线	3A
electrical wire	电线	8B
electromagnetic field	电磁场	7A
electromagnetic radiation	电磁辐射	7B
electromagnetic spectrum	电磁波频谱	7A
electronic circuit	电子电路	6A
electronic map	电子地图	3B
embedded operating system	嵌入式操作系统	6A
embedded system	嵌入系统	6A
end up	结束，死	1B
energy harvesting	能量采集	6A
entertainment system	家庭影院	8B
environmental condition	环境条件，环境状况	6A
Environmental Sensor Network	环境传感器网络	6B
ephemeris data	星历数据	3B
equipment rack	设备架	5B
error checking	误差校验，错误校验	5B
error correction	纠错，数据纠正	9B
error-correcting code	纠错码	9B
event handler	事件处理器	6A
event-driven programming model	事件驱动编程模型	6A
ever since	从那时到现在	9A

续表

词组	意义	课次
except for …	除……以外	5B
expansion slot	扩充插槽	7A
explosive growth	爆炸性增长	2B
external device	外部设备	5B
factory automation	工厂自动化	2A
fall back	后退	5B
fall outside	超出……超越	4A
fall under	受到（影响等），被归入	9A
fan out	扇出	5B
fault tolerance	容错	6A
fault tolerant	容错	1B
fiber optics cable	光导纤维电缆	5A
figure out	计算出，断定	5A
file server	文件服务器	5A
fire alarm	火警	3A
fire brigade	消防队	6B
fit into	插入，装入	5A
flat rate	统一费用	10B
floppy disk drive	软盘驱动器	5A
flow control	流控制	4A
focus on	致力于；使聚焦于；对（某事或做某事）予以注意；把……作为兴趣中心	6A
for short	简称，缩写	1A
form factor	物理尺寸和形状，规格	5B
format information	格式信息	9B
forwarding plane	转发平面	5B
fragment free	无分段	5B
free rein	完全的行动自由	9A
full duplex	全双工	5B
fumble for	笨手笨脚地去摸索，摸索	3A
games console	游戏控制台	1B
garbage truck	垃圾车	1A
geo information	位置信息，地理信息	9B
get on with	继续做	8B
get sick	生病	1A
global roaming	全球漫游	10B
go beyond	超出	10B
go off	离开，消失	9A
government agency	政府部门	2B
gravity feed water system	重力给水系统	6B
guaranteed time slot	有保证时隙	10A
half duplex	半双工	5B
hard drive	硬盘驱动器	5A

续表

词　　组	意　　义	课次
hardly ever	难得，几乎从来不	9A
heart patient	心脏病患者	2B
heart rate	心率	1B
high performance	高精确性，高性能	5B
home network	家庭网络	3A
home theater	家庭影院	3A
hybrid network	混合网络	10A
in a manner	在某种意义上	10B
in an emergency	在紧急的时候	3A
in case of	假设，万一	6A
in conjunction with …	与……协力	1B
in contrast to …	和……形成对比，和……形成对照	4A
in embryonic form	在酝酿之中	1A
in essence	实际上	10B
in one's infancy	初期，早期	2A
in practice	在实践中，实际上	9A
in recent years	最近几年中	9B
in relation to	关于，涉及，与……相比	8A
in sequence	顺次，依次	4B
in terms of …	根据，按照，用……的话，在……方面	10A
in the background	在背后，在幕后，作为后果	9B
in the case of	在……的情况	7A
in the event of …	如果……发生	3B
in the extreme	非常，极端	5B
in the form of …	以……的形式	6A
in the midst of	在……之中，在……的中途	7B
in the presence of	在面前	7B
in theory	理论上	1A
in truth	实际上	7A
in unison	一致地	8B
independent of …	不依赖……，独立于……	4A
information traffic	信息流量	5A
infrared light beam	红外线光束	8B
infrared signal	红外线信号	8B
in-store product labeling	在库产品标签	9B
integrated circuit	集成电路	7B
intend for …	打算供……使用	4A
interact with …	与……相合	1B
interface card	接口卡	5A
interfere with	妨碍，干涉，干扰	8B
International Organization for Standardization	国际标准化组织	4A
International Society of Automation	国际自动化学会	6A
Internet Engineering Task Force	因特网工程工作小组	6A

续表

词　　组	意　　义	课次
Internet of Things (IoT)	物联网	1A
interpret…as	把……看作；把……理解为	3A
interrogation zone	读取器询问区，侦测区	7B
intrusion detection system	入侵检测系统	5B
in-vehicle solutions	车载解决方案	2A
inventory management	库存管理	2A
irrigation automation	自动灌溉	6B
just about	几乎	7A
keep up	维持，继续	10B
kilobits per second	每秒千比特	10A
laptop computer	膝上型计算机	5A
Latency-Sensitive Application	传输延迟的网络应用	8A
law enforcement agency	执法部门	2B
leakage detection	泄露检测	6B
licensing fee	授权使用费用，许可证费用	3A
light industry	轻工业	2A
light margin	空白区	9A
limited range	有限范围	8A
line of sight	视线，瞄准线	7B
load distribution	负荷分配	5B
Local area network	局域网	4A
local power source	本地电源	7B
local regulation	局部调节	8A
lock on	锁定，用雷达跟踪	3B
logical addressing scheme	逻辑寻址方案	4A
logical topology	逻辑拓扑	4B
logistics management	物流管理	2A
low cost	低成本	10B
low transfer data rate	低传输数据率	10A
lower-case letter	小写字母	9A
machine health monitoring	机器的健康监测	6A
machine to machine	机器对机器	1A
magnetic card	磁卡片，磁性卡片	9B
magnetic reed switch	磁簧开关	10A
magnetic stripe	（卡片或文件上的）磁条	9A
magnification factor	扩大因数，放大倍数，放大系数	9A
make alliances with	与……结成联盟；与……联合	3A
make sure	确信,证实，确保	8B
make up	构成	8B
make use of	使用，利用	8B
manage to	达成，设法	8B
management station	管理站	5B
mask pattern	掩模图案	9B

续表

词　　组	意　　义	课次
m-business solutions	移动商务解决方案	2A
meal plan	用餐计划	1A
Media Access Control	媒体存取控制，媒体访问控制	4B
Media Access Unit	媒体存取单元，媒体访问单元	4B
media player	媒体播放器	1B
mesh network	网状网络	3A
Metcalfe's Law	麦特卡夫定律	4B
microwave oven	微波炉	8A
mirror image	镜像，映像	5B
misting system	喷雾系统	6B
mobile device	移动设备	2A
mobile learning	移动学习	2A
mobile phone	移动电话，手机	10B
money market	金融市场，货币市场	9A
motion sensor	运动传感器	1A
move away	离开	9B
move off	离开	9A
multihop wireless mesh network	多跳无线网状网络	6A
multilayer switch	多层交换	5B
nail down	钉牢	4B
natural disaster	自然灾害	6B
near field	近场	7B
network adapter	网络适配器，网卡	7A
network address translation	网络地址转换	5B
network bridge	网桥	5B
network card	网卡	5A
Network Interface Card (NIC)	网卡	5A
network layer	网络层	4A
network operating system	网络操作系统	5A
network plan	网络套餐	10B
network segment	网段	5B
network sensor	网络传感器	5B
network switch	网络交换	5B
nothing more than	仅仅，只不过	1A
nuclear power plant	核电站	6B
numbering system	编号系统	9A
numerical code	数字编码，数字代码	3A
nursing home	疗养院	3A
oil drill site	石油钻井现场	2B
on a regular basis	经常，例行的，有规律的	8B
on average	平均起来	3B
on both sides	双方，两边	5A
on its own	本身	1A

续表

词 组	意 义	课次
on one's behalf …	为……的利益，代表	1A
on safari	外去远足，远行狩猎	10B
on-board battery	板载电池	7B
on-board computer	车载计算机	1B
Open Systems Interconnection model (OSI model)	开放式系统互联参考模型	4A
opposite direction	反向，相反方向	4B
optical cable	光缆	4A
originate from	发源于	10A
out of the box	开箱即用	8A
outflow pipe	出水管	2B
output power	输出功率	10A
outsourcing troubleshooting	外包的故障排除	2A
overall performance	总性能，全部工作特性	7A
overlay network	覆盖网络，重叠网络，叠加网络	4A
packet sniffer	封包监听器，封包探测器	5B
packet switching	包交换技术	4B
parallel port	并行端口	5A
particle concentration	粒子浓度	6B
peer-to-peer network	点对点网络	10A
performance figure	性能指标	7A
personal computer	个人计算机，缩写为 PC	2B
physical layer	物理层	4A
physical topology	物理拓扑	4B
pick up	捡起，获得	8A
plug and play	即插即用	5B
plug into	把（电器）插头插入，接通	7A
Point-to-Point Protocol (PPP)	点对点协议	4A
poor geometry	不良几何条件；不良几何图形	3B
port control center	港口管理中心	10A
port management	端口管理	5A
port mirroring	端口镜像，端口映射	5B
portable phone	手提电话	8B
power consumption	能量消耗，功率消耗，动力消耗	6A
power line	电力线，输电线	8A
Power over Ethernet	用以太网供电	5B
power supply	电源	6A
power-saving mode	省电模式	10A
presentation layer	表示层	4A
prevent sb. from doing sth.	阻止某人做某事	7A
preventive maintenance	预防性维修，定期检修	2A
proceed to …	向……进发	1B
processing unit	处理部件，处理器	6A

续表

词　　组	意　　义	课次
product lifecycle	产品生命周期	2A
production plant	生产工厂	2B
proprietary technology	专利技术	3A
public wireless network	公共无线网络	2A
publishers association	出版者协会	9A
pull wire	拉线	7A
quality of service	服务质量	8A
quiet zone	静止区	9A
quite a bit	相当多	10B
rack mounted	安装在机架上的	5B
radio frequency	无线电频率	7B
radio signal	无线电信号	7B
radio wave	无线电波	3A
raw water	未净化的水	2B
read only	只读	7B
real estate	房地产	2A
real time	实时	2A
reclaimed land	开垦地，开荒地，新生地	1A
Reed–Solomon error correction algorithm	里德-所罗门纠错算法	9B
refer to	指；涉及；查阅；有关	2A
regardless of	不管，不顾	4B
regulatory agency	管理机构	10A
relate to	涉及	3A
relative position	相对位置	3B
relative size	相对大小，相对值	9A
rely on	依赖，依靠	1B
remote access control	远程访问控制	2A
remote control	遥控，遥控装置，遥控操作	3A
remote diagnostics	远程诊断	2A
rental company	租赁公司	2B
repeater hub	转发集线器	5B
research and development	研究与开发，研发	6A
residential gateway	家庭网关	5B
result in	引起，导致，以……为结局	2B
retail store	零售店	9A
rocket booster	火箭加速器，火箭助推器	3B
rotating machinery	回转式机器	6B
run out of	用完，耗尽	1A
rush hour	高峰时间	5A
safe mode	安全模式	3A
sat nav	卫星导航	1A
satellite TV receiver	卫星电视接收机	8B
save sb. from	省得某人做某事，使某人摆脱……	1A

续表

词 组	意 义	课次
security alarm	安全警报器	3A
self repair	自修复	1A
sensing device	灵敏元件，传感器	6A
sensitive data	敏感数据	9B
sensor monitoring	传感器检测	2A
sensor node	传感器节点	6A
serial number	序号，序列号	7B
serial port	串行端口	5A
serve as	充当，担任	1B
session layer	会话层	4A
set aside	留出	8B
set-top box	置顶盒	10A
ship control center	船舶控制中心	10A
shopping list	购物单	2B
short message	短信	3A
shut off	关掉，切断	3A
signal strength	信号强度	8A
sit through	一直挺到结束，耐着性子看完（或听完）	10B
sleep in	多睡一会	1A
sliding window	滑动窗口	4A
slip into	分成	5A
smart city	智慧城市	1A
smart home	智能家居	3A
smart switch	智能交换机	5B
social media	社交媒介	1B
software application	软件应用程序	5A
solar eclipse	日食	3B
solar energy	太阳能	3B
solar panel	太阳电池板，太阳能电池板	3B
solid object	固体	3B
Source Routing Algorithm	源路由算法	3A
spanning tree protocol	生成树协议	5B
spare part	备件	3A
special component	专有部件，专用附件	6A
spread over…	遍布在……	2B
spread-spectrum frequency hopping	扩频跳频，展频跳频	8B
stackable switch	可堆叠交换机	5B
star network	星型网络	6A
star topology	星型拓扑	4B
stateful inspection firewall	状态检测防火墙	5B
stay in touch	保持联系	8B
step by step	按部就班的	2B
stick with	[口]坚持做（某事）	10B

续表

词　　组	意　　义	课次
stock level	库存水平	9A
stock number	物料编号	7B
storage area networks	存储区域网	5B
storage space	存储空间	5A
store and forward	储存和转送	5B
strategic location	优越的地理位置，战略要地	2B
stream of bits	比特流	4A
streaming video	流视频	10B
subscription fee	预付费	3B
suitable for …	适合……的	4A
supply chain	供应链	2A
surf the net	网上冲浪	10B
switch port	交换端口	5B
take advantage of	利用	3B
take care of	照顾	3A
tape back-up unit	磁带备份机	5A
technical specification	技术规范	10B
text message	文字信息	10B
the bulk of	大半，大部分的	10A
time difference	时差	3B
timing error	同步误差，定时误差	3B
token ring	令牌网	4B
traffic cop	<美口>交通警察	5A
traffic volume	交通量，运输量，运输密度，行车量	2B
transfer rate	传输率	10B
transmission medium	传输介质，传送介质	4A
transmission power	发射功率，传输功率	8B
transmission rate	传输率	4B
transport layer	传输层	4A
treatment plant	污水处理厂	2B
tune in	收听	8A
turn on	开启，开始	8B
turn out	结果	8B
twisted pair	双绞线	5A
twisted pair Ethernet	双绞线以太网	4B
two-dimensional code	二维码	9B
tyre pressure	轮胎气压	1B
unbroken rule	完整的破折号	9A
underground water	地下水	6B
uninterruptible power supply	不间断电源（UPS）	5B
Universal Remote Control	通用远程控制	10A
unshielded twisted-pair	非屏蔽双绞线	5A
up and down	上下地，到处，前前后后	1A

续表

词 组	意 义	课次
user intervention	用户干涉，用户介入，用户干预	8B
utility company	公共事业公司	2B
validity check	有效性检查	9B
vary with …	随……而变化	8A
vending machine	自动贩卖机	2A
video calling	视频电话	1A
video recorder	录影机	9A
video sender	视频传输装置	8A
video surveillance	视频监视	2A
video-game console	视频游戏控制台	8A
virtual circuit	虚拟线路，虚拟电路	4A
virtual memory	虚拟内存	6A
wait in lines	排队等候	10B
warn of	警告，告诫	1B
water quality monitoring	水质量监测	6B
water treatment	水处理，水的净化	2B
web address	网址	9B
web browser	网络浏览器	5B
web cache	网页快照，网页缓存	5B
web server	网络服务器	3A
weed out	清除	8B
wired broadband network	有线宽带网络	1A
wired network	有线网络	7A
wireless access point	无线接入点	5B
wireless network access point	无线网络接入点	8A
wireless personal network	无线个人网络	3A
within the confines of …	在……（范围）之内	5B
without regard to	不考虑，不遵守	4B
word processor	文字处理软件	5A
write-once, read-multiple	单次写入多次读取（WORM）	7B

缩写表

缩 写	意 义	课次
2D (2 Dimension)	二维	3B
3D (3 Dimension)	三维	3B
3G (Third Generation)	第三代通信	10B
4G (Fourth Generation)	第四代通信	10B
AIM (Automatic Identification and Mobility)	自动识别和移动	9B
AP (Access Point)	访问接入点	7A
API (Application Programming Interface)	应用程序编程接口	9B
app (application)	应用	9B
ASCII (American Standard Code for Information Interchange)	美国信息交换标准码	4A

续表

缩　　写	意　　义	课次
ASIC (Application Specific Integrated Circuit)	特定用途集成电路	6A
AT&T (American Telephone & Telegraph)	美国电话电报公司	1A
ATM (Asynchronous Transfer Mode)	异步传输模式	5B
AUI (Attachment Unit Interface)	连接单元接口	5A
BAP (Battery Assisted Passive)	电池辅助无源	7B
BNC (Bayonet Nut Connector)	同轴电缆接插件	5A
CBM (Machinery Condition-based Maintenance)	基于状态维修	6B
CDMA (Code Division Multiple Access)	码分多址	2A
CLI (Command-Line Interface)	命令行界面	5B
CPI (Characters Per Inch)	每英寸字符数	9A
dBm	分贝毫瓦	10A
DC (Direct Current)	直流电	7B
DDOS (distributed denial-of-service)	分布式拒绝服务	9A
DES (Data Encryption Standard)	数据加密标准	9B
DGPS (Differential GPS)	差分 GPS，微分 GPS	3B
DIN (Deutsche Industrie-Norm (德文))	德国工业标准	5A
EAN(European Article Number)	欧洲商品编码	9A
EBCDIC (Extended Binary Coded Decimal Interchange Code)	扩充的二进制编码的十进制交换码	4A
EC (Electrical Conductance)	导电率	6B
EDGE (Enhanced Data rates for GSM Evolution)	GSM 增强数据率演进	10B
EIRP (Equivalent isotropically radiated power)	等效全向辐射功率	8A
EPC (Electronic Product Code)	电子产品代码	7B
EPCGlobal	国际物品编码协会（EAN）和美国统一代码委员会（UCC）的一个合资公司	7B
EU (Energy Unit)	能量单位	8A
FCC (Federal Communications Commission)	（美国）通信委员会	8A
GP (General Practioner)	全科医生	1A
GPRS (General Packet Radio Service)	通用分组无线业务	10B
GPS (Global Positioning System)	全球定位系统	3B
GS1 (Globe standard 1)	国际物品编码协会	9A
GUI (Graphical User Interface)	图形用户界面	8A
HBA (Host Bus Adapter)	主机总线适配器	4A
HF (High Frequency)	高频	7B
HRC (Human Readable Characters)	人类可读的字符	9A
HTTP (Hypertext Transfer Protocol)	超文本传输协议	8A
I/O (Input/Output)	输入输出	6B
ID (IDentification, IDentity)	身份	7B
IEEE (Institute for Electrical and Electronics Engineers)	电气和电子工程师协会	3A
IGMP (Internet Group Management Protocol)	因特网组管理协议	5B
IM（Instant Messenger）	即时消息，即时通信	9B
IMP (Interface Message Processor)	接口信息处理器	4A

续表

缩　写	意　义	课次
IMT (International Mobile Communication)	国际移动通信	10B
IP (Internet Protocol)	网际协议	10B
IPTV (Internet Protocol television)	网络电视	8A
ISBN (International Standard Book Numbering)	国际标准图书编号	9A
ISM (Industrial，Scientific and Medical)	工业，科学和医学	8A
ISSN (International Standard Serial Number)	国际标准连续出版物编号	9A
ITF (Interleaved Two and Five)	交插二五	9A
ITU (International Telecommunication Union)	国际电信联盟	5B
JIS (Japanese Industrial Standard)	日本工业标准	9B
kbps (kilobits per second)	千位每秒	10B
LAN (Local Area Network)	局域网	4B
LF (Low Frequency)	低频	7B
LLC (Logical Link Control)	逻辑链路控制	4A
M2M (Machine to Machine)	机器对机器	2A
MAC (Medium Access Control)	媒体访问控制	10A
MB (MegaByte)	兆字节	5A
Mbps (Megabits per second)	兆位每秒	7A
MEMS (MicroElectroMechanical Systems)	微型机电系统	6A
MSTP (Multi-Service Transfer Platform)	多业务传送平台	5B
NBI (Philippines National Bureau of Investigation)	菲律宾国家调查局	9B
NTT (Nippon Telegraph and Telephone Public Corporation)	日本电报电话公共公司	9B
O2	英国一家通信公司	1A
OCR-A (Optical Character Recognition-ANSI Standard)	光字符识别-美国标准协会标准	9A
OCR-B (Optical Character Recognition-International Standard)	光字符识别-国际标准	9A
OGC (Open Geospatial Consortium)	开放地理信息联盟	6A
PAN (Personal Area Network)	个人局域网	8B
PC (Personal Computer)	个人计算机	8B
PCMCIA (Personal Computer Memory Card International Association)	个人计算机储存卡国际联盟	5A
PSTN (Public Switched Telephone Network)	公共开关电话网络	2A
PVC (Permanent Virtual Circuit)	永久虚拟电路	4A
QR Code (Quick Response Code)	快速响应码	9B
RAID (Redundant Array of Inexpensive Disks)	冗余磁盘阵列	5A
RAM (Random Access Memory)	随机存储器	5A
RF (Radio Frequency)	无线电频率	7A
RFC (Request For Comments)	请求评议，请求注解	5B
RFID (Radio Frequency IDentification)	无线射频识别技术	1A
RMON (Remote Network MONitoring)	远程网络监控	5B
ROM (Read Only Memory)	只读存储器	7B
RSTP (Rapid Spanning Tree Protocol)	快速生成树协议	5B

续表

缩　　写	意　　义	课次
SA (Selective Availability)	选择可用性，选择性可靠度	3B
SCSI (Small Computer System Interface)	小型计算机系统接口	5A
SIM (Subscriber Identity Module)	用户身份识别模块	10B
SMON (Switch Monitoring)	交换机监控	5B
SNMP (Simple Network Management Protocol)	简单网络管理协议	5B
SOHO (Small office/home office)	小型办公室/家庭办公室	5B
SOI (Silicon-On-Insulator)	绝缘衬底上的硅	7B
SPB (Shortest Path Bridging)	最短路径桥接	5B
STP (Shielded Twisted Pair)	屏蔽双绞线	5B
TCP (Transfer Control Protocol)	传输控制协议	5B
TVOC (Total Volatile Organic Compounds)	总挥发性有机物	6B
UDP (User Datagram Protocol)	用户数据报协议	4A
UHF (UltraHigh Frequency)	超高频	3B
UMTS (Universal Mobile Telecommunications System)	通用移动通信系统	10B
URI (Uniform Resource Identifier)	统一资源标识符	9B
URL (Uniform Resource Locator)	统一资源定位符	5B
USB (Universal Serial Bus)	通用串行总线架构	6A
UV (UltraViolet)	紫外线	6B
VLAN (Virtual Local Area Network)	虚拟局域网	5B
VoIP (Voice over Internet Protocol)	网络语音，网络电话	10B
VP (Vice President)	副总裁；副总统	1A
VPN (Virtual Private Network)	虚拟个人网络	8A
WAAS (Wide Area Augmentation System)	广域增强系统	3B
WAN (Wide Area Network)	广域网	2A
WAP (Wireless Application Protocol)	无线应用协议	10B
WCDMA (Wideband Code Division Multiple Access)	宽带码分多址	10B
WEP (Wired Equivalent Privacy)	有线等效加密	7A
WiFi (WIreless FIdelity)	无线保真	8A
WLAN (Wireless Local Area Network)	无线局域网	7A
WME (Wireless Multimedia Extension)	无线多媒体扩展	8A
WPA (WiFi Protected Access)	WiFi 保护访问	7A
WPAN (Wireless Personal Area Networks)	无线个人局域网	10A
WSN (Wireless Sensor Network)	无线传感器网络	6A
XML (eXtensible Markup Language)	可扩展标记语言	4A

教学资源支持

敬爱的教师：

感谢您一直以来对清华版计算机教材的支持和爱护。为了配合本课程的教学需要，本教材配有配套的电子教案(素材)，有需求的教师请到清华大学出版社主页(http://www.tup.com.cn)上查询和下载，也可以拨打电话或发送电子邮件咨询。

如果您在使用本教材的过程中遇到了什么问题，或者有相关教材出版计划，也请您发邮件告诉我们，以便我们更好地为您服务。

我们的联系方式：

地　　址：北京海淀区双清路学研大厦 A 座 707

邮　　编：100084

电　　话：010-62770175-4604

课件下载：http://www.tup.com.cn

电子邮件：weijj@tup.tsinghua.edu.cn

教师交流 QQ 群：136490705

教师服务微信：itbook8

教师服务 QQ：883604

(申请加入时，请写明您的学校名称和姓名)

用微信扫一扫右边的二维码，即可关注计算机教材公众号。

扫一扫
课件下载、样书申请
教材推荐、技术交流